THE RIGHTS REVOLUTION

THE RIGHTS REVOLUTION

Lawyers, Activists, and Supreme Courts in Comparative Perspective

Charles R. Epp

THE UNIVERSITY OF CHICAGO PRESS

CHICAGO AND LONDON

rnment at the University of Kansas.

The University of Chicago Press, Chicago 60637
The University of Chicago Press, Ltd., London
© 1998 by The University of Chicago
All rights reserved. Published 1998

07 06 05 04 03 02 01 00 99 98   1 2 3 4 5

ISBN: 0-226-21161-4 (cloth)
ISBN: 0-226-21162-2 (paper)

Library of Congress Cataloging-in-Publication Data

Epp, Charles R.
   The rights revolution : lawyers, activists, and supreme courts in comparative
perspective / Charles R. Epp.
      p. cm.
   Includes bibliographical references and index.
   ISBN 0-226-21161-4 (cloth : alk. paper).—ISBN 0-226-21162-2 (paper : alk. paper)
   1. Civil rights—History.   I. Title.
   K3240.4.E65   1998
   342'.085—dc21   98-14170
                                                                              CIP

⊗ The paper used in this publication meets the minimum requirements of the
American National Standard for Information Sciences—Permanence of Paper for
Printed Library Materials, ANSI Z39.48-1992.

To Robert O. and Amelia Epp

CONTENTS

TABLES AND FIGURES

Acknowledgments

A comparative project of this scope depends on the support of many institutions and people. Foremost, I am deeply indebted to Joel Grossman and Herbert Kritzer for their encouragement, advice, comments, and critiques. Joel directed the dissertation from which this book evolved, and his generous support and encouragement over the course of many years made the project possible. He prodded me, in particular, to develop and refine the idea of a support structure. Bert, too, actively supported and encouraged my research and writing in big and little ways. His advice for conducting research in Britain aided my work there, and his wonderful course on qualitative research methods inspired my comparative research design. In addition, Don Downs, Marc Galanter, and Graham Wilson, my other advisers at the University of Wisconsin, offered very helpful suggestions and criticisms, and Marc's advice regarding India and his contacts there proved essential for the research conducted in that country. I am also grateful to Gerald Rosenberg and Peter Russell for offering many helpful comments and suggestions on the manuscript. I thank Gerald Rosenberg, in particular, for generously offering advice and encouragement that went beyond the usual responsibilities of a manuscript reviewer.

I am also indebted to a number of other people for many helpful comments and contributions at various stages of the project. Richard Pacelle generously allowed access to his data on the U.S. Supreme Court's agenda. Ted Morton, Ian Brodie, and Shannon Ishiyama Smithey provided comments and suggestions that strengthened my treatment of the Canadian case; I am especially grateful to Ted Morton for his generous contributions. Jim Christoph, Carol Harlow, and Susan Sterett provided comments and suggestions that improved my discussion of the British case. For other comments and contributions, I am indebted to Burt Atkins, Jeff Ayres, W. A. Bogart, Ruth Buchanan, Chris Burke, Dana Chabot, Cornell Clayton, Freddie Diamant, Tim Epp, John

Esser, Don Farole, Roy Flemming, Todd Foglesong, Robert Geyer, Micheal Giles, Howard Gillman, Stacie Haynie, J. Woodford Howard, Jeff Isaac, Dan Levin, Steven Maynard-Moody, John Sayer, Sigrun Skogly, the obstreperous Daniel A. Smith, Mark Suchman, Neal Tate, Tracy Wahl, Jerold Waltman, Stephen Wasby, and Gerald Wright. My colleagues at Indiana University and the University of Kansas, in particular, offered congenial atmospheres for completing the analysis and writing.

Undoubtedly some of the people to whom I am indebted will disagree with parts of my analysis. Their comments and suggestions in the context of disagreement provide a model of the scholarly community, and I can only hope to be as fortunate in the future. Any remaining errors of fact or interpretation are, of course, mine.

My research in Britain, Canada, and India would not have been possible without the advice and support of many people and several institutions in those countries. In India, Rajeev Dhavan generously provided invaluable support, advice, and contacts; the Indian Law Institute provided access to research sources; and the staff in the Office of the Registrar, Supreme Court of India, answered many questions and generously provided access to statistical sources. In Britain, the Institute for Advanced Legal Studies provided a research base for several months, and the staff of the House of Lords Records Office kindly provided access to useful sources. In Canada, the Human Rights Research and Education Centre and the Fauteaux Hall Law Library, both at the University of Ottawa, and the library of the Supreme Court of Canada offered access to many documentary sources. Additionally, many individuals in each of these countries generously consented to interviews, and many rights-advocacy organizations allowed access to their files. I am humbled by the generous and patient guidance and support of my hosts in these countries.

The research for this book depended on financial support from several institutions. The University of Wisconsin, Madison, was a congenial and supportive home for interdisciplinary research on law, and I am grateful in particular for a Legal Studies Fellowship from the Institute for Legal Studies and a dissertation fellowship from the university. My work on this project was made possible as well by a Canadian Government research grant, a National Science Foundation grant (No. SES 9225087), and a summer faculty fellowship from Indiana University.

In the final stages of the process, this book has benefited from the careful and attentive efforts of several people at the University of Chi-

cago Press. In particular, I am grateful to John Tryneski for intelligent and conscientious direction and to Leslie Keros for patient and helpful coordination. And I am indebted to Becky Laurent for unusually perceptive and constructive editing on matters of both style and substance.

I am grateful to the American Political Science Association for permission to incorporate material from my article, "Do Bills of Rights Matter? The Canadian Charter of Rights and Freedoms," *American Political Science Review* 90:765–79 (1996), into chapters 9 and 10.

In the end, though, I am especially indebted to my wife, Lora Jost, for her support and ever-sharp critic's eye, both of which helped me to maintain this course over what has now been, I realize, a long time. And I dedicate this book to my parents, whose efforts on behalf of human rights have made a difference.

ONE

Introduction

Sed quis custodiet ipsos custodes?
(But who will guard the guardians?)

—Juvenal

On October 29, 1958, at 5:45 in the morning, nine Chicago police officers acting without a warrant forced their way into James and Flossie Monroe's home, pulled the Monroes and their six children out of bed, and forced them to stand half-naked in the living room while they ransacked the home, dumped out the contents of drawers, tore clothes out of closets, and slit open mattresses. Officer Pape, the leader, beat James Monroe with his flashlight and called him "nigger" and "black boy"; another officer pushed Flossie Monroe; and several officers kicked and hit the children and pushed them to the floor. The officers eventually took Mr. Monroe to a station house, where he was forced to appear in a lineup and was questioned for ten hours about a recent murder. Throughout the ordeal, the officers refused to allow Monroe to call a lawyer or his family. In the end he was released—the victim of a story about a "Negro robber" concocted by the real murderers. The Monroe family sued the officers under a federal civil rights statute, but the federal district court and the court of appeals rejected their right to sue in federal court. In 1961, to the surprise of many, the United States Supreme Court reversed and granted them this right.[1]

A few years later a decision like *Monroe v. Pape* would seem routine. But in early 1961 the Court had yet to establish its reputation as a consistent defender of individual rights against official abuses of power.[2] Only a few years earlier, for instance, in *Screws v. United States*, a criminal case brought against a Georgia sheriff who had brutally beaten a black man to death, the Supreme Court overturned the sheriff's conviction and created a difficult standard for convicting perpetrators of police brutality.[3] The sheriff was acquitted on retrial under the new standard. The *Monroe* decision, by contrast, opened the door to civil lawsuits to redress official abuses of individual rights.[4]

The decision, moreover, was part of a much larger transformation in

which the Supreme Court, for the first time in its history, began deciding and supporting individual rights claims in a sustained way. As
late as the mid-thirties, less than 10 percent of the Court's decisions
involved individual rights other than property rights; the Court instead devoted its attention to business disputes and often supported
property-rights claims brought by businesses and wealthy individuals.[5] The Court's attention and support eventually shifted to modern
individual rights.[6] By the late sixties, almost 70 percent of its decisions
involved individual rights,[7] and the Court had, essentially, proclaimed
itself the guardian of the individual rights of the ordinary citizen. In
the process, the Court created or expanded a host of new constitutional rights, among them virtually all of the rights now regarded as
essential to the Constitution: freedom of speech and the press, rights
against discrimination on the basis of race or sex, and the right to due
process in criminal and administrative procedures. Undoubtedly the
depth of this transformation is limited in important ways: some rights
have suffered erosion, and, as many Americans know, judicial declara-
tions of individual rights often find only pale reflections in practice.[8]
But as I demonstrate in more detail shortly, the transformation has
been real and it has had important effects. This transformation is commonly called the *rights revolution.*

Why did the rights revolution occur? What conditions encouraged
the Supreme Court to regularly hear and support individual rights
cases after largely ignoring or spurning them for 150 years? And why,
after many years of hearing claims by powerful businesses, did the
Court regularly turn its attention to the claims of "underdogs"? In
sum, *what were the sources and conditions for the rights revolution?*

Sources and Conditions for the Rights Revolution

The U.S. rights revolution is usually attributed to one or more of the
following: constitutional guarantees of individual rights and judicial
independence, leadership from activist judges (particularly Supreme
Court justices) who have been willing to use those constitutional provisions to transform society, and the rise of rights consciousness in popular culture. Conventional explanations tend to place particular emphasis on judicial leadership as the catalyst for the rights revolution.
Constitutional guarantees, judicial leadership, and rights consciousness certainly contributed to the U.S. rights revolution. This book
shows, however, that sustained judicial attention and approval for individual rights grew primarily out of pressure from below, not leadership from above. This pressure consisted of deliberate, strategic or-

ganizing by rights advocates. And strategic rights advocacy became possible because of the development of what I call the support structure for legal mobilization, consisting of rights-advocacy organizations, rights-advocacy lawyers, and sources of financing, particularly government-supported financing.

This support structure has been essential in shaping the rights revolution. Because the judicial process is costly and slow and produces changes in the law only in small increments, litigants cannot hope to bring about meaningful change in the law unless they have access to significant resources. For this reason, constitutional litigation in the United States until recently was dominated by the claims of powerful businesses; they alone commanded the resources necessary to pursue claims with sufficient frequency, acumen, and perseverance to shape the development of constitutional law. And for this reason, too, constitutional law and the courts largely ignored the potential constitutional rights claims of ordinary individuals. The rights revolution grew out of the growing capacity of individual rights advocates to pursue the forms of constitutional litigation perfected by organized businesses, but for very different ends. The growth of the support structure, therefore, significantly democratized access to the Supreme Court.

Others have posited, of course, that political pressure and organized support for rights litigation influence judicial attention and approval for civil rights and liberties.[9] My analysis builds on such research. But what is distinctive about my analysis is its emphasis on material resources, on the difficulty with which those resources are developed, and on the key role of those resources in providing the sources and conditions for sustained rights-advocacy litigation. Many discussions of the relationship between the Supreme Court and litigants assume that the resources necessary to support litigation are easily generated and that, as a result, litigants of all kinds have always stood ready to bring forward any kind of case that the Court might indicate a willingness to hear and decide. But that presumes a pluralism of litigating interests and an evenness of the litigation playing field that is wholly unjustified. Not every issue is now, nor has been in the past, the subject of extensive litigation in lower courts, due in part to limitations in the availability of resources for legal mobilization.

Implications of the Support-Structure Explanation

The support-structure explanation for the U.S. rights revolution is significant for two closely related debates in contemporary politics and constitutional law: (1) whether (or to what extent) democratic pro-

cesses must be sacrificed in order to achieve protection for individual rights, and (2) how best to protect individual rights in modern society. Many people perceive a deep tension between rights and majoritarian democracy and believe that, if we wish to "guard the guardians" (the police and other public officials), we must turn unaccountable power over to judicial guardians. Some critics have claimed that the Supreme Court's decision in the *Monroe* case, for instance, amounts to a judicial usurpation of power because under the *Monroe* precedent, courts have constrained the discretion of public officials without regard to the wishes of democratic majorities.

The rights revolution, either implicitly or explicitly, is at the heart of the debate over the relationship between rights and democracy. For it was during the rights revolution, according to the advocates of contemporary individual rights, that courts finally began properly defending and protecting such rights. And according to the critics of the new rights, it was during the rights revolution that judicial power grew out of control and eroded the democratic process. Robert Bork, a leading critic of the new rights, has described the rights revolution as "the transportation into the Constitution of the principles of a liberal culture that cannot achieve those results democratically." Creating rights through judicial interpretation, he declares, is "heresy," and "it is crucial to recognize a heresy for what it is and to root it out."[10] His use of the term "heresy" is deliberate, for the key problem, in Bork's view, is a heretical judicial interpretation of a foundational written text, the Constitution. In the judges' hands, Bork charges, the Constitution has been transformed from a mechanism for limiting arbitrary governmental power into a source for arbitrary judicial power. As Bork observed, "the Constitution is the trump card in American politics, and judges decide what the Constitution means."[11] This is a judge-centered analysis of the rights revolution, but it also asserts that judicial power depends on constitutional structure.

To a remarkable degree many defenders of contemporary rights accept the judge-centered interpretation of the rights revolution and of rights protection in general; they acknowledge that the rights revolution grew out of fundamentally undemocratic processes. But they defend many of the new rights on the ground that the results, in the end, strengthened democracy.[12] In this view, for instance, the electoral reapportionment rulings of the early sixties[13] deeply interfered with the democratic political process but did so in order to enhance the fairness of that process.[14]

If my thesis is correct, however, the common emphasis on constitutional provisions and judges is exaggerated and the concern about undemocratic processes is ill founded. Of course it is unlikely that a majority of the population, if polled, would have supported each judicial decision in the rights revolution. But many legislative policies could not survive a popular referendum either. The meaning of "democracy" is thus complex and nuanced, and the critics recognize that fact by focusing mainly on the issue of process—claiming that the process of rights creation is judge-dominated and therefore is *intrinsically* less a result of broadly based action than is legislative policy making.

This book is intended in part to refute that persistent claim by showing that the rights revolution depended on widespread support made possible by a democratization of access to the judiciary. Cooperative efforts among many rights advocates, relying on new resources for rights litigation—financing, organizational support, and willing and able lawyers—provided the raw material for the rights revolution. Many of those resources either were legislatively created or reflected a democratization and diversification of the legal profession and the interest-group system. Neither judges nor constitutional guarantees are irrelevant; judges ultimately decide whether to support rights claims, and constitutional guarantees may become rallying symbols for social movements and may provide footholds for lawyers' arguments and foundations for judicial decisions. But both the policy preferences of judges and the meaning of constitutional rights are partly constituted by the political economy of appellate litigation, particularly the distribution of resources necessary for sustained constitutional litigation. If the rights revolution developed out of the growth of a broad support structure in civil society, if rights litigation commonly reflects a significant degree of organized collective action, and if judicially declared rights remain dead letters unless they gain the backing of a broad support structure, then the rights revolution was not undemocratic or antidemocratic, even in the processes that created it. And if the evidence and analysis in support of that proposition is persuasive, then critics bear the burden of explaining why we should return to a time when only large businesses and the wealthy commanded the organizational strength, resources, and legal expertise to mobilize constitutional law in their favor.

The support-structure explanation is likewise pertinent to the other rights-related debate mentioned above—how best to protect individual rights in modern society. In the United States, great political battles

are fought over judicial nominees. In other countries, some citizens wish for a John Marshall or an Earl Warren (great American Supreme Court Justices) to breathe life into their moribund constitutional law. And constitutional lawyers from the United States jet about the world engaging in "constitutional engineering," the process of creating new constitutions for other countries—on the assumption that new or revised constitutional structures and guarantees will re-form other societies.

Under the support-structure explanation proposed here, however, proponents of expanded judicial protection for rights should not place *all* hope in judges or constitutional reform but should provide support to rights-advocacy lawyers and organizations. If a nation—the United States or any other—wishes to protect individual rights, it would do well not to confine its efforts to encouraging or admonishing its judges, fine-tuning its constitution, or relying on the values of popular culture to affect rights by osmosis. Societies should also fund and support lawyers and rights-advocacy organizations—for they establish the conditions for sustained judicial attention to civil liberties and civil rights and for channeling judicial power toward egalitarian ends.

The Genesis of the Support-Structure Explanation

The standard emphases on judges, constitutional text, and popular culture reflect a nearly exclusive focus in past research on the U.S. case. In the United States, liberal judges, constitutional rights guarantees, and growing popular support for individual rights coincided at the time of the rights revolution, and so commentators attempting to interpret or explain the rights revolution commonly looked no further than those influences. But as I started to study the U.S. rights revolution I became aware of similar (or apparently similar) rights revolutions in other countries. In Britain, for instance, a country with a conservative judiciary and no constitutional bill of rights, individual rights nonetheless are gaining increasing judicial attention and support.[15] Such developments encouraged me to look for other possible influences, and my focus here on resources for legal mobilization is the result. The four common-law countries selected for my comparative analysis—the United States, India, Britain, and Canada—have gained reputations as sites of rights revolutions (of varying strengths and focuses, to be sure) but differ in a number of dimensions, particularly in their constitutional structures, the reputations of their judges for creativity and ac-

tivism, the presence of rights consciousness in popular culture, and the strength of their legal mobilization support structures.

In such a comparative investigation, clarity about what is being compared is essential. *Rights*, as I use the term here, consist of the new rights that emerged in judicial interpretation of U.S. constitutional law and statutes in this century. Constitutional rights in the past had been primarily the rights of property and contract. The new rights encompass, among other rights, freedom of speech and the press; free exercise of religion and prohibitions on official establishment of religion; prohibitions against invidious discrimination on the basis of race, sex, and a few other more or less immutable characteristics; the right of privacy; and the right to due process in law enforcement and administrative procedure. What precisely these new rights include and how they are to be applied in practice of course remain matters of some dispute.

I have focused, in particular, on women's rights and the rights of criminal defendants and prisoners. These two issues are especially useful lenses through which to analyze rights revolutions, for their status varies significantly from country to country and also over time. Criminal procedure is an issue within the traditional purview of common-law courts, yet until recently it received little attention in supreme courts. Criminal defendants form a diffuse, unorganized class; I examine how, in some countries and under some conditions, the rights claims of criminal defendants nonetheless came to form a major element of the rights revolution. The issue of women's rights, by contrast, is relatively new to judicial systems. Many countries' courts initially resisted the development of women's rights, yet those rights are now a significant part of the rights revolution in some of these countries. Moreover, the level of organized support for women's-rights litigation has varied significantly among countries and over time.

The *rights revolution*, as I use the term, was a sustained, developmental process that produced or expanded the new civil rights and liberties. That process has had three main components: judicial attention to the new rights, judicial support for the new rights, and implementation of the new rights. This book examines each of the four countries in terms of these components. Judicial attention (or the "judicial agenda") is measured as the proportion of cases decided by a court per year focusing on particular issues, among them the new rights. Judicial support is gauged more informally, by examining the general direction of a court's policies with regard to rights. Implementation of

judicial decisions is a complex and multifaceted matter and, with respect to implementation, this book focuses on the extent to which
courts have issued a continuing stream of judicial decisions that enforce or elaborate on earlier decisions.

Do Rights Matter in Practice?

It is important to emphasize that developments in the first two components—greater judicial attention to individual rights, and greater judicial support for them—may not lead to greater protection for those
rights in practice. As Gerald Rosenberg has argued, the enforcement
powers of courts acting on their own are relatively weak, and some
of the key rights announced by the Supreme Court during the rights
revolution were not implemented and had little of their intended
effect.[16]

Nonetheless, there is good reason to believe that an expansion of the
support structure for legal mobilization may significantly enhance the
implementation of judicially declared rights in practice. Rosenberg
showed that the Supreme Court's decision in *Brown v. Board of Education*[17] striking down racial segregation in public schools was implemented far more rapidly and substantially in the southern states that
bordered the north than in the deep South because many officials in
the border states favored desegregation and used the *Brown* decision
to push for it.[18] Similarly, Michael McCann found that union advocates
of comparable worth policies used judicial rulings as leverage in private bargaining to gain favorable changes in work contracts.[19] Those
studies suggest that implementation of judicial decisions is greatly influenced by the acts and strategies of public officials and rights advocates. Yet the effectiveness of rights advocates in these endeavors is
likely to be conditioned by their knowledge and resource capabilities.
As Marc Galanter has written, "the messages disseminated by courts
do not carry endowments or produce effects except as they are received, interpreted, and used by (potential) actors. Therefore, the
meaning of judicial signals is dependent on the information, experience, skill, and resources that disputants bring to them."[20] The presence and strength of a support structure for legal mobilization enhances the information, experience, skill, and resources of rights
claimants and thus likely affects the implementation of judicial decisions on rights. The American Civil Liberties Union (ACLU), for instance, provides individuals with assistance in asserting and defending judicially declared rights in a wide variety of situations.

The dramatic expansion of the United States Supreme Court's atten-

tion to liberal rights, then, in conjunction with a vibrant support structure, provided a new assembly of bargaining tools and symbolic resources to a wide array of previously "right-less" individuals and groups. There are limits to the social changes produced by judicial rulings, and those rulings depend on support from government officials and on private parties having the capability to use them well. But judicial rulings may be used to great effect by rights organizers. The rights revolution in the United States did not merely result in judicial recognition of the existence of individual rights; it also gave rights advocates bargaining power and leverage that enabled them to expand protection for individual rights in practice.

An Illustration

The importance of the support structure for legal mobilization may be illustrated by the addition of a few details to the story of *Monroe v. Pape*. James and Flossie Monroe, it turns out, were not exactly lone individuals facing a hostile government on their own. The National Association for the Advancement of Colored People Legal Defense and Educational Fund (NAACP-LDF) for years had pushed a campaign of strategic litigation and political pressure against police brutality and racial discrimination in the criminal justice system, and it had gained the support of the Civil Rights Section of the United States Department of Justice.[21] Then, in the late fifties, the Illinois chapter of the ACLU funded a large study of the problem of illegal detention and questioning by the Chicago police. In 1959, the organization published the study, titled *Secret Detention by the Chicago Police*, which documented, on the basis of a random sample of court cases, that more than half of all persons arrested in Chicago were held and questioned in police stations for more than seventeen hours without any formal charges being filed; 10 percent were held for more than forty-eight hours.[22] The report showed that James Monroe's situation—at least from the time he reached the police station—was not unusual: the Illinois ACLU estimated that twenty thousand people in Chicago suffered similar illegal detention and questioning annually. Supreme Court Justices William O. Douglas and Tom Clark requested copies of the report, and Douglas soon cited it in a speech.[23] Two years later, after the Monroes' appeal had wound its way up through the court system, Justice Douglas wrote the Supreme Court's majority opinion in the case. The NAACP-LDF and Justice Department work, and the Illinois ACLU study in particular, provided the background to the *Monroe* case.

And then there is the matter of how the Monroes managed to pursue

their case up through the judicial hierarchy and present a persuasive legal argument, in an area of the law fraught with esoteric precedents and rules, before the Supreme Court. The main author of their brief before the Court, it turns out, was Morris Ernst, who had been one of the ACLU's leading lawyers since the twenties. The ACLU, then, provided direct support for the *Monroe* case.

The story of *Monroe v. Pape* gets even more complicated. Justice Douglas's opinion in favor of the Monroes was a classically incrementalist decision. By exposing the Chicago police officers to financial liability for their actions, the decision constituted a victory for individual rights advocates and a defeat for their opponents. But Douglas declined to take the additional step of exposing city *governments* to liability for the actions of their officers. And so civil rights advocates criticized the Court for not going far enough, for failing to give cities any incentive to properly train and discipline their officials. The NAACP-LDF, in particular, pursued a legal campaign to convince the courts to take that next step, which the Supreme Court eventually completed in 1978.[24]

The right (really a remedy) won by James and Flossie Monroe thus rested on far more than judicial power and constitutional promises (although both were crucial), and the judicial decision that declared the right was not in any ordinary sense tyrannical. The new right grew out of the collective efforts of a large number of people who relied on organizational, legal, and financial resources that had been created by broad, collective efforts.

The Conditions for the Rights Revolution: Theory

Conventional interpretations of the rights revolution identify several key factors—constitutional guarantees, judicial leadership, and popular rights consciousness—that have a venerable place in theories of constitutional democracy. The thesis of this book is not that these factors are irrelevant but that they are insufficient to explain the rights revolution. In this chapter I examine the theoretical logic of the conventional interpretations and show how the support-structure explanation supplements them in crucial ways. Although the various factors interact in practice, many commentators give primacy to one or another, and it is useful to discuss each one separately.

Conventional Interpretations

The Constitution-Centered Explanation: Judicial
Independence and Bills of Rights

In the constitution-centered view, the crucial conditions for a rights revolution are structural judicial independence and a foundation of constitutional rights guarantees; given those conditions, judges are free to devote sustained attention and approval for civil rights and liberties. The judicial system's structural independence from direct political pressure is widely recognized as a necessary condition for any significant judicial check on arbitrary power. Courts are structurally independent to the extent that the job security and salaries of their judges, and the decision-making process, are insulated from political manipulation.[1]

Apart from judicial independence, the presence or absence of constitutional rights guarantees is widely believed to be the most important influence on the extent of judicial policy making on rights. In the popular imagination, there is no doubt that judicial support for rights flows from a bill of rights. Many scholars, too, view constitutionally en-

trenched bills of rights as significant influences on judicial policies. (The term "entrenched bill of rights," though not common in the United States, is widely used elsewhere to refer to constitutional rights guarantees that authorize judicial review of ordinary statutes). Standard comparisons of the United States and other countries, for instance, typically trace the extraordinary vibrancy of judicial review of state action, judicial attention to rights, and judicial policy making on rights in the United States to the presence of an entrenched bill of rights in the United States Constitution.[2] The U.S. experience, indeed, has powerfully shaped standard conceptions of the influence of constitutional rights guarantees. The common addition of bills of rights in the last several decades to constitutions around the world is surely due in part to admiration of the U.S. model.[3]

Nonetheless, proposals to adopt a bill of rights have often provoked heated debate in many countries. In France, for example, Edouard Lambert opposed establishment of a constitutional bill of rights in the early decades of this century because he feared it would enable French judges to mimic American judges' opposition to economic regulation and planning.[4] The framers of the Indian Constitution in the late forties deliberated at some length on the dangers of American-style judicial activism and then, following the advice of United States Supreme Court Justice Felix Frankfurter, eviscerated a proposed due process clause in order to limit the Indian Supreme Court's power.[5] Canadian debates over adoption in 1982 of the Charter of Rights and Freedoms focused in large part on the desirability of authorizing judges to review legislation; a number of Canadians vigorously opposed the Charter for fear that it authorized what they called American-style judicial activism.[6] In Britain, debates over whether to establish a written bill of rights continue to revolve around the degree to which judges may be trusted with expanded powers.[7]

Debates over proposed bills of rights are vigorous because the documents are widely believed to produce profound effects. One presumed effect, as the foregoing survey suggests, is an expansion of judicial power.[8] Bills of rights undoubtedly seem to grant great but poorly defined powers to the judiciary. It is widely assumed that judges cannot resist the temptation to use those powers broadly and, further, that a bill of rights stymies the legislature from curbing judicial action. Thus, James Madison speculated that a bill of rights would "naturally" lead courts to "resist every encroachment upon rights" by legislatures and executives.[9]

Bills of rights are also thought to encourage the growth of many

competing interest groups. In systems without a bill of rights or judicial review, policies are made primarily in the legislative and executive
branches of government. In those forums, groups must form broad
coalitions to advance their interests. But some observers have argued
that, in systems with an entrenched bill of rights, groups have an incentive to avoid the task of coalition building because they can go it alone
in the courts.[10]

Additionally, bills of rights are believed to powerfully shape popular
culture. Thus, James Madison argued that "[t]he political truths declared in that solemn manner [in a bill of rights] acquire by degrees
the character of fundamental maxims of free Government, and as they
become incorporated with the national sentiment, counteract the im-
pulses of interest and passion."[11] Similarly, others have argued that a
bill of rights may promote the development of "rights consciousness"
in popular culture. That is, the existence of constitutional rights guarantees may encourage individuals to interpret harms to their interests
as violations of "rights" and, because of this changed consciousness,
constitutional rights may become rallying points for social movements
and popular pressure on government. The U.S. Constitution's rights
guarantees, according to Vivien Hart, encouraged a popular belief in
the right to a minimum wage; and Hendrik Hartog has argued that
adoption of the Fourteenth Amendment in 1868 provided a new rallying point for political and social movements by African-Americans,
women, and others.[12] In Canada, a supporter of the ill-fated 1960 Bill
of Rights argued that "the real significance of the Canadian Bill of
Rights lies not in its content but in the way in which it has served as a
focal point for and stimulus to arguments about civil liberties. . . . The
very existence of this Bill of Rights . . . both acts as a milestone on the
road to increased consciousness of civil liberties and itself serves to
encourage their further development."[13]

But the effects of a constitutional bill of rights are commonly exaggerated. Among the many new bills of rights created since 1945, some
are shams, and even those that are not are quite flexible in practice.
Both the U.S. Bill of Rights and the Indian Constitution's anemic due
process clause were ignored for many years but have since become
foundations for much judicial policy making. The fate of a bill of rights
thus depends on forces outside of it. In the United States, at least, the
relatively broad arena of judicial action and the limits on legislative
power are plausibly due less to the Bill of Rights alone than to the
many veto points in the legislative process and the practical difficulty
of passing court-curbing actions.[14] And judges are likely to use their

powers under a bill of rights only if they oppose public policy, yet many judges support public policies against rights claims. Additionally, from the perspective of the ordinary individual, a bill of rights, by itself, offers only promises but no resources or remedies for mobilizing those promises in the judicial system. Thus, A. V. Dicey argued that constitutional rights guarantees were meaningless in the absence of ordinary legal remedies to invoke them.[15] Similarly, James Madison warned that a bill of rights would be ineffective *"particularly . . . where the law aggrieves individuals, who may be unable to support an appeal [against] a State to the supreme Judiciary."*[16] It thus takes more than judicial independence and a bill of rights to make a rights revolution.

The Judge-Centered Explanation: Judicial Leadership and Docket Control
According to the judge-centered explanation for rights revolutions, significant judicial protection for individual rights results primarily from supportive judges who have the power to focus on the cases that interest them. Judges, of course, ultimately decide who wins and who loses in appellate cases and whether a particular rights claim is accepted or rejected. Over time, the accretion of such judicial decisions shapes the development of the law. Thus, rights revolutions undoubtedly cannot happen without rights-supportive judges. In the U.S. case, in particular, judicial leadership has always seemed crucial to the genesis of the rights revolution. In 1953 Earl Warren assumed leadership of a Supreme Court that contained only a few consistent supporters of civil liberties and civil rights, and within a few years enough other supporters of those rights joined the Court to form a solid liberal majority. The decisions of that majority greatly expanded the scope of constitutional rights and significantly contributed to the U.S. rights revolution.

As illustrated by the Warren Court, judicial attitudes undoubtedly influence judicial decisions, but judicial leadership, by itself, cannot create a rights revolution. The influence of judicial attitudes is likely to depend on structural judicial independence (as discussed in the last section) and on the extent to which judges can choose which cases to decide.[17] Judicial freedom to choose cases varies from country to country and from court to court, depending on the extent of legislatively granted docket control. Some courts must decide nearly every case that comes to them; those courts typically become overloaded with routine disputes between private parties and therefore cannot focus on cases they might regard as especially important. Other courts, for instance the United States Supreme Court, enjoy nearly complete control over their dockets and, therefore, may choose which issues they

will decide. Greater discretion at the agenda-setting stage enhances the influence of judicial attitudes more generally. At the extreme, a court that enjoys complete discretion over its docket and that receives a wide array of cases may create whatever agenda it wishes. At the least, it is clear that when the United States Supreme Court gained control of its agenda in 1925, the Court used that discretion to increase its attention to constitutional and other public law issues and decrease its attention to mundane disputes between private parties.[18] Similarly, as state supreme courts in the United States have gained discretionary control over their dockets, their agendas have shifted away from private economic disputes and toward public law.[19]

If a court has structural independence and control of its docket, then its decisions—in theory— may become a matter of personal idiosyncrasy and historical accident—a matter of who is chosen to sit on a court and how long it takes the judge to retire or die. As Robert Yates, an antifederalist critic of the United States Constitution, predicted of Supreme Court judges: "There is no power above them, to controul any of their decisions. There is no authority that can remove them, and they cannot be controuled by the laws of the legislature. In short, they are independent of the people, of the legislature, and of every power under heaven. Men placed in this situation will generally soon feel themselves independent of heaven itself."[20] With an expansive view of the Supreme Court's freedom and a recognition of the growing liberalism of its justices in the fifties and sixties, some proponents of the judge-centered explanation have characterized the U.S. rights revolution as the virtually independent creation of a few Supreme Court justices.[21]

Like the constitution-centered explanation, the judge-centered explanation for rights revolutions undoubtedly has much validity, especially in the United States. Even liberal judges armed with control of their dockets and an entrenched bill of rights, however, cannot make rights-supportive law unless they have rights cases to decide, and the process of mobilizing cases rests on far more than judicial fiat. The judge-centered explanation, alone or in combination with the constitution-centered explanation, is incomplete.

The Culture-Centered Explanation: Culture and Rights Consciousness
Under the culture-centered explanation for rights revolutions, popular culture is thought to influence judicial protection of individual rights in several ways. First, judges are themselves shaped by a society's cultural assumptions and are therefore unlikely to either create rights not

recognized by their society or undermine rights highly valued by their society. Second, courts lack the institutional power to enforce decisions that run contrary to widely held beliefs. Third, the number and kinds of issues that citizens take to the courts as rights claims depend on whether and how the society's culture frames disputes in terms of rights.

These three influences are commonly highlighted by proponents of the culture-centered explanation. Thus, Louis Hartz argued that the power of the U.S. Bill of Rights and the Supreme Court resulted not only from the Constitution but, more importantly, from Americans' "Lockian creed" of liberal individualism, which encourages Americans to frame their political ideals in terms of individual rights, to take their concerns to courts, and to expect courts to make policy on such questions.[22] Mary Ann Glendon has similarly claimed that a popular culture of liberal "rights talk" in the United States has increased the emphasis on rights in American constitutionalism and has thus encouraged and reinforced the Supreme Court's focus on individual rights.[23] And although Glendon emphasizes the continuing uniqueness of the liberal language of rights in the United States, she recognizes that the rights agenda is growing elsewhere, and she attributes this growth to the globalization of human rights discourse.[24]

But the influence of American-style "rights talk" is not the only factor that has affected global awareness of individual rights. The spread of rights consciousness is also likely related to the "democratic deficit" of the modern bureaucratic state. In the twentieth century, particularly since 1945, state bureaucracies have grown far beyond the capacity of the electoral and legislative process to exercise anything approaching direct control, and critics in many countries have bemoaned that lack of democratic accountability. Individual-level checks on the administrative process—in addition to collective control over it—have therefore become increasingly attractive. And individual-level checks are articulated in the language of rights. As Jack Donnelly has argued, the repressive capacities (or, more benignly, the bureaucratic capacities) of the modern state virtually demand a response emphasizing individual rights.[25] That response, in turn, arguably has helped to legitimate judicial oversight over the administrative process. Mauro Cappelletti, for instance, has argued that the growing intervention in individuals' lives by national state bureaucracies, combined with the difficulty of using the electoral process to correct abuses, has encouraged the development of rights discourse and legitimated the growth of judicial oversight over the administrative process.[26] Indeed, in each of the countries

in this study, as government grew, there also began to develop a pervasive sense that unrestrained governmental power threatened important values and that at least some governmental power should be harnessed to serve egalitarian purposes. In each country, the courts and individual rights were seen to be possible institutional mechanisms for achieving those goals.

The culture-centered explanation for rights revolutions is thus partly correct. Cultural frames undoubtedly shape the kinds of claims that individuals can even conceive, as well as the kinds of changes that they view as within the realm of possibility.[27] Individuals, whether ordinary citizens or judges, cannot assert or sanction a right unless they can conceive of the idea of a "right" in general and also of the particular right in question. And so surely the growing attention paid by supreme courts to rights claims would not have developed in the absence of the concept of "rights" or the extension of that concept to areas of life previously untouched by it. Protection of women's rights, for example, depended in part on a growing recognition that gender discrimination is a problem. That recognition is such a recent development that, when Herbert Wechsler gave his famous lecture in 1959 on "neutral principles" in judicial decision making, he offered classification by sex as an example of a type of discrimination that was beyond reproach.[28] The perception that gender discrimination is a problem, however, has grown, and women's-rights claims are now heard and upheld by judges. A minimal recognition of rights, therefore, is a necessary condition for development of a judicial rights agenda and, for that reason, the spread of rights consciousness throughout much of the world has undoubtedly contributed to the development of judicial attention to rights.

But rights consciousness alone is likely to be insufficient to produce an expansion in judicial attention and support for rights, because cases depend on material support, and material support does not flow automatically from changed perceptions.[29] Combining rights consciousness with a bill of rights and a willing and able judiciary improves the outlook for a rights revolution, but material support for sustained pursuit of rights cases is still crucial. A support structure for legal mobilization provides this missing ingredient.

The Support Structure for Legal Mobilization

The unstated premise of the conventional explanations for rights revolutions is that lawsuits and appeals easily arise as a reflection of constitutional provisions, judicial policies, and/or cultural changes. Thus, in

the standard theories, a rights-friendly culture naturally generates rights cases; litigants easily and naturally rely on constitutional rights guarantees; and litigants pursue rights claims if judges indicate a friendliness toward those claims.

But cases do not arrive in supreme courts as if by magic. The premise of the alternative explanation proposed here is that the process of legal mobilization—the process by which individuals make claims about their legal rights and pursue lawsuits to defend or develop those rights—is not in any simple way a direct response to opportunities provided by constitutional promises or judicial decisions, or to expectations arising from popular culture.[30] Legal mobilization also depends on resources, and resources for rights litigation depend on a support structure of rights-advocacy lawyers, rights-advocacy organizations, and sources of financing.

The logic behind the support-structure explanation consists of two interrelated points. First, rights revolutions depend on widespread and sustained litigation in support of civil rights and liberties. Supreme courts that can choose their cases usually will not hear an issue unless cases presenting the issue have reached critical mass in the judicial system; the United States Supreme Court hesitates to hear an issue that has not, in Supreme Court parlance, "percolated" in lower courts.[31] Moreover, even landmark decisions are isolated symbols unless they are supported by a continuing stream of cases providing clarification and enforcement. For example, the implementation of *Brown v. Board of Education*,[32] the 1954 United States Supreme Court decision overturning racial segregation in public schools, depended in large part on a number of later cases (as well as support from Congress and the presidency).[33] Widespread and sustained litigation, therefore, is crucial to a rights revolution.

The second point is that successful rights litigation usually consumes resources beyond the reach of individual plaintiffs—resources that can be provided only by an ongoing support structure. The judicial process is time-consuming, expensive, and arcane; ordinary individuals typically do not have the time, money, or expertise necessary to support a long-running lawsuit through several levels of the judicial system. For this reason, Marc Galanter argued that "one-shotters"— ordinary individuals with little experience in the courts—typically fare poorly in comparison to seasoned, well-resourced organizational litigants ("repeat players") unless the one-shotters can gain the resource-related advantages held by repeat players.[34] Moreover, successful rights litigation depends on a steady stream of rights cases that press

toward shared goals, for changes in constitutional law typically occur in small increments. A support structure can provide the consistent support that is needed to move case after case through the courts. Although one might expect the contingency fee system to provide needed financial support to rights litigants in the United States, it actually provided little support for civil rights and liberties cases during the formative years of the rights revolution. The fruits of constitutional rights victories are essentially "public goods," legal guarantees that benefit a population much broader than the immediate plaintiff seeking to create or expand the right. So at the broadest level, the benefits to rights advocates have outweighed the costs of cases. But at the level of the individual cases, the cost of pursuing a rights case has usually exceeded any monetary award to the plaintiffs (at least in the early phases of a rights revolution), so lawyers have had little monetary incentive to take such cases on a contingency basis. Organized rights advocates, however, have developed a range of sources of support—comparable to the resources held by repeat players—and have made them available to potential rights claimants. These sources of support, consisting of rights-advocacy organizations, willing and able lawyers, financial aid of various types, and, in some countries, governmental rights-enforcement agencies, form what I call the support structure for legal mobilization.

Each of the main components of the support structure has contributed to the process of legal mobilization in significant ways. Organized groups help to provide expert legal counsel and to develop and coordinate legal research and strategy; they provide financing or aid in finding sources of financing; they sponsor or coordinate nonlegal research, particularly in the areas of social science, history, and medicine, that support particular legal claims; they provide publicity; and they provide networks of communication and thereby facilitate the exchange of ideas.[35]

Some governmental rights-enforcement agencies have played a role very similar to private groups. In the United States, the Justice Department at some points in its history has directly supported lawsuits, conducted and coordinated legal research and strategy, and filed supportive briefs as an *amicus curiae* (a nonparty "friend of the court").[36] In some other countries, too, the support of government agencies has been crucial for the development of civil liberties and civil rights litigation.

Funding has come from private foundations, wealthy individuals, and some government programs, particularly legal aid in some countries.[37] Funding from these sources has provided crucial start-up costs

for organizations as well as ongoing support for litigation campaigns. More recently, in the United States some financing has come from fee-shifting statutes that authorize judges to award attorneys' fees to rights plaintiffs whose claims succeed.

Willing and able lawyers, too, have played a crucial role. Lawyers speak for rights plaintiffs in court, contribute to legal strategy, and provide much of the network through which information about rights litigation travels.[38] Rights-supportive lawyers and law schools have also built a body of scholarship on individual rights and legal remedies, which aids others in learning how to successfully pursue rights-advocacy litigation. The availability of such lawyers depends in large part on the diversity and organization of the legal profession in a given country at a given time.[39] The extent to which a legal profession is racially and ethnically diverse and open to women significantly influences the extent to which it provides access to the courts to women and members of racial and ethnic minorities. And the extent to which lawyers practice in firms rather than alone influences their ability to specialize, to work on nonremunerative cases, and to take advantage of economies of scale.

The support structure for legal mobilization is neither a judicial creation nor a direct result of a bill of rights. Opportunities provided by judges and by a bill of rights certainly influence the extent to which people invest time and resources in developing parts of the support structure. But the components of the support structure reflect other influences as well. Rights-advocacy group organizing has historically reflected changes in public policy, the availability of resources, and the growth of knowledge about how to form citizen-action groups.[40] The diversity of the legal profession has reflected patterns of immigration and access to higher education. And the availability of financing has reflected the rise of private foundations and changes in government policy.

Support Structures and Rights Revolutions

Throughout this book, analysis of the relationship between the support structure for legal mobilization and sustained judicial attention and support for rights focuses on the timing of developments in these two areas. Vibrant support structures are a relatively new development—but *they preceded and supported the development of rights revolutions.* Most of the significant developments in the support structure in the United States—including the birth of organized rights-advocacy groups—began shortly after 1910. In other countries, significant developments

came after 1965. The NAACP, the ACLU, the International Labor Defense, and other litigation support groups were formed in the early decades of this century; they organized, financed, and provided legal counsel for many of the most important civil rights and liberties cases to reach the United States Supreme Court.[41] More recently, in a number of other countries interest groups have played an increasingly important role in supporting civil rights and liberties litigation. For instance, in Canada, early developments in freedom of speech and religious liberty resulted from the efforts of Jehovah's Witnesses,[42] and in Britain, litigation by the Child Poverty Action Group overturned some sex discrimination in the Social Security Act of 1975.[43] Similarly, sources of financing for civil rights and liberties cases have become more widespread and substantial in recent years. Private foundations have grown significantly in wealth and size in this century, particularly in the United States. Legal aid in civil cases and the most important forms of aid for criminal defendants are relatively new developments. In the United States, governmental aid began growing only in the last sixty years; in other countries the growth of legal aid has been even more recent. But, again, the expansion of financial resources preceded development of the rights revolution. The legal profession has also become increasingly diverse and has organized in firms. Those developments date to the early years of this century in the United States and occurred much later in other countries;[44] but again, the key developments in the legal profession preceded and supported developments in the rights revolution. The support structure, then, is relatively new: but rights revolutions are more recent yet.

Admittedly, in some instances, judges have created new rights in advance of sustained litigation on the subject by rights advocates, but even then the presence of a vibrant support structure is a necessary condition for rights advocates to capitalize on new legal opportunities offered by judges. As I shall show, for instance, the weakness of the support structure in India is precisely the explanation for why no rights revolution emerged there after Supreme Court justices tried to create one.

None of this means that organized rights advocates, given adequate support, can control and manipulate the nature and timing of the issues appearing on the judicial agenda. As Stephen Wasby has observed, the complexity of the litigation process, the number of litigants, and the inevitability of historical accident and unintended consequences all conspire to limit the extent of deliberately planned control of litigation by organized groups.[45] Thus the support-structure expla-

nation does not replace a theory of judicial control of the agenda with its mirror image, a theory of complete control by strategic litigators. A support structure merely gives rights advocates access to the judicial agenda. But that has been a significant development.

If the existence of a support structure is necessary for rights advocates to have access to the judicial agenda, we should expect developments in the support structure to be matters of political strategy and controversy. Indeed this is the case. Much of the support structure's development in the United States and in other countries has reflected the political strategies of liberals and egalitarians to use the courts for political change. Recently in some countries political conservatives have responded by developing competing legal advocacy organizations and by attempting to cut governmental funding for legal services. These controversies reflect a recognition that the development of law in general, and of rights in particular, is shaped by the nature and extent of the support structure.

In sum, if the support-structure hypothesis is correct, neither particular civil liberties or civil rights lawsuits nor the rights revolution in general resulted in any direct way only from judicial fiat, the opportunities provided by constitutional rights guarantees, and/or rights consciousness in popular culture. Instead, the development of a support structure for civil rights and liberties litigation propelled rights issues into the higher courts, encouraged the courts to render favorable decisions and, at least to some extent, provided the judiciary with active partners in the fight against opponents of implementation of the new rights. As Ruth Cowan observed regarding women's-rights litigation, "Success in the judicial arena, as in other political forums, hinges on the organization and mobilization of resources."[46] Similarly, as a civil rights litigator told Stephen Wasby, "What there's money for, you tend to do."[47]

Alternative Expectations for Comparative Research

The foregoing discussion leads to a number of alternative expectations for the comparative study of rights revolutions. Assuming a necessary minimum level of structural judicial independence (and that other factors are held equal) the expectations can be summarized as follows: (1) If the *constitution-centered* explanation is correct, we should expect that rights revolutions have occurred only where there exist constitutional rights guarantees, only after adoption of those guarantees, and only on the particular claims supported by those guarantees. We should also expect that popular rights consciousness increases after

adoption of constitutional rights guarantees. (2) If the *judge-centered* explanation is correct, we should find that rights revolutions have occurred only where judges support civil liberties and civil rights, only after development of that support, and only on claims that judges clearly support—at least if the conditions for broad judicial discretion are present. (3) If the *culture-centered* explanation is correct, we should find that rights revolutions have occurred only where popular rights consciousness is widespread, only after development of popular rights consciousness, and only on those claims recognized in popular rights consciousness.

If, however, the elements of the standard explanations, taken singly or together, provide an incomplete explanation of the rights revolution, then we should consider the following proposition: If the *support-structure* explanation is correct, we should find that rights revolutions have occurred only where and when and on those issues for which material support for rights litigation—rights-advocacy organizations, supportive lawyers, and sources of financing—has developed.

Structure of the Study and Overview of Findings
My analysis rests on a comparison of rights revolutions in the United States, Canada, India, and Britain in the period 1960–1990 (although my analysis of the United States begins much earlier). These countries differ in the extent and nature of their rights revolutions, as well as in the structure of their constitutions, the extent to which judicial liberals have dominated their supreme courts, and the extent of their support structures for rights litigation. This study design facilitates analysis of the sources and conditions for the rights revolution.[48]

This analysis has led to the following general observations: First, the growth of judicial protection for individual rights is indeed a widespread, but not universal, development. It has been greatest in the United States and Canada and weakest in India, and it is present but not vibrant in Britain. In the following chapters, variations among countries and over time form the basis for my analysis. Second, in each country, the language of rights became increasingly widespread by the mid-sixties. It flourished in the United States as early as the mid-nineteenth century but developed only after the early sixties in the other countries in this study. Third, although each country's constitutional structure provides a threshold level of judicial independence, the existence of constitutional rights guarantees differs significantly from country to country: the United States has had a bill of rights for more than two hundred years; India adopted a constitution, including

a bill of rights, in 1950; Canada adopted a bill of rights in 1982; Britain has no constitutional bill of rights. The Canadian experience, in particular, offers the chance to assess the effect on the judicial agenda of adoption of a constitutional bill of rights. Fourth, in each country the supreme court has been dominated by activist, rights-supportive judges at one or another point in the recent past. In the United States, that occurred most clearly under the leadership of Chief Justice Earl Warren from 1953 to 1969. In Britain, the Appellate Committee of the House of Lords, under the leadership of Lord Reid, developed a modestly activist posture in the sixties and early seventies. In Canada, judicial supporters of expansive protection for individual rights controlled the Supreme Court after the early eighties. And in India, leading justices on the Supreme Court created a revolution in constitutional law in the late seventies and early eighties, greatly expanding the constitution's formal protection for equality rights and for the less fortunate classes in Indian society.

Finally, the strength and the timing of growth in the support structure for rights litigation varies significantly among the countries. That support structure is larger and more diverse in the United States than in the other countries. The United States has a large legal profession but, more importantly, the profession is ideologically diverse, organizationally adept, and adversarial in orientation; this is increasingly true of the legal profession in Canada, but the profession in Britain remains relatively homogeneous, and Indian lawyers practice individually, thus gaining none of the advantages of specialization and the like that accrue in the firm setting. The United States has a wide array of private foundations that finance a relatively large number of public interest organizations. The other countries in the study almost entirely lack such systems. The United States has large and relatively mature systems for providing legal defense to poor criminal defendants; such systems are newer in the other countries in the study. Although there are important differences among countries in the extent of the support structure for legal mobilization, those structures have changed in similar directions over recent decades. In each country in this study the support structures have deepened and diversified. In the United States the origins of that deepening and diversification began as early as the first and second decades of this century, in the development of the first public interest groups to use litigation as part of their political efforts, in the growing size and diversity of the legal profession, and in the development of official policies requiring the legal representation of

indigent criminal defendants. In other countries such changes began much later, primarily after 1970.

Throughout this study I have relied as much as possible on data from a variety of sources to facilitate triangulation, or double- and triple-checking. The data for the dependent variable, the judicial agenda, consist of cases heard by each high court in 1960, 1965, 1970, 1975, 1980, 1985, and 1990. There are several sources for the data. The agenda data for the United States were obtained from Pacelle's study of the United States Supreme Court's agenda.[49] The data for Canada, India, and Britain were gathered for this study from published court records (the Canadian Supreme Court Reports, All India Reporter, and Law Reports: Appeal Cases). The published records for India and Britain do not include information on all cases heard by their high courts, and so I supplement information gathered from published sources with information from some unpublished sources held at the courts themselves.[50]

The data for the independent variables come from a variety of sources, which I document in each of the chapters. In general, I rely on the large legal and social scientific literature on the legal systems of each of the countries, supplemented by interview and documentary sources that I gathered in visits to Canada, England, and India.

My analysis proceeds country by country. For each of the four countries, I devote a chapter to the political and legal context for judicial protection of individual rights and a chapter to the nature and timing of developments in the rights revolution and the influence of the support structure. As I show, in most places, until relatively recently, the support structure for pursuing rights cases has been weak and access to courts has been limited to a small proportion of the population and to the issues they wish to litigate. Most individuals, and the legal claims they might wish to make, have been ruled out of the contest virtually from the start. The growth of support structures for legal mobilization, as I show in the following pages, however, has democratized access to supreme courts in recent years and has provided a principal condition for the judicial rights revolution.

THREE

The United States: Standard Explanations
for the Rights Revolution

The United States, in a popular and influential view, is "The Land of Rights."[1] The language of rights seems to pervade popular discourse, political disputes, and judicial decisions; Americans have come to believe that freedom of speech, freedom of religion, and equality are the central values of their political system. The United States Supreme Court, moreover, is among the most active courts in the world, and its intervention in policy debates is typically justified as necessary for defending individual rights. The Court's "key role in American government," according to Jesse Choper, "is to guard against governmental infringement of individual liberties secured by the Constitution."[2]

Yet the Supreme Court began turning its attention to individual rights only recently. As late as 1916, 125 years after adoption of the Bill of Rights, the Court focused its attention largely on resolving commercial disputes and virtually never examined issues related to individual rights. Partly as a result, protection for civil liberties and civil rights in American society suffered. As late as 1950 state laws relegated most black schoolchildren to separate, poorly funded schools and discriminated against African Americans in public accommodations. State laws also prohibited the sale and use of birth control devices and most states prohibited abortions except in limited circumstances. State police authorities could, by law, use nonphysical coercion in extracting confessions or incriminating information from criminal defendants, and defendants could, by law, be prosecuted, convicted, and sentenced to prison for serious crimes even if they lacked an attorney. In many states, authorities acting without court authorization could search a person's home and seize anything they deemed to be evidence.

By 1975 none of those things remained legal; all were banned by the Supreme Court as violations of fundamental constitutional rights. In a span of about fifty years, the Supreme Court went from virtually ignoring civil rights and liberties to devoting the majority of its attention to

such issues. The constitutional rights revolution constituted a major revolution in the meaning of constitutionalism itself. Where once constitutionalism's central ideal had been limited government, now its central ideal had become the protection of individual rights. As noted in the previous chapters, these dramatic changes are usually attributed to a favorable constitution, leadership by liberal Supreme Court justices, and popular support for civil liberties and rights in American culture. Each of these explanations is partly correct. But, even taken together, they are greatly incomplete as an explanation for the rights revolution.

The U.S. Rights Revolution

A necessary first step in examining the U.S. rights revolution is to clarify the timing of developments in that revolution. My analysis in this chapter and the next is devoted to explaining three developments in the rights revolution, which are partially illustrated in figure 3.1.[3] First, the Court's agenda on civil liberties and civil rights as a whole began to grow early in this century, long before the ascendance of a liberal majority on the Court, which is usually dated either to 1937 or to the period after Earl Warren's appointment as chief justice in 1953. The Court's attention to civil liberties and civil rights began to grow even before the 1933 court term, the first year illustrated in figure 3. 1. Second, the Court's agenda on criminal procedure began to grow in the early thirties, again, long before justices with liberal attitudes toward criminal procedure gained control of the Court. Third, the Court's agenda on women's rights began to grow in the early seventies, just after liberals lost control of the Court to conservatives. Let us consider each of these developments in turn.

First, the Court's attention to civil liberties and rights as a whole grew in fits and starts until the beginning of its well-known, dramatic climb in the sixties. The magnitude of the change is surprising. In the 1933 term, civil liberties and civil rights constituted about 9 percent of the Court's agenda; by the 1971 term, they constituted about 65 percent of the agenda.

Because systematic data on the Court's agenda are available only after 1932, figure 3.1 misses important changes before that year. Indeed, the Court's attention to civil liberties and civil rights began to grow almost twenty years earlier. Dating the origin of an important development is always a tricky business. Nonetheless, in the matter of the Court's attention to individual rights, there is a fairly clear beginning point in the years following the First World War.[4] Before 1917,

Figure 3.1 Rights Agenda of the U.S. Supreme Court

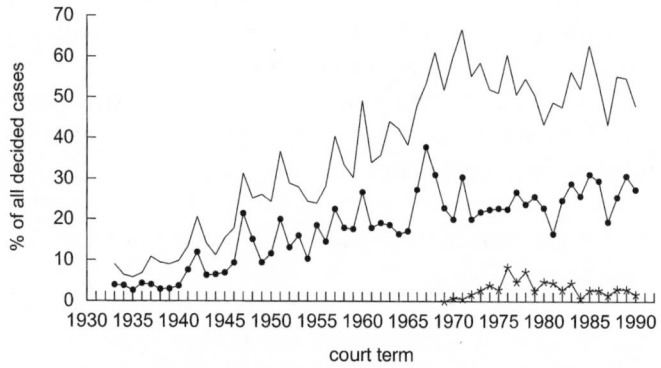

court term

— aggregate rights agenda •– rights of accused ✳– women's rights

Source: Pacelle, *Transformation*, and data provided by Pacelle.

the Court rarely decided civil liberties cases. Beginning in that year, however, the Court began deciding such cases relatively regularly. In 1917, the Court overturned Louisville's racially exclusionary zoning law (*Buchanan v. Warley*).[5] In 1919 the Supreme Court decided four important freedom of speech cases (*Schenck v. United States, Abrams v. United States, Debs v. United States, and Frohwerk v. United States*), in each rejecting claims that convictions under the Espionage Act of 1917 violated the First Amendment.[6] After those restrictive decisions, however, the Court handed down several decisions that suggested that freedom of speech might receive some level of constitutional protection. In 1920 the Court suggested, but did not rule, that the First Amendment's guarantee of freedom of speech restricted state action as well as federal action (*Gilbert v. Minnesota*); in 1925, the Court again advanced that suggestion (*Gitlow v. New York*); finally, in 1927 in *Fiske v. Kansas*, the Court ruled that the First Amendment's guarantee of freedom of speech indeed restricts state action.[7] Meanwhile, the Court expanded constitutional protection for some personal liberties not even mentioned in the Constitution's text. In the mid-twenties, the Court affirmed that the Fourteenth Amendment's due process clause protects the liberty of parents to send their children to private schools (*Pierce v. Society of Sisters*) and of schools to teach modern languages other than English (*Meyer v. Nebraska*).[8] In 1931, the Court ruled that freedom of the press applies to the states (*Near v. Minnesota*); in 1932, the Court ruled that the right of fair trial and the right to counsel apply in capital trials in state courts (*Powell v. Alabama*).[9] In addition to these famous

and important cases, the number of less important decisions on civil rights and liberties also began increasing after about 1917.

Undoubtedly the Court heard and decided some civil liberties and rights cases before 1917.[10] In the area of freedom of speech in particular, David Rabban has argued that the Supreme Court's attention to the issue preceded the famous World War I-era cases by several decades.[11] Rabban documented eighteen freedom-of-speech cases decided by the Court in the years before 1917.[12] In relation to the Supreme Court's overall agenda, however, civil liberties and civil rights cases remained lonely exceptions. By the beginning of the twenties civil liberties and civil rights cases appeared with increasing frequency on the agenda.

Although judicial attention to civil liberties and civil rights as a whole began to grow after 1917, not all components of the rights agenda grew at the same time or same pace. The Supreme Court's attention to the rights of the accused and prisoners began to grow as early as the forties, long before the landmark due process decisions in the sixties. At its height in the 1967 term, the criminal procedure agenda commanded just under 38 percent of the agenda space, compared to a low of under 3 percent in the 1935 term. But fully half of that eventual growth–17 percentage points—had occurred *before* the appointment of Earl Warren in 1953.

In the area of women's rights, the Supreme Court had virtually no agenda until 1971 but after that year began devoting increasing attention to the issue. The pattern is intriguing because the Court's attention to women's rights began to grow just after the transition between the liberal Warren Court and the more conservative Burger Court. The Warren Court heard only one case explicitly raising a women's-rights claim and rejected that claim,[13] (although *Griswold v. Connecticut*[14] may also be considered a women's-rights case due to the centrality of reproductive freedom in the women's movement). The Burger Court, by contrast, took up the issue of sex discrimination and heard dozens of cases in the seventies and eighties. The new agenda, furthermore, involved more than a scattering of routine cases: it was a momentous intervention into highly contentious issues, among them equal treatment under the law and abortion.[15] Nonetheless, the agenda space devoted to women's rights has remained far less than the space devoted to the rights of the accused and prisoners.

Why did the Supreme Court's attention to civil liberties and rights begin growing after 1917, long before judicial liberals gained control of the Court? Why did the Court's attention to criminal procedure begin

growing after the early thirties, and why did the Court's attention to women's rights begin growing rapidly only after 1970? In the remainder of this chapter I consider and reject as incomplete the conventional explanations for these developments.

The Limitations of Standard Explanations

The Constitution-Centered Explanation

The United States Constitution and its Bill of Rights have significantly affected the political and legal process in the United States, but the effects have been indirect. The Constitution is less an ironclad framework for government than a set of resources to be used by political actors as best they can. As a consequence, the Constitution has proven to be enormously elastic over time. Its formal structure and provisions, with a few exceptions, have changed little, yet its meaning has changed dramatically.[16] The most significant changes have been the vast expansion in the powers of the national government and the great broadening and deepening of the meaning of individual rights as limitations on the powers of both the national and state governments. One of the most important aspects of that transformation was the application of most provisions in the Bill of Rights to the states, a process that began after 1920.

In the nineteenth century, it was widely accepted that the Bill of Rights placed no limitations on the power of the states. In *Barron v. Baltimore* (1833)[17] the Supreme Court ruled that the Bill of Rights applied only to the federal government; that ruling clearly was consistent with the dominant view in the late 1700s among the framers and ratifiers of the first ten amendments, and the ruling was reaffirmed in several other cases in the nineteenth and early twentieth centuries. The passage of the Fourteenth Amendment in 1868, of course, provided a potential foundation for applying the Bill of Rights to the states, because it explicitly placed rights-based limitations on the states. Yet which rights were guaranteed by the Fourteenth Amendment remained notoriously unclear, for the amendment referred only in relatively vague and general terms to "the privileges or immunities of citizens of the United States," "life, liberty, or property," "due process," and "equal protection of the laws." Although some judges and politicians argued that those words protected a broad range of rights and, in particular, applied the provisions of the Bill of Rights to the states, many others disagreed, and the matter remained a subject of great

dispute well into the twentieth century.[18] The formal constitutional change wrought by the Fourteenth Amendment, then, did not by itself decisively change the meaning of the rights protected by the Constitution, at least as understood by legal elites. Moreover, the growth in judicial attention to individual rights began long after passage of the Fourteenth Amendment, indeed as much as fifty years later. Adoption of the amendment, then, simply is not plausible as a complete, or even nearly complete, explanation for the growth of the rights revolution.

Many of the important developments in the rights revolution in the twentieth century nonetheless were based on the Fourteenth Amendment, and therefore passage of the amendment was a contributing condition. As Hartog has suggested, passage of the Civil War Amendments, arising as they did from the long slave-emancipation struggle in which the language of rights figured prominently, contributed greatly to the connection between the Constitution and rights aspirations in popular culture.[19] That connection has provided a uniquely powerful organizational resource and lever of influence for rights-seeking social movements. Nonetheless, as I show in the next section, those movements existed before passage of the Fourteenth Amendment, and new ones developed in the late nineteenth and early twentieth centuries, and yet the Supreme Court recognized virtually none of their claims until after World War I. That lack of recognition was due in part to the weakness of the support structure for rights litigation in the nineteenth century, as discussed in the following chapter. To a significant extent, of course, it was also due to the Supreme Court's deliberately narrow reading of the Fourteenth Amendment in the 1870s and 1880s. In several key cases, particularly the *Slaughterhouse Cases* (1873), *Minor v. Happersett* (1876), and the *Civil Rights Cases* (1883), the Court virtually defined the Fourteenth Amendment's newly declared rights out of existence.[20] The Court, dominated by judicial conservatives, had great misgivings about demands for a growth of federal power and federal rights. However the weakness of the support structure for civil liberties and civil rights in the late nineteenth century, discussed in the next chapter, also helps to explain the anemia of the new rights in those years.

In any event, the mere presence of rights guarantees in the United States Constitution, although surely contributing to rights consciousness in popular culture, cannot by itself explain the dramatic growth of the rights revolution in the twentieth century, for the text of the key constitutional rights have remained unchanged since 1870.[21]

The Culture-Centered Explanation

As passage of the Fourteenth Amendment contributed only indirectly to the Supreme Court's growing attention after 1917 to rights cases, that growth is commonly attributed either to the policy preferences of the Court's justices (discussed in the next section) or to changes in American political culture, particularly popular attitudes toward rights. It is useful to distinguish two components of popular attitudes. One component, "rights consciousness," is simply the recognition that a particular claim may be formulated in the language of rights. Clearly no rights agenda on a particular topic is possible if there is no recognition that the issue involves "rights." The other component of popular attitudes is "public opinion," the perception (justified or not) that a majority of people support a particular rights claim.

Rights consciousness, although necessary for the development of a rights revolution, is hardly sufficient. Americans were fascinated by rights, made extravagant claims in the name of rights, and developed social movements behind the banner of rights long before the Supreme Court began showing much interest in civil liberties or civil rights cases. Contrary to the view that there has been a recent proliferation of "rights talk" and that only recently have Americans become nearly obsessed with making rights claims, the language of rights has been widely used in popular struggles for at least a century and a half, and perhaps longer. Constitutional interpretation in the United States, as Hartog observed, has been a "contested terrain" over which popular groups and legal elites struggle, and in this struggle, popular groups typically have formulated their claims in the language of rights.[22] "Liberty" and "equality" were profoundly important principles to many of those participating in the antislavery fight before the Civil War.[23] After the war, the freed slaves, participants in the women's movement, and political dissenters in general, all demanded greater respect for civil liberties and civil rights. Thus, rights "consciousness has thrived among those who did not benefit from mainstream interpretations of the Constitution."[24]

Long before the Supreme Court turned its attention to civil liberties and civil rights, moreover, dissident rights claims gained surprisingly wide support among public officials and the general public. The Fourteenth Amendment's ringing promises, as William Nelson has shown, reflected a widespread, if amorphous, popular ideology of "liberty" and "equality" that existed before the Civil War.[25] After that war, proponents of freedom of expression, for instance, regularly used the rhetoric of constitutional rights and gained widespread support.[26] Between

1909 and 1913, the International Workers of the World (IWW), a radical labor organization, aggressively championed freedom of speech, and its members ("Wobblies") made provocative speeches on street corners throughout the country. In what came to be known as the free speech fights, many local officials tried to ban the speeches, but some officials refused to prosecute Wobblies on the grounds that doing so would violate constitutional rights, and other officials who tried to crack down on IWW speakers were surprised by the level of support for the Wobblies' right to speak.[27] In 1913, a leading journalist wrote that, in the free speech fights, "a very vital principle of American life [was] at stake—the right of free speech, of public discussion, and protest."[28] Not all officials and members of the broader public were so tolerant, and the Wobblies themselves proved to be relatively intolerant of dissent against their views. But the IWW free speech fights clearly indicate that there was a strong rights consciousness regarding freedom of speech among the U.S. population in the decades before World War I.

Nor is it true that ordinary people only recently have come to use "rights talk" to justify all manner of claims. For at least a century Americans appear to have been willing to use the language of rights in attempts to justify a wide variety of claims that no court even today would recognize. A man charged with blackmail in Louisiana in 1885, for instance, argued that the Louisiana law prohibiting blackmail was an unconstitutional infringement of freedom of speech.[29]

Nor can it be said that recourse to the courts was not recognized as a possibility before 1917, when individual rights cases began to gain significant attention in the Supreme Court, because those who used the language of rights in the last decades of the nineteenth century and the first decades of the twentieth occasionally pursued their claims in court. As I shall discuss further in the following chapter, the Free Speech League, a loose collection of free speech advocates, supported several appeals against criminal convictions of speakers, writers, and publishers,[30] and the early moving-picture industry, free-thought radicals, and socialists also pursued litigation before 1917 attempting to expand constitutional protection for freedom of expression.[31]

Thus, although there was widespread rights consciousness regarding freedom of speech and the possibility of pursuing free speech claims in the courts, the Supreme Court began turning attention in a sustained way to freedom of speech only after the beginning of World War I. Widespread, popular rights consciousness predated the development of the rights revolution by many decades, perhaps even by a century.

On the other hand, it might be suggested that although "rights talk" has been around for a long time, the majority of the public has supported expansion of constitutional rights only relatively recently (and that the rights revolution reflected trends in public opinion). Many sophisticated observers of the Court have indeed suggested that the Court responds to public opinion.[32] As early as the 1830s, Alexis de Tocqueville observed that, in America, the justices' "power is immense, but it is power springing from opinion. . . . Often it is as dangerous to lag behind as to outstrip it."[33] Similarly, Robert McCloskey, echoing Tocqueville, wrote, "the Court has seldom lagged far behind or forged far ahead of America," largely because the Court's power depends on popular legitimacy.[34]

Although the Court undoubtedly responds to broad changes in public opinion (the justices, after all, are part of the public), any explanation centered on public opinion has great difficulty explaining the three broad changes in the Court's agenda that are the subject of this analysis. Undoubtedly a liberalization in popular attitudes toward women's rights preceded the Court's growing attention to that issue.[35] Similarly, the Court's support for desegregation is sometimes attributed to growing popular support in the fifties and sixties for civil rights.[36]

Nonetheless, changes in public opinion cannot fully explain all significant changes in the Court's agenda. This may be illustrated most clearly by the Court's agenda on the rights of the criminally accused. Although the Court's attention to criminal procedure grew dramatically between the early thirties and the mid-sixties, criminal defendants nonetheless have never received much sympathy from the American public. Instead, since 1918, just after World War I, there have been a number of periods of widespread concern over a "crime wave."[37] More significantly, there has long been a widespread belief that criminal defendants receive unfair advantages in the judicial system. As early as 1937—long before the due process revolution in criminal procedure—two law professors referred to the "widely held" belief that "trial procedure gives to the criminal defendant an unfair advantage."[38] Indeed, articles in popular periodicals have regularly criticized the legal system as going easy on criminals or, worse, aiding them.[39]

On the other hand, concern about police brutality and racial discrimination in the criminal justice system began to develop after the late twenties and thereafter grew increasingly strong. In popular magazines and journals, the number of articles on police brutality, in particular, jumped significantly beginning in 1929. Suddenly article titles

like "Use of Torture in America's Prisons" and "Brutalities by the Police" began appearing frequently.[40] As following chapter shows, the growing publicity about police brutality and racial discrimination in the criminal justice process did not happen by accident: it resulted directly from pressure and research by rights advocates.

In sum, although popular fear of a "crime wave" and concern about the "Unreasonable Leniency of Criminal Justice"[41] seem to have been present from the twenties through the fifties, after the late twenties a counter-argument, raising concerns about police brutality and racial discrimination in the criminal justice system, began to develop in the popular press. The counter-argument undoubtedly offered a new opportunity for judicial attention to criminal procedure; but the opposing concern, the belief that courts remained too lenient and offered too many loopholes for clever defense attorneys, seems to have retained greater popular strength. Public opinion did not drive the growing judicial attention to criminal procedure, at least not in any direct or simple way.

The Judge-Centered Explanation

Perhaps the most common explanation for the judicial rights revolution is that the Supreme Court gained discretionary control over its docket in 1925, and that political liberals who wished to create and expand constitutional rights gained control of the Court after the mid-thirties and used their new discretionary control over the agenda to expand their attention to civil liberties and civil rights.[42]

Undoubtedly the justices of the United States Supreme Court have greater discretion over their agenda than do the supreme court judges of most other countries and, therefore, the conditions exist in the United States for a judge-led transformation of the judicial agenda. The Supreme Court gained substantial control over its agenda in 1925 as part of a set of reforms intended to help the Court better manage its workload. In the early decades of the twentieth century the Supreme Court faced mounting numbers of appeals, and the Court was required by law to decide virtually all of them. As a result, by 1925 the Court was two years behind in processing cases on its docket.[43] Congress responded to demands for judicial reform (urged by Chief Justice Taft and members of the Supreme Court, among others) by passing the Judiciary Act of 1925, which greatly restricted the types of cases the Court was required to hear.[44] In 1924, 40 percent of the cases coming to the Court were under its mandatory jurisdiction; by 1930, only 15 percent were under that jurisdiction.[45] The Judiciary Act's purpose was

to enable the Court to shift its attention away from ordinary business disputes, which had inundated its docket, and toward public law.[46]

The Judiciary Act seems to have largely accomplished its purpose: after 1925 the Court began refusing to hear ordinary business disputes and focused increasing attention on major disputes over public policy. Since 1925, the number of cases brought to the Supreme Court has increased substantially, which has further increased the justices' control over their own agenda. Of the seven thousand or more cases now filed with the Supreme Court each year, the Court grants full hearing, usually, to less than 150, and that number dropped well below one hundred in the early nineties.

As the Court's selection mechanism is discretionary and the available cases so numerous, proponents of the judge-centered explanation have reasoned that the Court's agenda largely reflects the justices' policy preferences. Undoubtedly that is true to some extent. Individual justices tend to vote to grant certiorari more often for cases in which they disagree with the lower court's ruling or for cases in which they can expect their preferred outcome to win in the Supreme Court.[47] Moreover, recent research by Caldeira, Wright, and Zorn shows that the justices' decisions to place cases on the discuss list and their votes on cases on the discuss list exhibit patterns that are consistent with a significant role for policy preferences and strategic decision making.[48] Agenda-setting decisions, then, are clearly influenced by the justices' policy preferences.

Nonetheless, the justices' beliefs about the Supreme Court's institutional role constrain the influence of raw preferences. First, the justices are constrained by the sua sponte doctrine, one variant of which discourages courts from deciding substantive issues not raised by at least one of the parties to the case. Although the doctrine is not universally followed, it appears to be an important constraint on the justices' willingness to create their own agenda apart from the issues presented by litigants.[49]

Second, the justices have developed an institutionalized reluctance to decide issues that have been the subject of little sustained litigation in lower courts. The likelihood that the Court will grant certiorari in any particular case is increased by the presence of the United States as petitioner, legal conflict among lower courts (conflict between federal appellate circuits is especially important), or dissent among judges on a lower appellate court.[50] In addition, H. W. Perry's interviews with justices and their clerks indicate that the justices are reluctant to take cases that have not "percolated" sufficiently in lower courts.[51]

Third, in order for an issue to reach the agenda, the issue typically must be taken repeatedly to the Supreme Court itself. Because of the large number of certiorari petitions, as a clerk told Perry, "there is enormous pressure not to take a case."[52] For this reason, early certiorari petitions on an issue are likely to be denied. The rationale, according to one of Perry's interviewees, is that "it's going to come up again if it's really an important issue. In fact a test to see if an issue is really important is to see if it comes up again."[53]

With some exceptions, a case must have issues that meet all these threshold requirements—conflict among lower courts, dissent in a lower court, extensive percolation, and repeated appearance on the docket—in order to be considered seriously as a candidate for a place on the agenda. The significance of these threshold requirements is that the justices' discretion over their docket is not nearly as unconstrained, and the number of cases among which the justices may choose is not nearly as large, as the judge-centered model assumes. In fact, Perry's interviews suggest that the number of certiorari petitions open for serious consideration is typically only a small fraction of the total docket.[54] Most petitions do not meet the threshold requirements and are rejected from the start.

Moreover, the process by which the justices select their agenda does not facilitate coherent, deliberate, policy-driven control of the agenda. The justices delegate a great deal of the case-screening process to their clerks, and decisions about which cases to select are made periodically over the course of each term rather than at one common point in time. As a result, the Court's agenda is built gradually and in a bureaucratic process in which there is a large number of contributing actors.[55] For various reasons, then, the path of the Supreme Court's agenda over time is likely to be connected, but only weakly, to the justices' policy preferences.

Some observers nonetheless have characterized the dramatic growth in judicial attention to civil liberties and civil rights as resulting primarily from changes in the justices' attitudes.[56] Thus, Jeffrey Segal and Harold Spaeth argue that the civil liberties agenda arose out of the liberal takeover of the Court in 1937, with *Palko v. Connecticut* (1937) and Footnote Four of *United States v. Carolene Products* (1938) signaling the opening of the new agenda; they characterize *Mapp v. Ohio* (1961) as the origin of an agenda on criminal procedure, and so on.[57] Segal and Spaeth thus argue that the development of the civil liberties and civil rights agenda was largely a judge-driven process.

Nonetheless, as we would expect if the justices' control over the

agenda process is attenuated, the judicial rights revolution has developed somewhat independently of changes in the Court's attitudinal composition. The Court's modern rights agenda, as I emphasized above, began to grow almost twenty years before the shift in the Court's majority in 1937. Moreover, it is not at all clear that the growing attention to rights can be attributed primarily to changes in the Court's attitudinal composition before 1937. Undoubtedly Justice Louis Brandeis, who joined the Court in 1916, was a strong early advocate of expanded judicial protection for civil liberties and rights. But only one other justice on the Court at the time, Oliver Wendell Holmes, Jr., can be considered a civil libertarian, and even his support wavered from issue to issue.[58] No other justice who consistently favored expansion of constitutional protection for civil liberties joined the Court until Hugo Black's appointment in 1937.[59] Yet the number of rights cases coming to the Court, and the proportion of its agenda devoted to such issues, began to grow after 1917.

Moreover, there is some direct evidence that the rights agenda's origins in the twenties and early thirties resulted less from the justices' decision to increase attention to such cases than from the growing presence of rights cases on the docket. In the October 1930 term the Court considered eight petitions for a writ of certiorari raising Bill of Rights issues and fifteen petitions relating to the Fourteenth Amendment's due process and equal protection guarantees, rejecting all of them.[60] The acceptance rate was higher in the October 1934 term, when the Court accepted three of five petitions concerning the Bill of Rights and four of thirty-six under the Fourteenth Amendment. But even in the 1934 term, the overall acceptance rate for civil liberties and rights petitions, 17 percent, was *lower* than the 20 percent acceptance rate for nonconstitutional petitions.[61] In brief, *although the Court's acceptance rate for rights petitions remained very low in the early thirties—indeed lower than the acceptance rate for nonconstitutional petitions—the agenda space devoted to civil liberties began to grow. It grew because litigants brought an increasing number of civil liberties and civil rights petitions to the Court.* The earliest developments in the rights revolution, then, resulted not from growing receptivity by the justices but from growing pressure by litigants.

Eventual judicial support for the new rights claims, of course, was necessary for development of the rights revolution. Had the justices continued to reject the new rights claims late into the thirties and forties, the growing pressure from below likely would have shifted toward tactics other than litigation aimed at the Supreme Court. But by the mid-thirties, the Court had rendered liberal decisions favoring the

new rights in several key cases, and so rights litigants knew that their efforts might not be wholly in vain.[62]

The most prominent period of liberal dominance on the Court occurred under the leadership of Chief Justice Earl Warren from 1953 through 1968. Warren joined a court deeply divided between judicial liberals and conservatives, and his appointment shifted the balance of power toward those favoring an expansion of judicial support for individual rights. In 1954, in *Brown v. Board of Education*, Warren led the Court to a unanimous decision striking down racial segregation in public schools.[63] But the decision, as expected, provoked a firestorm of controversy and the Court, to avoid further confrontation, allowed implementation of its ruling to proceed haphazardly. Judicial conservatives retained significant power on the Court until the replacement of several conservative justices with liberals in the late fifties and early sixties finally gave a decisive majority to the liberals. For much of the fifties, indeed, the Warren Court made few waves apart from the desegregation rulings. But in the sixties (indeed, beginning about the time of the *Monroe* decision in early 1961), Warren, along with Hugo Black, William Brennan, William O. Douglas, Abe Fortas, and Thurgood Marshall, fashioned a great transformation in many areas of constitutional law. The Warren Court extended most of the rights contained in the Bill of Rights to the states through incorporation in the Fourteenth Amendment's due process clause (thereby revolutionizing state criminal procedure in particular), gave clear and strong support to the civil rights movement, expanded protections for freedom of speech and the press, and created a new constitutional right to privacy. The Warren Court's reputation for creative judicial leadership is well deserved.[64] Nonetheless, at least *half* of the total growth in judicial attention to the new rights that eventually occurred between 1917 and the mid-sixties, as figure 3.1 illustrates, had already occurred by the time Earl Warren joined the Court. Thus, although the Warren Court produced a revolution in the meaning and scope of constitutional rights, earlier growth in the Court's attention to civil liberties and civil rights provided a foundation for that revolution.

THE CRIMINAL PROCEDURE AGENDA.   The limitations of judge-centered explanations of the rights revolution are particularly clear if we examine components of the judicial agenda. In the area of criminal procedure, the Supreme Court struggled over the extent of constitutional protection that should be applied to state trials, never fully extending to defendants in state courts the guarantees in the Bill of

Rights until the sixties.[65] In a scattering of other cases, the Court, while still rejecting the theory that the Fourteenth Amendment incorporated the protections in the Bill of Rights, began to supervise limited aspects of the state criminal process more actively.[66] Before 1961, the largest minority in favor of applying the criminal procedure guarantees in the Bill of Rights to state trials came together in 1947 in *Adamson v. California;* [67] by the end of 1947, however, two members of the liberal minority had died and were replaced by more conservative justices. Finally, in 1961, in *Mapp v. Ohio,* a new liberal majority on criminal procedure solidified and led the Court in a revolution in criminal procedure that extended to state trials most of the constitutional rights that applied in federal trials.[68] Among the more important decisions in that revolution was *Gideon v. Wainwright* (1963), which created a constitutional right to legal representation for felony defendants in state trials.[69]

A great disjuncture thus exists between the development of an agenda on criminal procedure, on the one hand, and, on the other, the Court's hesitance to intervene in state criminal proceedings. Between 1933 and 1961, the size of the criminal procedure agenda grew significantly; about three-quarters of the total growth in that agenda, up to its eventual peak in the late sixties, had occurred by the time the liberal majority solidified in 1961 (fig. 3.1). Yet the Court did not *invite* the new federal appeals of state criminal convictions; in fact, the Court hesitantly extended only a very limited federal review over only the most extreme abuses in the state criminal process. Instead, federal appeals of state criminal convictions virtually *forced* the Court to elaborate a limited set of federal protections against egregious abuses of due process. In *Brown v. Mississippi* (1936), for instance, the Court overturned the murder convictions (and death sentences) of three African Americans whose convictions had been based primarily on confessions extracted through brutal whippings.[70] The Court's development of only limited rights against egregious abuses of due process strongly suggests that the Court was not aggressively attempting to build a criminal procedure agenda. Instead, as I show in the following chapter, in the area of criminal procedure, until 1961, the Court mainly reacted to rising pressure from litigants.

THE WOMEN'S-RIGHTS AGENDA. The timing of growth in the women's-rights agenda presents different, but equally vexing, problems for a judge-centered explanation. The principal problem is not that growth in the agenda *preceded* liberal control of the Supreme Court but that the agenda did not take off until *after* liberals had lost control

of the Court in 1969. In 1969, Chief Justice Warren and Justice Fortas, both staunch liberals, retired. President Nixon nominated judicial conservatives Warren Burger and Harry Blackmun to fill their seats (Nixon's first two nominations to fill Fortas's seat were rejected by the Senate). In 1971 Hugo Black, another liberal, and John Marshall Harlan II, a conservative, retired and were replaced in January 1972 by Lewis Powell, a moderate conservative, and William Rehnquist, a conservative. Thus by early 1972 the Court, by any standard measure, had shifted decisively to the right. Nonetheless, in what might have at first appeared to be an inhospitable judicial environment, the women's-rights agenda grew explosively for several years.

This anomaly in the judge-centered explanation is not entirely without a solution, of course. The judge-centered explanation asserts that judicial attitudes are relatively fixed, and that judicial policies change only as a result of the replacement of justices. It thus might be argued that the justices who joined the Court after 1968 were more supportive of women's rights than the justices they replaced, and that this change produced the new women's-rights agenda. Some evidence seems at first to be consistent with that proposition. The Warren Court, in *Hoyt v. Florida* (1961), rejected a claim that Florida's practice of excluding women from jury pools (unless they specifically requested to be included) was unconstitutional.[71] By contrast, some of the justices appointed to the Court after 1968, particularly Blackmun and Stevens, proved to be liberals on women's rights and so the Burger Court was fairly receptive to expanding the women's-rights agenda. In fact, in a number of important cases, beginning with *Reed v. Reed* in 1971 (striking down Idaho's statutory preference for male executors of estates), the Burger Court expanded protection for women's rights by majorities of seven or more justices.[72] Thus, at the least it is clear that some of the otherwise-conservative justices in the new Burger Court were persuaded to support some sex discrimination claims.

But the converse—that the otherwise-liberal Warren Court justices were unalterably opposed to women's rights and therefore built no agenda on the issue—is not equally plausible. Indeed, the justices' attitudes toward sex discrimination, contrary to the assumptions of the judge-centered explanation, appear to have been quite malleable and unsettled during this early period, and the judicial agenda seems to have responded more to the litigation environment than to the justices' policy preferences. For example, three of the justices who had joined in *Hoyt*'s rejection of a relatively narrow sex-discrimination claim (Brennan, Douglas, and Stewart) embraced a sex-discrimination claim

in *Reed* that had far broader implications. Thus their attitudes toward sex discrimination seem to have shifted in the intervening years.

Given that malleability, it is possible to piece together a potential judicial majority in favor of striking down at least some sex-discriminatory laws much earlier than *Reed* in 1971. William Brennan, William Douglas, and Potter Stewart, all of whom joined in the *Reed* decision, likely could have been persuaded to support a sex-discrimination claim far earlier than 1971 (certainly Brennan and Douglas were well known for their liberal views). That makes three potential supporters before 1971. Further, if Potter Stewart, a justice with a moderate-to-conservative voting record on individual rights, could come to support sex-discrimination claims (as he did in the early Burger Court years), it is likely that Earl Warren and Abe Fortas, justices with very liberal records on individual rights, also would have supported such claims.[73] That makes five potential supporters long before 1971. Additionally, two other justices on the unanimous *Reed* Court were already serving by the end of 1967 (Byron White and Thurgood Marshall, appointed in 1962 and 1967, respectively). That makes seven potential supporters for sex-discrimination claims by the end of 1967. Thus, had many women's-rights claims reached the Court before 1971, it is at least possible, even easy, to piece together a majority of sympathetic justices.[74]

My point is that the justices' policy preferences, as indicated by their votes in cases, may be very poor predictors of the development of the judicial agenda. The development of the women's-rights agenda in the early seventies, in particular, was a surprising development that could not have been predicted by looking only at the Court's political or attitudinal composition.

Conclusion

The development of the rights revolution in the United States poses important and vexing puzzles. For almost a century and a half after ratification of the Bill of Rights, the Supreme Court largely ignored civil liberties and civil rights. Then, towards 1920, the Court began to devote increasing attention to civil liberties and civil rights, and that attention eventually grew into sustained support for a host of new rights. The earliest phases of the rights revolution, then, began long before the Warren Court's dramatic rulings in support of civil liberties and civil rights; they began even before the famous "switch in time" in 1937 when judicial liberals first gained control of the Court. Similar puzzles appear in particular areas of the agenda. The earliest phases

of the criminal procedure revolution began long before the Warren Court's landmark criminal procedure decisions in the sixties. The judicial revolution in women's rights, by contrast, began in 1971, just as the Court's composition began to shift sharply to the right. I have suggested that several common explanations for these developments, particularly the growth of rights consciousness and other shifts in public opinion, as well as the Supreme Court's growing liberalism after 1937, are greatly incomplete. As I show in the next chapter, changes in the support structure for legal mobilization provided key conditions for the U.S. rights revolution.

The Support Structure
and the U.S. Rights Revolution

The uneven development in phases of the U.S. rights revolution that I described in the last chapter cannot be understood as a result only of the adoption of the Civil War Amendments, liberal judicial leadership, or popular culture. The new rights were propelled onto the judicial agenda, in addition, by a great expansion in the availability of resources to potential litigants. The first organizations actively litigating on civil liberties were formed just before 1920, and they provided support for the early civil liberties cases that reached the Supreme Court. Similarly, the resources available to defend criminal defendants began to grow in the late twenties, propelling criminal procedure cases onto the Court's agenda. The resources available to women's-rights litigants began to grow relatively late, in the late sixties but, once they emerged, they propelled women's-rights cases onto the Court's agenda. Each of the puzzles, then, is solved by looking to the growth of the support structure for legal mobilization. This chapter provides evidence in support of that proposition.

The Support Structure for Legal Mobilization

The Supreme Court's case selection process and norms significantly affect the relationship between the Court's agenda and outside actors. As was noted in the last chapter, cases generally are not heard by the Supreme Court unless they present issues that represent conflict among and extensive percolation in lower courts. The Court's agenda (with some exceptions) is thus limited to cases that emanate from broad legal conflict in the lower courts. The development of such broad legal conflict on any particular issue, in turn, typically depends on the existence of substantial resources for litigating the issue. For this reason, the development of the support structure for litigation has been especially important in the United States for providing access to the Supreme Court's agenda. For much of U.S. history, only issues directly

related to economic and property disputes enjoyed sufficient support among organized litigants to reach the Supreme Court with any regularity and sophistication. But after 1915, an expanding and diversifying support structure for civil liberties and civil rights began to develop lower-court conflict and extensive litigation on the new issues; as a consequence, various civil liberties and civil rights issues increasingly reached the judicial agenda.

The Domination of Litigation by Managerial Businesses before 1915
The earliest developments in the support structure in the United States occurred between 1870 and 1910 in the organizational structures of businesses. Before 1870, most business enterprises were relatively small family-run operations with ad hoc, nonbureaucratic organizational structures and few professional managers. After 1870, during what business historians call the "managerial revolution," the American business sector began converting rapidly to large, bureaucratically structured, professionally managed organizations.[1] In the United States, the managerial revolution began and flourished first in the railroad industry after 1870; in the 1880s, it spread to areas of the economy involving production of goods; in the late 1890s, it expanded into a merger revolution in which bureaucratic enterprises joined to form still larger organizations. By the middle of the second decade of the twentieth century, the managerial revolution had ended, having transformed organizational structures in many areas of the American economy.

The managerial revolution in American business produced the first nongovernmental organizations with the capacity and the interest to pursue long-term, strategic litigation. Their interest in strategic litigation grew out of the growth in government regulation. To influential political thinkers, as well as large sections of the population, the growth of large business organizations threatened traditional conceptions of the primacy of the individual and the importance of individual initiative in the economy.[2] Legislatures responded by attempting to regulate the power of the new business organizations, leading to a massive change from previous conceptions of the limited constitutional powers of government.[3] Business organizations, naturally, had an interest in manipulating the new regulations in their favor.

The new managerial structure, moreover, provided businesses with the capacity to plan strategically and to allocate resources for the implementation of long-term strategic plans.[4] Additionally, the professional managers in the new organizational sector of the economy formed professional associations and networks of communication that

allowed them to learn from each other and to coordinate political strategies.[5] Many businesses, particularly the railroads, used their newfound capacity for coordinated action to pursue strategic litigation to influence state regulations. Between 1880 and 1900, a number of the new business organizations devoted significant resources to litigation campaigns intended to influence the path of government regulation.

The railroads, as Richard Cortner has observed, mounted the most extensive litigation campaigns during the period.[6] Several railroads challenged the so-called Granger Laws, state statutes that subjected railroads to rate regulation, but they lost their first important challenge (the *Granger Cases*) in 1877, when the Court ruled that private property "affected with a public interest" may be subject to public regulation unhindered by judicial review.[7] In response, the railroads mounted a systematic litigation campaign intended to reverse that unfavorable decision. "The litigation campaign of the roads," Cortner observed, "exhibited a mastery of many of the tactics [test cases, careful development of supporting evidence, and pressure on the judicial appointment process] that have been characteristic of constitutional litigation conducted by interest groups during more recent times."[8] During that campaign, the railroads won several landmark decisions that subjected state policies to judicial review under the Fourteenth Amendment.

Although the Supreme Court rejected the vast majority of constitutional challenges brought by business litigants,[9] businesses nonetheless continued to take large numbers of cases to the Court. They did so because they could: business litigants dominated the field of constitutional litigation in the late nineteenth and early twentieth centuries because of their nearly unique organizational and resource capacities. Scholarship on the legal profession during the first several decades of the century amply demonstrates the new managerial businesses' capacity to control the field of legal resources. As one scholar observed, for instance, the list of lawyers serving the railroads in their strategic litigation campaign consisted of a "Who's Who" of the bar.[10] Similarly, Louis Brandeis, in a speech in 1905, declared that "lawyers have, to a large extent, allowed themselves to become adjuncts of great corporations. . . . The leading lawyers of the United States have been engaged mainly in supporting the claims of the corporations; often in endeavoring to evade or nullify the extremely crude laws by which legislators sought to regulate the power or curb the excesses of the corporations."[11] And Woodrow Wilson in a 1910 speech declared that "we have witnessed in modern business the submergence of the individual within the organization," and that "in gaining new functions, in being

drawn into modern business instead of standing outside of it . . . the lawyer has lost his old function"; therefore, Wilson concluded, the country "distrusts every 'corporation lawyer.'"[12]

The alliance between leading lawyers and the leading managerial businesses of the day is not especially surprising. John Heinz and Edward Laumann's pathbreaking study on the social structure of the bar in Chicago revealed that the legal profession remains divided between an upper hemisphere of lawyers who serve large organizations, particularly corporate businesses, and a lower hemisphere of lawyers who serve individual clients.[13] One of the more significant findings of the study is that lawyers who serve organizational clients have far less professional autonomy than lawyers who serve individual clients, largely because of the managerial power of the organizational clients. This pattern of the legal profession's subservience to managerial organizations dates to the emergence of such organizations in the 1870s and 1880s. Theron Strong, a prominent lawyer who experienced the organizational transformation, observed in 1914 that client relations "had undergone a complete and marvelous change. The advent of the captains of industry, the multi-millionaires, the mighty corporations and the tremendous business enterprises, with all the pride of wealth and luxury which have followed in their train, have reversed their relative positions, and the lawyer, with a more cultivated intellect than ever and as worthy of deference and respect as formerly, is not treated with the deference and respect of early days."[14] The development of large organizations had transformed the legal world by dominating the work of lawyers and the development of litigation.

The extensive litigation campaigns mounted by businesses significantly influenced the Supreme Court's agenda, particularly by pushing the Court to address issues of interest to businesses. This is especially clear with regard to the Court's agenda under the new Fourteenth Amendment. "The Supreme Court began to elaborate doctrines resolving issues of priority [under the Fourteenth Amendment]," William Nelson observed, "only when a flood of cases in the closing decades of the nineteenth century made the inevitability of conflict fully apparent."[15] The Court's evolving interpretation of the Fourteenth Amendment in the late nineteenth and early twentieth centuries, of course, encouraged businesses to continue to bring challenges to legislation and regulatory action. Although many businesses lost their cases, leading decisions like *Hammer v. Dagenhart* (1918) (striking down a ban on the interstate shipment of the products of child labor) clearly indicated the general direction of the Court's policies.[16]

Yet even as managerial businesses dominated the field of constitutional litigation, several changes occurred in the availability of resources for legal mobilization that began to democratize access to the Supreme Court's agenda by transforming the capacity of nonbusiness interests to pursue sustained, strategic litigation. The most important changes were the development of rights-advocacy organizations, the diversification and organizational development of the legal profession, the gradual development of financial resources for civil liberties litigation, and the development of the Civil Rights Section in the Justice Department.

Rights-Advocacy Organizations

Effective rights-advocacy organizations such as the ACLU, the NAACP, and the American Jewish Congress began to appear after 1909. Some rights-advocacy groups, admittedly, existed before this time, but there are crucial differences between the earlier organizations and the later, more successful ones. The Free Speech League, which formed in 1902 and disintegrated in 1918 and 1919, was a loose association of activists and intellectuals under the leadership of Theodore Schroeder, an eccentric but brilliant civil liberties advocate.[17] The League, and Schroeder in particular, became heavily involved in a wide range of free speech disputes in the prewar years, particularly disputes over the spread of sex education materials, related anti-Victorian literature, and socialist discourse. In 1909 a benefactor gave Schroeder a "secret fund" for the purpose of supporting the organization and defending people prosecuted for their speech.[18] Schroeder used the fund, along with voluntary support from lawyers who were members of the League, to support First Amendment challenges to the prosecution of a number of activists for libel or for violating various antiobscenity laws or local ordinances against disorderly conduct and the like.[19] One such case, Fox v. Washington (1915), reached the Supreme Court, where Justice Holmes (before his conversion to free speech libertarianism) penned a unanimous decision upholding conviction of an anarchist for encouraging nude sunbathing.[20] Although the Free Speech League participated in a wide range of free speech causes, its influence in the courts remained limited. Undoubtedly one reason was a widespread judicial skepticism toward free speech claims. Nonetheless, the League's limited organizational capacities also crippled its potential influence. The League was organized in prebureaucratic fashion as a loose association of individual free speech advocates, and Schroeder's personal efforts and files seem to have constituted the en-

tirety of the formal organization.[21] As a Schroeder biographer noted, "the League was so much a reflection of Schroeder's personality and activity that in effect he carried it with him wherever he went."[22] Similarly, Roger Baldwin, founder of the ACLU, later observed simply that "Schroeder *was* the Free Speech League."[23] Schroeder and the League seem to have influenced the development of ideas about freedom of speech, but their support for appellate litigation remained limited by a lack of organizational and financial resources.

A few other prewar organizations advocated expansion of civil liberties or civil rights, but their influence, too, remained limited for one reason or another. The early moving-pictures industry attacked censorship of movies, in one case supporting appeals to the Supreme Court.[24] The Court decisively rejected a movie company's free speech claim against movie censorship, and the movie industry did not again pursue litigation on the matter until the forties. Similarly, the International Workers of the World aggressively advocated freedom of speech as part of its labor-organizing efforts, but it pursued few legal appeals due to both a lack of financial resources and an ideological opposition to use of the capitalist legal system.[25]

In one way or another, then, litigation on civil liberties and civil rights remained infrequent and isolated before World War I because potential rights litigants enjoyed only limited organizational and financial support. In the immediate prewar and post-war years, by contrast, several organizations developed stronger organizational structures and bases of support, with the result that they could support more cases and could pursue issues repeatedly, even if initially rebuffed by the courts.

Of these organizations, the ACLU, founded in 1920, undoubtedly has had the greatest impact, both by pressing issues onto the Supreme Court's agenda and by developing an effective organizational model— one that has been widely followed by other groups.[26] Roger Baldwin, the ACLU's first leader, recognized the growing importance of organizations in American public life, and he became committed to institutionalizing the ACLU to increase its effectiveness. "It was no accident that the organization was referred to as a 'union,'" Paul Murphy observed, "or that it sought to function on a national scale and implement centrally determined programs through a national organization."[27] In 1922, the ACLU began to receive limited financial support for its activities from the American Fund for Public Service, of which Baldwin was director.[28] Nonetheless, funding remained scarce, and the ACLU developed alternatives to the direct financing of cases, particularly the

use of a network of "cooperating attorneys," lawyers who were not directly employed by the ACLU but who provided legal advice and representation for ACLU-supported court cases, often without charging a fee. Baldwin used the term "cooperating attorney" as early as 1920;[29] since that time cooperating attorneys have proved to be one of the significant strengths of the organization. Additionally, state ACLU affiliate organizations grew out of the main organization over the years, significantly increasing the organization's reach throughout the country.[30]

The ACLU's support for constitutional litigation significantly affected the Supreme Court's agenda. The ACLU (or its pre-1920 predecessor, the National Civil Liberties Board) provided the primary support and coordination for the initial burst of civil liberties litigation between 1917 and the early thirties. Although ACLU strategists had misgivings about financing litigation in the face of conservative courts, the ACLU and its cooperating attorneys financed, provided legal counsel, or otherwise supported a remarkable number of important civil liberties cases in the twenties and early thirties.[31] In fact, most of the Supreme Court's early civil liberties decisions were made in cases that were ACLU-supported and likely would not have reached the Court had not that organization or its cooperating attorneys supported the appeals. The organization sponsored a number of key cases in which the Supreme Court made significant advances in constitutional law, among them decisions relating to incorporation of rights contained in the Bill of Rights into the Fourteenth Amendment as limitations on the states. These cases include *Gitlow v. New York* (1925) (in dicta,[32] incorporating the First Amendment's free speech clause);[33] *Whitney v. California* (1927) (in which Justice Brandeis, concurring, joined by Justice Holmes, argued that the free speech clause allows governments to criminalize only action, and not pure speech);[34] *Fiske v. Kansas* (1927) (incorporating the free speech clause);[35] *DeJonge v. Oregon* (1937) (incorporating the First Amendment's freedom of assembly clause);[36] *Everson v. Board of Education* (1947) (incorporating the First Amendment's establishment of religion clause);[37] and *Wolf v. Colorado* (1949) (incorporating of the Fourth Amendment's search and seizure clause).[38] The ACLU, together with the International Labor Defense, also sponsored *Stromberg v. California* (1931) (extending First Amendment protection to symbolic speech),[39] and ACLU lawyers argued *Powell v. Alabama* (1932) (creating, for capital cases, the right of indigents to counsel provided by the state)[40] and filed an *amicus* brief in *Cantwell v. Connecticut* (1940) (incorporating the First Amendment's free exercise of religion clause).[41]

The ACLU also offered to sponsor appeals in *Near v. Minnesota* (1931) (incorporating the First Amendment's freedom of the press clause),[42] but a wealthy publisher stepped in and took over financing.[43]

Similarly, the NAACP, formed in 1909, greatly affected the Court's civil rights agenda by supporting litigation against racial segregation. Prominent lawyer Moorfield Storey became the NAACP's first president and, virtually from the organization's inception, he encouraged the use of test cases. The NAACP supported and won test cases in the Supreme Court, in 1915 (striking down Oklahoma's grandfather clause for voting),[44] in 1917 (striking down Louisville's exclusionary zoning law),[45] and in 1926 (striking down Texas's white primary law).[46] By 1930 black lawyers constituted the active center of the organization and, in that year, the organization was awarded a $100,000 grant from the American Fund for Public Service that allowed its leaders to develop its now well-known systematic litigation strategy against segregation in public life.[47] In 1939 the NAACP created, for tax purposes, a separate Legal Defense and Educational Fund, which took over most of the NAACP's litigation efforts.[48] Between 1909 and about 1960, either the NAACP or the LDF supported the leading race-discrimination cases before the Supreme Court.[49]

The International Labor Defense (ILD), another litigation-support organization, was formed by the Communist Party in 1925. In the late twenties the ILD supported criminal defense campaigns for Sacco and Vanzetti and for labor organizers. Undoubtedly its biggest case was the defense of the "Scottsboro Boys," nine young black men who, in a sham trial in 1931, were convicted and sentenced to death on a charge of raping two white women while riding on a freight train in Alabama. The ILD hoped to use the case to gain support for its broader political agenda of organizing against American capitalism. Eventually the case became a tug of war between the NAACP and the ILD, with the former eventually ousting the ILD from control of the case.[50] The case produced several landmark Supreme Court decisions, particularly *Powell v. Alabama* (1932), which established a constitutional right to counsel in capital cases.[51]

The Jehovah's Witnesses, a religious sect, sponsored a number of other important Supreme Court decisions on both the free exercise of religion and freedom of expression in the years before the Warren Court. The sect's role in the development of U.S. constitutional law preceded a parallel and equally important role in the development of civil liberties law in Canada. The Jehovah's Witnesses originated in the United States in 1884, but only began supporting court cases after

World War I.[52] Two developments appear to have influenced the Jehovah's Witnesses' approach to the legal system. The first was the selection of Judge Joseph Franklin Rutherford, former general counsel
to the sect, to lead the sect after the death of its founder in 1917.
The second was the increasingly harsh reaction, beginning in World
War I, with which authorities responded to Witnesses' proselytizing
and antiwar activities. Federal authorities responded vigorously to the
organization after it published and widely disseminated *The Finished
Mystery* in 1917, a book that argued, among other things, that patrio-
tism and the demands by governments that their citizens engage in
"butchery" during wartime violated the principles of the Bible.[53] Federal authorities, armed with the Espionage Act of 1917, brought
charges against the eight main leaders of the Witnesses. They were
convicted and received 20-year prison sentences in 1919. In response,
the Witnesses began pursuing legal appeals.[54] Shortly after their brush
with the Espionage Act, the Jehovah's Witnesses began their well-
known practice of house-to-house proselytizing, which led increasingly to confrontations with local authorities. The number of arrests
related to such mission work rapidly increased between 1928 and the
mid-thirties. In response, under Judge Rutherford's leadership the
group developed a legal defense strategy that culminated in a number
of leading Supreme Court cases on freedom of expression and the free
exercise of religion. By 1986 the Jehovah's Witnesses had sponsored or
otherwise participated in thirty-six full decisions in the Supreme
Court.

   After the early fifties, the number of organizations supporting constitutional rights litigation began to increase.[55] This is especially clear
in the area of women's rights. The women's movement of the sixties
and seventies, unlike earlier women's movements, produced lasting
organizations with professional staffs and substantial resources.[56] Most
of the growth in the movement and in the number of organizations
occurred rapidly in the ten years following 1966 (fig. 4.1).

   Some of the organizations were dedicated specifically to financing
and supporting women's-rights litigation.[57] The first few women's organizations formed specifically for litigation support—the Legal Defense and Education Fund of the National Organization for Women,
the Women's Legal Defense Fund, and the Women's Rights Project of
the ACLU—were created in 1971.[58] After that year, the number of such
organizations grew significantly, to almost fifteen by 1973 and almost
twenty by 1979.[59] Some of the organizations played key roles in propelling women's-rights claims onto the Supreme Court's agenda. The

Figure 4.1 The Women's Movement in the United States: Number of National and Regional Organizations

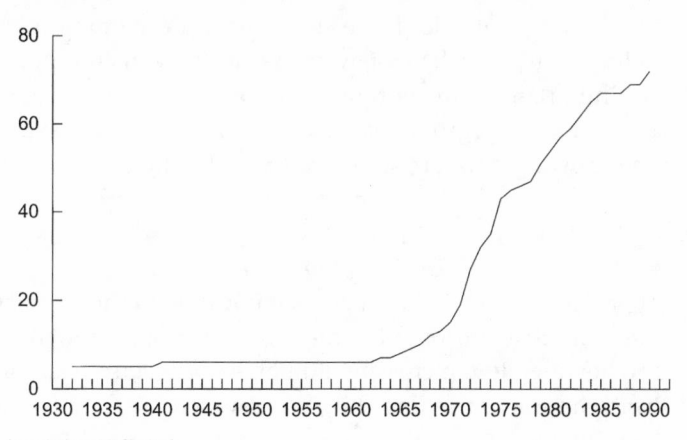

Source: *Associations Unlimited.*

ACLU's Women's Rights Project, for instance, played a leading role in directing the development of test-case litigation both in lower courts and in the Supreme Court,[60] and the Center for Constitutional Rights, founded in 1966, developed the research behind privacy rights challenges to state abortion laws.[61]

Although earlier in this century there were some tensions between several of the leading rights-advocacy organizations,[62] over time they have developed a great deal of cooperation. The American Fund for Public Service provided financial support to both the ACLU and the NAACP; and the ACLU, NAACP, and ILD cooperated to provide support for a number of cases in the twenties and early thirties. Indeed, the ACLU, the NAACP, and the American Jewish Congress formed the foundation of civil liberties and civil rights organizing for the first half (and more) of this century. They sponsored the leading cases in the Supreme Court on civil liberties and civil rights. In their briefs, they provided the arguments that the Court used when it supported civil liberties or rights claims; and, crucially, their efforts predated supportive decisions from the Supreme Court: as histories of the organizations reveal, they brought numerous cases in lower courts before they eventually won landmark decisions in the Supreme Court. The efforts of the early rights-advocacy organizations were a necessary condition for the development of the judicial rights revolution: without those efforts, there would have been virtually no civil liberties or civil rights cases for the Court to decide. It is no exaggeration to say that the early history of the Supreme Court's agenda on civil liberties and rights is

largely the history of the strategic efforts of civil liberties and rights organizations to influence the Court. Moreover, the ACLU, as noted above, played a crucial role in the seventies in developing organizations for litigation on behalf of women's-rights, which supported a number of important women's-rights cases in the Supreme Court. The expansion of organized group resources, then, constituted a significant part of the growing support structure for rights litigation in the Supreme Court.

The Legal Profession

The legal profession, too, has changed significantly in this century, and the changes greatly contributed to the growing support for civil liberties and rights litigation. Increasing numbers of lawyers began practicing in firms, the site of training shifted to law schools, and the lawyer population diversified.

Law firms provide economies of scale and a capacity for specialization and long-term strategic planning, all of which are valuable assets in supporting strategic litigation campaigns.[63] The widespread presence of law firms, like the other developments in the support structure, is a relatively new phenomenon. In 1872 there were only 15 firms with 4 or more lawyers in the entire country; between 1892 and 1903 the number of such firms jumped from 87 to 210; by 1924 there were well over 1000. As the number of firms grew, so did their size. In 1903, no firms consisted of ten or more lawyers; by 1914, there were six such larger firms; in the following years the number and size of large firms continued to grow.[64] Rights-advocacy organizations commonly have drawn cooperating attorneys from law firms that free up their attorneys to do such work. In addition, liberal rights advocates in the sixties and seventies developed public interest law firms to gain the benefits of the firm structure. The development and spread of the law firm as a principal form of legal practice after 1900, then, contributed to the growing support structure for rights litigation.

Additionally, in the 1880s the site of legal training began to shift from apprenticeship under established lawyers to formal education in law schools. In the nineteenth century, most lawyers were trained in apprenticeships; by 1915, most lawyers were trained in law school.[65] That change had important effects on the legal profession. First, the decline of apprenticeship and the rise of law schools disconnected training from the conservative interests of the practicing legal profession and provided the institutional basis for the development of theoretical study of law and for reform-oriented political efforts.[66] The de-

veloping legal professoriat, for instance, was the source for sociological jurisprudence and legal realism, two important movements in the study and practice of law that advanced the then-novel theory that legal decision making is policy making in disguise, and that, therefore, judicial policies should be developed self-consciously for political ends. The changes in legal education thus provided one of the foundations for the change in the justices' conception of their role as the defender of static constitutional limits on legislative power to a new role as guardian of evolving fundamental rights.[67] The law schools, moreover, also provided institutional support for clinical programs and legal research that supported some rights-advocacy litigation. The Court's decision in *Gideon v. Wainwright* (1963),[68] for instance, was widely expected at the time because of sustained litigation on the issue by, among others, several law professors from the University of Virginia.[69]

In addition, the growth of law schools provided entry into the legal profession to an increasingly diverse range of people who had difficulty getting apprenticeships under the old training system. As late as 1910, the legal profession remained, as Richard Abel writes, "overwhelmingly Protestant and native born."[70] The new law schools, however, were open to all whites, regardless of ethnic or religious background (although many schools, particularly in the South, continued to exclude blacks for several decades), and many of the schools offered night classes, which increased their accessibility to members of the lower classes.[71] These changes led to a dramatic and substantial diversification of the lawyer population, as new Jewish and Catholic immigrants from eastern and southern Europe, among others, got law degrees.[72] In New York City, for instance, between 1924 and 1929, 56 percent of new lawyers were Jewish; between 1930 and 1934 the percentage reached 80 percent. Moreover, between 1920 and 1930, the number of lawyers as a whole also grew rapidly, by 31 percent.[73]

The growing presence of Jewish, Catholic, and black lawyers in the United States in the years following World War I provided a growing base of legal representation for previously unrepresented groups. The new lawyers represented conscientious objectors, radical labor organizers, criminal defendants, communists, free speech advocates, and other unpopular figures and causes.[74] The significance of the change is revealed in part by its opponents' response. A prominent lawyer, for instance, railed against "the great flood of foreign blood . . . sweeping into the bar . . . [with] little sense of fairness, justice and honor as we understand them."[75] Another (George Wickersham) wrote, "To think

that those men, with their imperfect conception of our institutions, should have an influence upon the development of our constitution, and upon the growth of American institutions, is something that I shudder when I think of."[76] In response, the established bar formed professional associations, worked to increase bar admission standards, and used character tests in an attempt to maintain the legal profession's allegiance to the fading traditional conception of the constitutional order.[77] Moreover, some lawyers for the new interests faced disbarment proceedings; some even suffered beatings.[78] For instance, when a New York attorney presented evidence to J. Edgar Hoover of beatings and other repressive actions by federal agents against labor organizers in 1919, Hoover responded by urging that the attorney be disbarred for publicizing the evidence.[79]

By the mid-thirties, the changes in the legal profession began to take institutional form. In 1936, the National Lawyers Guild was formed. The Guild was created by progressive and radical lawyers who saw a need for an organizational alternative to the conservative American Bar Association, particularly as the latter continued to engage in racial discrimination in the thirties.[80] Yet the American Bar Association itself increasingly was pressed by its members to take up the issue of civil liberties and civil rights. In 1938, the organization created its Bill of Rights Committee, which greatly increased the symbolic prominence of the civil liberties issue in the broader organization. The Bill of Rights Committee's work was not only symbolic: it encouraged the Roosevelt administration's Justice Department to work more proactively in favor of protection of civil liberties, and it collected complaints of violations of civil liberties and passed them on to state and local bar associations for investigation and action.[81]

The changes in the legal profession in the years between the turn of the century and the beginning of the New Deal, then, constituted the beginning of the powerful tradition of progressive "cause" lawyering that reached its peak during the Warren Court era and shortly after it. The growing diversity of the U.S. legal profession in the teens and twenties thus provided an important source of support for the cases that constituted an emerging judicial rights agenda after 1917.

Just as the U.S. legal profession became significantly more ethnically diverse after 1900, it became dramatically more diverse along gender lines after 1965 as women increasingly chose law as a career. The number of women entering the legal profession began growing after the early sixties and, by the mid-seventies, women had become a primary source for the very rapid growth in the number of lawyers as a whole.[82]

Figure 4.2 Women Entering the Legal Profession in the United States

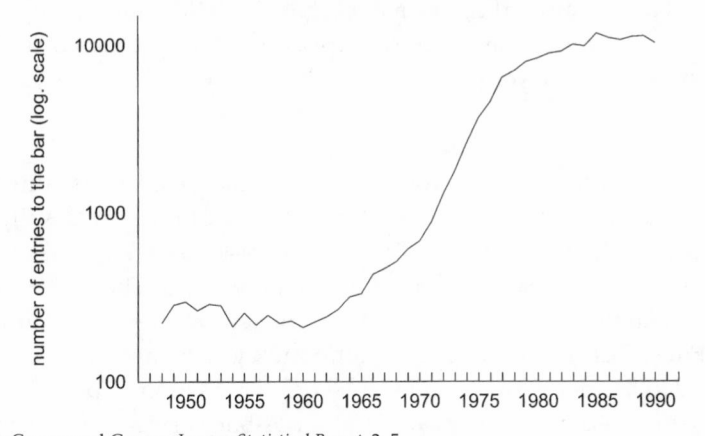

Source: Curran and Carson, *Lawyer Statistical Report,* 2, 5.

The rapid growth in the number of women entering the legal profession in the late sixties and seventies is illustrated in figure 4.2.[83]

The entry of substantial numbers of women into the profession transformed the base of support for women's-rights litigation. Certainly there were a few women lawyers in earlier years, and occasionally they supported cases, even to the Supreme Court. In 1948, Anne R. Davidow, for instance (who, along with her brother, served as general counsel to the Reuther brothers and helped to organize the United Auto Workers), took the case *Goesaert v. Cleary* to the Supreme Court (unsuccessfully challenging a Michigan law banning from bartending any woman who was not the wife or daughter of the bar owner).[84] But Anne Davidow was an exception in these early years. Many of the much larger number of new women lawyers in the seventies supported the women's-rights cause and women's-rights litigation, and their efforts generated litigation campaigns that otherwise would not have existed. Early women's-rights lawyers expressed frustration with what they regarded as male lawyers' lukewarm support and narrow conception of women's rights; to fill the void, the new women lawyers vigorously pursued women's-rights litigation on a number of fronts.[85] Thus, two female women's-rights lawyers who had just graduated from law school argued the landmark abortion rights case *Roe v. Wade* (1973).[86] Ruth Bader Ginsburg, a prominent attorney appointed to the Supreme Court in 1993, directed the ACLU's Women's Rights Project in the seventies and argued or otherwise supported many of the sex-discrimination cases that reached the Supreme Court during that time, among them the key early case *Reed v. Reed* (1971).[87] The growth in the

number of women lawyers beginning in the late sixties, then, provided a new base of support for women's-rights litigation, just as the newly diversifying profession a half-century earlier had pioneered the process of "cause" lawyering.

Sources of Financing for Litigation Campaigns

Organized civil liberties groups provided the institutional direction and support for rights litigation after 1916 but they lacked sufficient resources to finance more than a few court cases. The financial support for court cases came from one of two main sources. The first was private philanthropy, in the early years donated by the American Fund for Public Service and some wealthy individuals, and in later years provided by major foundations, the Ford Foundation in particular.

Charles Garland's American Fund for Public Service was created in 1922, and for a short time it supported key rights-advocacy efforts.[88] Roger Baldwin, the director of the ACLU, became the director of the new fund as well, and the original board of directors consisted largely of members of the ACLU's national committee.[89] Under Baldwin's leadership, there was little strategic focus; the Fund supported a wide array of left-wing causes in the twenties and thirties. Nonetheless, the Fund was the primary source of financial support for court battles directed by the ACLU in the twenties.[90] In addition, as noted in my discussion of the NAACP, the American Fund for Public Service, although lukewarm in its support for the NAACP, provided the financing for that organization's early legal research and litigation campaigns against racial segregation. The stock market crash of 1929 devastated the Fund, however, and as a consequence its support for litigation dropped dramatically in the thirties. In 1942 the Fund's board of directors dissolved it.

Other foundations, particularly the Ford Foundation, provided major grants to organizations working in favor of civil liberties and civil rights. The Ford Foundation gave $7.4 million to the National Legal Aid and Defender Association from 1953 to 1972; $15 million to create the pro–civil liberties Fund for the American Republic in 1952–53; $8.6 million to the Southern Regional Council from 1953 to 1977; $3.3 million to the NAACP-LDF from 1967 to 1976; and $13 million for the development of public interest law centers from 1970 to 1977.[91]

In addition, various states developed right-to-counsel policies that provided support for legal defense and appellate litigation on behalf of the criminally accused. The provision of counsel to poor people in civil cases and to indigent defendants in criminal cases is a relatively

old development in the United States. German immigrants developed the earliest forms of legal aid in the late 1800s in New York City for the purpose of protecting new immigrants from being victimized by fraud. An early champion of legal aid, Arthur von Briesen, however, expanded and institutionalized programs specifically to discourage new immigrants from joining radical movements by persuading them that the American legal system was fair. He argued that legal aid "keeps the poor satisfied, because it establishes and protects their rights; it produces better workingmen and better workingwomen, better houseservants; it antagonizes the tendency toward communism; it is the best argument against the socialist who cries that the poor have no rights which the rich are bound to respect."[92] The earliest forms of legal aid in civil cases were informally organized, and it was not until the sixties that a comprehensive national system was developed.

Providing defense counsel to indigent defendants developed later than civil legal aid, largely after World War I. The first organization providing counsel to indigent defendants was created in 1911 in Oklahoma, followed by one in Los Angeles in 1914.[93] Undoubtedly the Supreme Court's *Powell v. Alabama* decision in 1932 (and the publicity around the Scottsboro case in general) reinforced and invigorated the development of state policies on the right to counsel.[94] Supporters of legal aid and the right to counsel argued that policies providing legal representation to the poor were an effective rebuttal to criticisms that the judicial system served only the wealthy. The *New York Times*, for instance, declared that the Court's decision in *Powell* "ought to abate the rancor of extreme radicals while confirming the faith of the American people in the soundness of their institutions and especially the integrity of the courts."[95] The *Christian Century* agreed, arguing that had the Supreme Court upheld the convictions and death sentences, "a pronounced swing toward economic and political radicalism . . . would have been the inevitable result."[96]

As these pressures grew, states passed laws expanding the provision of counsel to indigent defendants. As early as the late twenties, and continuing through the late fifties, various states began adopting laws that required the provision of counsel to indigent criminal defendants. Some provided counsel only in capital cases, as required by *Powell*; other states went further, providing counsel to any indigent defendant charged with a felony. Although these state programs were grossly inadequate given the needs of vast numbers of poor defendants, particularly in states that provided counsel only in capital cases, they nonetheless provided a financial base for growing numbers of criminal

appeals to the United States Supreme Court decades before similar developments occurred in other countries.[97] By the late fifties, so much had changed that advocates of a right to counsel for all felony defendants could confidently declare that "the necessity for [legal] representation is generally recognized today" and that "any society which does not afford the right to counsel gravely endangers judicial search for truth and risks its replacement by the purge or the ceremonial trial."[98]

The diffusion of state right-to-counsel policies covering felonies is illustrated in table 4.1. By the late fifties, as the table shows, only six states limited their right-to-counsel policies to capital cases; most states guaranteed the right to counsel in felony cases, the standard that the Supreme Court eventually constitutionalized in 1963 in *Gideon v. Wainwright*.[99] The spread of such policies propelled a growing number of criminal procedure cases onto the Supreme Court's agenda. From 1957 through 1966 a significant proportion of criminal defendants before the Supreme Court were represented by government-provided attorneys.[100]

Finally, in 1965 the federal government launched a major initiative, the Legal Services Program, to supplement the spotty civil legal aid programs provided on the state and local level. In the late sixties and early seventies, the Legal Services Program developed a systematic test-case campaign to bring about legal reform in policies directly affecting the poor. As Susan Lawrence has shown, eighty cases financed by the Legal Services Program reached the Supreme Court's agenda; in many, the Court announced landmark decisions that significantly influenced the development of the due process revolution.[101] In the absence of the Legal Services Program it is highly likely that many of the cases never would have reached the Court, as few such cases reached the Court either before the Program was formed or after it was replaced in 1974 by the more conservative Legal Services Corporation.[102]

Additional financing for rights litigation has come from "fee shifting"—use of defendants' funds to pay attorneys' fees for successful plaintiffs—which is authorized in certain cases under both state and federal legislation. By the early eighties, some 150 federal statutes authorized the award of attorneys' fees to private litigants who prevail in court when seeking to enforce federal law, and many states had similar legislation.[103] The most important federal authorizations for fee shifting are found in the Civil Rights Act of 1964, the Civil Rights Attorney's Fees Award Act of 1976, and the Equal Access to Justice Act of 1982. These statutes are explicitly intended to encourage rights litigation for the purpose of enforcing federal civil rights. Fee shifting

Table 4.1 Proliferation of State-Level Right-to-Counsel Laws Covering Accused
Felons, 1929–1959

Nevada	1929	Utah	1943
Idaho	1932	West Virginia	1943
Washington	1932	Minnesota	1945
Indiana	1933	Iowa	1946
Tennessee	1934	Kentucky	1946
Colorado	1935	Arkansas	1947
Delaware	1935	Vermont	1947*
Georgia	1935	Wisconsin	1947
Illinois	1935	Wyoming	1947
Kansas	1935	Connecticut	1949
Montana	1935	Virginia	1950
New Jersey	1937	Michigan	1954
Oklahoma	1937	Texas	1954
Arizona	1939	New Hampshire	1955*
Missouri	1939	North Carolina	1955
Ohio	1939	Maine	1956†
South Dakota	1939	Rhode Island	1956
California	1941	Maryland	1957
New Mexico	1941*	Alabama	‡
New York	1942	Florida	‡
Louisiana	1943	Massachusetts	‡
Nebraska	1943*	Mississippi	‡
North Dakota	1943	Pennsylvania	‡
Oregon	1943	South Carolina	‡

Sources: Beaney, Right to Counsel, 84–87; Special Committee, Equal Justice, appendix.
*Included only capital crimes and crimes punishable by three or more years imprisonment.
†By judicial decision.
‡These states had not created comprehensive right-to-counsel policies by the end of the fifties. Several other states that had already created right-to-counsel policies ran afoul of the Supreme Court's decision in Gideon v. Wainwright (1963) requiring states to provide counsel for indigents facing felony charges. In the three years following the Gideon decision, the Court set aside convictions on the basis of the new Gideon rule in cases arising from Alabama, Florida, Illinois, Louisiana, Maryland, Missouri, North Carolina, Ohio, Oklahoma, and Pennsylvania. See Lewis, Gideon's Trumpet, 214.

clearly provides significant assistance to some rights litigants: several public interest litigation groups have derived substantial portions of their budgets from attorney fee awards.[104] Nonetheless, the extent of support provided to ordinary litigants should not be exaggerated, as some research shows that, at least in constitutional tort cases, attorneys' fees are rarely awarded to plaintiffs.[105]

The Federal Government

Federal policies, particularly those of the Department of Justice and the solicitor general, the second-ranking Department official, also have significantly influenced the Supreme Court's agenda. The solicitor general screens cases lost by the federal government in lower courts, deciding which to petition the Supreme Court to hear. In 1984, for in-

stance, then–Solicitor General Rex Lee screened almost seven hundred government cases, taking only forty-three to the Court.[106] Of those forty-three, the Court granted certiorari in thirty-three cases, a 76 percent success rate for the solicitor general—far higher than the 4 percent success rate for other petitions in the same term.[107] For the 1925–1988 period, the Court granted certiorari in over 70 percent of the cases supported by the Justice Department.[108] Indeed, studies of the Court's certiorari process agree that the presence of the solicitor general as petitioner greatly increases the likelihood that a case will be placed on the Court's agenda.[109] Moreover, between 1959 and 1989, solicitors general won over two-thirds of the Supreme Court cases in which they participated.[110] The policies pushed by the federal government in its litigation before the Supreme Court, therefore, have had a great impact on the Court's agenda and policy decisions.

Beginning in the thirties, the Justice Department increasingly advocated clear policy programs in the Supreme Court, and its strong support for civil rights in the late forties, fifties, and sixties encouraged the Supreme Court to devote sustained attention to civil rights.[111] After initially rebuffing pressure from civil rights groups for federal prosecutions of civil rights violations in the South, the Justice Department gradually began developing a civil rights program in the late thirties in response to growing pressure from organized labor, African Americans, and some elements of the legal profession.[112] In 1938, the Justice Department initiated a prosecution against coal companies in Kentucky for violating the rights of coal miners to speak and hold public meetings.[113] In 1939 Attorney General Frank Murphy, following suggestions by President Roosevelt as well as his own political commitments, created the Civil Liberties Unit of the Department's Criminal Division (soon renamed the Civil Rights Section and now called the Civil Rights Division) and charged it with enforcing long-dormant Reconstruction-era federal civil rights laws.[114] The new section developed a careful strategy to expand federal protection for civil liberties and civil rights: under Murphy's direction, section lawyers developed an analysis of federal enforcement power under old Reconstruction-era statutes, and then pursued test cases in the courts to vindicate their positions. In the test-case strategy, the section worked primarily to bring cases concerning lynchings, police brutality, and involuntary servitude and peonage in the South, several of which reached the Court in the forties and fifties.[115] In the late forties, Attorney General Tom Clark reinvigorated federal support for civil rights as part of an effort to shore up support for Truman's administration among northern

blacks.[116] As Clayton shows, the Justice Department's new commitment to civil rights led to its development of an amicus brief in support of the NAACP's case in *Shelley v. Kraemer* (1948),[117] which was followed by similar briefs in a string of other NAACP cases. In the Eisenhower administration, the Justice Department under Attorney General Herbert Brownell continued its support of civil rights, filing crucial briefs in *Brown* (1954) and other civil rights cases.[118] Moreover, during the crucial period leading up to the Court's decision in *Brown*, Justice Frankfurter and Philip Elman, a lawyer in the solicitor general's office (and former Frankfurter clerk) cooperated closely in developing strategies and counting votes in pursuit of a pro–civil rights decision on school segregation.[119]

After *Brown*, the Justice Department's influence over the Court's rights agenda deepened even further. The Department played a major role in the late fifties and sixties in pushing the civil rights agenda by supporting litigation against racial segregation and by pushing legislation that both expanded its own powers to fight segregation and also broadened the scope of civil rights.[120] As Robert Dixon observed, participation by the Justice Department in civil rights cases brought by private plaintiffs "strengthen[ed] their cases through the addition of federal legal resources."[121] After the Department pushed for and gained the authority under the 1964 Civil Rights Act to bring suit in its own name in discrimination cases, its direct participation in civil rights litigation before the Court grew dramatically.[122] In addition, in the sixties the Justice Department supported major expansions in the scope of statutory protection for civil rights, thereby providing the foundation for a new wave of litigation.

Thus, as Cornell Clayton has argued, "[t]he executive branch originally supported—even drove—the Supreme Court in its new political role" particularly by pushing civil rights cases onto the Court's agenda and by urging the Court to broaden its support for civil rights.[123] On the other hand, the Justice Department's early enforcement of civil rights in local communities should not be exaggerated. In the forties, even after creation of the Civil Rights Section, the Justice Department hesitated to intervene vigorously in actions against lynching in the South and, as Michal Belknap observed, "characterized its own policy as one of 'strict self-limitation.'"[124] Nonetheless, in the late forties, Truman's Justice Department became increasingly active on the issue, particularly by pressing race-discrimination cases onto the Supreme Court's agenda.

By the late sixties, actions by the federal government also contrib-

uted to the support structure for women's rights. In 1964, Congress passed Title VII of the Civil Rights Act, which banned employment discrimination against women and became the basis for Supreme Court case law on sexual harassment. Title VII's establishment of the Equal Employment Opportunities Commission (EEOC) to implement the law, and Congress's authorization in 1972 of the EEOC to initiate lawsuits in its own name, affected the judicial agenda.[125] Like the Equal Opportunities Commission in England, the EEOC in the United States provided an important extrajudicial source of financial and legal resources for appellate litigation.

Supplementing such legislation, Presidents Johnson and Nixon issued a number of executive orders directing the federal bureaucracy to implement rules against sex discrimination. The Nixon administration directed a review of the hiring practices of higher education institutions and, on the basis of the review, brought hundreds of suits in lower courts against such institutions.[126] While such policies did not directly affect the Supreme Court's agenda, they shaped the legal and political environment in which the Court began to take women's-rights cases.

The Impact of Judicial Policies on the Support Structure
The broadest changes in the U.S. support structure thus have sources in civil society and governmental policy that are largely independent of the Supreme Court's influence. Nonetheless, some Supreme Court policies have influenced developments in the support structure. Both Wasby and McCann have explored in rich and nuanced detail the various effects of judicial policies on rights-advocacy organizations and movements.[127] First, favorable judicial decisions typically have encouraged rights-advocacy organizations and lawyers to invest further resources in rights litigation. For instance, the Court's pro–civil liberties decisions in the early thirties—*Near v. Minnesota* (1931), *Stromberg v. California* (1931), and *Powell v. Alabama* (1932)[128]—encouraged the ACLU and its cooperating attorneys to continue their litigation campaigns;[129] similarly, *Brown v. Board of Education* (1954)[130] and subsequent decisions encouraged civil rights organizations and private foundations to invest substantial resources in further litigation campaigns.[131]

Additionally, some judicial decisions have contributed directly to the creation of resources for litigation. The Court's right-to-counsel decisions in *Gideon v. Wainwright* (1963)[132] and subsequent cases contributed directly to the deepening of institutional resources for criminal procedure litigation. The Court's decision protecting the right of organ-

izations (specifically the NAACP) to support litigation on behalf of
their members, and the decision upholding the award of attorneys'
fees under the Civil Rights Act of 1964, directly encouraged litigation
by rights-advocacy organizations and contributed to their resource
base.[133] Similarly, the Court's various decisions in the sixties loosening
the rules on standing and class actions broadened access by organized
group litigants to the judicial agenda. Nonetheless, in 1975, a more
conservative Supreme Court undermined previous judicial expansions
of the fee-shifting system by ruling that courts had no authority to
award attorneys' fees to successful plaintiffs unless specifically authorized by statute to do so.[134] Congress responded by enacting the Civil
Rights Attorney's Fees Award Act, discussed earlier.

Although favorable judicial decisions have clearly contributed to the
support structure, decisions against rights claims, perhaps surprisingly, often have not directly eroded that structure. This phenomenon
supports my contention that the support structure's base is broader
than judicial policies alone. In the twenties, the ACLU faced repeated
negative decisions from the Supreme Court, only to return to the Court
with additional cases. Had the ACLU's strategies been determined by
the Court's policies, *Stromberg* would never have reached the Court.
Similarly, as a civil rights litigator told Wasby, "Many cases have gone
forward anyhow [in spite of apparent opposition from the Supreme
Court], or *Brown* wouldn't have happened."[135] Thus, although the
Supreme Court's decisions matter, "litigators may attempt to change
such patterns."[136]

The Impact of the Support Structure

The developments in the support structure for legal mobilization that
are described earlier in this chapter have been crucial to the emergence
of judicial revolutions in freedom of speech and the press beginning
around 1918, in criminal procedure beginning in the early thirties, and
in women's rights in the early seventies. In each era, the Court's agenda
responded to litigants availing themselves of newly developed resources for litigation.

The growing support structure for legal mobilization provided a key
foundation for the rights revolution in two ways. First, the development of support for constitutional rights litigation propelled new civil
liberties and civil rights claims onto the Court's agenda. Few civil liberties or civil rights cases reached the Court's agenda before about 1918.
The few that reached the agenda remained isolated complaints, hardly
part of a sustained uprising of organized litigation. By around 1918,

however, an increasing number of organized groups, aided by an increasingly diverse legal profession, forcefully began pressing rights cases onto the Court's agenda. The ACLU led the effort, and other organizations followed or worked closely with the ACLU. By the early thirties, the NAACP had launched its strategic campaign against racial segregation, and the Jehovah's Witnesses had begun their campaign to defend door-to-door and street-corner proselytizing.

Developments in the support structure also propelled criminal procedure cases onto the Court's agenda. By the late twenties, several organized groups began attacking, partly through litigation, abuses in the criminal justice process, particularly racial discrimination by police and courts. In 1929, President Hoover created the Wickersham Commission to report on the state of the criminal justice system.[137] The ACLU's director succeeded in having leading members and supporters of the ACLU appointed to write the portion of the Commission's study devoted to the police. The ACLU researchers drew on previous research by the ACLU and released a report titled *Lawlessness in Law Enforcement*, which, as Samuel Walker observed, "created a national sensation, overshadowing all the other ten commission reports."[138] The report shocked many people, particularly legal and judicial elites, because it documented that police departments regularly used the "third degree"—physical and psychological coercion—against criminal suspects. The second key development that placed law enforcement practices on the national agenda was the Scottsboro case. The litigation around the Scottsboro case continued for years after the initial Supreme Court decision in 1932 and helped to focus attention in the legal community on various problems in the criminal justice process. Additionally, the Justice Department's Civil Rights Section, as noted earlier, supported civil rights and liberties litigation on a range of matters, particularly discrimination in the criminal justice process, and a number of the cases reached the Supreme Court. The Section heavily publicized its work against racial discrimination in the South and pursued a number of cases arising from problems in the justice system in southern states.[139] Finally, the growth of state right-to-counsel policies provided new resources for criminal appeals, so much so that many of the criminal procedure cases reaching the Supreme Court by the fifties were argued by government-sponsored attorneys. In the absence of these various sources of support, it is very likely that few criminal procedure cases would have reached the Supreme Court.

Similar developments in the support structure for women's-rights litigation help to explain the judicial revolution in women's rights just

as the Court's majority began shifting toward the right. Before 1970, a broad base of support for women's-rights litigation simply did not exist. But, as the women's movement developed after the mid-sixties, several new developments occurred—the number of women's-rights organizations and the number of women entering the legal profession grew dramatically—creating, for the first time in American history, a strong support structure for women's-rights litigation. The new support structure propelled a range of women's-rights issues onto the Supreme Court's agenda and thus, just as the Court's majority became increasingly conservative, it faced a rising tide of women's-rights litigation and a public mood increasingly supportive of women's rights.

By 1971 women's-rights litigators, unlike earlier civil rights and liberties litigators, were not inventing a new weapon against discrimination: they could model their litigation campaigns on earlier successful campaigns in many other policy areas. The Warren Court's egalitarian rulings on racial discrimination, and the litigation campaign of the NAACP-LDF, provided inspiration and practical guidelines for the women's-rights litigators in the seventies.[140] For these reasons, the judicial revolution in women's rights advanced far more rapidly than had the earlier developments in freedom of speech and race discrimination. Although some legal issues remained open to debate, both the justices and the litigators knew well the nature of the process in which they were participating, for it had been done many times before. Thus, once the Court had signaled clearly its willingness to question sex discrimination on constitutional grounds, litigation moved rapidly.

In early developments in each phase of the rights revolution, the justices often had not clarified and solidified their attitudes on a particular issue before its regular appearance on their agenda. Justice Holmes' flip-flop on freedom of speech is perhaps the most famous example of this judicial uncertainty. In 1919 Holmes wrote the Court's opinion in a unanimous decision upholding Charles Schenck's criminal conviction, over First Amendment objections, for distributing anti-draft leaflets.[141] Holmes's opinion held that Congress had the authority to criminalize criticism of the military draft during wartime. As several legal scholars and historians have recently observed, Holmes's opinion in *Schenck* followed conservative prewar free speech jurisprudence, which authorized government restrictions of any speech having a "bad tendency."[142] Yet litigants continued to bring free speech cases arising out of antiwar protests to the Court. Harvard professor Zechariah Chafee developed a strong defense of freedom of speech, and Holmes soon reversed his conservative position and began to use dissenting

opinions to articulate a libertarian defense of free speech.[143] Holmes's judicial attitude toward freedom of speech seems either remarkably malleable or, more plausibly, not clearly developed before the prolif- eration of free speech litigation confronting the Court in the post- war years. The birth of other issues through newly developing litiga- tion similarly has forced the justices to develop new jurisprudential and policy positions. *Everson v. Board of Education* (1947),[144] as J. Wood- ford Howard showed, presented the Court with establishment clause claims that it had not previously faced, and the justices, with no prior experience in the matter, shifted votes and jurisprudential positions during conference discussions of the case. "Ideological hardening came later," as Howard observed; "time and litigation may be neces- sary for implications to be perceived and attitudes to harden in a case- law system."[145] As these examples illustrate, the justices' policy prefer- ences, at least during the early development of a new judicial agenda, developed in response to new cases placed on their agenda by out- side litigants.

In the context of frequent litigation on any particular issue, of course, the justices typically have developed clear attitudes and sharp divi- sions. And in those circumstances, the replacement of justices may pro- duce substantial effects on the judicial agenda. In the area of criminal procedure, for example, the replacement of liberal justices by conserva- tives in the late sixties and early seventies produced a dramatic shift in the agenda. The liberal justices of the sixties had granted certiorari in criminal cases mainly to claims brought by defendants for the pur- pose of overturning convictions and expanding procedural rights; the new conservative majority, by contrast, began granting certiorari in cases brought by prosecutors for the purpose of reinstating convictions and narrowing procedural rights. But such a dramatic shift was pos- sible only because there existed a steady stream of criminal appeals supported by a broad support structure.

The second way in which the growing support structure for legal mobilization influenced the rights revolution is by supporting contin- ued litigation, in response to landmark decisions, that capitalized on openings offered by the justices. In the absence of a vibrant support structure, landmark decisions remain isolated events, neither imple- mented nor developed through further litigation. The Supreme Court's early decision in *Strauder v. West Virginia* (1880) banning race discrimi- nation in jury selection, for instance, remained a lonely, isolated pre- cedent before the development of a support structure for litigation

against race discrimination in the criminal justice system.[146] Similarly, as we shall see in the following chapters on India, after 1977 the Indian Supreme Court's decisions on due process have been as revolutionary as the leading decisions of the Warren Court, but the Indian rights revolution has failed to develop because of the support structure's weaknesses. By contrast, the U.S. support structure responded with speed and vigor to the Court's landmark rights decisions of the sixties.

Conclusion

The rights revolution in the United States, as I have shown in this chapter, has developed within a broader political economy of litigation. The growth of a support structure for legal mobilization—consisting of rights-advocacy organizations, a diverse and organizationally sophisticated legal profession, a broad array of financing sources, and federal rights-advocacy efforts—propelled new rights issues onto the Supreme Court's agenda.

Although judicial policies undoubtedly contributed to the development of that support structure, changes in the support structure have typically resulted from forces that are broader than the Court's policies alone. The major rights-advocacy organizations were formed during the wave of institution building in the early twentieth century, and the interest group system diversified tremendously as part of broader changes in American society in the post–World War II period; the legal profession diversified due to the development of law schools and major demographic changes in American society; and the growth of foundation funding for rights advocacy reflected the rise of the foundations themselves.

The great expansion of support for rights litigation could not, by itself, have produced the transformation of the Court's agenda. The Court has aided some developments in the support structure and not others and has thereby influenced long-term developments in the agenda. Thus the Court's civil liberties decisions of the early thirties encouraged ACLU lawyers to continue pursuing rights litigation. By the fifties, the support structure for rights litigation had deepened and broadened significantly; in that context, the liberal court majorities of the fifties and sixties produced a major transformation in the agenda. The *Brown* decision transformed the entire field of civil rights litigation, and the Court's procedural decisions of the sixties on standing, class actions, and the award of attorneys' fees provided significant support for liberal rights-advocacy organizations and lawyers. But the de-

velopment and persistence of a broad support structure for rights litigation was a crucial condition for even those supportive judicial
decisions. Of the countries in this study, and arguably of the countries
in the world, that support structure developed the earliest and the
most substantially in the United States, and on its foundation the Supreme Court has built the U.S. rights revolution.

FIVE

India: An Ideal Environment
for a Rights Revolution?

In the late seventies, Indian journalists revealed evidence of shocking abuse in the nation's prisons. Prison guards beat and tortured prisoners, sometimes using bicycle spokes and battery acid to cause blindness, and some prisons kept the criminally accused behind bars for years without trials, often far beyond the maximum sentence for their alleged crimes. The Supreme Court of India heard several cases arising from these allegations and handed down landmark decisions extending constitutional rights to prisoners.[1]

The prisoner rights cases were part of a dramatic attack on violations of individual rights begun by the Indian Supreme Court in the late seventies. The supposed judicial activism of American courts seems almost conservative by comparison to the Indian Court's leading decisions. By 1987 the Indian Supreme Court had ordered a complete reform of the country's prison administration and created, among other things, a constitutional right to a minimum wage,[2] a constitutional right to counsel ("free legal aid") in criminal cases,[3] and broad new remedies against destruction of the environment (for instance, in 1987 the Court ordered the immediate shutdown of twenty tanneries emitting pollutants into the Ganges River).[4] The Indian Supreme Court clearly *tried* to spark a rights revolution—*but little happened.*

As I shall show in the next chapter, the Indian rights revolution remained stunted, limited to a few Supreme Court decisions that were in large part neither fleshed out by later cases nor implemented in practice. The best explanation for that lack of energy, I shall show, is the weakness of the Indian support structure for legal mobilization. But first, this chapter shows that the key conditions identified by the conventional explanations—rights consciousness, judicial independence and the presence in the constitution of rights guarantees, and rights-supportive judges—all were met by 1978. Indians have increasingly framed their aspirations in the language of rights, the Indian

Constitution guarantees a basic set of liberal rights, and the Indian Supreme Court is independent of the legislative and executive branches of government, both by tradition and by constitutional guarantee (indeed, according to one scholar, it is "the most powerful court in the world"[5]). Perhaps most importantly, after 1977, leading judges on the Supreme Court became deeply committed to the protection of individual rights. If the standard explanations for the rights revolution are true, then India is an ideal site for a rights revolution.

Indian Society and Rights Consciousness
India is a country of startling diversity. It has a large industrialized economy and a growing computer industry, yet the majority of the population lives in rural villages and participates in a simple, agrarian economy. The urban middle class is large and growing, yet the majority of the population remains very poor. The population is large, over 930 million in 1995, and growing rapidly. There are hundreds of languages and a number of ethnic and religious groups. Even the most common religion, Hinduism, which influences much of Indian life, is deeply divided by more than two thousand castes that vary greatly by locality.

The major divisions in Indian society run along religious lines. Muslims make up a little over 10 percent of the population, Sikhs about 2 percent, and Hindus over 80 percent. Shortly after Indian independence from Britain in 1947, two regions dominated by Muslims became independent of India, forming the countries of Pakistan and Bangladesh. There remain deep tensions and resentments in India over that fragmentation. Some elements of the Hindu majority wish to increase the country's devotion to Hindu traditions; some elements of the Muslim and Sikh minorities—who constitute majorities in several states—wish to gain independence. In recent years militant Muslims and the Sikhs in India's northwestern states of the Punjab and Jammu/Kashmir have mounted violent independence movements and the Indian security forces have responded, sometimes with great brutality.[6] Nonetheless, although there is an increasingly powerful Hindu nationalist movement, the Hindu majority remains deeply divided along traditional caste lines.

Large segments of India's poorest classes also have grown increasingly frustrated with their position and increasingly are mounting grassroots movements demanding rights to land ownership, protection for environmental resources that provide their livelihood, and rights to acceptable pay and working conditions.[7] These movements

appear to be posing increasingly important challenges to local power holders as well as to the national power structure.[8]

There are sharp tensions along gender lines as well. The place of women in Indian society presents an oft-remarked paradox: they are both subjected to extreme brutality and held in great reverence and respect.[9] Brides in middle-class homes may be threatened, injured, or even murdered at the hands of future in-laws attempting to extract a larger dowry;[10] the police rape women in their custody;[11] men aggressively harass women in public places, verbally abusing women or even physically groping them, in what is mildly termed "eve teasing";[12] and there is a Hindu tradition of burning a widow on the funeral pyre of her husband, which is now largely defunct in practice but is resurfacing in Hindu communalist ideology; to the great horror of many Indians, religious and secular alike, a widow was burned on her husband's funeral pyre as recently as 1987. Although women thus face much discrimination and abuse, they also are revered throughout Indian society. Hindus include within their pantheon of gods several important goddesses, principal among them Lakshmi, the bringer of prosperity; women are often considered to have a special connection to Lakshmi. A number of important political leaders, among them former Prime Minister Indira Gandhi, have been women. Some lawyers practicing before the Supreme Court have been women. The mainstream political parties explicitly support the improvement of conditions for women. Criticizing women in public is considered a great offense against social taste. Gender lines thus form a major source of tension in Indian society.

In all of these tensions—caste-based, ethnic, religious, and gender-based—the Indian state looms large. Since 1950 Indian politics have been dominated by the creation of a large state bureaucracy and by its attempts to encourage economic development through control of industries and aggressive regulation of the economy. The Indian state has grown tremendously, now employing two-thirds of all workers in what is called the economy's "organized sector."[13] As Paul Brass observed,

> The state was perceived as the instrument which would establish India's sovereign presence in the world, would preserve its unity against foreign enemies and internal secessionists, ensure authority, order, and discipline in a society perceived as always on the brink of disorder and violence, promote economic development through centralized planning which would bring India out of the

backwardness of agrarian life and free it of a social order dominated by feudal institutions and practices and by religious super-
stitions, and make it possible for Indians also to maintain an effective parliamentary system.[14]

Internal security forces, among them the police and the army, make
the Indian state a formidable and growing presence in Indian society.
There is, according to one observer, "an increasing reliance on police
and other such organizations for effective governance . . . [and a] con-
siderable expansion in the police forces throughout the country."[15] The
Indian government has significantly increased the size of various components of the security forces in recent years, among them the conventional police and several paramilitary forces. Similarly, the Indian army
has increasingly been used to maintain order over recent decades,
from 476 occasions in the whole 1951 to 1970 period to 369 occasions
in the 1981 to 1984 period.[16] Kuldeep Mathur observes, "Undoubtedly,
there has been a proliferation in the coercive apparatus of the state,
and the symbols of state power have become more visible."[17]

The Indian state often uses preventive detention. For every year except for three between 1950 and the last year of this study (1990) one
or another national law authorizing preventive detention has been in
effect.[18] The Indian Supreme Court, though periodically asked to strike
down laws authorizing preventive detention, consistently has upheld
such laws. As early as 1950, in the landmark case *A. K. Gopalan v. State
of Madras*, the Supreme Court upheld the first national preventive detention statute and affirmed its rationale.[19]

Not surprisingly, various regimes have used their powers of preventive detention primarily to confine their political opponents. The widespread and common use of preventive detention appears to have developed in the late sixties and early seventies as the government
attempted to control a violent rebellion by leftist guerillas in West Bengal. Since then, regimes have used preventive detention with alarming
frequency and magnitude. Amnesty International has found as many
as twenty thousand political prisoners held at one time, among them
guerillas, students, trade unionists, and members of opposition political parties. Since the late seventies, the human rights organization's
reports have consistently charged both national and state governments
with brutality, including torture and killing, towards those held in preventive detention.[20]

Apart from preventive detention, police and security forces under
both the national and state governments routinely brutalize individuals they view as opponents. There is overwhelming evidence that In-

dia's various police forces beat, torture, or kill at the very least hundreds of people per year in response to petty insults, political activism, or organized crime.[21] The People's Union for Civil Liberties documented some six thousand killings by police from 1979 to 1982.[22] There is much evidence that police torture and killings continue to the present throughout large areas of India, among them the economically depressed states of Bihar and Uttar Pradesh, the areas of tribal conflict in the northeast, and the areas of separatist guerilla activity in the northwest states of Punjab and Jammu/Kashmir.[23]

The justification for such tactics, when one is given, is that the police must use vigorous methods to respond to organized and violent criminals. There is no doubt even among civil liberties advocates that India faces a mounting problem of organized private crime and violence, that the police have inadequate resources to deal with the problem, and that powerful individuals often escape justice in the courts. Articulate members of the police justify their tactics as necessary, in the absence of other solutions, to control violent criminals.[24] Similarly, judges sometimes justify preventive detention as a means for limiting the power of organized, powerful criminals.[25] Nonetheless, civil liberties advocates have documented that the vast majority of cases of torture and killing involve either petty criminals or political organizers of social movements among the poorest castes and classes.[26]

Moreover, the police significantly violate women's rights, both directly through abuse and harassment and indirectly through acquiescence to the crimes of others. There is evidence that police place some women in custody primarily to rape them.[27] And, along with the judiciary, they generally turn their backs on dowry-related abuse and murder.[28]

The Indian state also perpetuates discrimination against women through employment practices. As the Indian state employs a large proportion of workers in the economy's organized sector, state employment practices affect many women. A serious problem for women workers is that employers in India in the past have commonly required women to retire upon marriage, and some governmental employers have participated in this requirement. For instance, Air India has had a policy of firing stewardesses when they marry.[29] Another serious problem for women workers is the significant inequities that exist in wages and salaries. Some government agencies have had explicit policies of paying women less than men for the same work.[30] Additionally, women in government employment face sexual harassment by colleagues and supervisors.[31] Much of the evidence for the various prob-

lems facing women workers is anecdotal, but observers so universally attest to these problems that there can be little doubt that the problems are pervasive.

There is yet one final element of this rather gloomy litany of rights abuse by the Indian state. Indira Gandhi, prime minister for much of the late sixties, seventies, and early eighties, greatly centralized political power in the seventies, which culminated in election corruption in 1975. In that year, a political opponent filed a lawsuit challenging the legality of her 1975 election victory, and a High Court judge ruled against her. In response, Mrs. Gandhi imposed emergency rule for two years from 1975 to 1977, imprisoning thousands of political opponents. Amnesty International called the declaration of emergency rule "the most significant event of the year in terms of human rights in Asia."[32]

The period of emergency rule was a watershed in Indian politics.[33] The Emergency fragmented the Congress Party, which was voted out of power in 1977 for the first time since Indian Independence. Perhaps more importantly, the Emergency provoked the urban middle class and intelligentsia to begin questioning the value of a strong, unchecked Indian state.[34] For the first time since Independence, leaders of the state had used its arbitrary power not against the poorest members of society and separatist movements but against urban intellectuals, political opponents, and dissenters, many of whom were arrested and detained without trial for long periods of time. During the Emergency the national and state governments detained at least forty thousand political opponents and held most for the entire two-year period.[35] The arrests spread fear among intellectuals and political leaders. As one leading lawyer said of moves by the government to consolidate its power, "If I say anything about the recent amendments in public I shall be probably arrested. In fact, the only place where there is freedom of speech in this country is the few hundred square feet of various courtrooms."[36] As that observation suggests, intellectuals and political leaders began looking to the courts, particularly the Supreme Court, for a means of checking the power of the state.

The language of rights is increasingly used in these myriad tensions.[37] Muslim separatists in Jammu/Kashmir claim they have a right to a referendum on whether the state should remain part of the Indian union; victims of the Indian security forces make complaints in the language of rights; members of the "scheduled castes" (the term that replaced "untouchables" when the latter was banned) claim rights to public employment or a place in the educational system as part of India's affirmative action policies; and members of India's women's

movement claim rights to be free of harassment and violence perpetrated by the police, and as well as rights to equality in employment.

Moreover, India remains a democracy and, "in its adherence to legal forms and loyalty to legal procedures," as Marc Galanter has observed, "India is quite unique among Third World countries. . . . Courts and lawyers are a highly visible part of Indian life, frequently resorted to in matters ranging from great public issues to village disputes."[38] The all-too-present threats to individual rights thus conflict greatly with both a growing rights consciousness and a traditional respect for legal formalities and procedures. In India, the cultural prerequisite for a rights revolution seems to be amply present.

The Indian Constitution and the Legal Context

When India gained independence from Britain in 1947, the new nation's leaders had a deep commitment to establishing a constitutional democracy, and so their first project was to draft a constitution. The constitutional framers treated their task very seriously, consulting a wide range of constitutions, constitutional scholars, and jurists from other countries and engaging in debates over the course of almost three years, from 1946 through 1949.[39] The resulting constitution includes both continuities with the British legacy and clear departures from it. All in all, it provides a nearly ideal constitutional foundation for a rights revolution.

Imitating Britain, the Indian framers adopted a parliamentary system, with the national executive and the ruling party closely connected, and with broad powers granted to the central government. The Indian framers feared the possibility of conflict and fragmentation due to India's regionally and communally divided society and, consequently, granted much authority to the central government. That authority includes the power to amend the Constitution by a simple majority in the national parliament, and also the power of the central government to take over state governments under emergency circumstances.

The Indian Constitution, however, also rejected the British model in some important respects. Most importantly, the Constitution contains a declaration of Fundamental Rights and also a list of what are called "Directive Principles." The Fundamental Rights, following the American liberal tradition, place limits on state power; they include rights to equality, freedom of religion, cultural and educational freedom, rights against exploitation by the state or by private persons, and the right to constitutional remedies. The Fundamental Rights apply to both the

national and state governments. The Constitution explicitly qualifies these rights, however, by allowing restrictions related to agrarian reform, the implementation of any of the Directive Principles, and the maintenance of public order and morality, among other things. Additionally, the Constitution grants to the government the authority to suspend the Fundamental Rights entirely if it declares a state of emergency. The Directive Principles outline the government's obligation to enhance the welfare of the society and its citizens. The Directive Principles are not enforceable in court and therefore are understood simply to be broad guidelines for government policy.[40] By contrast, the Constitution provides that any claim of violation of a Fundamental Right may be taken directly to the Supreme Court.

Rights of the Accused and Prisoners

In the area of criminal procedure and the rights of the accused, the Indian Constitution provides a somewhat inconsistent foundation for rights litigation. On the one hand, the Constitution authorizes both national and state governments under specified circumstances to exercise "preventive detention"—the imprisonment of persons without charge or trial. The national government may use preventive detention to aid in the defense and security of the nation, and both the national and state governments may use the mechanism to aid in security of a state government, the maintenance of public order, or the provision of essential supplies and services.[41] Preventive detention, as has been noted, has also been used by regimes to arrest and confine their political opponents.

On the other hand, the Indian Constitution and statutory law also place limits on the arbitrary exercise of power by police and other security forces. The Constitution forbids preventive detention for longer than three months unless an advisory board authorizes the detaining authority to continue the detention longer than that period; it requires that the detaining authority communicate to the detainee the grounds for detention "as soon as may be"; and it requires that the detainee be allowed to respond to the order.[42] The Constitution's equality provisions, particularly in Article 14, prohibit discrimination on the basis of a range of ascribed characteristics. More importantly, Article 21 requires that liberty or life be taken only through procedures established by law. Moreover, statutory law, backed up by Supreme Court decisions, attempts to limit the use of torture in police investigations. For the purpose of limiting the incentive of police to torture suspects, the Indian Code of Criminal Procedure since 1853 has barred the admis-

sion in court of *any* statement made by an accused to the police, and the Supreme Court has extended the prohibition to include statements made to the police in the presence of a magistrate.[43] Ironically, there is some speculation that such a prohibition has the effect of limiting lawyers' concerns about police torture because torture has come to seem inevitable given the admitted ineffectiveness of removing the presumed principal incentive for torture.[44]

Women's Rights

In the area of women's rights, the Indian Constitution and the country's laws also provide a somewhat inconsistent foundation for rights litigation. Article 14 of the Constitution's Fundamental Rights specifically prohibits the government from discriminating on the basis of sex. Additionally, the Constitution's Directive Principles call for the government to work to eliminate discrimination against women in the private sector. There also is legislation addressing the most serious problems facing Indian women, among them discrimination in employment, the practice of dowry (which systematically victimizes new brides), and rape by police officials. For instance, the Equal Remuneration Act of 1976 prohibits pay discrimination on the basis of sex. Its requirements cover a wide range of work settings, including both agricultural work and work in the industrialized sector. The Act also authorizes the government to create advisory committees for the purpose of developing programs to increase employment opportunities for women. Taken together, these various provisions of Indian law provide a strong foundation for litigation on women's rights. As one scholar observed, "On paper, India now boasts some of the more advanced legislation in the world pertaining to equality rights for women."[45]

On the other hand, Indian laws governing marriage, divorce, and inheritance greatly discriminate against women in some religious groups. Indian law distinguishes between ordinary civil law and what are called "personal laws" associated with each of the major religious communities in India (Hindu, Muslim, Christian, and Parsi).[46] Each religious community has its own personal laws governing what is ostensibly the private sphere of marriage, divorce, inheritance, and adoption. The various personal laws differ in the rights they grant to women. For example, under the Hindu system there are fourteen grounds for divorce, but for Christians there is only one ground and "divorce is almost impossible."[47] Similarly, the Indian Code of Criminal Procedure, generally understood as applicable to any individual, grants to women a right to adequate maintenance from their husbands

in the event of divorce, but the law governing Muslims grants maintenance for a period of only three months after the divorce, in addition
to the minimum lump sum of her dower ("mahr").[48] For Muslim
women, the Muslim code prevails. Regardless of these differences, the
personal laws disadvantage women. For instance, each of the systems
of personal laws grants either full or predominant inheritance rights
to sons rather than to the wife and daughters. The system of personal
laws, then, directly contradicts a standard of formal equality before the
law, both by providing different legal rights depending on community
membership and by providing fewer rights to women than to men.

Such a system appears to contradict the Indian Constitution's explicit fundamental rights to equality before the law contained principally in Articles 14 and 15. In addition, one of the Constitution's Directive Principles directs the government to establish a uniform civil code;
while Directive Principles are not enforceable, the Supreme Court in
other matters has declared that they must be used to interpret the nature of the Fundamental Rights. The Indian Constitution, then, appears
to provide a foundation for rejection of the system of personal laws.[49]
On the other hand, one of the compromises reached in framing the
Constitution appears to have been that the judiciary would not have
the authority to abolish the system of personal laws.[50] The system en-
dures, and no scholar of the subject expects a uniform civil code at
in the foreseeable future due to the continuing religious tensions in
Indian society.

In theory, at least, the Indian Constitution and statutory law thus
provide at least a basic foundation for the development of a judicial
rights revolution. The Constitution explicitly guarantees a broad set
of rights against state action, and statutory law in some respects has
broadened those rights. There are firm constitutional guarantees, in
particular, for both women's rights and due process in criminal procedure. As noted, however, India's Fundamental Rights are qualified
in some very important respects. The Constitution has generally been
understood to authorize the system of personal laws that deeply dis-
criminates against women; and the Constitution authorizes governments to imprison persons without charge or trial for certain specified
reasons. Nonetheless, the Indian Constitution's rights guarantees,
taken as a whole, are remarkably robust.

The Indian Supreme Court

The Supreme Court is an important element of the Indian constitutional structure and is greatly revered among the educated classes.
Galanter has observed that the Indian judiciary is accorded "extraordi-

nary respect" and "enormous popular regard."[51] For instance, when Indira Gandhi violated legal tradition in 1973 by advancing a loyal junior justice on the Supreme Court to the position of chief justice, bypassing three senior justices, the bar and members of the educated classes vigorously criticized her action as an attack on the Court, its independence, and its traditions.[52] In recent years, Indians routinely have turned to the Court to provide independent investigations into all manner of political scandals and crises. The Court, without any doubt, is a major political institution with broad powers and great popular support.

In contrast to the United States Constitution, which does not explicitly grant to the Supreme Court the power of judicial review, there has never been any doubt that the Indian Constitution granted the Indian Supreme Court that power. Granville Austin observes that, from the earliest days of independence, the Indian judiciary was regarded as "an arm of the social revolution" and that members of the Constituent Assembly believed judicial review to be an "essential power" of the new country's courts.[53] Article 13 declares that any law that encroaches on any of the Fundamental Rights shall be void, although it does not declare who has the authority to make such a determination. Additionally, the earliest proposals on Fundamental Rights emphasized that they must be enforceable,[54] and the resulting Constitution included among the Fundamental Rights the right to petition the Supreme Court directly in matters relating to these rights. Article 32 reads:

> (1) The right to move the Supreme Court by appropriate proceedings for the enforcement of the rights conferred in this Part [the section on Fundamental Rights] is guaranteed.
> (2) The Supreme Court shall have power to issue directions or orders or writs, including writs in the nature of *habeas corpus, mandamus, prohibition, quo warranto* and *certiorari*, whichever may be appropriate for the enforcement of any of the rights conferred by this Part.

Dr. B. R. Ambedkar, the chair of the drafting committee, declared of this right to petition the Supreme Court directly on Fundamental Rights, "If I was asked to name any particular article of the Constitution as *the most important*—an article *without which this Constitution would be a nullity*—I would not refer to any other article except this one. It is the very soul of the Constitution and the very heart of it."[55] This "soul of the Constitution" makes the Indian Supreme Court the most accessible of the four supreme courts in this study, and arguably of any supreme court in the world.

Additionally, the Indian Supreme Court's jurisdiction is remarkably

broad. It has original jurisdiction over disputes between the national government and the states and between different states;[56] it has appellate jurisdiction over criminal and civil cases, although since 1972 appeal to the Supreme Court in civil cases has been limited to those certified by a state High Court to involve a "substantial question of law of general importance;"[57] and it has advisory jurisdiction to render its opinion on any question of law or fact referred to it by the president. The Court also has a special leave jurisdiction that grants it discretion to hear appeals involving "any judgment, decree, determination, sentence or order in any cause or matter passed or made by any court or tribunal in the territory of India" except for matters relating to the Armed Forces.[58] Thus the Supreme Court may decide nearly any issue that arises in Indian politics.

Although the Constitution grants broad powers to the Supreme Court, two constitutional provisions originally placed significant limitations on the Court's power. The Court, however, has effectively neutralized both. First, the constitutional framers, on the advice of Felix Frankfurter that substantive due process posed a threat to the state's regulatory power, replaced a proposed due process clause in Article 21 with the bland guarantee that "No person shall be deprived of his life or personal liberty except according to the procedure established by law."[59] In an early decision the Supreme Court dutifully followed that wording in rejecting a substantive challenge to a law allowing detention without trial,[60] but later, as I shall show shortly, the justices aggressively developed an American-style substantive due process, in which they used Article 21's clearly procedural guarantee to protect substantive rights. Another limitation on the power of the judiciary is the ease of amending the Constitution. Amendments that do not affect the structure of government (the process of electing the President, the distribution of legislative power between the states and the Union, and the powers of the Supreme Court and the state High Courts, among other things) require only the assent of a majority in each house of Parliament (but at least two-thirds of those present and voting).[61] Amendments that affect the structure of government must also be ratified by the legislatures of at least half the states. Thus the process of amendment is relatively easy to accomplish. Nonetheless, as I shall discuss shortly, the Court has ruled on several occasions that amendments that violate the Constitution's basic structure are void.

The Supreme Court's power is undoubtedly attenuated, however, by an unclear and fragmented agenda. This results from several factors. For one, the Court's workload is staggering. During the calendar year 1990 the Supreme Court disposed of an impressive 56,343 cases; but at

the end of that year 185,108 other cases still waited decision.[62] The second, and perhaps most important, reason for incoherence in the agenda is that the Indian government has responded to the Court's growing workload not by granting the justices discretion over which cases to decide (as is the case in Canada and the United States) but by increasing the number of justices on the Court.[63] Originally the Constitution provided for eight justices including the chief justice; in 1956 this was increased to eleven; in 1960 to fourteen; in 1977 to eighteen; and in 1986 to twenty-six.[64] The Supreme Court hears and decides cases by panels, most of which are composed of only two or three justices. Important constitutional benches may be composed of five, seven, or occasionally nine justices. The large number of justices and the fragmentation into small panels allows a great degree of inconsistency to creep into decision making.[65] A third factor contributing to incoherence in the agenda is the relatively short term served by most justices, sometimes only a year or two. Terms of service tend to be short because there is a mandatory retirement age of sixty-five, and because, by accepted practice, a person is appointed to the Supreme Court only after serving on the High Court of one of India's states. Consequently, a person must have been appointed to a High Court relatively early in life to have any chance of reaching the Supreme Court and serving there very long before mandatory retirement.[66] Chief justices, in particular, commonly serve very short terms, sometimes only a few months. This is because usually only the most senior associate justice on the Supreme Court is elevated to the position of chief justice. Deviations from the practice of elevation by seniority have produced extremely sharp objections from the bench and bar.[67] These factors—the large caseload, the large number of justices and fragmentation of the Court into numerous small panels, and the relatively short terms of the justices and even shorter terms of chief justices—contribute to inconsistency, uncertainty, and conflict in Supreme Court decision making.

Although the Supreme Court's powers are thus limited in a number of ways, the lawyers, intellectuals and political leaders who opposed Indira Gandhi's emergency rule had some justification for placing hope in the courts. The Supreme Court has been an active policymaker since Independence, often opposing the policies of the national government. The ideological direction of the Court's policies may be divided roughly into two periods, one in which leading justices championed property rights but not due process and equality, and the second in which the reverse has been true.[68]

During the first period, roughly from 1950 through the mid-

seventies, the Supreme Court had engaged in a running dispute with various governments over the issue of property rights.[69] The national government had developed a nationalization program which it justified as necessary for implementing the Constitution's Directive Principles, but the Supreme Court, in a series of decisions, held that the right to property, one of the Fundamental Rights, required the Indian government to pay owners full market value for property taken for nationalization. The Indian government refused and passed the Fourth Amendment in 1955, which changed the constitutional text that formed the basis for the Court's decisions, and the Twenty-Fifth Amendment in 1971, which removed the property right from the jurisdiction of the courts. After the 1971 amendment, a constitution bench of the Supreme Court, over two dissents, responded with a stunning decision that struck down those parts of the amendment that precluded judicial review of property rights claims, on the ground that judicial review is a part of the basic structure of the Indian Constitution.[70] Under this "basic structure" doctrine, the Court claims the authority to reject constitutional amendments if they are inconsistent with the Constitution's basic structure. The Gandhi government responded by announcing that it would seek justices committed to the ideals of socialism, and it largely fulfilled that promise.[71] The court-packing plan provoked an outcry alleging the erosion of judicial independence.

The period of emergency rule from 1975 to 1977 marks the turning point between the Supreme Court's first and second eras. During the Emergency, the Gandhi government took a number of steps that directly challenged the Court's authority. For instance, the government passed the notorious Forty-Second Amendment that purported to immunize any future amendments from judicial review.[72] The government also called on the Supreme Court to abandon its "basic structure" doctrine to give the government a free hand to legislate by constitutional amendment. The Court convened a constitutional bench in order to take that step but then dissolved the panel when none of the participants—neither those loyal to the government nor those opposed to it—appeared willing to legitimate the regime's demand for unchecked power to change the Constitution in any way it wished.[73] The regime then stepped up the pressure on the Court. As Upendra Baxi later recalled, "there was no knowing whether the Supreme Court building might be locked on one 'fine' morning . . . . [T]here were hints that judicial power might be curbed in the days to come."[74] Not surprisingly, the Court acquiesced in many of the government's demands. The

Court validated (for practical purposes) Gandhi's challenged election, and it upheld, in sweeping fashion, the government's suspension of habeas corpus and Fundamental Rights. But as a consequence, respect for the Court among the legal profession and educated classes declined significantly.

The Court's second ideological era, marked by judicial activism in favor of equality and due process, began after the end of the Emergency.[75] The new judicial policies have been characterized as "a populistic quest for legitimation"—an attempt to regain the public favor that was lost when the Court acquiesced in the abuses of the Emergency.[76] The Court rejected important parts of the Forty-Second Amendment as unconstitutional and reaffirmed its claim that Parliament may not change the basic structure of the Indian Constitution.[77] Additionally, the Court abandoned its earlier limited conception of administrative and criminal due process and created a substantive due process standard that the justices used to strike down a range of administrative and law enforcement practices.[78] The new approach closely connected the values of due process and equality, so that the equality standard no longer merely requires that equally situated parties be treated equally, but also that any "arbitrary or unreasonable actions . . . are *per se* discriminatory."[79] For instance, the Court struck down arbitrary limitations on international travel,[80] the extended imprisonment of defendants facing trial,[81] the conditions of prison confinement and discipline,[82] mandatory death sentences for prisoners who commit murder while sentenced to life in prison,[83] and arbitrariness in the negotiation and granting of government contracts.[84]

In addition, the Supreme Court tried to increase its accessibility to ordinary people. The Court created a constitutional right to legal aid in criminal cases.[85] Additionally, the leading justices, in particular Bhagwati, actively encouraged public interest lawsuits and then ruled on them.[86] In addition to directly encouraging petitions, Bhagwati served both as the head of the government's legal aid bureaucracy and as a Supreme Court justice. In his position as chair of the Committee for Implementing Legal Aid Schemes (CILAS), Bhagwati developed programs to educate the Indian citizenry about its constitutional rights and to provide them with the means to claim those rights in the courts, and under his direction CILAS helped to facilitate external support for public interest litigation; in his position as justice of the Supreme Court, Bhagwati was a leading judicial advocate of public interest litigation and he ruled in favor of the claims brought as a result of his efforts as head of CILAS.

In 1982 the justices loosened standing requirements to allow law-suits by publicly interested individuals or groups wishing to bring cases on behalf of others.[87] Justice Bhagwati held that "Any member of the public having *sufficient interest* can maintain an action for judicial redress for public injury arising from breach of public duty or from violation of some provision of the Constitution or the law" and that "sufficient interest" included a genuine concern for the rights of others who were unable to assert their own claim.[88] The justices apparently took this step because it was clear to proponents of the new egalitarian activism that the justices could not for long create cases for themselves and, if the social action litigation was to continue, a mechanism would have to be created for bringing the new kinds of cases to the Court. In addition, to encourage access to the Court by previously excluded groups, Justice Bhagwati began transforming newspaper articles, let-ters to the editor, and letters to the Supreme Court into writ petitions under Article 32.[89] Such cases brought on behalf of others came to be called "public interest" cases or "social action litigation."

The leading justices also developed extended and detailed policy prescriptions for government officials to fulfill. For instance, the jus-tices created new environmental standards for mountainside quarries, and they required that housing be provided for street dwellers. In a pair of especially far-reaching decisions intended to improve water quality in the Ganges River, the Court ordered about twenty tanneries to cease operations until they had instituted adequate waste treatment procedures, and it likewise ordered a major city (Kanpur) to institute a range of policies to reduce water pollution originating from the city.[90] The justices occasionally appointed lawyers, academic scholars, or rep-resentatives of interest groups to monitor the implementation of such orders.[91]

The Supreme Court focused in particular on abuses of power by police and prison officials. For instance, in a highly publicized early landmark case the Court ordered the state of Bihar to pay compensa-tion to a number of prisoners blinded by police with bicycle spokes and battery acid.[92] The Court was particularly active in its prison re-form efforts. Before the Emergency, the Supreme Court's policy was that individuals lost their fundamental rights under Article 19 upon entering prison.[93] But in early post-Emergency cases, the Court re-versed that policy and ruled that prisoners retain all of their funda-mental rights except for those necessarily surrendered as part of incar-ceration and consequently that prison discipline must remain within the bounds of due process.[94] Shortly after the Emergency the Supreme

Court attacked the use of torture in prisons.[95] The Court also ruled that, beyond elimination of torture, conditions of prison life must not violate a right to "human dignity and all that goes along with it, namely, the bare necessities of life such as adequate nutrition, clothing and shelter over the head and facilities for reading, writing, and expressing oneself in diverse forms, freely moving about and mixing and commingling with fellow human beings."[96] The Court also attacked the common practice of holding defendants, often for years, in prison ostensibly awaiting trial, and it required the state of Bihar to release tens of thousands of such "undertrial" prisoners.[97]

On women's rights, the Supreme Court has had a mixed record. On the issue of violence against women, the Court increasingly has responded vigorously to crimes against women and abuses by police and other officials. For instance, the Court has ordered vigorous investigations of dowry deaths,[98] has ordered investigation of and compensation for assaults by police of imprisoned women,[99] has ordered the improvement of "protective homes" for women taken from prostitution,[100] and has actively monitored state governments' response to allegations of rape in police custody.[101]

In some leading decisions, the Supreme Court has struck down statutes and policies that discriminate on the basis of sex. In 1982, in a major ruling, the Court declared that although the Directive Principle calling for equal pay for equal work is not itself enforceable in court, it should be used to guide interpretation of the Fundamental Right to equality in Articles 14 and 16.[102] This means, according to the Court, that the Fundamental Right to equality, which is enforceable, requires equal pay for equal work. The Court thus turned an unenforceable guideline for the government into an enforceable right. Additionally, the Court has struck down statutes or policies that discriminated against married women or that authorized lower pay for women than for men engaged in the same work.[103] For instance, in 1986 the Court rejected as a violation of the constitution's equality rights a state law requiring married women applying for public employment to obtain their husbands' consent.[104]

Additionally, the Court has inched toward limiting the extreme discrimination embodied in the country's system of personal laws, even though the Constitution appears to authorize those laws. In a landmark decision (the *Shah Bano* case), the Court overturned settled law and held that the Muslim personal laws required a man to provide maintenance for his divorced wife.[105] In another key decision (*Mary Roy v. State of Kerala*), the Court expanded a Christian woman's right to

inherit family property.[106] Nonetheless, the *Shah Bano* decision provoked a dramatic backlash from conservative Muslims, who forced Parliament to enact a statute undoing the main holding of the case.[107] Since then, the Court has delayed action on further challenges to the personal laws by failing to bring them up for hearing.[108] Perhaps surprisingly, however, there is some evidence that lower courts now follow the Supreme Court ruling in *Shah Bano* rather than the more recent statute, due to the sympathies of lawyers and judges.[109]

On the other hand, the Court has upheld some forms of sex discrimination. In several key cases the Court upheld sex discrimination in the airline industry. In one case, for instance, the Court upheld a mandatory retirement age of fifty-eight for male "pursers" and thirty-five for female "hostesses" and a rule that hostesses must quit if they marry within four years of being hired.[110]

Apart from these exceptions, the new activism was clearly creative. Yet it had its limits. The Court focused largely on abuses of power and discrimination by low-level officials, rather than on corruption or policy failures at higher political levels. As Baxi remarked, "The respondents in the SAL [social action litigation] matters are always political small fries."[111] Additionally, by the late eighties judges claimed that they were swamped with public interest cases, which they claimed overwhelmed their ability to function effectively.[112] The Court, moreover, was unable to develop strategies for enforcing its orders in the many cases where orders were skirted or simply ignored.[113]

Apart from those limitations, within the sphere of activity staked out for social action litigation, the justices did all they could to develop an egalitarian, due process revolution. And there is little doubt that judges, rather than public interest activists, originated the development.[114] Former Chief Justice Bhagwati has claimed that "public interest litigation in India is primarily judge-led and even to some extent judge-induced, the product of juristic and judicial activism on our Supreme Court."[115] Similarly, Smitu Kothari, a scholar and organizer of a social movement umbrella organization, observed, "there is absolutely no question in my mind that public interest litigation was at the behest of activist judges."[116] Rajeev Dhavan, a scholar, Supreme Court lawyer and organizer of a public interest litigation center, likewise concludes that public interest litigation was judge-led in all relevant aspects, from the "juristic imagination" that developed the plan for such litigation, to the creation of cases, to the favorable rulings in those cases.[117]

It is clear, then, that a number of Supreme Court justices, using a variety of activist tactics, worked vigorously after 1977 to develop pub-

lic interest litigation and a heightened egalitarian rights agenda. The Court's degree of support for rights claims is a graphic measure of the post-Emergency judicial transformation. Based on my sample of published cases, the period of the Emergency marked a near-low in the Court's support for rights claims, with the Court supporting only a little over 35 percent of such claims; from there, the level of support rose steadily until it reached a high of nearly 70 percent in 1990 (the last year of my study).[118]

Conclusion

A number of conditions in India seem to have been ideal for the emergence of a rights revolution. The Indian Constitution guarantees a broad list of rights; the Indian state increasingly has come to violate many of those rights; Indians have used the language of rights in response; and the Supreme Court after 1978 handed down a number of landmark decisions that dramatically expanded the scope of promised protection for constitutional rights. In particular, the extent of change in constitutional interpretation wrought by the Supreme Court is difficult to overstate. Commentators typically describe it in revolutionary terms. Baxi, for example, called the new jurisprudence a "remarkable development" and nothing less than the Supreme Court's "transition from a traditional captive agency . . . into a liberated agency."[119] Indeed, it may be that the Supreme Court, for the first time in its history, had a clear political program and that litigants were well aware of it. Nonetheless, as I show in the next chapter, the landmark rights decisions remain isolated; no sustained rights agenda has grown up around them. The explanation, I shall show, is the weakness of the support structure for legal mobilization.

SIX

India's Weak Rights Revolution and Its Handicap

Although all key conditions for a rights revolution identified in conventional analyses—a favorable constitutional structure, judicial support, and rights consciousness—were met in India, India's nascent rights revolution has failed to develop. The primary explanation for that failure is the weakness of India's support structure for legal mobilization.

The Nascent Rights Revolution

Overview

In spite of all the sound and fury after 1977 regarding the Supreme Court's egalitarian judicial activism, the Court has not developed sustained attention to individual rights. After 1977, as before, economic interests and ordinary economic disputes dominated the agenda and individual rights remained relatively ignored.

Nonetheless, the Indian Supreme Court's agenda has a dual nature, and rights cases have indeed become more prominent in one part of the agenda—a fact that has led some observers to conclude erroneously that India has experienced a rights revolution. On the one hand, the Court pronounces on the major issues of the day; on the other, it processes tens of thousands of routine cases. The "public agenda," as I call the decisions falling in the former category, consists of decisions that are published in law reports. The "routine agenda" consists of the tens of thousands of unpublished decisions. Because of the massive workload of the Indian Supreme Court, only a small fraction of its decisions are ever published; the other decisions are known to no one but the lawyers and the parties to the case.

Since 1977 the Supreme Court's public agenda has indeed shifted toward a greater focus on egalitarian rights and due process, although the shift has not been as dramatic as in the other supreme courts in

Figure 6.1   Rights Cases on Public Agenda of the Indian Supreme Court

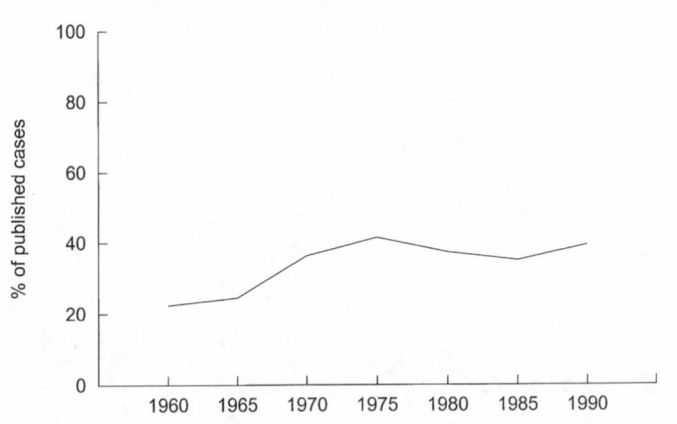

Source: Compiled from *All India Reporter.*
N = 1960, 98; 1965, 106; 1970, 113; 1975, 99; 1980, 102; 1985, 100; 1990, 112.

this study.[1] But in 1990 the much larger and arguably more important routine agenda focused no more on individual rights than it did in 1965.[2]

The proportion of the Supreme Court's public agenda devoted to rights cases over time is presented in figure 6.1. The Court's attention to rights cases increased over the period of the study, but the increase was gradual and not great. Moreover, the Court's level of attention to rights cases declined after 1975, just when we should expect it to have increased due to the justices' growing egalitarian activism.

The proportion of the Supreme Court's routine agenda devoted to rights cases is presented in figure 6.2. The data reveal a startling observation: *the peak of the Supreme Court's attention to fundamental rights claims was in the mid-seventies but, during the period of the Court's egalitarian activism after the Emergency, there was no substantial increase in the incidence of such claims.*[3] Admittedly, after 1979 there was moderate growth in the absolute number of fundamental rights cases coming to the Supreme Court. But that growth is minuscule compared to the dramatic growth that occurred between 1975 and 1978. Moreover, the number of rights cases as a proportion of all cases coming to the Supreme Court did not grow at all after 1978. Thus, in spite of several landmark individual rights decisions beginning in 1978, the Court's *routine* agenda has remained relatively unchanged except during the period of the Emergency.

To return to the Court's public agenda, other measures of change in that agenda generally corroborate that some changes have occurred,

Figure 6.2   Rights Cases on Routine Agenda of the Indian Supreme Court

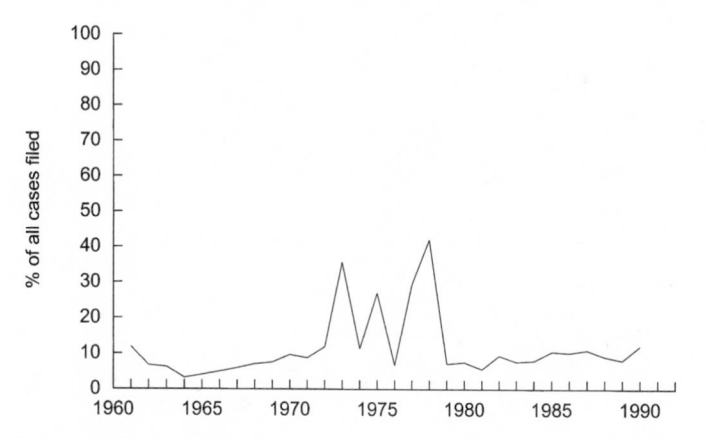

Source: Registrar, Indian Supreme Court.

but that they have been relatively insubstantial. One such indicator consists of the use of constitutional or other higher law foundations for the Court's decisions. Cases resting on constitutional foundations typically are more important, and involve greater intervention into ordinary political processes, than cases resting on statutory foundations; thus trends in the use of constitutional foundations are an indicator of the level of activist judicial intervention in political and administrative processes. The evidence from the Indian Supreme Court is mixed (fig. 6.3). There has been some growth in the Court's reliance on constitutional foundations. But the pattern of change is entirely unrelated to variations in the Court's level of activism on rights questions. The proportion of all decisions that were based on constitutional foundations actually declined from previous years in both 1980 and 1985, the period of greatest egalitarian activism. This observation strongly suggests that even the Court's public agenda has not been responsive to the justices' growing activism after 1978.

Nonetheless, the Court's egalitarian activism after 1978 affected the level of attention to two components of the judicial rights agenda— equality rights cases and property rights cases (fig. 6.4). The agenda space devoted to property rights claims, while never large, nonetheless became virtually nonexistent after the Emergency, at the same time that the Court's attention to equality rights claims grew somewhat. Those trends, in contrast to much of the data reported here, are quite consistent with the accepted wisdom that the Supreme Court's egalitarian activism shifted the Court's agenda to the left. But that shift occurred in only two relatively minor components of the Court's aggre-

Figure 6.3   Decisions by the Indian Supreme Court Based on Constitutional Grounds

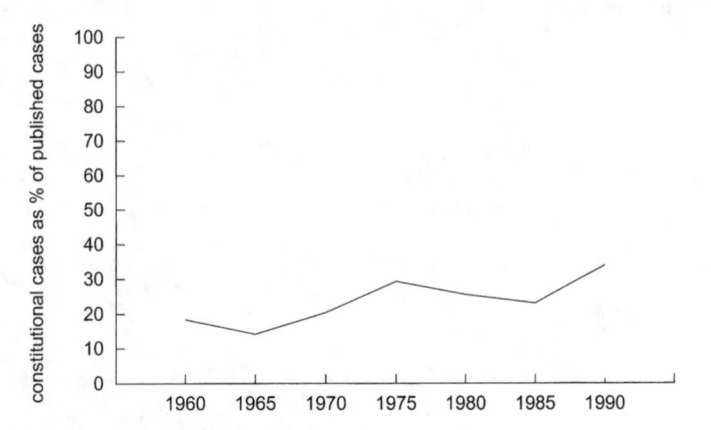

Source: Compiled from *All India Reporter.*
N = 1960, 98; 1965, 106; 1970, 113; 1975, 99; 1980, 102; 1985, 100; 1990, 112.

Figure 6.4   Property Rights and Equality Rights Cases on Public Agenda of the Indian
Supreme Court

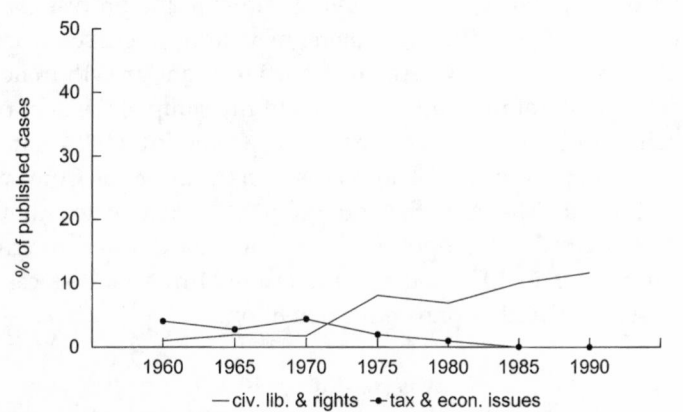

Source: Compiled from *All India Reporter.*
N = 1960, 98; 1965, 106; 1970, 113; 1975, 99; 1980, 102; 1985, 100; 1990, 112.

gate agenda and, even in those components, the change remained relatively small.

The Criminal Procedure Agenda

Although the leading Supreme Court justices directed much of their
populist judicial activism in the late seventies and early eighties
against what is commonly called governmental lawlessness—the arbitrary and brutal acts of minor police and prison officials—such issues
remain a very small part of the Court's agenda. The proportion of cases

Figure 6.5   Criminal Procedure and Preventive Detention Cases on Public Agenda of
the Indian Supreme Court

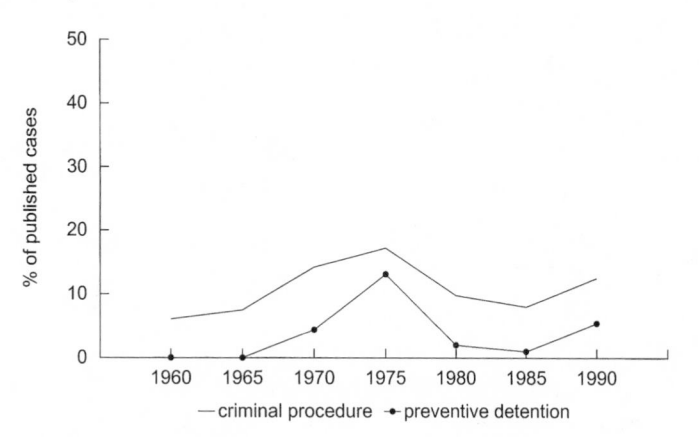

Source: Compiled from *All India Reporter.*
N = 1960, 98; 1965, 106; 1970, 113; 1975, 99; 1980, 102; 1985, 100; 1990, 112.

on the Court's public agenda involving criminal due process claims is
relatively small and, although there may have been some growth
around 1975 and after 1985, there is no significant growth trend over
the whole period of the study (fig. 6.5). In my sample, the only period
in which significant growth occurred was from 1970 to 1975. In 1975,
the number of preventive detention cases in the Supreme Court mush-
roomed (fig. 6.5). That growth in attention to preventive detention substantially affected the proportion of the agenda devoted to criminal
due process, for in 1975, most of the criminal due process cases involved issues related to preventive detention.

The Women's-Rights Agenda

As shown in the last chapter, the Indian Constitution and legal context
provides a firm foundation for women's-rights litigation, the Indian
state contributes to continued discrimination against women, and the
Supreme Court has given growing support to women's rights. Thus we
might expect that the Court's agenda on women's rights has grown,
especially since the surge in the Court's egalitarian activism after 1978.

Women's-rights cases appear in all of the sample years beginning
with 1975, but their portion of the agenda has not grown, remaining
at less than 3 percent of all cases on the public agenda. The Court has
heard cases in each of the major areas of interest to women in India,
particularly violence, the continued existence of the personal laws, and
discrimination in employment, and some of the cases may be consid-

ered of major significance. But the number of women's-rights cases per year remains very small, far below the level of importance of the problems facing women in Indian society, and litigants appear to have little success in systematically bringing cases to enforce or expand upon past precedents, or in systematically enforcing legislative victories.

The Weak Support Structure

In spite of the existence of constitutional and legal guarantees, the continuing denial of constitutional and legal rights to many Indians, and the clear anguish expressed by members of the Supreme Court after 1978 over this denial, the rights revolution—if it can even be called that—is limited to a few key decisions by the Supreme Court. There has been no development of sustained, deep judicial policy making on individual rights. If anything, contrary to all expectations there was a decline in the representation of rights cases on the judicial agenda in the late seventies and early eighties. Moreover, the high point in the Court's attention to rights cases, ironically, occurred during the period of emergency rule from 1975 through 1977. The Court's attention to criminal due process, in particular, grew during the Emergency and declined thereafter. On the other hand, the Court's attention to women's rights began to develop after the mid-seventies but, even on this issue, the Court's rights agenda remains small and disorganized.

The best explanation for these patterns—absence of growth in the aggregate rights agenda, growth in the criminal procedure agenda in the mid-seventies and decline thereafter, and weak growth in the women's-rights agenda after 1975—is the patterns of development in the Indian support structure for legal mobilization. The Indian interest group system is fragmented, the legal profession consists primarily of lawyers working individually, not collectively, and the availability of resources for noneconomic appellate litigation is limited. I shall examine, first, the broadest contours of the support structure, and second, the particular areas of rights of the accused and women's rights.

The Support Structure's Main Components

INTEREST-GROUP SYSTEM. Indian society is composed of a complex pluralism of groups and movements—and it therefore might at first appear to be fertile ground for the development of litigation support groups.[4] Nonetheless, rights-advocacy groups in India remain woefully weak and fragmented.

By the late sixties, intellectuals and middle-class students became increasingly disenchanted with the Indian government's failure to improve the lives of the poorest classes as well as the government's increasing use of repression. Moreover, many believed that the conventional political parties were failing to address those problems.[5] As a result, a new wave of social movements and nonparty political organizing developed. The first regional civil liberties organizations were formed at the same time, the late sixties, to respond to state repression of reform and revolutionary movements.[6] In the seventies, foreign contributions to Indian social action organizations began to increase, growing eventually to $400 million in 1991–92.[7] By the late seventies "support" organizations developed to conduct research and provide network connections for grassroots organizations; the newer support organizations in particular pursued public interest litigation.[8]

Indira Gandhi's imposition of emergency rule in 1975 energized the growing social movements and civil liberties organizations. For one thing, the Emergency transformed the political consciousness of some members of the urban intellectual and political class. For the first time since Independence, the government used its powers of preventive detention against members of the middle and upper classes, exposing thousands of them to conditions they found horrifying. Previously, the few middle-class political prisoners had been held in special cells that were relatively uncrowded and clean. The vast numbers arrested during the Emergency forced prison officials to place political prisoners with the ordinary prison population, where the intellectuals and political leaders directly experienced desperate conditions and vicious abuse by police and prison officials.

For instance, the government imprisoned Snehalata Reddy, a well-known actress and intellectual, apparently for her association with leading socialist politicians. While in prison, Reddy saw firsthand the inhumane treatment of many women prisoners, and she tried to publicize the problem. Eventually she was released due to deteriorating health and shortly thereafter she died of a heart attack. Reddy's case became a cause célèbre in the Indian press, where much of the coverage noted her horror over the conditions endured by other women prisoners. After her death, the Human Rights Committee (a short-lived rights-advocacy group), for instance, published excerpts from her prison diary.[9]

As other political leaders and intellectuals emerged from prison after the Emergency they spread similar stories and apparently carried a new empathy for the plight of India's poorest classes. As Upendra

Baxi has noted, the Indian press also adopted a more aggressive stance after the Emergency, cooperating with the intellectuals and social action organizations in publicizing abuses of power by government officials. The new empathy with the poorest classes encouraged a growing sense that something had to be done about what came to be called, in various terms, "repression and governmental lawlessness."[10]

Thus, as Smitu Kothari states, "the experience with the Emergency and its aftermath was fundamentally politicizing. Political awareness expanded and rural and urban struggles widened. In the urban areas numerous new organizations were established. . . ."[11] For instance, the first national human rights organization, the People's Union for Civil Liberties and Democratic Rights, was created in 1975. It was followed by similar organizations throughout the country.[12]

The Emergency, in addition to transforming the middle class's political consciousness, also generated a great infusion of resources into rights-advocacy organizations. For a short time during and just after the Emergency, powerful organizations and individuals provided financing to increase the institutional strength of rights-advocacy organizations.[13] In particular, opposition political parties, whose members the Gandhi government imprisoned, extended much support to rights-advocacy organizations. Many such organizations were formed during and just after the Emergency in response to Emergency-related repression. In 1977, a meeting of civil liberties organizations in New Delhi drew almost sixty such organizations.[14]

Unfortunately, the Emergency marked a high-water mark for the organization of civil liberties groups; the later decline was due in large part to the loss of funding and support from powerful elements of India's upper classes and political parties. With the end of the Emergency, many rights-advocacy organizations disbanded as quickly as they formed. Of the sixty organizations that met in New Delhi in 1977, less than twenty still existed ten years later.[15] After the leading opposition politicians were swept to power in the Janata Party victory after the Emergency, they withdrew their support for the civil liberties organizations. Some leading politicians even declared that organizations advocating civil liberties had become obsolete with the election of a pro-democracy party,[16] an assumption belied by the explosion of post-Emergency police brutality noted in the previous chapter. The People's Union for Civil Liberties, the main national organization, almost collapsed as a result of the withdrawal of support.[17] As one organization's newsletter noted, the shifting support by political parties greatly weakened civil liberties organizations:

[T]he parliamentary parties are consistently seeking to influence such organisations and utilize them to serve their party interests, at the cost of the civil liberties movement. This aggravates tensions within the organisations (specifically at such times as during elections) and splits the movement.[18]

Nonetheless, after the end of the Emergency and the fragmentation of the civil libertarian opposition, a number of civil liberties groups, women's-rights groups, environmental groups, and organizations supporting the rural poor continued to exist. Even these groups, however, have failed to provide significant support for strategic litigation. Two factors have contributed to this failure. The first is the preponderance of what scholars variously call "demand groups"[19] or "grassroots social movements,"[20] to the near-exclusion of well-institutionalized organizations. Such demand groups or movements frequently arise and just as frequently fade away. They develop on an ad hoc basis around a single issue or cluster of issues and exert pressure through tactics related to mass mobilization rather than expert knowledge. The dominant place of demand groups results from the huge size of the unorganized sector (outside of government and large industry), which comprises two-thirds of the Indian economy.[21] Such movement groups, due to their transitory nature and their lack of emphasis on expert knowledge for influence, provide the occasion for ad hoc litigation, but they provide no sustained support for long-term, systematic litigation strategies.

Additionally, Indian rights-advocacy organizations remain deeply fragmented and marginalized.[22] Many have suffered from internal conflict that periodically threatens their institutional life. The original civil liberties organization in the state of Andhra Pradesh (the Andhra Pradesh Civil and Democratic Rights Association), for instance, split into two separate organizations during its first year of existence (1973), and "[a]fter the Emergency embittered relations existed between [the two]."[23] In 1981, one of the breakaway factions itself split in two.[24] Similarly, the main national organization at the time of the Emergency, the People's Union for Civil Liberties and Democratic Rights, split into two organizations, one more concerned with abuses of civil liberties and the rule of law and the other more concerned with social inequality.[25]

Indian rights-advocacy groups are also handicapped due to their dominance by charismatic leaders. As D. L. Sheth and Harsh Sethi state,

> Many of the organisations, including the more modern and professional ones, revolve around the founding, often charismatic personalities. Rarely are they able to transcend them, either in devel-

oping a second-tier leadership or in producing new leaders after the original set had departed. This high degree of transience has serious implications, not just for institutionalisation, but also for formulating long term programmes.[26]

Similarly, Smitu Kothari, while generally hopeful that the new social movements will contribute to a deepening of Indian democracy, identifies as a significant weakness "the problem of voluntarism resulting in a lack of sustained effort by a committed and recognized cadre of activists."[27] The dominant role played by charismatic leaders is a handicap particularly for organizations that attempt to support rights litigation. In such organizations, the leader takes on the responsibility of raising the funds, devising litigation strategies, conducting the bulk of the legal research, drafting submissions to the courts, promoting the cases or causes in the press, presenting arguments in court, and, if successful in court, monitoring implementation of court decisions. Moreover, many such leaders do not specialize by issue but instead attempt to cover the whole gamut of public interest issues. The problem of overload is obvious.

Thus, although Indian rights-advocacy organizations have made some significant contributions, they remain handicapped by weak institutionalization and excessive dependence on charismatic leadership. As one analysis concluded, civil liberties organizations

> have never enjoyed a stable institutional existence. Groups come up at points of crisis, survive for a period of time, and "in the tradition" of most such institutions in this country, become inactive, fade away, even die out, only to resurface, often in a new form at another time of crisis. More stable probably have been the individuals, the activists who form the core of such organizations.[28]

THE INDIAN LEGAL PROFESSION. A significant proportion of individual rights cases—perhaps even a vast majority—have been supported largely through the voluntary efforts of lawyers. Indian lawyers have made heroic efforts, often risking their lives, to provide legal representation for unpopular causes or for those accused of crimes or guerilla activity.

The Indian legal profession is quite large, in terms of sheer numbers as well as measured in relation to India's population.[29] As in the United States, educated Indians seem to believe their society is overrun with lawyers and, as in the United States, stories of frequent and frivolous litigation are common. The Indian legal profession, then, at first may

appear to provide a ready source of support for rights-advocacy litigation.

Surprisingly, that is not the case. The Indian legal profession, as Galanter has observed, remains highly fragmented and individualized.[30] There are very few law firms or partnerships. Most lawyers practice alone or with only one or two assistants. The efforts of these individual lawyers lead to litigation that is largely reactive and ad hoc. Thus the Indian legal profession suffers from structural weaknesses similar to those that handicap Indian interest groups. As Marc Galanter observed, the fragmented structure of the Indian legal profession limits its capacity to pursue strategically planned litigation:

> Among the prominent features of Indian lawyers are their orientation to courts to the exclusion of other legal settings; litigation rather than advising, negotiating or planning; their conceptualism and orientation to rules; their individualism; and their lack of specialization. . . . Thus we get a picture of legal services supplied by relatively unspecialized lawyers, involved in little coordination of effort, offering a relatively narrow range of services. Relations with clients are episodic and intermittent. The lawyer addresses discrete problems in isolation from the whole situation of the client and uninformed by considerations of long-range strategy. This kind of *atomized* legal service accentuates the disadvantages of the poor and disadvantaged in using the legal system.[31]

Legal education and scholarship contributes to this orientation. Legal realism and sociological jurisprudence—movements calling attention to the social and political context of judicial decisions—significantly affected legal education in the United States but remain largely ignored in Indian legal education. As a consequence, law schools teach students only the law, with very little attention to its social and political context. Moreover, Indian scholars of law, in attempting to understand the significance of judicial decisions, only rarely look beyond the words of judges.

The Indian legal profession, moreover, is highly stratified and elitist, mirroring the caste stratification and sex discrimination of Indian society generally. Members of the dominant castes, particularly Brahmins, are heavily represented in the Supreme Court bar, and Brahmins and locally powerful castes dominate the bar in local areas.[32] Although formal access to the legal profession is far less demanding than access to the medical or engineering professions, the legal profession's fragmented, individualized structure greatly hinders access by members of the poorer classes. Few poor individuals have the resources necessary to set up their own practice or the social connections necessary

to build a client base or to gain access to another's office as an assistant.[33] The Indian legal profession also consists almost exclusively of men. In 1961, only 1 percent of Indian lawyers were women; the percentage remained unchanged by 1971.[34] By the early eighties, after a decade of social upheaval, including the development of a broad women's movement, women still accounted for less than 3 percent of all lawyers.[35] The glacial rate of change in the profession, in spite of substantial social change, suggests that the Indian legal profession is likely to remain an exclusive domain for some time.

SOURCES OF FINANCING.   Perhaps the most significant weakness of the Indian support structure is the dearth of financial resources for rights litigation. Rights cases are supported primarily either by the aggrieved party or by voluntary efforts by a lawyer. The near-total absence of other sources of financing has greatly limited the number of individual rights cases. The lack of financing is not due to any lack of formal provisions for legal aid. The Forty-Second Amendment to the Indian Constitution, passed during the Emergency, among other things added to the Constitution's Directive Principles a provision calling on the government to provide free legal aid to the poor.[36] After the Emergency, the Supreme Court by judicial fiat converted that unenforceable Directive Principle into a constitutional right.[37] Additionally, for decades there have been government reports and legislative bills proposing the establishment of legal aid plans, but only after the mid-seventies have any been implemented.[38] Two reports, prepared under the leadership of Justice Krishna Iyer in 1973, and Justices Bhagwati and Krishna Iyer in 1978, provided the impetus for the new programs.[39] The national government now has a working legal aid plan in place, as do several of the states.

Although the long-awaited legal aid programs finally became a reality, they suffer from a number of problems. First, the legal aid programs support only a minuscule number of cases, both in absolute and relative terms. The limitations of legal aid are particularly clear in the Supreme Court. Legal aid in the Supreme Court is administered by the Supreme Court Legal Aid Committee, which originated in 1981 as part of that period's flurry of activity around access to justice. The Committee, composed of members of the Supreme Court bar, examines applications for aid and selects from them about five hundred to eight hundred per year for funding, a number that seems to have peaked in the mid-eighties and declined somewhat by the early nineties.[40] Figure 6.6 presents the number of Supreme Court cases supported by legal aid

Figure 6.6   Legal Aid Cases Compared to Total Workload, Indian Supreme Court

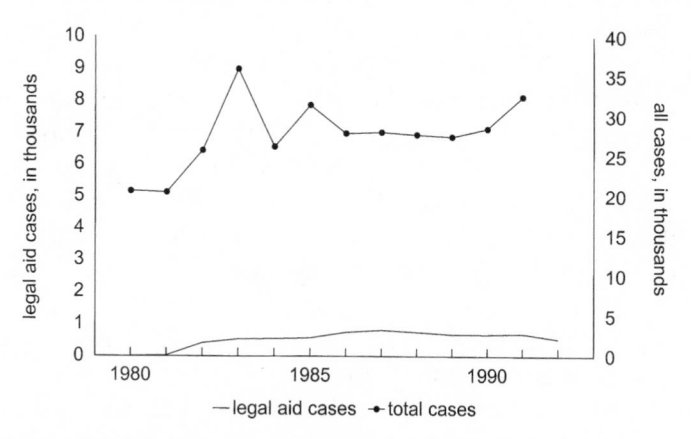

—legal aid cases   ◆ total cases

Source: Registrar, Indian Supreme Court; and Supreme Court Legal Aid Committee.

in relation to the total number of cases filed annually. Cases financed by legal aid clearly represent a minimal contribution to the Supreme Court's agenda. Lawyers who practice before the Supreme Court who were interviewed for this project universally declared that legal aid provided little assistance in generating fundamental rights cases.[41]

The Indian legal aid programs are limited in another respect as well. They tend to be passive, taking cases on a largely ad hoc basis, rather than as part of a broad policy-oriented strategy. As Galanter observed, official legal aid programs "eschew . . . any deliberate impact on the design or administration of government policy."[42] Although some legal aid programs in other countries have been similarly reactive and ad hoc in their orientation, others, as I shall suggest in the following chapters, have provided much support for strategic litigation.

Unfortunately, the Indian government has handicapped social movements, rights-advocacy groups, and strategic litigation in various ways. According to Dhavan, after Gandhi returned to power in 1980 her government mounted a "massive, long and tendentious investigation" of grassroots organizations; the succeeding government (led by her son Rajiv Gandhi) attempted to enact a legal code governing the conduct of such organizations; and the government reduced the tax exemption for donations to charitable organizations.[43]

Rights-advocacy organizations, in particular, face hostility and even brutal repression by police officials. For instance, in the early seventies the Andhra Pradesh police arrested and beat a number of members of the state's civil liberties organizations, and the police killed one pro–civil liberties lawyer who had defended individuals accused of partici-

pating in a guerilla movement.[44] In 1982 members of the Tamil Nadu police force beat V. M. Tarkunde, President of the People's Union for Civil Liberties, while he was leading an independent investigation into charges that the police forces were executing members of a resistance movement.[45] In 1985, members of the Andhra Pradesh police murdered Dr. A. Ramanathan, the Vice President of the Andhra Pradesh Civil Liberties Committee.[46] In 1987, the Andhra Pradesh police arrested and beat Dr. K. Balagopal, a leading civil liberties activist.[47]

Additionally, the almost heavy-handed leadership of Supreme Court justices appears to weaken initiatives for legal change from outside the judiciary. For example, when the Indian Law Institute was created in 1957 as a legal reform body analogous to the American Law Institute, the justices of the Supreme Court insisted on placing it across the street from the Supreme Court and on having control over it. The chief justice is the honorary chair of the Institute, and the choice of director is influenced by the justices. Similarly, Supreme Court justices, upon hearing of the growing public-interest law movement in the seventies, worked aggressively to take control of the movement. Prominent justices traveled to visit the lawyers involved and to learn about their casework. Then, in highly publicized developments, the justices directly placed some of the public interest cases on their docket and named friends or associates as legal counsel. Although such strong interest in the early cases signified an admirable interest in cultivating the movement, the effect seems to have been to undercut the original decentralized sources of the movement. Additionally, the country's legal aid system is directly under the control of a Supreme Court justice. To an extent not known in other countries, then, Supreme Court justices oversee important components of the support structure for legal mobilization. As a consequence, nonjudicial actors tend to follow the lead of the judicial hierarchy and hesitate to initiate strategies for legal change.

The Support Structure and the Rights of the Accused
The Court's agenda on the rights of the accused, as I showed earlier, remains very small and indeed has declined since 1975. Yet, during one period—roughly 1975 to 1977—the Court's agenda on criminal procedure grew rapidly. A large proportion of those cases involved prisoners challenging their imprisonment under the preventive detention laws. Although official court reports provide little information on the circumstances of such cases, there is little doubt that many consisted of preventive detentions under Gandhi's emergency rule. Yet the

practice of preventive detention was widespread long before the Emergency and continued to be used heavily after the Emergency. Why, then, were preventive detention cases suddenly a significant part of the Supreme Court's agenda during the Emergency, but basically not present before or after that period?

The relative absence of such issues on the judicial agenda results not from any lack of legal foundations (the Constitution contains explicit guarantees of procedural rights), nor from any failure of commitment on the part of the justices (who appear very concerned about such issues in the few cases coming before them), nor from structural hindrances in the judicial system (such cases have immediate access to the Supreme Court), nor from any lack of rights consciousness among the victims of state repression.

The explanation for the general absence of such issues outside of the Emergency is clear: preventively detained persons and the criminally accused typically have no access to the organizational, financial, and legal resources that would enable them to take their cases to the Supreme Court (or to any court, for that matter). Preventive detention typically (with some significant exceptions) has been used against the relatively weak and poor.

During the Emergency, however, judicial attention to preventive detention grew because the government detained members of an entirely different class. For the first time, many were prominent politicians and members of the educated classes, and they had access to substantial personal and organizational resources for judicial appeals. For instance, as noted earlier, the cases of some leading intellectuals became causes célèbres. Opposition parties rallied to the support of civil liberties organizations. The Emergency, then, occasioned a massive infusion of support into the support structure for rights litigation. The result was a flurry of litigation, particularly over preventive detention cases. But, with the end of the Emergency, the support structure collapsed as quickly as it grew, and support for legal challenges around the thousands of routine preventive detention cases dwindled.

The small proportion of Supreme Court cases devoted to the rights of the accused and of prisoners, then, results, to an important extent, from the weakness of the support structure. The nature of the Indian criminal process and prisons virtually demands a rights-based response. The justices have demonstrated concern for the issue and have handed down a number of landmark decisions expanding the scope of constitutional due process guarantees. But without a stronger and more organized support structure to bring greater numbers of such

cases to the Supreme Court, the possibility of greater judicial attention
to the issue seems limited.

The Support Structure and Women's Rights
The development of the support structure for women's-rights litigation
has followed a slightly different track. Since the mid-seventies a new
wave of "autonomous women's organizations" has developed.[48] These
were the first women's-rights organizations to be independent of political parties. The development of the autonomous women's organizations immediately preceded and supported the recent appearance of
women's-rights cases on the judicial agenda. The autonomous women's
organizations focused their work specifically on the problem of violence against women and they pressed the Supreme Court to take up
the issue and to convict and punish the perpetrators.

The Supreme Court's decision in what is called the Mathura rape
case[49] in 1979 focused the efforts of the new wave of the women's movement on the issue of violence against women.[50] The case concerned the
rape of Mathura, a fourteen-year-old girl, by two police constables.
The trial judge acquitted the defendants on the grounds—astoundin-
gly—that consent could be presumed, but the High Court reversed
and entered convictions. On appeal by the defendants, the Supreme
Court in 1979 reversed and reinstated the acquittals. Upendra Baxi and
three other legal scholars protested the Supreme Court's decision in an
open letter to the Supreme Court.[51] Eventually various women's groups
mounted a vigorous campaign of publicity and mass demonstrations
to force the Court to reconsider.[52] Their organizing around the issue
served to catalyze growing concern within the women's movement
over violence against women. The Supreme Court failed to respond,
but the national government passed the Criminal Code (Amendment)
Act 1983, which shifted the burden of proof in allegations of rape from
the accuser to the accused once sexual intercourse had been established.

The Mathura rape case achieved prominence in large part because
it occurred at roughly the same time as the development of the new,
more militant wave of the women's movement. The new organizations
picked up the issue of violence against women, and their organizing
around the issue helped to consolidate the new movement. Only four
years before the Mathura case no such organizations existed to respond to a similar Supreme Court decision in which two Supreme
Court justices (Bhagwati and Faizal Ali), relying on their own specula-
tive reconstruction of the facts that emphasized the victim's character,

had acquitted several men charged with a gang rape.[53] By contrast, the Mathura case catalyzed the movement and produced a focus on violence that remained the center of the movement's concerns for a number of years.

Following the Mathura rape case, the women's movement began supporting court cases with greater frequency and focused most of its litigation efforts on violence against women. Women's-rights advocates supported prosecutions of other rapes,[54] dowry-related deaths,[55] and of maltreatment of women in prison or "protective custody."[56] Such a strategy was consistent with the dominant focus of early public interest litigation suits, as noted above, on the actions of minor officials.

Nonetheless, the vast majority of women's-rights cases in the Supreme Court have been supported only by the aggrieved parties and their lawyers acting entirely independently of any larger strategy. Indeed, there is little evidence of any larger strategy surrounding any of the Court's women's-rights cases, particularly with regard to the systematic pursuit and development of issues over time. For example, while several early cases focused publicity on the conditions of women's confinement in prison and protective custody, that attention has all but disappeared although the problem remains serious.

In legal challenges to India's discriminatory personal laws, too, most cases have gained little real support from women's-rights organizations and instead have been supported primarily by individual litigants and their lawyers. Apart from one of the cases the Court refuses to bring up for hearing, *All India Women's Federation v. Union of India,* individual litigants acting largely on their own have brought all of the challenges to the system of personal laws. As they reached the Supreme Court, some of the cases, in particular *Shah Bano* and *Mary Roy,* became causes célèbres within the women's movement. But there is little evidence that women's organizations provided any significant financial or legal support or coordination of legal strategies.

Similarly, in the area of employment discrimination, individual women (or small, unorganized groups) have brought virtually all of the cases. Women's-rights organizations have made no effort to litigate on this matter. Partly as a result, the case law is poorly developed, pursuing no set of issues consistently across time. The closest approximation to a consistent theme is the matter of discrimination against married women, but even there some of the Court's rulings directly contradict others. Apparently women's-rights groups have opted to devote their attention elsewhere, leaving the field to the ad hoc activities of individual lawyers.

Nonetheless, even on the issue of violence against women, on which the women's movement has worked with great dedication, women's-rights organizations seem to have had a peripheral role in generating litigation and coordinating legal strategies. Although there is a relatively large number of organizations working on women's rights, there is virtually no cooperation in developing cases for the Supreme Court.[57] In part this may be due, as the lawyer and scholar Ratna Kapur suggests, to a failure by the women's movement to view the process of judicial interpretation as an arena influenced by political struggle.[58] But in large part the failure of women's organizations to provide institutional strength to women's-rights litigation results from the institutional weaknesses of the organizations due to their limited funding, their low levels of professionalization or, when professionalized, their fragmentation into competing organizations. The women's movement has succeeded in identifying the problem of violence against women and, through protest activity, has succeeded in influencing newspaper coverage on the issue "far in excess of its numerical strength or organizational cohesiveness."[59] But unlike creating newspaper coverage, influencing the judicial agenda requires a great commitment of institutional resources over an extended period of time, which is beyond the current capacity of the Indian women's movement.

Many women's-rights advocates attest to the handicap posed by limited resources. The journal *Manushi* was one of the few organizations to attempt a sustained focus on women's-rights litigation, but its efforts were limited to championing the *idea* of rights-based litigation, providing continuing publicity to court cases, and connecting potential litigants with women's-rights lawyers. As the journal's editor, Madhu Kishwar, said, reflecting on the role of *Manushi* in supporting court cases, "We may have inspired some cases, like the *Mary Roy* case, and we may have directed some women to lawyers, but most of the women's-rights cases have been brought by individual women fighting for their own rights."[60] Geeta Luthra and Pinky Anand, two leading women's-rights lawyers, concurred that organizations acted to connect litigants with lawyers ("for example, *Manushi* sends all of their cases to us"). However, they affirmed that organizations could offer little funding, that rights cases depended on voluntary work by lawyers, and that virtually none of the Supreme Court's women's-rights cases depended on support from women's organizations.[61] Other participants in women's-rights litigation concur in that assessment. Chandramani Chopra, a leading women's-rights lawyer, in assessing the role of organizations said, "What is the role of women's groups in Supreme

Court cases? Useless. Funding? They do not give funds, they expect us [the lawyers] to work for free."[62] Similarly, Shyamla Pappu, a Senior Advocate in the Supreme Court,[63] although not critical of women's-rights organizations, stated that when she takes a rights case she virtually always volunteers her services because of the lack of organizational funding. Jyotsna Chatterji, Director of the Joint Women's Programme, one of the principal national women's organizations involved in women's-rights litigation, stated that her organization worked repeatedly to pressure the Supreme Court to hear some of the early cases involving violence against women, but that the lack of adequate organizational funds limited her organization's efforts. She concluded, "If we had greater resources, we would take more cases."[64]

On the other hand, the women's groups have failed to pursue litigation in part because they have not recognized its potentially great importance. As Ratna Kapur observes, the women's movement has focused on gaining legislative victories and on occasional test cases but often fails to recognize that the implementation of legislative reforms may depend on litigation and other forms of pressure on administrators.[65]

These observations are by no means intended to diminish the value of the efforts by legal scholars, lawyers, journalists, and women's-rights groups supporting women's-rights cases. These efforts have been important both for their message and their support for individual women. Nonetheless, the efforts of discrete, unorganized individuals have been insufficient, and there is thus no foundation for sustained judicial attention and support.

Conclusion

The Indian Supreme Court surely is among the most active courts in the world, and it also is among the most supportive of egalitarian and procedural rights. But it has been unable to develop a sustained and deep agenda on individual rights. The best explanation for that paradox is that the Indian support structure for legal mobilization—the complex of financial, legal, and organizational resources necessary for appellate litigation—remains weak and fragmented.

Surely the structural characteristics of the Indian Constitution and judicial system and the activist judges offered ample opportunity for rights-based litigation. The Indian Constitution explicitly guarantees a broad range of fundamental rights, and the Supreme Court has broadened the list beyond the explicit constitutional guarantees. Structurally, the Court is very accessible: individuals raising any Fundamen-

tal Rights claim may approach the Court directly rather than pursue their claim first through lower courts, the Court has broadened standing requirements to allow activists to bring claims on behalf of others, and the Court has developed mechanisms to allow it to entertain tens of thousands of cases annually.[66] And since 1978, egalitarian activists on the Court have transformed the Court's jurisprudence in favor of the rights of previously excluded groups in Indian society. Most of the key conditions identified by conventional explanations of the rights revolution were thus met in India. Nonetheless, the Supreme Court's agenda remained largely unchanged across the period of the study. With the exception of the period of the Emergency from 1975 to 1977, Fundamental Rights claims constituted a small proportion, about 10 percent, of the Court's total caseload.

Limitations on the Court's discretionary control over its own docket surely hinder its capacity to develop a sustained agenda on any particular issue, for instance individual rights. The Court decides well over 30,000 cases annually. Unlike other supreme courts in this study, the Indian Supreme Court is not authorized to weed out insignificant cases brought to it on appeal; indeed, the Court's justices and members of the Indian legal elite more generally believe that the Court has a responsibility to the public not to weed out insignificant cases. Thus Chief Justice M. N. Venkatachaliah stated, "the Court should not try to limit the sorts of cases that are decided. . . . Our needs are different than yours in the United States. We have chosen to make our Court more responsive to the pressures rising from society."[67] Although the choice to remain responsive may enhance the Court's legitimacy, it comes at a cost to the Court's ability to focus sustained attention on particular issues.

Development of sustained judicial attention to personal rights has been limited, in addition, by the weakness of the Indian support structure for legal mobilization. The support structure gained significant strength only during the Emergency from 1975–1977; then, as the government threatened the rights of many powerful people, they and organizations allied with them devoted substantial resources to bringing civil liberties cases, particularly appeals against preventive detention. Although the Emergency provoked the formation of a rights-advocacy support structure that still exists, after the government lifted emergency rule the wealthy and opposition political parties pulled their financial support. As a consequence, the support structure nearly collapsed. Legal aid exists, but it is terribly underfunded, and lawyers commonly doubt its usefulness. Some lawyers regularly volunteer

their services for arguing rights-based claims, but the fragmented, individualized structure of the legal profession limits the overall impact of their efforts. Rights organizations exist, but their funding is inadequate to finance continuing litigation campaigns. The efforts of the leading rights advocates have been heroic, but the structure of their organizations limits those efforts to relatively ad hoc pressure on the Supreme Court.[68] Voluntary efforts by a few individual lawyers and resource-poor rights-advocacy groups have simply been insufficient to generate a rights revolution.

SEVEN

Britain: An Inhospitable Environment
for a Rights Revolution?

Britain is an important case in this comparative study because, unlike India, it appears at first to be an *in*hospitable environment for the development of a rights revolution.[1] The key conventionally identified conditions for a rights revolution are not met in Britain or exist only to a greatly attenuated degree. Rights consciousness has developed in popular culture, and European economic and human rights law increasingly places something like a constitutional check on the British government; nonetheless, Britain has no constitutional bill of rights, its judges are remarkably conservative, and its legal culture greatly favors parliamentary sovereignty to the nearly complete exclusion of judicial creativity.

Yet in the last several years the British courts and, in particular, the Appellate Committee of the House of Lords, Britain's supreme court, have handed down several surprising decisions expanding judicial protection for civil liberties and civil rights. In *Derbyshire County Council v. Times Newspapers Ltd.*, the court created a common-law right of free speech that significantly increased protections against libel actions.[2] The decision contradicted the conventional wisdom that the British courts, lacking a constitutional bill of rights, are incapable of generating protections for fundamental rights. In the second case, *In re M.*, involving the deportation of an immigrant, the House of Lords (as the court is often called) asserted its authority to subject not only lower administrative officials but also Cabinet ministers to judicial injunctions and contempt of court for violations of administrative due process.[3] The decision attacked one of the basic doctrines of parliamentary government—that the highest political officers of the government are subject only to electoral, not judicial, sanction. And in *R. v. Secretary of State for Transport, ex parte Factortame Ltd.* (1991) and *R. v. Secretary of State for Employment, ex parte EOC* (1994) the House of Lords struck down parts of parliamentary statutes, in the latter case because the

offending statute was inconsistent with the rights of women under European Community law.[4] The decisions directly contradicted the most basic doctrine of parliamentary sovereignty, that only Parliament can repeal the laws it has created. Describing the latter decision, the *Times* of London declared, "Britain may now have, for the first time in history, a constitutional court."[5]

In this chapter I explain why standard explanations for rights revolutions should lead us to expect that none of this should happen in Britain. In the next chapter I show that the landmark rights decisions are not aberrations but are part of a broader and growing rights revolution, and that Britain's support structure is an important part of the explanation for both that development as a whole as well as variations in the kinds of rights that have developed.

British Society and Rights Consciousness

British society and politics have been characterized by increasing conflict since the post-war consensus began to break down after the sixties. The growing conflicts have produced a new politics of rights, which is clearly evident in several areas.

One conflict is the emergence of a war-like state of affairs in Northern Ireland.[6] In the late sixties, the Northern Ireland Civil Rights Association was formed to work against discrimination suffered by the Catholic minority in housing, employment, and the exercise of political rights. Frustrations developed into a civil rights movement that organized street marches and protests. By the early seventies, many of the street marches had occasioned bloody confrontations between Catholics and Protestant unionists, and the British government sent troops to restore order. Catholic republicans viewed the troops as an occupying army, and the long-simmering tensions between the British government and nationalists in Northern Ireland erupted into a guerilla war. The British government responded with a number of measures that have been vigorously criticized as violations of civil liberties: security forces have used highly questionable tactics in conducting investigations and arrests, and the government in the eighties prohibited the public broadcast of communications by people associated with the nationalist movement. In addition, the appellate courts have been very reluctant to overturn trial courts' questionable convictions of alleged terrorists.

A second important development is the growth of controversy over race relations. Since the fifties there has been a substantial influx of nonwhite immigrants, typically from Britain's former colonies in Af-

rica, the Caribbean, and south Asia, with a substantial proportion of the immigration occurring between the mid-sixties and the mid-seventies.[7] The proportion of the British population from ethnic minority backgrounds jumped from about 2 percent in 1971 to almost 5 percent in 1991.[8] By the mid-sixties the issue of immigration became increasingly politicized, as well as increasingly defined in racial terms. Significantly, although many immigrants are white, and although many members of racial minority groups were born in Britain, the term "immigrants" is commonly used to refer to Britain's racial minorities. Thus, some elements of the British population and some politicians have attributed to "immigrants" a range of Britain's growing social problems, among them growing crime, drug abuse, and social unrest.[9] Britain's various racial minority communities have become increasingly mobilized in election campaigns, often challenging the main political parties which have neglected the concerns of racial minorities.[10] Rights-advocacy organizations have also formed to work on the issue. The Joint Council for the Welfare of Immigrants and the Immigration Law Practitioners Association, for instance, have been active in supporting litigation on due process in deportation proceedings.[11] The British government attempted to respond to the growing conflict over the race issue with several successive Race Relations Acts in 1965, 1968, and 1976, banning race discrimination in housing, employment, and the like. The 1976 Act attempted to increase organizational resources for enforcement of antidiscrimination law, particularly by creating the Commission on Racial Equality (CRE). But the CRE has been widely criticized for organizational problems and weak enforcement initiatives. There is no doubt that race will continue to be an increasingly important component of British politics, both in the form of racism against nonwhite groups and as a source of solidarity among those groups.

Third, the British women's movement, like similar movements in other Western countries, entered a new phase in the seventies, marked by greater militance, less willingness to play politics within traditional party structures, and growing interest in fundamental change in social policies and gender relations. Women's-rights advocacy is discussed in more detail in the following chapter.

Fourth, there have been growing rights-based criticisms of the British criminal process and prisons. The rights of defendants gained much public attention after the mid-seventies due to allegations of injustice in the prosecution of a number of suspected Irish Republican Army bombers and other political activists. By the eighties it was clear

to most observers that "miscarriages of justice," as they were called, occurred frequently in the prosecutions and trials of suspected political activists as well as in convictions on other serious charges.[12] Moreover, in the sixties, seventies, and eighties there was a large increase in the number of convictions for serious ("indictable") offenses, the population from which we might expect criminal appeals to develop, from a little over 150,000 in 1960 to almost 500,000 per year by the early eighties.[13] The miscarriages of justice became causes célèbres and drew attention to unfairness in the criminal justice process and to appalling conditions, overcrowding, and fundamental denials of due process in Britain's prisons.

In each of these areas of conflict and social change, prominent actors have increasingly used the language of rights to characterize their demands and aspirations. The renewed tensions in Northern Ireland, for instance, began with a Catholic civil rights movement there in the late sixties.[14] The Campaign Against Racial Discrimination in the sixties actively promoted civil rights for nonwhite immigrants.[15] In the women's movement, although leftists have been sharply critical of what they view as an individualizing tendency in the language of rights, the language of rights is increasingly prominent.[16] Moreover at a very general level, by the mid-sixties there was widespread and growing concern over abuse of rights in the British administrative process and the need for checks on executive power.[17] Thus, as Bernard Crick, a leading British political scientist, observed as early as 1964, the "very concept 'civil liberties' until quite recently seemed somewhat un-British . . . [b]ut recently the concept is on everyone's lips."[18]

The Constitutional and Legal Context

Unlike most modern industrialized countries, Britain has no modern bill of rights, and the British legal tradition and culture discourage courts from intervening in the policy-making process. In A. V. Dicey's classic discussion (which has had a revered, yet contested, place in British legal culture) Parliament alone is sovereign. Dicey's view of parliamentary sovereignty has two elements: first, Parliament is omnicompetent, in that it may create or undo any law it wishes; and, second, Parliament has a monopoly on legitimate law-making power, in that no subordinate governmental body may legitimately create law.[19] The role of courts is limited to applying the common law (so long as Parliament has not superseded it by legislation) and ensuring that administrative officials act no more broadly than authorized by parliamentary statute (the latter is called "judicial review" in Britain).

If Parliament is sovereign, however, how might civil liberties be protected? Presumably Parliament may legislate a right out of existence (as it did in 1994 when it eliminated the traditional right of criminal defendants to silence). Dicey's response to that problem was that parliamentary sovereignty would be self-correcting: if governmental power is truly limited by judicial review to only those actions authorized by Parliament, then governmental power will grow no broader than desired by the people—and, presumably, the people will never destroy their own liberties. Dicey also argued that the common law would, in practice, be more effective at protecting individual rights than a bill of rights. This is so, he argued, because a bill of rights, by simply declaring rights, provides no effective remedies in law, and because a government may easily ignore or suspend a bill of rights. By contrast, the common law embodies a range of remedies for violations of rights and, in order to ignore or suspend the myriad and complex protections for individual rights embodied in the common law, a government would have to entirely destroy a whole culture and customary system of law.

As critics of Dicey have observed, however, those asserted mechanisms for protecting individual rights have serious weaknesses. A political majority may well decline to oppress itself—but it surely is capable of oppressing a minority. Additionally, the common law's complex protections for individual rights come to mean nothing if the courts conclude that administrative bodies need not meet judicial standards of fair procedure—in other words, that complaints about the fairness of administrative procedure should be addressed to Parliament, not the courts. That is precisely what the House of Lords decided in a famous case in 1915: administrative bodies need follow only the procedural standards required by Parliament, not common-law standards of fair procedure as required in the courts.[20] That case brought to the surface a fundamental tension in Dicey's thought: on the one hand, the courts were to protect liberty against arbitrary government action but, on the other, Parliament is sovereign and government officials are answerable primarily to Parliament. In the crunch, Dicey—and much of British constitutional thought after him—went with parliamentary sovereignty.

In short, although Dicey celebrated the judiciary and the common law as a bastion of liberty, the undoubted tendency of the system has been to reign in, circumscribe, and subordinate judicial power. Thus, proponents of a broader judicial role in the late twentieth century lament the "long sleep of judicial review in Britain."[21] British lawyers

and scholars have traditionally struggled to construct a theory by which individual rights may be protected in a system that, in theory at least, allows no check other than the ballot box on the power of government. The labored nature of their theories attests to the difficulty of the enterprise.[22] The British constitutional context thus seems to provide an inhospitable climate for a rights revolution.

The policy process is much less centered in Parliament, however, than the classic theory assumes: instead, policies are made in deals between powerful interest groups and party leaders. Most policy in the modern British state has been developed by the civil service in cooperation with powerful private organized interests, and parliamentary deliberation is merely a formality that largely rubber-stamps cooperative administrative–interest group agreements into law. As Samuel Finer observed in 1970, "Increasingly what the minister presents to the Commons is a package arrangement agreed between his civil servants and the representatives of outside groups."[23] The British policy-making process thus consists of more or less informal, but institutionalized, arrangements between administrative officials and organized interests.[24] That fact poses problems for Dicey's theory that the system is democratically self-correcting.

Ironically, the importance of those extra-parliamentary deals has also worked to minimize the policy-making role of the judiciary, because, in contrast to the relatively loose policy coalitions in the United States, the tight relations in Britain strongly discourage groups from going outside the leadership process to achieve changes in public policy. Some groups, admittedly, have used an "outside" adversarial approach to the policy process but typically they have turned not to the courts but rather to the media or individual members of Parliament.[25] But generally (at least in the past), in the conventional wisdom, groups have avoided litigation because of the basic nature and structure of the British state.[26] The power of the governing party to override court decisions by passing new legislation has encouraged interest groups to press their influence where it matters, which is in the process of drafting legislation within government ministries.

Some Britons, animated by the growing popular concern for civil liberties and rights, have pushed aggressively for creation of a bill of rights for the purpose of giving judges a check on the power of officials.[27] In 1988 prominent intellectuals and opinion leaders created an organization called "Charter 88"—so named in commemoration of the three hundredth anniversary of the Glorious Revolution—whose main purpose was to press for adoption of a bill of rights.[28] The Charter 88

movement has been the leading force behind the rise of the issue on the public agenda. Proponents of a bill of rights favor a variety of approaches. The most common is explicit incorporation of the European Convention on Human Rights, along with additional rights, into British law, as ordinary statutes, as a superstatute (one requiring an extraordinary majority for repeal or amendment), or as a formal constitutional guarantee. The most controversial parts of the proposals, naturally, deal with the role of the judiciary in relation to parliamentary sovereignty. Most of the proposals would allow Parliament to override judicial decisions by an extraordinary majority. By 1990, however, no proposal for a bill of rights had gained support from the government. Additionally, important elements of the Labour Party withheld support from the proposals, fearing that unelected judges would use judicial review—in the American sense of the word—to undermine the interests of organized labor. The Labour Party, in the wake of its decisive victory in the 1997 elections, now seems to be heading toward passage of a nonconstitutional bill of rights—likely the incorporation of the European Convention on Human Rights into domestic law—without authorizing judges to overturn statutes found to be contrary to the bill of rights.[29] Although there has been pressure for adoption of a modern bill of rights, Britain thus remained without one throughout the period of this study. If a constitutional bill of rights is a necessary condition for the development of a judicial rights revolution, there should be no rights revolution in Britain.

Admittedly, some observers argue that several recent legal developments in Britain—the development of administrative law and the growing impact of European law—fill the gap left by the absence of a bill of rights.[30] First, in recent years British law has offered growing protection for procedural rights in the administrative process.[31] Since the sixties British courts have developed a modern system of administrative law for the purpose of controlling discretionary action by government officials. As late as 1965, a legal writer could lament the "absence of a system of public law in the United Kingdom."[32] By 1990, however, British judges had created or expanded a range of remedies aimed at providing judicial oversight of administrative and government action.[33]

In an important decision in the *GCHQ* case in 1984, Lord Diplock developed an influential summary of the grounds of judicial review that had developed in British law.[34] First, courts could overturn administrative acts on the grounds of illegality. Thus whether a "decisionmaker . . . understands correctly the law that regulates his decision-

making power and . . . gives effect to it" is a matter open to judicial review.[35] In extreme cases earlier in this century the courts struck down social welfare policies adopted by local authorities on the grounds of illegality. A particularly startling use of the doctrine had occurred, for instance, in *Roberts v. Hopwood* (1925),[36] in which the House of Lords ruled that a local borough council had exceeded its legal authority by establishing an excessively high minimum wage for its employees.

A second ground for judicial review is procedural impropriety that violates either statutory standards of fair procedure or a common-law standard of fairness now commonly called "natural justice." There are important parallels between natural justice and the U.S. doctrine of due process. In a classic landmark case on natural justice, *Ridge v. Baldwin*, the House of Lords ruled that a local constable was entitled to a hearing before being dismissed from his job.[37] Building on that precedent, the courts have held that the "legitimate expectations" of persons influence the nature of the procedures that may be required before administrative action is authorized. For instance, in the *GCHQ* case, the House of Lords ruled that public-sector unions had developed a legitimate expectation to be consulted before administrative actions withdrawing union recognition could occur. In the last thirty years, the natural justice standard has evolved into something akin to a fundamental right to fairness that is wholly independent of statutory foundation.

Third, the British courts have developed a doctrine that administrative discretion must be exercised rationally. The Court of Appeal created the doctrine in *Associated Provincial Picture Houses Ltd v. Wednesbury Corporation* (1948),[38] which involved a municipality's decision to allow cinemas to open on Sundays only on the condition that no child under age fifteen could be admitted. The court, in the end, found the condition not to be wholly unreasonable; but Lord Greene MR,[39] in reaching that conclusion, declared that "the decision of the local authority can be upset if it is proved to be unreasonable in the sense that the court considers it to be a decision that no reasonable body could have come to."[40] That declaration has expanded into a broad judicial check on administrative discretion. In some recent cases, courts have used the reasonableness doctrine with sweeping effect. For instance, in 1983 the House of Lords struck down a decision by the Greater London Council to heavily subsidize public transportation in London because of a campaign promise; the Lords ruled that that this was "unreasonable" because responsible exercise of policy discretion precludes automatic implementation of such a campaign promise.[41]

Judicial review in Britain, then, has evolved from a rather timid attempt to keep administrative agencies within their statutory authority to a much broader and more ambitious practice of reviewing the substance and procedure of government decisions. Two points are worthy of emphasis. First, British judicial review increasingly involves judicial evaluation of the substantive correctness of government decisions. Second, many important judicial decisions have been directed at actions of local authorities (local governments) and not simply at actions of administrators. Local authorities in Britain are not legally autonomous from the central government as are American state and local governments, and so British judicial decisions that overturn the actions of local authorities are not precisely equivalent to American judicial decisions overturning state or local policies. Nonetheless, British judicial review, particularly when directed at local authorities (or even, as is now possible, at high government ministers), is now clearly more intrusive than a benign checking of administrative discretion.

In addition, in Order 53 of 1977 the House of Lords consolidated various common-law remedies into one streamlined procedure, the application for judicial review. Subsequent revisions of the rule created a special set of High Court judges specializing in administrative law.[42] Some observers view the procedure as facilitating the development of administrative law.[43] Others claim, to the contrary, that the new procedure enables judges to control and limit applications for judicial review, that only a few issues (primarily immigration and homelessness) have been affected by the new procedure, and that it has been used primarily against local authorities and not the central state.[44] Although that is true, the number of judicial review applications has grown dramatically since creation of the procedure. The consolidated procedure, if only by uniting previously disparate mechanisms for appeal into one unified process and giving it the name judicial review, has drawn attention to administrative law and created out of it something like a "case congregation" that has developed a life of its own.[45]

In addition to the new administrative law, European law increasingly offers several foundations for rights litigation. One of those is European human rights law. Since 1966, when Britain accepted the jurisdiction of the European Court of Human Rights in Strasbourg, the Court has been the last step in an appeals process for claims under the European Convention on Human Rights. Its decisions are not binding on member states but nonetheless have great informal influence over domestic law. Persons making claims under the European Convention on Human Rights must exhaust all national appeals before going to

the European Commission and the Court of Human Rights, and so must appeal to the House of Lords, thereby affecting its judicial agenda.

There have been more complaints lodged against the U.K. with the European Commission on Human Rights than against any other country.[46] The relatively high level of complaints arising from Britain is due in part to that country's relatively well-developed support structure for legal mobilization, which enables British claimants to mobilize the human rights enforcement process more easily than residents of some other European countries; but, as Donald Jackson has shown, it also results in part from the British government's tactics in Northern Ireland and the intransigence of British prison authorities in the face of unfavorable European Court of Human Rights rulings in the seventies and eighties.[47] Relatively few of the complaints originally lodged with the Commission, however, proceed through all of the steps necessary to reach the Court. In 1990, for example, the Commission received 202 complaints against the U.K., but it admitted only 38 as within the Convention's jurisdiction.[48] But once a complaint has reached the court itself, the decision often has gone against the U.K.: between 1959 and 1990, the Commission referred forty-one cases to the Court and the Court determined that British authorities had violated the Convention in thirty of them.[49] Parliament typically has responded by revising the offending statute or practice, although in a number of instances the revisions have provoked further lawsuits.[50]

British courts increasingly refer to the Convention,[51] both for the purposes of interpreting vague domestic statutory language and for developing the common law.[52] But British courts also seem determined to show that British law provides adequate protections for human rights *independently* of the European Convention. The House of Lords, for example, in a case noted at the beginning of this chapter, recently ruled that speech that is critical of government receives common-law protection from libel actions.[53] If anything, this underscores the influence of the European Convention on Human Rights.

European Community (EC) rules have also had increasing influence on British law. The United Kingdom joined the European Community (which until 1986 was called the European Economic Community) in 1973.[54] As required by the Treaty of Rome of 1957, the foundation for the European Community, Parliament incorporated into British law fundamental parts of the Treaty and agreed to honor its commitments under the Treaty. EC rules take two forms, regulations and directives,

both of which are mandatory upon member states, although by different processes. Regulations have immediate effect in member states, while the far more common directives have effect only upon the enactment of legislation by member states. Nonetheless, in the event of a member state's failure to enact the legislation as required by a directive, domestic courts are to give the directive "direct effect" in any litigation in which the member state is a party. If a court is uncertain of the correct application or interpretation of an EC rule, it is required to refer the question to the European Court of Justice (ECJ). The ECJ has developed a reputation for liberalism, and indeed in recent decades it has created a body of rulings that increasingly resembles constitutional law.[55] Inevitably, British courts are asked on occasion to require the British government to come into compliance with an EC directive—and thus EC law has come to take on a quasi-constitutional supremacy that is enforceable in the British courts.

Rights of Accused and Prisoners
British law has a comprehensive statute governing police and criminal procedure. The Police and Criminal Evidence Act (PACE), passed in 1984 in response to criticisms about the "miscarriages of justice" discussed earlier, was an attempt to clarify the authority of the police and the rights of suspects in criminal investigations. Even after that substantial revision, however, critics charged that defendants' rights continued to be violated in various ways. Under increasing pressure, the government charged a Royal Commission on Criminal Justice with examining the issue and proposing reforms.[56] Although PACE failed to eliminate miscarriages of justice, it nonetheless provided, for the first time, a unitary statutory foundation for criminal appeals on matters of police and trial procedure. PACE included rules on a wide range of criminal procedure issues, among them provisions on search and seizure, legal representation, and confessions.[57] The statutory rules were based on the common law regarding the gathering and introduction of criminal evidence. The statute, however, did more than consolidate: it weakened some of the procedural protections. For example, it granted a significant extension of time in which the police could interview suspects without the benefit of an attorney. PACE's defenders claimed that it would lead to greater protection of criminal defendants because it distilled common-law rules scattered among many judicial decisions into a single documentary format. Its critics naturally focused on the weakening of some of the procedural protections. None-

theless, some research suggests that appellate courts have used PACE as a statutory foundation for examining the actions of the police more closely than they have in the past.[58]

Procedural rules, as well as substantive law, have influenced the development of criminal law in Britain. As Michael Zander observed, "the English appeal system manifests a marked reluctance to make itself too available" to criminal defendants.[59] Until 1960, British appellate procedures virtually prohibited criminal appeals to the House of Lords. The Administration of Justice Act 1960 removed or lowered several procedural hurdles: it abolished the requirement for the Attorney General's approval of criminal appeals to the House of Lords, lowered the standard for leave to appeal from matters of law of "exceptional" public importance to those of "general" public importance, and allowed appeals from the Divisional Court in addition to appeals from the Court of Appeal.[60] Largely as a result of the pre-1960 hurdles, only twenty-three criminal appeals reached the House of Lords between 1907 and 1960; after passage of the Act, the number of criminal appeals began to increase.[61]

Criminal appellants, however, face additional impediments. Those wishing to appeal to the Criminal Division of the Court of Appeal must first obtain leave to appeal, something not required of civil appellants.[62] More significantly, those wishing to appeal from the Court of Appeal to the House of Lords must, in effect, first gain permission from the Court of Appeal: that court must certify that a point of law of "general public importance" is at issue and either that court or the House of Lords must grant leave to appeal. Not surprisingly, the charge is often made that the Court of Appeal uses the certification mechanism to prevent the House of Lords from hearing criminal appeals.[63] In addition, applications for criminal appeal at each level of the judicial system must be filed within fourteen days of an adverse decision. Convicted prisoners often receive no post-trial advice from their barristers about appeals until after the deadline.[64]

In addition, the Court of Appeal has the power to order that the time spent appealing a criminal conviction not count toward the sentence of the defendant if he or she is in prison. Reportedly the Court of Appeal rarely uses the power, but prisoners apparently view it as a serious and substantial threat. According to one rights organization, "Many lawyers are ignorant of its [rare] use and advise their clients not to appeal because of the apparently drastic nature of the power."[65]

Finally, the law provides appellate judges with only limited remedies for correcting errors in lower courts. A conviction that suffers from

a procedural error can be either quashed—which has the effect of an acquittal—or affirmed on the ground that the error results in no miscarriage of justice. The best research on the topic has found that the Court of Appeal typically chooses to find no miscarriage of justice rather than to quash convictions.[66] This surely further discourages criminal appeals.

Women's Rights

A limited legal foundation for women's-rights litigation has developed in Britain. The Sex Disqualification (Removal) Act of 1919 provides that "A person shall not be disqualified by sex or marriage from . . . entering or assuming or carrying on any civil profession or vocation . . ." (among other things).[67] It is somewhat unclear whether the 1919 Act applies only to statutory disqualification on the grounds of sex or marriage or whether it applies more broadly to *any* disqualification on the grounds of sex or marriage; this crucial matter was never addressed directly in the case law.[68] In general, the 1919 Act has received very little attention outside the limited areas of jury duty and service in official positions.

Parliament passed legislation of far more importance in the 1970s. The Equal Pay Act of 1970 and the Sex Discrimination Act of 1975 are similar to some U.S. anti-discrimination statutes and, indeed, reflected a strong American influence.[69] The Equal Pay Act (which took force in 1975 after a delay to allow employers time to meet its requirements) required the equal treatment of women and men in all terms of the work contract. The Act made use of the collective nature of British employment patterns by granting a Central Arbitration Committee the authority to equalize provisions in collective labor agreements applying differentially to men and women. In a country where 70 percent of the work force has wages determined by collective agreement, this provision of the law produced relatively dramatic results, raising the female/male wage ratio from about 63 percent before 1975 to about 72 percent in 1980.[70]

The Sex Discrimination Act of 1975 bans discrimination in hiring, promotion, working conditions, housing, and services. The Act's creators followed the U.S. Supreme Court's decision in *Griggs v. Duke Power Co.*[71] by including provisions against "indirect" discrimination as well as "direct" (the British distinction is based on the distinction in U.S. law between disparate impact and intentional, invidious discrimination, but there are some differences; in particular, statistical evidence, which is central to disparate impact claims in the United States,

is not commonly used in British courts). The 1975 legislation also created the Equal Opportunities Commission, a quasi-governmental agency with powers to enforce the ban on sex discrimination. But in a significant departure from past practice, the legislation also authorized individuals to bring their own complaints to industrial tribunals, with appeal to the ordinary court system. By allowing individuals to pursue discrimination complaints through the court system, the Act reflected the strong influence of the American model of anti-discrimination enforcement which relies heavily on individual legal mobilization.[72]

European Community economic rules and regulations have also increasingly provided a foundation for litigation against discrimination in employment and pay. Article 119 of the Treaty of Rome of 1957 required member states to create legislation requiring employers to pay men and women equal pay for equal work. The Equal Pay Directive of 1975 extended that requirement to work of "equal value" and thus resembles comparable worth policies in the United States.[73] The Equal Treatment Directive of 1976 required member states to pass legislation guaranteeing equal treatment of the sexes in access to employment, training, promotion, and working conditions.[74] Subsequent directives extended these requirements to include social security and self-employed occupations, among other things.[75]

The landmark European Court of Justice decisions described above have allowed rights advocates to pursue claims in British courts demanding that British law be brought up to the standards set by the EC directives.[76] In a series of decisions, the European Court ruled that European law may be given "direct effect" in national courts in suits brought by individuals. In *Defrenne v. Sabena* the Court held that the EC ban on sex discrimination in pay was directly effective against member states,[77] and in *Marshall v. Southampton and South West Hampshire Area Health Authority*, it held that the requirement of equal treatment was directly effective.[78] The British courts, including the House of Lords, have recognized the authority of the European Court of Justice in matters of European law. European Court of Justice precedents have therefore become, for all practical purposes, part of British law; significantly, the precedents on fundamental rights, particularly the right against sex discrimination, are among the few principles of British law that have virtual constitutional status.

British anti-discrimination law nonetheless does not reach as broadly as comparable U.S. law. The British Sex Discrimination Act did not cover important forms of discrimination, and it did not apply to many areas of public life. It specifically did not apply to employment

provisions on death or retirement (thus allowing employers to establish different mandatory retirement ages for men and women), and it did not apply to relatively wide areas of British society, among them single-sex schools, charities, political parties, competitive sports, or insurance.[79] The Sex Discrimination Act also provides a very short time period for filing claims (three months), it grants to labor tribunals (the primary enforcement mechanism) only narrow powers, and it authorizes only limited remedies.[80] Although limited in these ways, the new anti-discrimination statutes nonetheless provided a foothold for litigation against sex discrimination.

Several "higher law" foundations for judicial review have thus begun to transform the role of British courts. The new administrative law is increasingly creating a "constitutional law without a constitution."[81] And the growing role of European human rights and economic law also increasingly offers foundations for judicial review of British law. European law affects British law even where it is not directly applicable in British courts. As one of the judges in the House of Lords, Browne-Wilkinson, has argued, British judges, under pressure from European law, increasingly may find in the common law the tools necessary to protect human rights, even in the absence of the adoption of a formal bill of rights.[82] Yet most observers seem to agree that these developments provide far less support for rights than would a bill of rights, and so debate continues over whether to create such a constitutional document.

The Appellate Committee of the House of Lords

British judges are remarkably conservative, and this conservatism greatly contributes to the traditionally inhospitable environment for rights litigation in Britain. This is especially true of Britain's highest court, the Appellate Committee of the House of Lords, one of the most conservative courts in the world.[83] For instance, until 1966 the House of Lords maintained a policy of never departing from precedents in its own previous cases. Eventually, mounting social change forced it to abandon some of this extreme conservatism. In its 1966 Practice Statement, the House of Lords declared that it would no longer be bound by precedent but would, when necessary, use its judicial powers to create new law.[84] Although the Practice Statement appeared to open the door to creative judicial policy making, the House of Lords remains very hesitant to depart from precedent.

In some respects the Appellate Committee is not a court but rather, as its name indicates, a committee of the House of Lords. Its members

(the "Law Lords") wear business suits and conduct their judicial hearings relatively informally, unlike the gowned and wigged judges of the other British courts. Nonetheless, there is little doubt that the Appellate Committee functions as a supreme court. Since the mid-1800s it has increasingly assumed the role and function of a final appellate court and its decisions constitute the authoritative interpretation of British law from which lower courts may not, by law, deviate.[85] In civil disputes, the Appellate Committee has been Britain's court of final appeal since 1876, when Parliament established it as a permanent, separate committee. In criminal matters, it has been the court of final appeal for England and Wales since 1960 (it still does not hear appeals in Scottish criminal cases). Although the House of Lords is the point of final appeal within the British judiciary, it is not necessarily the judicial leader in all areas of the law. Lower courts, particularly the High Court and the Court of Appeal, have been more creative than the House of Lords in some areas of the new administrative law.

Membership in the Appellate Committee is somewhat more fluid than in most supreme courts, consisting of the Lord Chancellor, nine Lords of Appeal in Ordinary and any number of additional members of the House of Lords qualified to sit as judges by virtue of past judicial experience. In practice the Law Lords consist primarily of the Lords of Appeal in Ordinary joined by several other Lords selected by the Lord Chancellor to hear particular cases. A person who is named a Law Lord cannot be removed from that status. When hearing cases, the Judicial Committee is divided into several panels, usually consisting of five judges each. Lord Chancellors have occasionally used their powers of selecting panels to limit the influence of certain Law Lords, but this is rare.[86]

The Law Lords' conservatism results in part from the nature of the pool from which they are drawn. The pool consists of Lord Justices, leading judges on lower appellate courts. These judges, in turn, are chosen from among judges lower in the judicial hierarchy, and lower judges are elevated from among Queen's Counsel. Queen's Counsel are elite, senior barristers; and barristers, in turn, are the relatively more elite and selective hemisphere of the British legal profession. The pool from which Law Lords are drawn is thus a very narrow, highly selective group of judges who have been filtered out in successive steps from groups that are only slightly less narrow and selective. Unlike in the United States, few politicians or political lawyers make their way into the British selection process.

The nature of the appointment process also contributes to the Law

Lords' conservatism. Formally, the Queen, on the advice of the Prime Minister, fills vacancies. In practice, the Lord Chancellor, who is the Speaker of the House of Lords, the country's chief judicial officer, and a member of the Cabinet, selects the names in consultation with his senior officials. The Prime Minister and the Queen routinely assent. The Lord Chancellor is a gatekeeper at several points in the hierarchy within the bar and judiciary, and members rise in that hierarchy through his discretion. To become a Queen's Counsel, a barrister must petition the Lord Chancellor, who investigates the applicant's character and legal reputation among other leading members of the bar. The same process is repeated for elevation from Queen's Counsel to a position in the higher judiciary. The overall process thus tends to exclude those who deviate from conventional legal and judicial norms and produces senior appellate judges and Queen's Counsel who share a conservative outlook on the proper role of the judiciary.[87] There are exceptions, of course. Some barristers and judges with more liberal attitudes have managed to rise through the hierarchy by virtue of their undoubted legal expertise. Nonetheless, British judges, by and large, remain remarkably conservative. Additionally, the British judiciary remains predominantly white and male. By 1990, only one of the twenty-nine lord justices on the Court of Appeal was a woman, and only one of the eighty-two High Court judges was a woman—and there were no women among the Law Lords in the House of Lords.[88]

Table 7.1 contains a list of the Law Lords at each of the years in this study and classifies them as either liberal or conservative in their judicial attitudes; it also identifies the Lord Chancellor[89] and Lords of Appeal in Ordinary (those who regularly sit in the Appellate Committee) in a given year. "Liberal" Law Lords have been more or less supportive of the new individual rights; "conservative" ones have been more or less unsupportive of the new rights.[90]

The table's classification reflects the common assessment by scholars that in the sixties the leading Law Lords supported the judicial development of individual rights but that after the mid-seventies they were replaced by more conservative judges.[91] Lord Reid led the Law Lords in the sixties and early seventies, both as its senior Lord of Appeal and as the philosophical leader of the trend toward greater (but still moderate) judicial liberalism. A relative rarity as a former politician (serving as Unionist party member in the House of Commons in the early thirties), he believed that more Law Lords should have political experience. At one point he stated that judges with such experience "know how the machinery of government works and are able to under-

Table 7.1   The Law Lords

1960	1965	1970	1975	1980	1985	1990
Kilmuir	*Gardiner*	*Gardiner/*	*Elwyn-Jones*	*Hailsham*	*Hailsham*	*MacKay*
Birkett	Cohen	*Hailsham*	**Cross**	**+Bridge**	**-Brandon**	**-Ackner**
Cohen	**+Devlin**	**+Denning**	**-Dilhorne**	**-Dilhorne**	**+Bridge**	**-Brandon**
+Denning	**-Dilhorne**	**-Dilhorne**	**+Diplock**	**+Diplock**	**-Brightman**	**+Bridge**
-Evershed	**+Donovan**	**+Diplock**	**+Edmund-Davies**	**+Edmund-Davies**	**+Diplock**	**-Brightman**
Goddard	-Evershed	**+Donovan**	**Fraser**	**Elwyn-Jones**	**+Edmund-Davies**	Elwyn-Jones
-Hodson	**Guest**	**Guest**	**Guest**	**Fraser**	**Elwyn-Jones**	Emslie
Jenkins	**-Hodson**	**-Hodson**	**-Hodson**	**-Keith**	**Elwyn-Jones**	**+Goff**
Keith	**MacDermott**	**MacDermott**	**Kilbrandon**	Lane	**Fraser**	**Griffiths**
Merriman	**+Morris**	**+Morris**	**+Morris**	Lowry	**Griffiths**	**Griffiths**
+Morris	Morton	**+Pearce**	**+Reid**	**-Roskill**	**-Keith**	**Jauncey**
Morton	**+Pearce**	**+Pearson**	**Russell**	**Russell**	**-Roskill**	**-Keith**
-Radcliffe	**+Pearson**	**+Reid**	**Salmon**	**Salmon**	**-Scarman**	Lowry
+Reid	**-Radcliffe**	**+Upjohn**	**Simon**	**+Scarman**	**-Templeman**	**+Oliver**
-Simonds	**+Reid**	**-Wilberforce**	**-Templeman**	**-Templeman**	**-Wilberforce**	**-Roskill**
Somervell	-Simonds	Wheatley	**-Wilberforce**			
Tucker	**+Upjohn**					
	-Wilberforce					

Notes: Lord Chancellors are listed at the top of each column. Lords of Appeal in Ordinary are boldface. Judicial liberals are designated by (+); judicial conservatives are designated by (−).

stand better issues concerning the administration."[92] Alan Paterson, relying on interviews with a number of the Law Lords, concluded that
Reid had been the driving force behind the development of the 1966
Practice Statement that freed the House of Lords from strict adherence
to *stare decisis* (judicial precedent).[93]

Since the mid-seventies, however, scholars have characterized the
House of Lords as increasingly conservative.[94] As early as 1978, Robert
Stevens predicted that a number of appointments since the mid-
seventies, barring changes in appointment policies, would shift the
House of Lords back toward judicial conservatism.[95] Lord Russell, for
example, was generally regarded as a judicial conservative;[96] and Lord
Hailsham's "judgments sometimes read like his speeches to associations of conservative ladies."[97] David Feldman recently surveyed the
attitudes of the Law Lords and concluded that, by retirement and replacement, the House of Lords had become significantly more conservative in the eighties.[98] Since then, the House of Lords is again developing a somewhat more liberal orientation, but the development
postdates 1990, the closing year of this study.

The structure of the decision process in the House of Lords may
attenuate the effects of judicial attitudes. The Law Lords, both when
considering leave-to-appeal petitions and deciding cases, sit not as one
unified body but instead in smaller panels. The division into panels
makes it more difficult for potential appellants to develop appeal strategies based on the Law Lords' attitudes. Thus appellants often do not
know in advance of petition or appeal which of the Lords will hear
their case. Even if some judges are known to be more liberal than others, appellants cannot predict from this whether their own bench will
consist of liberals or conservatives. This fact minimizes the possibility
of strategic planning based on perceptions about the Lords' judicial
activism and thus limits the effect of those perceptions on the judicial
agenda. If an overwhelming majority of the judges are either liberal or
conservative, however, then prospective appellants do not face such
problems of prediction.

Additionally, the House of Lords has less control over its docket than
do the U.S. or Canadian supreme courts. Cases reach the House of
Lords by two paths. The Court of Appeal, the workhorse of the British
appellate judiciary, has the authority to grant parties leave to appeal
to the House of Lords. From 1983 through 1985, 38 percent of the cases
on the House of Lords' docket that had come from the Civil Division
of the Court of Appeal were placed on that docket by the Court of
Appeal.[99] If the Court of Appeal refuses to grant such leave or if the

Figure 7.1   Judicial Workload of the House of Lords

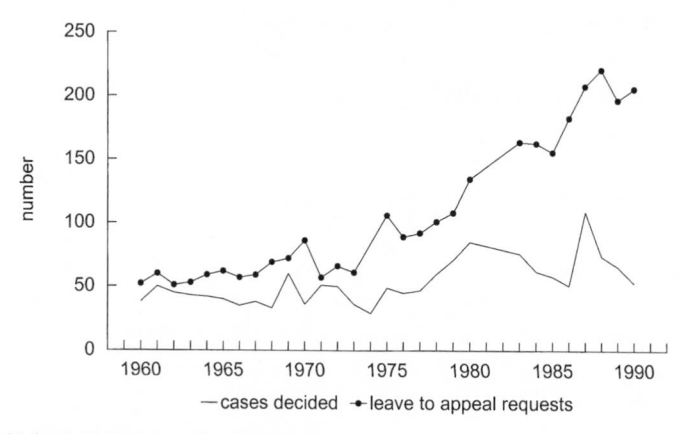

Source: *Civil Judicial Statistics* and *Judicial Statistics.*

case comes from another court, parties to civil cases may seek leave to appeal directly from the House of Lords.[100] The House of Lords generally must accept cases sent by the Court of Appeal, but it has full discretion to accept or reject other cases. In 1990, the House of Lords allowed thirty petitions for leave to appeal out of 170 filed.[101]

Although the House of Lords' agenda is shaped partly by the leave-to-appeal decisions of lower courts, its degree of discretion increased substantially over the period of the study due to increases in the number of cases on its discretionary docket. In 1960, the House of Lords agreed to hear virtually every case that came to it, but by 1990 it took only about one out of four cases (fig. 7.1). The number of cases decided after full hearing has increased over the thirty years of this study, but the increase has been very uneven, with the number decided in 1990 only marginally more than the number decided in 1960; nonetheless, there were several substantial surges in the eighties. The House of Lords, apparently, is placing firm limits on the number of cases it decides. Leave-to-appeal petitions have increased more substantially and consistently, particularly since the late seventies. Leave-to-appeal petitions are analogous to petitions for a writ of certiorari in the United States Supreme Court in that a grant of leave by the House of Lords is purely discretionary.[102] Due to the growing number of leave petitions and the marginal growth in the number of cases decided, the House of Lords has increasing discretion over the sorts of cases it will hear.

The House of Lords, then, became increasingly conservative over the course of the study period. Additionally, its discretion over its docket clearly increased over the course of the study. Increasing conservatism,

combined with increasing docket control, might be expected to produce a shift to the right in the court's decisions. On the other hand, British judges below the House of Lords level clearly supported an expansion of attention to rights, particularly by participating in the development of the law on administrative procedure. Nonetheless, if the judges' policy preferences alone determine the course of rights revolutions, we should not expect to find the Judicial Committee of the House of Lords participating in a rights revolution.

Conclusion

If we focus only on conventionally identified conditions for sustained judicial support for civil rights and liberties, then Britain appears to be an especially inhospitable site for the development of a judicial rights revolution. Admittedly, rights consciousness has grown and European economic law and human rights law provide firmer legal foundations for rights litigation than were available in the past and have required important expansions of protection for rights in British law. But those rights-supportive trends seem to be outweighed decisively by other factors. Britain has no bill of rights and, although there has been some pressure for adoption of a bill of rights, the government has declined to enact one. Perhaps more importantly, British legal culture and the judiciary are remarkably conservative. The legal culture rejects judicial policy making in favor of parliamentary sovereignty, and the judicial appointment process produces judges who are very hesitant to strike out in new directions in the law. Thus no rights revolution should be expected in Britain. In the next chapter, I show that a rights revolution has nevertheless developed and that the growth of a support structure for legal mobilization helps to explain that development.

EIGHT

Britain's Modest Rights Revolution and Its Sources

Although Britain's legal culture and constitutional structure seem to provide little support for the development of a rights revolution, by 1990 the agenda of the Appellate Committee of the House of Lords had shifted significantly toward rights cases. In 1960 the House of Lords' most important judicial decisions dealt with quibbles over tax law, but by 1990 its most important decisions shook the foundations of parliamentary sovereignty by expanding quasi-constitutional rights. Yet that is only part of the picture, for even by 1990, the majority of cases decided by the House of Lords involved relatively routine, relatively unimportant disputes, and rights cases accounted for less than one-third of the agenda. Cases relating to administrative procedure and women's rights figure prominently among the House of Lords' rights decisions, but decisions relating to criminal procedure are practically nonexistent.

Changes in the support structure for legal mobilization facilitated appellate litigation on women's rights but did not do so for criminal procedure. Certainly judicial attitudes cannot fully explain the differences: the Law Lords have not been particularly friendly to the rights of criminal defendants but, until very recently, the same was true of their attitude toward women's-rights claims. Additionally, although the growing influence of European labor standards in the eighties contributed to the growth of the women's-rights agenda, that agenda would not have developed without litigation sponsored by the British Equal Opportunities Commission (EOC). The EOC pursued a dual strategy in the European Court of Justice and in domestic courts for the specific purpose of influencing domestic British law. Without the resources for appellate litigation provided by the EOC, the influence of European law on British women's employment rights would have been significantly smaller. Thus variations in the support structure help to explain variations in the British rights agenda.

Figure 8.1   Issue Agenda of the House of Lords

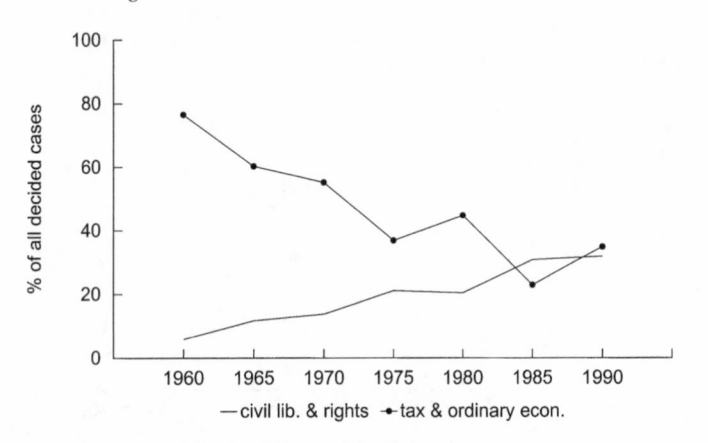

— civil lib. & rights   ●— tax & ordinary econ.

Source: Compiled from *Appeal Cases* and House of Lords records.
N = 1960, 68; 1965, 68; 1970, 87; 1975, 76; 1980, 103; 1985, 101; 1990, 101.

Rights Cases on the Judicial Agenda

Overview

Rights cases constituted just over 5 percent of the House of Lords' agenda in 1960, but this percentage rose steadily to just over 30 percent in 1990 (fig. 8.1).[1] Although the proportion of rights cases on the agenda by the end of the period was roughly half of that found on the agendas of the Canadian and U.S. supreme courts, the trend in the House of Lords was clearly toward expansion.

As the Law Lords devoted increasing attention to rights claims, their attention to tax and ordinary economic cases declined dramatically.[2] In 1960 tax cases and ordinary economic cases dominated the judicial agenda of the House of Lords, taking up 77 percent of the agenda space (fig. 8.1). But by 1985, after a precipitous drop, tax and economic cases claimed only 23 percent of the agenda space. In 1990 there was an unusual growth in ordinary economic disputes, increasing the agenda space of the two categories to about 35 percent.[3] Nonetheless, the decline in the agenda devoted to economic issues over the study period is dramatic, and it mirrors the growth in attention to rights claims.

Additionally, the number of listed parties to each case, an indicator of case complexity, has increased (fig. 8.2). In 1960 the average number of parties was just over two per case—most cases pitted a single individual against another. By 1990 the average had roughly doubled. While the growing number of participants in House of Lords cases remains substantially smaller than the the numbers found in U.S. and Canadian supreme court cases, the trend appears to be toward greater

Figure 8.2   Number of Parties to Cases before the House of Lords

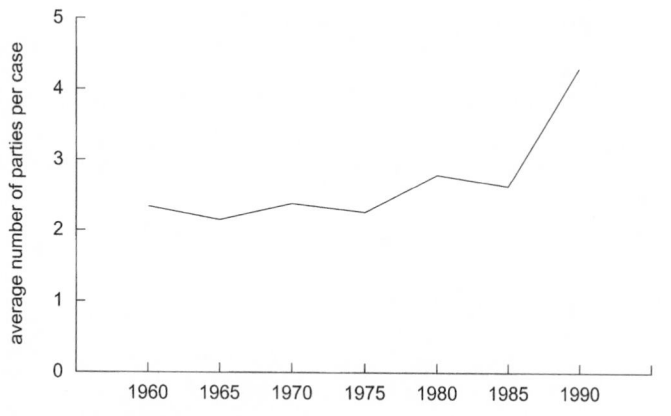

Source: Compiled from *Appeal Cases* and House of Lords records.
N = 1960, 68; 1965, 68; 1970, 87; 1975, 76; 1980, 103; 1985, 101; 1990, 101.

complexity. Unlike the U.S. and Canadian judicial systems, however, Britain has no formal mechanism for allowing persons with no direct interest in a dispute to participate in the argument of a case, and the absence of such a mechanism in Britain has limited the growth of case complexity.

Although there have been important changes in the Law Lords' agenda, including a general growth in attention to rights issues, not all rights issues have gained increasing judicial attention. For purposes of this comparison, rights cases are divided into three categories: procedural rights (limitations on the procedures of government agencies and officials), substantive rights (prohibitions such as those contained in the First Amendment to the United States Constitution), and equality rights. The House of Lords' rights agenda is composed largely of procedural claims, although equality rights cases began to appear in 1975 (fig. 8.3). This emphasis on procedural rights contrasts with the United States Supreme Court's agenda, in which procedural, substantive, and equality rights constitute more nearly equal components, and with the Canadian Supreme Court agenda which, while dominated by procedural claims, has experienced an increase in substantive and equality cases since 1980.

Moreover, the trends become even more curious if they are further subdivided. The equality cases on the House of Lords agenda have consisted almost exclusively of *sex* equality cases; there are virtually no racial equality claims on the agenda. The procedural rights cases have consisted almost exclusively of administrative procedure cases;

Figure 8.3   Rights Agenda of the House of Lords by Type of Right

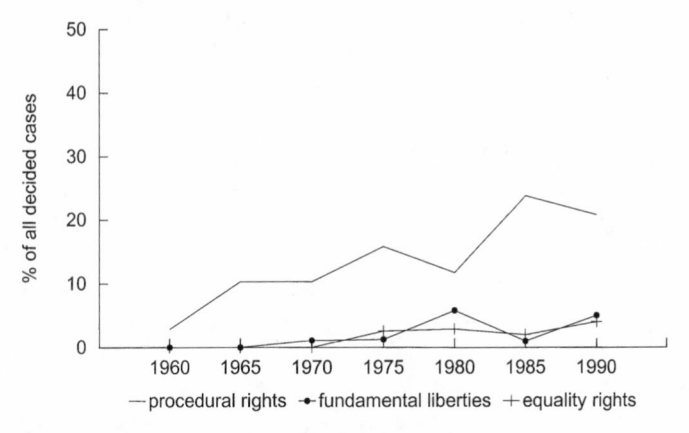

Source: Compiled from *Appeal Cases* and House of Lords records.
N = 1960, 68; 1965, 68; 1970, 87; 1975, 76; 1980, 103; 1985, 101; 1990, 101.

there are virtually no criminal procedure claims on the agenda. Thus, although undoubtedly there has been a rights-based transformation of the judicial agenda, it seems oddly skewed. These trends are discussed in more detail below.

The Criminal Procedure Agenda

The House of Lords devotes little attention to criminal procedure, particularly compared with the attention given the topic by the United States Supreme Court. Just as significantly, the proportion of the House of Lords' agenda devoted to criminal rights, unlike other rights issues, did not increase during the period studied here. Over the study period, criminal procedure cases never constituted more than 11 percent of the cases decided by the House of Lords, and in 1990 fewer than 3 percent of the cases involved criminal procedure.

The House of Lords occasionally hears criminal cases with important implications for procedural rights. In some cases it has expanded the options for appellate review and in some cases narrowed them. In *Connelly v. DPP* (1964), the Lords created an important avenue for criminal appeals by ruling that courts could stay criminal proceedings if they determined the authorities were perpetrating an "abuse of process" by violating standards of fairness.[4] But the Lords have also restricted defendants' rights. In *Stafford and Luvaglio v. DPP* (1974), the Lords addressed how the Court of Appeal should deal with new evidence of innocence presented on appeal after conviction, one of the areas of greatest controversy in the miscarriage-of-justice cases. The

Lords ruled that appellate courts must attempt to assess whether, in light of new evidence, the conviction was "unsafe or unsatisfactory" and not whether it might have led the original jury to have a reasonable doubt.[5] The "unsafe or unsatisfactory" standard, according to some scholars, has discouraged the Court of Appeal from ordering retrials in contested cases hanging on fresh evidence, hence compounding the failure of the appellate courts to address adequately the problem of miscarriages.[6] Similarly, in 1980 the Law Lords ruled that entrapment is not sufficiently unfair to justify a stay of proceedings.[7] Finally, the Law Lords appear to have relaxed the standards determining when police have authority to stop and search or arrest a person on the street. Before the early eighties, police could stop and search only if there was a reasonable suspicion of illegal activity; in *Mohammed-Holgate v. Duke* (1984) the Law Lords appeared to abandon that standard entirely, substituting instead the rule that stops and searches, and arrests, are prohibited only if wholly unreasonable.[8] The case involved a lawsuit for false imprisonment brought by a woman against a police detective who had stopped and arrested her, not in order to bring charges, but in order to question her under conditions of heightened emotional stress. The Law Lords ruled that arrest for the purpose of questioning was accepted practice and not a violation of standard administrative law principles governing official discretion. In the same year the Law Lords upheld the arrest of a man whom the arresting constable, on orders from a superior, honestly suspected of being a terrorist, although the evidence did not support the arrest order; the Lords held that since the statute under which the arrest was made did not explicitly require the suspicion to be based on reasonable grounds, there was therefore no such requirement.[9] The record of the House of Lords on significant criminal appeals, then, is mixed.

Even in areas of criminal procedure law that have gained new statutory bases, the House of Lords has heard few cases. For instance, the much touted Police and Criminal Evidence Act of 1984 (discussed in chapter 7) was thought to provide a new statutory foundation for important aspects of criminal procedure, and some observers expected it to generate new criminal defense litigation. Nonetheless, the portion of the House of Lords' agenda on police procedure (seizure of evidence, questioning of subjects, and the like) has remained at less than 5 percent of all cases throughout the study period and even declined by 1990.

By contrast, the House of Lords devoted significant attention in the eighties to prisoner rights, an area in which no change should have

been expected. Before the mid-seventies, British prisoners had few if any protections against the exercise of arbitrary power by prison administrators.[10] Courts refused to claim jurisdiction over prison administrators' decisions, and recourse through the prison administration system and the external administrative hierarchy was of no help. In one widely quoted case from 1972, Lord Denning MR rejected out of hand the possibility of judicial review of prisoners' claims: "If the courts were to entertain actions by disgruntled prisoners, the [prison] governor's life would be made intolerable. The discipline of the prison would be undermined."[11] Other judges used an analogy between prisons and British navy ships to refuse review, suggesting that, just as the nineteenth-century navy would have foundered had ship captains not had absolute authority on their ships, so prisons would collapse if prison governors lacked absolute authority.

That position began to erode in the mid-seventies and is now entirely abandoned. The British courts have intervened in some aspects of prison life, in particular prison discipline. But the courts also have not taken the U.S. route of judicial review of the broader conditions of prison life.

The new aggressiveness of the courts toward prison administration began with a European Commission on Human Rights decision in 1975 that prisoners must be allowed access to legal advice.[12] The British government had refused a prisoner's request to consult with a solicitor about an admittedly false charge left on his prison record. The British government responded to the Commission ruling with a new rule governing prisoner correspondence, under which prisoners could consult solicitors and seek review in the courts only after they had received a decision on their claim from the Home Office (the government department with authority over the prison system). In *Raymond v. Honey* (1983) the House of Lords used the rule to reject a prison governor's interference with a prisoner's communication with a solicitor.[13] The government responded by amending the rule to allow consultation with a solicitor only if the prisoner had at least notified the prison authorities of his complaint; that too was struck down.[14]

In the late seventies the first of several serious prison riots occurred. Each was followed by internal prison disciplinary hearings conducted by prison "Boards of Visitors." Several important British prisoner-rights cases developed out of the disciplinary hearings over a riot at Hull Prison. In those hearings, the Board of Visitors heard serious charges against hundreds of prisoners, imposing penalties ranging up to several years' additional sentence for some of the prisoners. The

hearings to determine guilt and determine penalties were perfunctory at best. In response, in *R. v. Board of Visitors Hull Prison, ex parte St. Germain* (1979), the Court of Appeal ruled that the courts have jurisdiction over the disciplinary decisions of Prison Boards of Visitors.[15] In that case and others after it, however, the courts distinguished the disciplinary authority of the boards from that of the governors, and refused to extend judicial review to decisions by governors. That refusal was overturned in *R. v. Deputy Governor of Parkhurst Prison, ex parte Leech* (1988), in which the House of Lords ruled that courts have jurisdiction to hear judicial review applications against governors' disciplinary decisions.[16]

In the eighties, then, the Appellate Committee of the House of Lords devoted increasing attention to the issue of prisoners' rights. As the preceding summary indicates, the Law Lords handed down several landmark decisions on prisoners' rights. Although the number of such decisions remains small, their presence belies earlier expectations about the autonomy of prison authorities. Most importantly, by 1990 the Law Lords had abandoned their earlier refusal to review prison discipline and had, instead, brought prison administrators under the authority of the courts.

The Women's-Rights Agenda

Cases involving women's rights on the House of Lords' agenda have never been numerous; before 1980, there were almost none. Indeed, one commentator noted that "the most remarkable thing about the [Sex Disqualification Act of 1919] is how little it has been relied upon as a means of establishing the unlawfulness of sex discrimination in employment. In nearly sixty years the parts of the Act which are of potential relevance in this context have been directly in issue in a court of law on only two occasions. . . ."[17]

But since 1980 the women's-rights agenda has grown slowly. No women's-rights cases appeared until 1980, but the number of such cases had risen, albeit modestly, to three in 1990, constituting 3 percent of the total agenda. Although small, this number was almost the entire agenda devoted to *all* equality issues, which is surprising in light of the racial tensions and other equality concerns discussed in the last chapter. Perhaps more surprisingly, although Britain has no constitutional right to equal protection, the House of Lords' women's-rights agenda is fully as large as the Canadian Supreme Court's women's-rights agenda (as we shall see in the following chapters), even though Canada has a Charter of Rights containing a guarantee of equal treat-

ment. Yet, even so, the number of cases focusing on women's rights is small relative to the other components of the House of Lords' rights agenda.

The British courts have become a principal forum for hearing criticisms of Britain's sex-discrimination laws. Over the course of recent decades, women's-rights advocates have criticized British sex-discrimination law on several grounds. First, for some years after the European Union's Equal Pay Directive of 1975, the British government did not amend British law to require equal pay for work of equal value (or "comparable worth"). Second, some lower courts had interpreted the Sex Discrimination Act of 1975 to allow "benign" discrimination that, in their view, benefited women, and some women's-rights advocates favored an interpretation banning "benign" discrimination as well. Third, it has been common practice in some businesses to require earlier retirement for women than men, and women's-rights advocates greatly opposed the government's decision to exclude retirement policies from coverage under the Sex Discrimination Act. Fourth, women's-rights advocates virtually universally condemn the limited nature of the remedies available under the sex-discrimination statutes.

In these and other matters, judicial decisions have had a significant impact on the meaning and implementation of the British sex-discrimination statutes. Although sex-discrimination law is still primarily a statutory undertaking, judge-made law has increasingly influenced the meaning of the statutes and has increasingly required Parliament to amend the statutes. The House of Lords, in particular, has handed down several important decisions on British sex-discrimination law. It twice declined to extend the Sex Discrimination Act's coverage to include discriminatory retirement policies;[18] it ruled that "benign" discrimination violates the Sex Discrimination Act's ban on "direct discrimination";[19] over the objections of women's-rights advocates it accepted the use of "market conditions" as a justification for policies that have a disparate impact on men and women;[20] and it interpreted "pay" under the Equal Pay Act broadly so as to include all compensation offered by employers.[21] Similarly, the Law Lords have agreed with women's-rights advocates that job comparison studies may compare the pay of jobs held predominantly by women with those held predominantly by men even if some men are employed in the predominantly female jobs.[22] That decision has endorsed relatively broad comparable worth policies. Of the major criticisms directed against the sex-discrimination statutes, only the issue of remedies did not appear on the judicial agenda during the study period. After 1990, however, that

issue was the subject of litigation in the European Court of Justice. Thus, although the record of the House of Lords on women's rights is mixed, the Law Lords have favored women's rights in a number of key cases.

The Impact of the Support Structure

Although few of the conventionally identified conditions for a rights revolution are present in Britain, the House of Lords nonetheless developed a judicial rights agenda after 1960. Only some potential rights issues, however, are on that agenda. The Law Lords have given much attention to administrative procedure but little to criminal procedure. Yet within the area of criminal procedure, the Law Lords have expanded their agenda on prisoners' rights. And the Law Lords have started to develop an agenda on equality rights, but that agenda consists almost entirely of sex-discrimination claims. These variations in the rights agenda reflect, to a great degree, the nature and strength of the support structure for legal mobilization.

The Support Structure's Main Components

ORGANIZATIONS. The number and strength of rights-advocacy groups has grown significantly in Britain in recent decades, but these groups address only a few issues and they remain much weaker than their counterparts in Canada and the United States. In Britain the number of organized groups using litigation as a tactic began to increase in the sixties.[23] Some of these organizations have used litigation only sporadically; others have mounted well-planned, strategic litigation campaigns. For instance, the Child Poverty Action Group, created in 1965, began using test cases strategically in the early seventies and continues to do so, primarily in the area of the interpretation of social welfare statutes.[24] The National Council for Civil Liberties (NCCL), formed in 1934, was until the sixties a shoe-string operation that seldom turned to the courts. But in the late sixties and seventies, the NCCL increased its use of litigation and its focus on educating the public about civil liberties and rights. The NCCL created a legal defense fund in 1969 and in 1972 published the first of many editions of a best-selling guide titled *Civil Liberties*.[25] The organization became increasingly active in the courts in the seventies and eighties; by the early nineties (when it changed its name to "Liberty"), the organization was the center of a network of several hundred solicitors and bar-

risters ("cooperating attorneys," as they are called in the United States) working on a range of rights issues.[26] Similarly, MIND, an organization championing the rights of mental patients, vigorously pursued a test-case strategy in the eighties.[27] The Joint Council for the Welfare of Immigrants, formed in 1967, and the Immigration Law Practitioners Association, formed in 1984, have pursued test cases on the fairness of procedures governing immigration.[28] In addition to these organizations, several others have worked specifically in the areas of women's rights and criminal procedure, as I shall discuss shortly.

To compound the tardiness in the development of litigation-oriented strategies, until the early seventies there were few educational or informational materials on civil rights and liberties in British law. As Dhavan and Partington observed, there was "a total lack of systematic information . . . no textbooks and hardly any practitioners' books . . . [few] courses . . . [and] no legal specialists."[29] Liberty, the group JUSTICE, and the Legal Action Group, an organization formed in 1971, now provide research and education on civil rights and liberties.[30]

Community Law Centres have also contributed to the support structure. The Centres are quasi-governmental organizations that provide legal assistance and advice, particularly in poor neighborhoods. In the late sixties, the Society of Labour Lawyers, inspired by the Legal Services Program in the United States, began pressing for a similar initiative in Britain. The first Centre was created in 1970, and by 1990 there were sixty Centres scattered throughout the larger cities.[31] Funding, which in recent years has become increasingly tight, comes primarily from the national government, although limited funds also come from local authorities, from foundations, and through taking legal aid cases.[32] Although the Centres primarily take routine cases involving rents, welfare, and the like, they also have supported some sex-discrimination and immigration litigation, and some of the Centres have tried to pursue cases that are likely to have a broad impact beyond the particular parties to the case.

Taken together, the various rights-advocacy organizations, and especially the Legal Action Group, provided the organizational base for networks of lawyers, researchers, and activists working to expand protection in British law for civil liberties and civil rights. No such organizational base existed before the late sixties, and thus the development was highly significant. Nonetheless it should not be exaggerated. Unlike similar organizations in the United States, for example the ACLU or the National Organization for Women, none of the British groups has had sufficient resources to hire more than one or two in-house

counsel. Moreover, the relatively weak base of financial resources has greatly limited the capacity of any of the organizations to sponsor test-case litigation.

SOURCES OF FINANCING.   Limitations in the availability of independent financing for litigation have driven rights advocates in Britain typically to rely on government-sponsored legal aid for support. Legal aid, or the provision of legal counsel or advice to civil litigants and criminal defendants, developed into a massive, state-funded program in Britain during the period of this study.[33] The current program dates to the Legal Aid and Advice Act of 1949. Although legal aid is state funded, it is administered by the Law Society of England and Wales, a voluntary professional association of solicitors. Legal aid committees, composed of solictors and barristers, screen applications for legal aid based on criteria regarding the applicant's financial need and the merit of the proposed legal claim. In its various forms, it provides financing for individuals to retain private lawyers.

Legal aid contributes more than simple financing for court cases: qualifying for legal aid for a case also shields the litigant from financial liability under the "loser pays" rule.[34] Under that rule, losing parties in either trial or appellate courts may be required to pay the lawyers' fees of their opponents. As a result, parties without substantial long-term financial resources may be less willing than parties with greater resources to take even meritorious cases because a single loss, even if unlikely, would be so devastating as to discourage gambling on a likely victory. Hence, strategic litigation by parties lacking substantial resources is discouraged. This fact compounds the weaknesses of the comparatively poorly funded rights-advocacy groups in British society.[35] But qualifying for legal aid ameliorates that difficulty and so the growth of legal aid in the sixties and seventies created a condition for the development of rights litigation. Success in gaining legal aid funding for a claim is typically the single most important factor for determining whether the claim goes forward. This is reflected in the fact that newspaper stories about lawsuits commonly focus on whether legal aid has been granted for a particular claim—for instance, "Legal Aid Has Been Granted to 200 Smokers Considering Suing British Cigarette Companies."[36]

The level of funding for civil litigation and criminal defense, and the number of cases supported by legal aid, began to grow substantially after the late sixties (fig. 8.4). This is particularly true of legal aid in criminal cases, for which government funding was very limited until

Figure 8.4 Cases Supported by Legal Aid: All Courts and the House of Lords

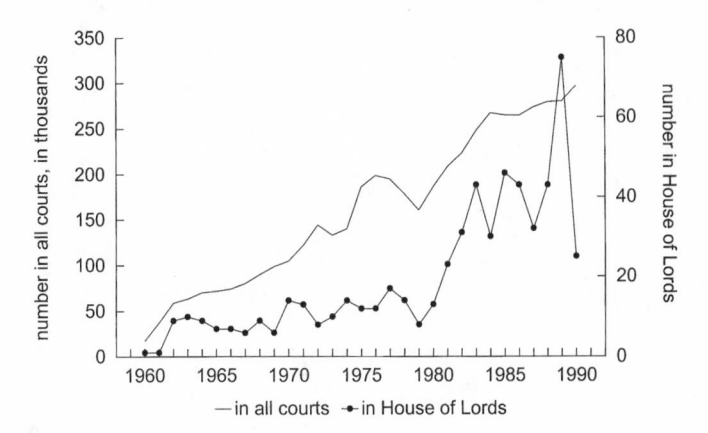

— in all courts -•- in House of Lords

Source: Civil Judicial Statistics, Judicial Statistics, and reports of the Law Society.

the early seventies.[37] Individuals qualify for legal aid if they meet a means test that has been relatively generous. In the late seventies and early eighties, about 70 percent of the population qualified for legal aid. In the late eighties, however, the Thatcher government's attempts to cut budgets extended to legal aid, with the result that the proportion of the population qualifying for aid declined. For example, one study concluded that eligibility for legal aid among all individuals fell from 80 percent of the population in 1979 to 51 percent in 1990, while among couples with two dependent children, the proportion eligible for legal aid dropped from 75 percent in 1979 to 34 percent in 1990.[38] The cuts produced a firestorm of controversy, particularly within the legal profession, that has yet to diminish.

In 1960 funding for legal aid was extended to appeals to the House of Lords and, since that year, the number of cases supported by legal aid in the House of Lords has grown dramatically (fig. 8.4). On the other hand, the number of legal aid cases in that court also dropped significantly in the late eighties. There is a close correspondence between the level of funding for legal aid cases in the House of Lords and the size of that court's rights agenda. As I showed above, the size of the aggregate rights agenda grew most rapidly in the early eighties, leveling off in the second half of that decade. That pattern closely follows the pattern of growth in the number of cases financed by legal aid both in the aggregate, and in the House of Lords.

THE LEGAL PROFESSION. The growth in legal aid contributed to a number of important changes in the British legal profession. Those

Figure 8.5   Growth of the British Legal Profession

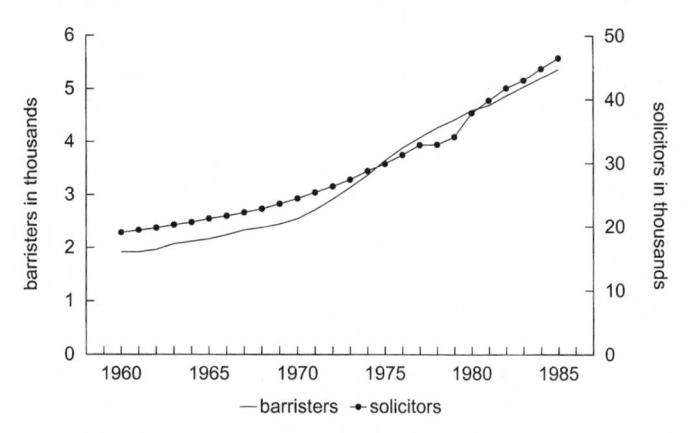

Source: Abel, *Legal Profession in England and Wales*, tables 1.16 and 2.14.

changes, with some exceptions, further expanded the support structure for legal mobilization. First, the growth of legal aid, along with a
growth in government assistance for education, fueled a growth in the
number of both barristers and solicitors after about 1970.[39] Figure 8.5
illustrates the growth in the two sides of the legal profession through
1985.

Perhaps more importantly, however, both sides of the legal profession began to diversify after the mid-seventies due to the entry of racial
minorities and women. Before the early seventies, the structure of entry to the bar had acted to exclude all but fairly wealthy, white male
aspirants who could afford the substantial fees and the risk of little
work in the first years of practice; but some of those barriers eroded
in the seventies with the growth of government assistance for education.[40] The class composition of the solicitor side of the profession has
not changed substantially, in part because the class backgrounds of
solicitors traditionally have been more diverse than those of barristers.
But the number of female solicitors has grown substantially, due to
greater access by women to higher education in the seventies and to
the work provided by legal aid.[41]

The growing size of the British legal profession, in turn, contributed
to a growth in the size of barristers' chambers and solicitors' firms. As
Abel reports, in 1960 only about 10 percent of barristers' chambers
contained ten or more barristers but, by 1979, that percentage had
climbed to 60 and, by 1984, 75 percent of barristers' chambers contained ten or more barristers; in fact, by 1984, 27 percent of chambers
contained more than twenty barristers.[42] Although those numbers remain very small in comparison to the size of the typical large American

law firm and, although barristers technically practice individually and not as part of their chambers, the shift from small chambers to larger ones contributed to growing legal specialization. By the eighties, some chambers were identified as focusing largely on civil liberties law and judicial review. Similarly, the size of solicitors' firms has grown. According to Abel, the median number of principal solicitors in the fifteen largest firms (as of 1983) grew from about eight in 1950, to thirteen in 1960, to twenty-one in 1970, to about forty-five in 1983, and to forty-six in 1985.[43] The new and growing firms of solicitors, unlike barristers' chambers, are corporate enterprises that foster internal cooperation and specialization both within and among firms. As with barristers' chambers, a small but significant number of solicitors' firms now specialize in civil liberties law.

The nature of legal education, too, has changed. Before about 1970, British legal education sharply distinguished law and the legal profession from other domains in society. In the years after about 1970, however, British legal education in the universities began to change in two important ways. First, law departments increasingly began to offer training in civil liberties and civil rights law. Second, influenced by trends in American legal education, law departments began offering interdisciplinary courses relating law to its social and political context. These developments in legal education have contributed to changes in the legal profession's self-understanding, primarily by encouraging solicitors and barristers to view litigation pragmatically, as a tool for achieving social and political purposes.[44]

The support structure for legal mobilization, then, deepened and diversified between 1960 and 1990. The developments in rights-advocacy organizations, sources for financing, and the legal profession all significantly departed from past patterns. Nonetheless, in comparison to its counterpart in the United States, the British support structure remains relatively small, weak, and resource-poor. In general, the broad trends in the support structure for legal mobilization closely correspond with broad trends in the House of Lords' agenda on rights. In the late seventies and eighties, both the support structure and the rights agenda grew significantly but modestly. Moreover, as I show in the next several sections, variations in the strength of the support structure help to explain variations in the judicial agenda on rights.

The Support Structure and the Rights of the Accused
In spite of general external pressures, among them the rising number of serious convictions and public controversy, and in spite of major statutory reform, the House of Lords agenda on defendants rights is

stagnant. By contrast, the Law Lords greatly expanded their attention to the issue of prisoners' rights. Those variations reflect both the structural characteristics of the judicial system described in chapter 7 and the nature of the support structure for criminal appeals.

The support structure for legal mobilization is significantly weaker for criminal appeals than for civil appeals. Although legal aid for criminal defendants increased dramatically over the period of the study,[45] there remain significant limitations on legal aid in the context of criminal appeals. Criminal applications for leave to appeal to the Court of Appeal are heard by a single judge, who generally refuses legal aid if he or she refuses the application.[46] Criminal appellants who finance their own cases may continue by petitioning the whole court. In addition, legal aid funds are generally available in appeals to both the Court of Appeal and the House of Lords to pay fees for barristers but not for solicitors, whose support in developing the case is often critical.[47] The limitations on legal aid restrict the upward flow of criminal appeals at both appellate levels of the judicial structure.

Another, perhaps more important, factor limiting the number of criminal appeals is the structure and culture of the British legal profession. Mike McConville and his colleagues, in an extensive interview-based study of British firms of solicitors specializing in criminal cases, discovered that most such firms provide disorganized, ineffective criminal defense services from the earliest stages of the criminal process through appeals. Most firms specializing in criminal cases train new solicitors by throwing them into the midst of active defense work with little or no guidance and training, and most rely heavily on such untrained or partly trained solicitors for work on the crucial early phases of cases. They rely primarily on evidence provided by the police and prosecutors rather than independently gathering their own evidence and checking the validity of the prosecution's evidence. Most firms provide disorganized, disjointed defense services in which different members of the firm handle different stages of the case-building and case-presenting process. They commonly stereotype criminal defendants as stupid and guilty. And most firms prefer to defend compliant defendants who plead guilty rather than defendants who vigorously protest their innocence and wish to contest the charges.[48] As a consequence, most defendants, even in rather serious cases, must rely on ineffective counsel who routinely fail to develop an adequate case of any sort before crucial court appearances. The relatively common miscarriages of justice in part reflect such patterns of inadequate case preparation.

McConville and his colleagues attribute weak defense services to a "culture" of nonadversarial criminal defense in Britain.[49] One of the most important sources, they argue, is the division of the legal profession between barristers and solicitors, and the associated celebration of the oral tradition of defense in court by barristers over the nitty-gritty, unglamorous, but crucial case-preparation work by solicitors. Barristers have a monopoly on representation of clients in all but the lowest courts in Britain and, as a consequence, solicitors have little incentive to develop cases adequately for effective appeals; the structure of incentives encourages solicitors, rather, to expend the least amount of effort necessary to see their cases through to completion in the magistrates' courts (where solicitors have rights to oral representation). This structure exacerbates the disorganization and discontinuity of defense services: "[t]he solicitor, frustrated by being unable to continue representation into the higher court, largely cedes control, both of the case and of the client, to the barrister."[50] Yet barristers, their role confined to oral advocacy in court, have no real role in building a case, with the result that the defense tends to rest on an inadequate factual case. Although McConville and his colleagues conclude that such weaknesses are common to most firms of solicitors specializing in criminal law, they also discovered that a minority of firms in their sample provided defense services that were more aggressive and effective. They concluded, therefore, that the culture developed by a firm strongly influences the extent to which it provides effective defense services. Most of the firms they surveyed adopted routinized, ineffective patterns; but some, for reasons centered on enhancing their managerial efficiency, provided somewhat more effective services and others, for reasons related to their commitment to a political ideal of adversarial justice, provided substantially more effective services.

The main exception to this pattern is the support by the group JUSTICE for a number of the worst miscarriage-of-justice cases. But JUSTICE itself has lamented the lack of support for appeals in criminal cases, particularly miscarriage-of-justice cases, and attributes this lack to the severe limitations on legal aid for appeals and the fact that "few other organisations are as fortunate as JUSTICE in having access to the legal and forensic help which makes the investigation of cases possible."[51]

Limited resources, the structure of the British legal profession, and the organizational culture and lack of commitment of defense solicitors to adversarial justice, then, compound the other factors that limit the incidence and effectiveness of criminal appeals. The importance of the

support structure may be illustrated by comparing ordinary criminal appeals with appeals regarding prisoner rights. As we saw above, prisoner-rights cases, although still small in number, grew significantly over the decade of the eighties. Why that is so relates directly to the support structure for legal mobilization.

The prisoner-rights agenda was strongly influenced by the strategic action of a relatively small number of legal activists who succeeded in pressing initial cases onto the judicial agenda and who followed the initial cases with others. The key actors included persistent prisoners,[52] several public interest groups, several solicitors, and several barristers. As one of the solicitors described the strategy, the legal activists sought first to overcome the prohibition on legal representation for prisoners in disciplinary proceedings and then sought to use that foothold to explore a range of issues relating to the conduct of discipline and communication. In particular, from the start of the strategy the key activists had hoped to bring the prison governors under the jurisdiction of the courts.[53]

The prison litigators had to cross two hurdles to develop their prisoner-rights agenda: a lack of financial resources and the unwillingness of the courts to question prison administrators. The solicitors found it difficult to obtain legal aid for their clients in the early cases but succeeded in convincing the Legal Aid Board to grant aid in several crucial cases, a process that became easier as the cases succeeded and the Legal Aid Board warmed to their success.[54] The main solicitor in the leading cases asserted that the cases would not have developed had they failed to receive legal aid.[55] In addition, the participants describe the courts and in particular the House of Lords, at the start of the strategic litigation, as unwilling to address the issue.[56] The initial cases were carefully selected so that the facts—the nature of the disciplinary hearings—were so shocking that the judges virtually would be forced to act. The participants were aided in this task by the vigorous responses of the Prison Boards of Visitors to the riots of the late seventies and by the willingness of prisoners to coordinate their efforts and to self-select only the most promising complaints. When the strategists, after sufficiently developing precedents, began attempting to bring cases directly against the prison governors, the Home Office conceded case after case before they reached the House of Lords, fearing an adverse ruling from the Law Lords.[57] But eventually prisoner-rights cases reached the House of Lords and, as discussed above, the Law Lords did indeed bring prison governors under judicial review.

In addition to the prison discipline cases the prisoner-rights activists

brought cases on sentencing, parole, and prisoner communication with the outside world. In those areas as well the participants describe strategic development of precedents in the face of initial opposition from the courts.

The Law Lords' agenda on prisoner rights, then, developed directly out of a strategic litigation campaign mounted by several solicitors and barristers. The main solicitors and barristers gained the benefit of organizational support from several prominent civil liberties firms, and their clients gained the financial support of legal aid. By contrast, ordinary criminal defense services are poorly organized and have a culture of nonadversarial passivity. These variations in the support structure help to explain the different trajectories of the prisoner-rights agenda and the ordinary criminal procedure agenda.

The Support Structure and Women's Rights

The nature of the support structure for women's-rights litigation similarly helps to explain the development of the House of Lords' agenda on women's rights as well as the limited nature of that agenda. Judicial attention to women's rights has grown somewhat, due in large part to strategic litigation by the Equal Opportunities Commission (the quasi-governmental agency created by the Sex Discrimination Act of 1975). But the agenda remains limited in large part because the support for women's-rights litigation, although growing, remains relatively modest. For one thing, legal aid is not available for representing sex-discrimination claimants in industrial tribunals, the courts of first instance for such claims.[58]

British women's-rights organizations, unlike their American counterparts, have virtually no capacity to mount strategic litigation campaigns. The women's movement in Britain, as in other countries, entered a second, more radical, phase in the late sixties and seventies, as women began pressing for fundamental changes in their legal and social position. In the United States, this new women's movement produced strong and stable organizations with the capacity to support and pursue strategic litigation, and the movement also gained the support of already existing organizations, particularly the ACLU. In Britain, by contrast, the new women's movement remained highly decentralized and informally organized.[59] Unlike the U.S. organizations' heavy emphasis on pressing for legal change, in Britain, the grassroots movement devoted more energy to internal debates about feminist philosophy.[60] Moreover, the British women's movement is not strongly institutionalized. Its organizational presence has consisted primarily

of local committees and weakly organized grassroots groups. The few national women's-rights organizations have not been closely involved in the development of national enforcement policies, due in part to an early lack of receptivity on the part of the Equal Opportunities Commission and the British government to involvement by women's groups.[61] In general, the contrast between the U.S. and British women's movements is substantial: British groups are comparatively poorly funded and poorly organized.[62]

The decentralization, lack of institutionalization, poor funding, and theoretical focus of British women's groups have had important effects on the development of women's-rights litigation. None of the women's-rights organizations has had sufficient resources to pursue cases systematically through the appellate courts; as a consequence, women's-rights groups have seldom played central roles in the development of court cases. In the few instances when women's groups have participated in litigation, their grassroots structure and theoretical focus have encouraged the use of unconventional tactics. For example, when the Greenham Common women protesters were prosecuted for trespassing at a defense base, in an action they defined as part of the movement for women's rights, they chose to continue the protest in court by singing rather than submit to the protocol of the courtroom.[63] This weak involvement by women's groups in strategic litigation cannot be attributed to any deliberate deference to government policy enforcement efforts because, until the late eighties, women's-rights groups were generally critical of the Equal Opportunities Commission's legal strategies.[64] Susan Atkins observed, "feminists have insisted on establishing their own methods of organization, deliberately challenging conventional strategies for reform, the use of the law included."[65] But lack of resources surely contributes to the tendency to downplay legal strategies. As a solicitor who is associated with several women's-rights groups explained, "if you want to develop test cases, you need loads of money, which we don't have."[66]

To remedy the lack of support for litigation by the women's movement, the Women's Legal Defence Fund (WLDF) was formed in 1989. The group's founders hoped to coordinate legal expertise and advice on women's rights and to provide funding for court cases. The organization created a network of women lawyers and hoped to use them to provide representation in women's-rights cases.[67] Thus the WLDF offered the potential for planned, strategic litigation for legal change, on the pattern that appears in the United States and Canada.

Nonetheless, the WLDF suffered from organizational and funding

weaknesses that eventually led to its collapse. The organization depended primarily on a single large grant from a private foundation.[68]
The limited availability of such grants in Britain before the creation of
the WLDF apparently was one of the key factors limiting the development of similar organizations and of women's-rights litigation in general. Harlow and Rawlings report that "the WLDF collapsed through
lack of funding in 1991."[69]

Although women's-rights groups have supported little women's-
rights litigation, the Equal Opportunity Commission began a new strategic litigation campaign in the eighties. That campaign propelled
women's-rights issues onto the judicial agenda. The EOC's new initiative was long in coming. Observers generally agree that the original
mandate of the EOC was not to support litigation but to educate and
persuade employers to end sex discrimination.[70] The EOC could also
pursue "formal investigations" in cases of systematic discrimination
by large employers, could issue "nondiscrimination notices" that if violated could result in court enforcement, and could, in the end, support
individual applicants in pursuing civil claims against discriminatory
employers. Several examinations of the policy record of the EOC in the
early and mid-eighties criticized the agency for failing to act more
aggressively to enforce the laws against sex discrimination. For example, Vera Sacks observed that the legal budget had never exceeded
five percent of the total budget and that "law enforcement generally is
seen by many in the Commission as a last resort."[71] As Evelyn Ellis
concluded, reviewing developments through the mid-eighties, "the
Commission has, in practice, preferred to exercise its strict legal powers sparingly and to proceed by encouraging and negotiating good
equal opportunities policies wherever possible."[72] Sally Kenney ex-
plains the agency's conservative posture as reflecting both the tripartite
composition of its leadership (with commissioners chosen roughly
equally from government, industry, and trade unions) and the government's appointment of conservative commissioners.[73] Thus in its early
years, the EOC fit the characteristically British cooperative, nonadversarial style of administrative policy making discussed in chapter 7.[74]

By the mid-eighties, however, as a result of extended discussions
within the EOC, the EOC began to call for a number of fundamental
changes in British sex-discrimination law and, when the government
declined to proceed with the reforms, the agency embarked on a new
strategy to produce law reform through test cases in the courts.[75] By
law, the EOC supports cases that otherwise would fail for lack of financing; the agency provides all of the financing for cases it chooses

Figure 8.6   Legal Expenditures of the Equal Opportunities Commission

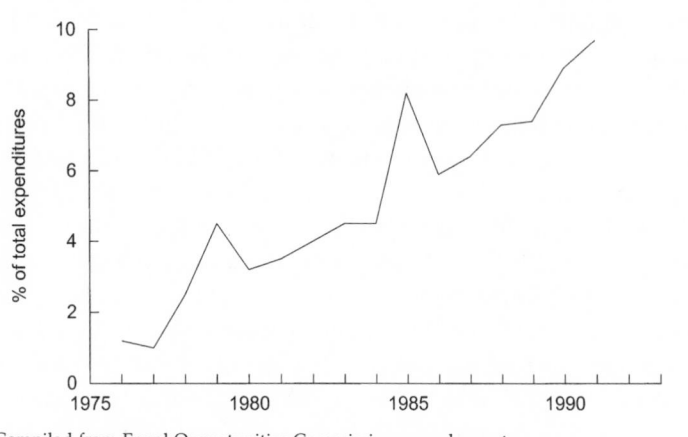

Source: Compiled from Equal Opportunities Commission annual reports.

to support.[76] The EOC's efforts focused on reforming the Equal Pay Act, which had prohibited contractual inequalities in pay between men and women. As noted earlier, criticisms of the Equal Pay Act in the eighties focused on the exclusion of retirement benefits from coverage under the Act and on the Act's failure to address sex-role segregation (the payment of poor wages and benefits to workers in jobs held primarily by women).[77] The EOC's litigation strategy since the mid-eighties has been directed at chipping away at the exclusion of retirement benefits from the provisions of the Act and at expanding protections for part-time workers and women in jobs that provided no benefits. The EOC's growing focus on litigation is illustrated by the growing proportion of its budget allocated to its legal section (fig. 8.6).

In pursuit of that strategy, the EOC sponsored cases in the European Court of Justice to develop favorable precedents there and then employed those precedents in the British courts. In its drive to reform British sex-discrimination law, the EOC sponsored a number of cases that led to important decisions by the European Court of Justice.[78] In at least one instance, the strategy forced Parliament to revise British statutes.[79] (Additionally, the creation in 1983 of the British law requiring equal pay for equal work—in the U.S. lexicon, "comparable worth"—was required by a European Court case brought by the Commission of the European Community.[80])

By the early nineties EOC strategy had become increasingly aggressive, involving another concerted attempt at law reform through the courts. The current effort, which is directed at the House of Lords and is based on EC treaty obligations that have become part of British law,

is an attempt to require the British government to amend its laws on the benefits of part-time workers, who disproportionately are women. For example, the EOC recently won a remarkable victory in the House of Lords that calls on the government to substantially improve its pension and layoff regulations for part-time workers.[81]

The EOC's support for test cases on women's rights has thus had a significant effect on the judicial agenda. In 1979 and 1980, the EOC supported several cases in the House of Lords, and those cases formed the entire women's-rights agenda of that court in 1980. In the second half of the eighties, the EOC supported cases in the House of Lords or in the EC legal process in every year but 1986 and supported four separate cases in the House of Lords in 1987 alone. In 1985, the EOC supported no cases in the House of Lords, as it was pursuing three in the European Court of Justice; no women's-rights cases appear on the House of Lords agenda in 1985. In 1989 and 1990, the EOC again supported several cases in the House of Lords, and those cases formed the entire women's-rights agenda of that body in those years.

The nature of the support structure for women's-rights litigation thus helps to explain both the growing presence of women's-rights cases on the House of Lords' agenda and the relatively small number of such cases. In comparative terms, the EOC supports about as many women's-rights cases in the House of Lords as do the U.S. enforcement agencies in the United States Supreme Court. In contrast to Britain, however, the United States has a substantial support structure for women's-rights litigation apart from the official enforcement agencies.

Conclusion

Although Britain has no bill of rights, and although judicial conservatives retained control of the Appellate Committee of the House of Lords until after 1990, there has been a modest rights revolution in Britain. Between 1960 and 1990 the agenda of the Appellate Committee of the British House of Lords changed, to a small but significant extent, away from a focus on routine economic disputes and toward a focus on public law and, in particular, rights claims.

Structural characteristics of the judicial system have greatly conditioned that growth. Criminal defendants must gain leave to appeal at two levels of the appellate process in order for their claims to proceed, and for appeals from the Court of Appeal to the House of Lords the appeal must, in effect, be approved by the Court of Appeal, the court whose decision is under challenge. Those hurdles have limited the development of a criminal procedural rights agenda. The development

of a consolidated procedure for judicial review, by contrast, has facilitated the development of an administrative procedural rights agenda.

Variations in the support structure for legal mobilization have also significantly influenced the judicial agenda. Without the resources of the Equal Opportunities Commission, both for coordinating legal strategy and for providing financing, the European Court rulings on women's rights discussed above almost certainly would not have occurred, and the judicial agenda on women's rights would have languished. Without vigorous efforts by several politically committed solicitors and barristers and without their success in gaining legal aid, the prisoner-rights cases would have been greatly diminished both in number and in impact on the agenda. The fate of criminal appeals illustrates that point: limitations on legal aid for criminal appeals and the low level of commitment among many solicitors who specialize in criminal defense have handicapped the judicial agenda on criminal procedure. The substantial growth in the support structure for some rights claims therefore provided the necessary foundation for the transformation of the House of Lords' judicial agenda and, where that support structure remains the weakest, potential issues do not appear on the agenda.

Although the rights agenda in Britain has grown significantly, future growth may be limited by the relative weakness of British rights-advocacy groups and limited sources of funding. The handicap imposed by the limited resources of British public-interest groups is compounded by the fee-shifting rule, which requires losers in civil litigation to pay winners' costs. Although the public-interest groups would not always lose if they litigated, their resources are so limited that the risk of loss discounts the probability of victory.

Certainly the absence of a constitutional bill of rights and the conservatism of the Law Lords are not irrelevant. Continued opposition by the Law Lords undoubtedly can halt the development of a line of cases. But the process of agenda setting is an interactive and subtle process. In part it is a process by which outside interests attempt to educate the judges about their concerns. Thus, a solicitor who worked on the prisoner-rights agenda described an important victory in the House of Lords in the late eighties as an indication that "the battle for control of the judicial mind was won."[82] Judicial attitudes, then, surely influenced the judicial agenda, but organized groups and lawyers influenced judicial attitudes by bringing cases that forced the judges to confront new and troubling issues.

The traditional contrast between an aggressive rights agenda in the

United States Supreme Court and, until recently, a weak one in Britain, may result as much from the greater availability and diversity of resources for appellate litigation in the United States as from that country's Bill of Rights and the well-known activism of its judges. What changed in Britain to produce an emergent rights agenda was neither the constitution nor the judges but the growing availability of resources and the growing aggressiveness of legal activists.

NINE

Canada: A Great Experiment in Constitutional Engineering

Canada has experienced a vibrant rights revolution since 1960: civil rights and liberties have become a sustained part of the judicial agenda, and courts, particularly the Supreme Court of Canada, have created and expanded a wide range of new rights, particularly in the areas of criminal procedure, sex discrimination, and equality more generally. Many of the new rights, moreover, have been implemented in practice—for instance, in the early nineties, Ontario dropped or stayed some forty thousand criminal charges in cases in which trial had been delayed longer than allowed by a recent Supreme Court ruling.[1]

The Canadian rights revolution is a crucial test case in my comparative study because, according to most observers, it resulted directly from the adoption in 1982 of Canada's new constitutional bill of rights, the Charter of Rights and Freedoms. Much of the rights revolution, indeed, occurred after 1982 and in matters covered in the Charter. By contrast, passage of Canada's statutory Bill of Rights in 1960 led to no sustained judicial attention to civil rights and liberties. A comparison of the negligible changes in attention to rights after passage of the statutory Bill of Rights in 1960 and the substantial judicial attention and approval to rights after passage of the Charter in 1982 commonly leads scholars to conclude that the new rights revolution resulted from constitutional engineering.[2]

There is no doubt that a great transformation, in fact, occurred. In the area of abortion, for instance, the Supreme Court of Canada reversed course in only a little over a decade. In 1976, shortly after *Roe v. Wade* in the United States, Canada's Supreme Court rejected Dr. Henry Morgentaler's claim that the Canadian law criminalizing abortion except in certain limited circumstances should be voided as a violation of the Canadian Bill of Rights.[3] But in 1988, after passage of the Charter, the Court reversed course and, in another case brought by Morgen-

taler, struck down the law as a violation of rights guaranteed by the Charter.[4] The Court accepted new rights in other areas as well.[5] Before the early eighties, the Court generally refused to exclude from criminal court any relevant evidence, such as a confession, even if obtained under great pressure and without the accused being allowed access to an attorney; but by the mid-eighties the Court began excluding evidence relatively routinely on the grounds that police procedure violated the Charter.[6] Adoption of the Charter in 1982 thus seems to mark a great watershed in Canadian judicial politics: out of the Charter, it is commonly believed, a tremendous rights revolution developed.

Matters are not so simple, however. The mere presence of a constitutional bill of rights may have little effect on the judicial agenda: before the third decade of this century, the United States Supreme Court paid little attention to civil liberties and civil rights, although the U.S. Bill of Rights had existed for nearly a century and a half. Similarly, the absence of a constitutional bill of rights has not entirely precluded judicial attention to rights claims in other countries: in Britain, as I showed earlier, a small but significant proportion of the House of Lords' judicial agenda is now devoted to rights claims.

Canada, then, presents a nearly ideal test of the various explanations for sustained judicial attention to civil rights and liberties.[7] Popular rights consciousness began growing in the sixties; in 1975 the Supreme Court gained nearly complete discretionary control over its agenda; in 1982 the Charter of Rights and Freedoms was adopted; and, in the mid-eighties, judicial liberals gained a majority on the Supreme Court. Thus, all conventionally identified conditions for a rights revolution have been met, but the last piece fell into place only after the early eighties. In this chapter I provide an overview of that cultural, constitutional, and institutional context. As I show in the next chapter, sustained judicial attention to civil rights and liberties began to develop significantly before 1982 in the context of a growing support structure for legal mobilization.

Canadian Society and Rights Consciousness

Although U.S. and Canadian societies share many surface similarities—both are relatively wealthy, well educated, ethnically diverse, and without ancient historical roots—scholars have traditionally emphasized differences between the two. In a nutshell, U.S. society is characteristically individualistic and liberal; Canadian society is characteristically communitarian and conservative.[8] As Seymour Martin Lipset, a leading proponent of the distinction, has argued, Canadian society

was created largely by conservative English Tories fleeing the American revolution and conservative Catholics fleeing the French revolution, while American society was created by a wide range of groups seeking freedom from political or religious domination.[9] In this view, then, Canadian political and legal culture is built around collective projects created in legislatures and implemented through governmental power and is relatively deferential to authority rather than ever willing to challenge that authority in the courts.[10] As I shall discuss shortly, Canadian judges until recently have indeed been relatively reticent to create new individual rights against governmental power.

Although both Canada and the United States are ethnically diverse, their diversity is manifested in very different ways. As Lipset has argued, American ethnic groups have intermixed far more freely than have Canadian groups; U.S. culture is a "melting pot," while Canadian culture is a "mosaic."[11] Perhaps most importantly, Canada is comprised of two dominant and very distinct cultural groupings, the English and the French. French Québec, distinguished not only by language and custom but by geographic area, government, and legal system, is a uniquely Canadian phenomenon. Moreover, Canada's prairie provinces have relatively large and distinct religious communities, and large geographic areas, particularly of the Canadian north, are settled primarily by aboriginals. In recent decades, immigrants from Asia, Africa, the Caribbean, and Eastern Europe have settled in increasing numbers in Canada's large cities, giving them a new multicultural atmosphere. The proportion of the population that is of neither French nor English background grew from about 8 percent in 1867 to about a third in the 1981 census.[12] Traditionally, Canada's diverse cultures coexisted in part due to the willingness of the dominant groups to allow the others authority within their own cultural spheres. Thus the French in Québec enjoyed an important degree of autonomy, and the religious sects in the western provinces largely governed themselves.[13]

Although Canada's legal culture traditionally made little room for civil liberties and rights, Canada's cultural mosaic may have created an important condition for the development in the seventies and eighties of a rights-focused legal culture. The unique position of Québec strongly influenced this development. Some French-speaking Québecers, increasingly emphasizing their distinct cultural heritage, began to credit with increasing legitimacy the idea of rights against the English majority in the country as a whole. Similarly, members of the English minority in Québec began to be concerned about *their* rights against the French majority within Québec. Additionally, in the sixties and sev-

enties, Canada's native groups became increasingly active by creating organizations and mounting demands for land and respect, and the newer immigrant groups have become more organized as well. This growing multiculturalism in Canada contributed to a heightened concern among both minority groups and liberal Canadians about human rights.[14]

At about the same time, many Canadians in general developed a growing interest in human rights. Although discussions of civil liberties began in the last years of the Great Depression and the early years of World War II, and although the government enacted the federal Bill of Rights in 1960, there was little popular interest in the issue until the mid-sixties.[15] For instance, when the government held public hearings on the proposed Bill of Rights in 1960, only nine individuals, six organizations, and the Minister of Justice testified.[16] In the sixties, however, popular interest in human rights exploded, accompanied by growing frustration with the narrowly drafted Bill of Rights and the unwillingness of courts to enforce it. In 1968, the government proposed fundamental constitutional reforms, including a constitutional charter of rights and in 1970 and 1971 the government held public hearings in forty-seven cities on the reform proposals and received over seventeen hundred briefs and interventions from a wide range of individuals and interest groups.[17]

The popular interest in human rights was not only growing but also taking on new forms. Before 1960, discussions of civil liberties occurred mainly among lawyers and some government leaders, and the issue was conceptualized largely in narrow, formal legal terms, particularly around the traditional negative liberties of freedom of speech and procedural due process. With the explosion of popular interest in the sixties, however, the issue of human rights increasingly came to be conceptualized as a matter of equality, particularly equal respect and dignity for the various non-English groups in the Canadian mosaic as well as the disabled. Even environmentalists pushed for environmental rights.[18] As Cynthia Williams observed, "the language of citizen rights had become a flexible and expansive garment for dressing up a number of citizen interests."[19]

The federal government actively tried to cultivate the new rights consciousness as a means of undercutting the centrifugal forces in Canadian federalism. The national government's concerns about Québec separatism provided some of the impetus for the inclusion of citizen rights, particularly language rights, in the 1968 constitutional reform proposals. Moreover, as I discuss in the next chapter, the federal gov-

ernment began aggressively financing various citizens' groups in the late sixties as a means for developing a national Canadian consciousness and loyalty.

By 1970, then, a vibrant and growing rights consciousness was beginning to permeate Canadian culture. As Maxwell Cohen observed in 1968,

> Human rights . . . within the past twenty years [have become] an important piece of "debating" language. . . . No one could have predicted in 1945–46 the power or semantic consequences of this kind of language, or its absorption into the wider arena of political debate in this generation, and the ease with which it has become part of the political dialogue, part of the debating experience of peoples in all parts of the world. . . . Canadians have been able to pour into these words rising standards of social, economic, political, and legal behavior, in rich variety, so that they have become a large "catchall" for social claims.[20]

The Charter of Rights and Freedoms and Legal Reform

Amidst great fanfare and a significant degree of political conflict, Canada adopted a constitutional bill of rights, the Charter of Rights and Freedoms, in 1982. Pierre Trudeau, who in the late sixties and the seventies served first as Canada's Justice Minister and then as Prime Minister, had pushed a constitutional bill of rights for a number of years after 1968 as part of a larger response to the growing threat of Québec separatism. Trudeau apparently hoped to accomplish several purposes, among them protecting English speakers from French-only laws in Québec, assuaging the fears of French speakers in other provinces, and, as Knopff and Morton have shown, encouraging the development of rights-based loyalties that would unite some Canadians across provincial boundaries.[21] After political maneuvering that is too complicated to relate here, the government succeeded in 1982 in passing a greatly revised Charter and a new procedure for amending the Constitution.[22] The final list of rights resulting from that historic struggle is about seven pages long and contains detailed language inserted to discourage the courts from adopting narrow interpretations of its guarantees.

Canadians commonly attribute enormous symbolic and practical importance to the Charter. At the most basic level, the Constitution Act 1982, which contains the Charter, marked Canada's final step of independence from Great Britain and rejection of parliamentary sovereignty. Until very recently, Canada's ties to Britain strongly influenced

Canadian government and politics and, in particular, the role of the Supreme Court. The original design of the Canadian government incorporated parliamentary sovereignty modeled after Westminster, modified by a federal structure reflecting the vast size of the country. As in England, the ruling party in the national parliament selects the prime minister and, with important qualifications, the prime minister and the ruling party face few constitutional limitations on the policies they may enact. Until passage of the Charter, the main limit to the national government's power was federalism. Unlike parliamentary sovereignty in England, where Parliament truly is the supreme law-making body in the country, in Canada the national parliament and prime minister are supreme only within the subject areas allotted to the federal government by the Constitution. The areas left to the provinces, including many areas of economic regulation, constituted important gaps in the authority of the national parliament. The Canadian system departed from the British tradition in one other way, by containing limited constitutional rights guarantees: the pre-Charter constitution explicitly protected the educational rights of religious minorities against provincial government actions and protected language rights against actions by both the national and the provincial governments.[23] Apart from those limited constitutional rights and federalism, however, Canada's national and provincial parliaments retained broad legislative powers.

The British tradition influenced Canadian government and politics in other ways as well. Canadian government remained formally subject to the British crown through several mechanisms that were only gradually abandoned. Until 1931, the Judicial Committee of the British Privy Council could invalidate any Canadian law that contradicted British law.[24] Until 1949, decisions of the Supreme Court of Canada could be appealed to the Judicial Committee of the Privy Council, whose interpretations, even of Canadian law, were final and authoritative. The Judicial Committee's invalidation in the thirties of a range of statutes attempting to regulate the economy indicates that the Committee's supremacy over Canadian law was not merely formal.[25] As Arthur Maloney, a leading constitutional lawyer and former member of Canada's Parliament observed, "I recall the optimism which existed when appeals to the Privy Council were abolished in 1949. The Supreme Court was then the highest court in the land. It was free to take a stand on Canadian issues without having to look over its shoulder."[26] Finally, until 1982, the Canadian constitution itself was a British parliamentary

statute, the British North America Act, 1867 (now the Constitution Act, 1867). Passage of the Constitution Act, 1982, then, was the last in a series of steps toward Canadian independence.

Perhaps more importantly, the Charter marked a significant departure from the Westminster style of parliamentary sovereignty by creating a number of significant, detailed limitations on the power of the provincial and national governments and by authorizing courts to strike down any legislation in conflict with those limitations. The Charter contains separate lists of rights under the headings "Fundamental Freedoms" (similar to the liberties contained in the First Amendment to the United States Constitution); "Democratic Rights" (the right to vote and limitations on the time in which the House of Commons may remain in authority without facing reelection); "Mobility Rights" (the right of citizens to leave and enter the country and to move and live in any province); "Legal Rights" (procedural due process); "Equality Rights" (equality before the law and equal protection of the law without regard to race, national or ethnic origin, color, religion, sex, age or mental or physical disability); and "Official Languages of Canada" and "Minority Language Educational Rights" (providing for the equal status of French and English). The Charter also guarantees the right to redress through the judicial system and declares that the Constitution is the supreme law of Canada and that any laws inconsistent with it are "of no force and effect." Significantly, the Charter's provisions formally authorize judicial review in cases brought by individuals.

Both critics and supporters of the Charter claim that it has produced a number of important changes in Canadian politics and society. The Supreme Court's current chief justice has called passage of the Charter "a revolution on the scale of the introduction of the metric system, the great medical discoveries of Louis Pasteur, and the invention of penicillin and the laser."[27] Political scientists have made more realistic but still sweeping claims about the Charter's effects. Knopff and Morton, for example, wrote that the Charter "is the occasion not just for new kinds of lawsuits, but also for a new form of constitutional politics. . . . In a myriad of ways, the Charter of Rights and Freedoms has truly transformed the Canadian political landscape since its enactment in 1982."[28]

The Charter is widely thought to have transformed, in particular, the Supreme Court's agenda, decisions, and workload. Most importantly, scholars argue that the Charter has increased the Court's level of attention to rights claims, its support for rights claims, its reliance on constitutional reasoning, and its exercise of judicial review.[29] Additionally,

several scholars have argued that the Charter encouraged interest groups to proliferate and to take their demands to the Supreme Court, thereby promoting growing complexity of conflict in cases.[30]

Additionally, proponents of the Charter hoped that it would provide the foundation for judicially led law reform on matters that the provincial and national governments had ignored. In particular, law reformers hoped that they could achieve neglected reforms in the areas of criminal procedure and women's rights.

Rights of Accused and Prisoners before 1982

Under the Constitution Act, 1867, authority over criminal law in Canada is left exclusively to the national government. Thus Canada's criminal law consists of the federally enacted Criminal Code, created in 1892. Additionally, the Constitution Act of 1867 grants the federal government exclusive authority over criminal procedure. Thus the Criminal Evidence Act creates the rules of evidence under which crimes are to be investigated and prosecuted. On the other hand, one of the peculiarities of the Canadian federal system is that much of the business of enforcing the federal Criminal Code is left to provincial officials and courts.

The Criminal Code, 1892 was the more conservative and authoritarian of two alternative proposals in the late 1800s for a Canadian criminal code.[31] Accordingly, reforms in the law since then generally have liberalized it, both substantively and procedurally. Capital punishment has been abolished in practice since 1962.[32] Additionally, until 1923, there was no automatic right to appeal criminal convictions. Those wishing to appeal had to obtain permission either from the trial judge who had presided over their conviction, or from both the Attorney General and the Court of Appeal.[33] Statutory amendments in 1923 created an automatic right to appeal. Not surprisingly, there were very few criminal appeals before 1923.

Apart from expanding access to legal appeals, there have been surprisingly few changes in recent decades in Canada's statutory law on criminal procedure. The federal government embarked on a plan in the early seventies, through the creation of the Law Reform Commission of Canada, to fundamentally reform both the substantive and the procedural parts of Canada's criminal law. The Commission drafted a number of reports and called for important changes in the law, particularly legislation authorizing trial judges to exclude evidence obtained in violation of due process.[34] Parliament, however, enacted none of the important proposed changes in either the substance of the criminal

law or in criminal procedure. In 1992 the government closed down the Commission for budgetary reasons. But long before 1992, advocates of reform in criminal procedure had become increasingly frustrated with the complete absence of parliamentary action. As I shall show in the next chapter, much of the pressure for the reform of criminal procedure came to be channeled through the courts.

Women's Rights before 1982

Canada, like the other countries in this study, has a history of discrimination on the basis of sex. As late as 1928, the Canadian government tried to prohibit women from being appointed to the Senate, and the Supreme Court agreed, ruling that women were not "persons" qualified to serve in the Senate within the terms of the British North America Act.[35] Henrietta Muir Edwards, the plaintiff in the 1928 case, appealed the Supreme Court's decision to the Judicial Committee of the British Privy Council, which overturned the Canadian Supreme Court's ruling and ordered her seated.[36]

In some important respects, however, Canadian law began to reflect a concern about sex discrimination earlier than the law of the other countries in this study. Between 1950 and 1962, eight of the twelve Canadian provinces passed legislation banning sex discrimination with regard to pay.[37] Additionally, in 1956, eight years before similar action by the United States Congress, the Canadian Parliament created legislation banning sex discrimination in pay (which applies to limited labor matters under federal control).[38] Moreover, the statutory Canadian Bill of Rights of 1960 prohibited discrimination on the basis of sex in the exercise of a range of other basic rights.

Nonetheless, pressure from women's-rights organizations demanding further law reform grew in the sixties, leading the government to appoint a Royal Commission on the Status of Women in 1967. The Royal Commission was charged with studying the matter and issuing a report outlining needed reforms. The report, issued in 1970, made over one hundred proposals for changes in Canadian law and policy toward women.[39] The report focused primarily on economic issues, particularly discrimination in wages, the need for greater governmental support for child care, and matrimonial property rights. The latter issue was a major concern of the Royal Commission, as provincial laws gave married women few rights to matrimonial property in the case of divorce. The Commission recommended law reform to give women and men equal property rights in such instances, and the provinces responded to varying degrees. The issue was dramatized by a

divorce case, *Murdoch v. Murdoch* (1978), in which the Supreme Court upheld an Alberta court's refusal to give the wife equal property rights to the family ranch despite her contribution to ranch work over the course of the marriage.[40] Additionally, the report recommended creation of a permanent commission to study women's issues, which resulted in the creation in 1974 of the Canadian Advisory Council on the Status of Women. The Royal Commission also recommended that the Criminal Code of 1892 be amended to legalize abortions, on the woman's request, in the first twelve weeks of pregnancy, but the Canadian government pursued no reforms on that front, prompting litigation that I will discuss in the following chapter.

There were several important waves of legislative reform on women's issues in the sixties and seventies. First, in those years the provinces and the Canadian government created human rights codes that banned discrimination on a number of grounds, among them sex. The human rights legislation also created quasi-judicial commissions that were charged with enforcing the provisions of the codes by entertaining individual complaints. Second, in 1978, 1979, and 1980 all of the provinces reformed their statutes governing marital property, to the effect that husbands and wives have nearly equal property rights upon divorce or death.[41] This had been a major focus of the Royal Commission on the Status of Women, but provincial governments had not moved ahead with legislation until prodded by the popular outrage over the *Murdoch* decision in 1978.

As the foregoing discussion indicates, the Canadian government and the provinces responded somewhat more actively to the recommendations of the Royal Commission on the Status of Women than did the Canadian government to the recommendations of the Law Reform Commission with regard to criminal procedure. In the area of women's rights, law reformers created new statutory foundations for litigation, particularly in the form of human rights codes. In the area of criminal procedure, however, little legislative reform has occurred.

The Supreme Court of Canada
Reformers working on criminal procedure and women's rights increasingly turned toward the Supreme Court for solutions after the early seventies. In retrospect, that is somewhat surprising because the Supreme Court had demonstrated a resolute conservatism and unwillingness to create new judicial policies in response to reform pressures. On the other hand, Canadian reformers saw the United States Supreme Court under the leadership of Chief Justice Earl Warren in the fifties

and sixties leading the way in law reform, and the Canadians could look back to a period of relatively important civil liberties decisions by their own Supreme Court in the fifties.

Moreover, the Canadian Supreme Court resembles the United States Supreme Court in a number of respects. It is composed of one chief justice and eight associate ("puisne") justices. Before elevation to the Supreme Court, justices typically have been leading judges on appellate courts, sometimes politicians, and sometimes law professors. The Court's jurisdiction, while including some matters under original jurisdiction, is primarily appellate. As with the United States Supreme Court, its role is generally recognized as one of law clarification rather than error correction. It decides about one hundred cases per year on the merits, through full hearing and opinion; in the cases considered on the merits, it hears oral arguments but relies heavily on arguments presented in written briefs. Decisions frequently appear as a single opinion of the majority, are written by one justice, and are often accompanied by the concurring and dissenting opinions of other justices (in some recent cases the majority has been deeply divided into several competing opinions). Additionally, the Canadian Court has the power of judicial review, although until recently it limited its conception of that power largely to matters related to federalism.

Perhaps most importantly, in 1975 the Canadian Supreme Court gained significant discretionary control of its docket. Before then, the Court was required to hear the great majority of cases appealed to it because they came under its mandatory jurisdiction. Civil cases involving more than $10,000 (before 1956, $2,000) and capital criminal cases were appealable as a matter of right. By the early seventies appeals by right began overwhelming the Court and, to remedy the problem, Parliament passed a revision of the Supreme Court Act that gave to the Court much greater discretion over its docket by eliminating appeals by right in civil cases.[42] Since 1975, most appeals have come to the Court as applications for leave to appeal, which the Court has full discretion to accept or reject, in the same way that the United States Supreme Court has discretion over petitions for writ of certiorari. The Supreme Court of Canada is still required to hear any criminal appeal on a matter of law where the court from which the appeal arises has overturned an acquittal or has been divided. Nonetheless, the 1975 legislation significantly expanded the Court's discretionary control over its docket. Supporters of the change, including Chief Justice Bora Laskin, believed that it would allow the Supreme Court to focus on matters of public importance and would increase the stature of the

Court as a national policy-making institution.[43] In 1974 and 1975 the number of appeals as of right began to decline and the number of leave-to-appeal applications began to increase. While the number of leave petitions grew, the Supreme Court limited the number of cases decided by full opinion to under about 120 per year. The result was as planned: the Court could pick from among a range of cases coming to it those that it regarded as the most important. Thus 1975 marked a significant turning point in the Canadian Supreme Court's institutional history.

The U.S. and Canadian Courts, however, differ in some significant ways. The Canadian Supreme Court, unlike the United States Supreme Court, routinely renders advisory opinions on some of the most important political issues of the day, in so-called "reference cases." The reference procedure might appear to predispose the Canadian Supreme Court to take on an active law-making role. The Canadian Supreme Court also differs from its counterpart in the United States in several ways that may have contributed to a hesitancy to develop an activist jurisprudence. The total number of cases filed in the Supreme Court is relatively small, under six hundred per year, compared to the roughly seven thousand cases now filed in the United States Supreme Court annually. While clerks assist the Canadian justices, their role appears to be much less important than in the U.S. Court, where they appear to keep the justices abreast of innovative approaches in the law schools. Most importantly, until 1982 the Canadian Supreme Court rested on only a statutory foundation and, perhaps related to that fact, its justices held a relatively narrow conception of their role in the law-making process.[44]

For whatever reason, until the mid-eighties the justices of the Supreme Court remained far more conservative than law reformers had hoped. Although the Supreme Court in the fifties, in the absence of a bill of rights, handed down a number of landmark decisions on civil liberties, those decisions rested on very narrow grounds related to the jurisdiction of provincial governments within the federal system.[45] After the fifties, the most important test of the Canadian Supreme Court's willingness to engage in law reform occurred in a series of cases brought under the Canadian Bill of Rights. Although the drafters of the Canadian Bill of Rights apparently believed that it provided the authority for courts to nullify legislation,[46] the Supreme Court interpreted the Bill of Rights very narrowly in virtually every case that raised the issue. In the Court's first decision under the Bill of Rights, *Robertson and Rosetanni v. The Queen* (1963), the Court (over one dissent) developed the controversial position that the document created no

new rights but only reemphasized those already existing under Canadian law.[47] After that key decision the Court consistently declined to use the Bill of Rights to strike down legislation. By the mid-sixties, civil liberties advocates were beginning to express extreme disappointment that the Court's support for civil liberties had even diminished after passage of the Bill of Rights. As one observer lamented, "[the] first flowering of truly independent and supreme judicial power seems to have wilted. The sixties have . . . witnessed the onset of reaction."[48] The only exception to that apparent judicial hostility to rights claims was *The Queen v. Drybones* (1970), in which the Court struck down, as racially discriminatory, parts of the Indian Act that created a rule regarding public drunkenness applicable only to Indians, and that subjected Indians to harsher penalties than non-Indians for liquor violations.[49] That decision followed a period of vigorous criticism of the Supreme Court for its restrictive interpretations of the Bill of Rights. Nonetheless, after *Drybones* the Court did not again use the Bill of Rights to uphold a rights claim until after 1982.[50]

The Court's conservative rulings reflected its ideological makeup. Judicial conservatives clearly dominated the Canadian Supreme Court before the mid-eighties and judicial liberals gained a majority on the Court only after 1985. Table 9.1 illustrates the changing composition of the Court by characterizing the justices as liberal or conservative in their attitudes toward the new individual rights claims. Before 1982 there were three leading proponents of an expanded civil liberties agenda on the Supreme Court—Ivan Rand (serving from 1943 to 1959), Emmett Hall (serving from 1962 to 1973), and Bora Laskin (serving from 1970 to 1973 as associate justice, and from 1973 to 1984 as chief justice). Nonetheless, no majority of justices consistently supported the expansion of judicial policy making on civil liberties and civil rights until the late eighties.

On the other hand, the Supreme Court began tentatively liberalizing judicial doctrines in other areas in the late seventies. In particular, the Court significantly expanded standing to sue, a key factor influencing the openness of the courts to new issues. The most important developments occurred before 1982 in a series of cases commonly called the "standing trilogy."[51] In each, a plaintiff lacking the traditional characteristics for standing to challenge the validity of a law—personal or economic injury related to implementation of the law—attempted to raise a constitutional challenge. In each, the Supreme Court granted standing, thus expanding the ability of citizens to mount general attacks on legislation that did not directly affect them. In *Minister of Jus-*

Table 9.1 The Supreme Court of Canada

1960	1965	1970	1975	1980	1985	1990
−*Kervin*	−*Taschereau*	−*Fauteaux*	+*Laskin*	+*Laskin*	+*Dickson*	+*Dickson*/
−Abbott	−Abbott	−Abbott	−Beetz	−Beetz	−Beetz	+*Lamer*
+Cartwright[1]	+Cartwright	+Hall	+Dickson	−Chouinard	−Chouinard	−Cory
−Fauteaux	−Fauteaux	−Judson	−Grandpre	+Dickson	−Estey	−Gonthier
−Judson	+Hall	−Laskin	−Judson	−Estey[2]	−LaForest	−LaForest
+Locke	−Judson	−Martland	−Martland	−Lamer	+Lamer	+/− L'Heureux-Dubé[3]
−Martland	−Martland	−Pigeon	−Pigeon	−Martland	−Le Dain	+McLachlin
−Ritchie	−Ritchie	−Ritchie	−Ritchie	−McIntyre	−McIntyre	+/− Sopinka[4]
	+Spence	+Spence	+Spence	−Pigeon	+Wilson	−Stevenson
				−Ritchie		+Wilson

Sources: Bushnell, "Leave to Appeal Applications"; Heard, "Charter"; Morton, Russell, and Riddell, "Descriptive Analysis"; and Tate and Sittiwong, "Decision Making."

Notes: Chief justices are italicized at the top of each column; (+) indicates liberalism on civil liberties and rights, (−) indicates conservatism on civil liberties and rights.

[1]Bushnell places Cartwright in the group of justices who were opposed to the use of fundamental rights in judicial review; see Bushnell, *Captive Court*, 317. Nonetheless, Tate and Sittiwong report a high civil liberties score for Cartwright; see "Decision Making." I follow Tate and Sittiwong here.

[2]According to Bushnell (*Captive Court*, 487–88), Estey opposed the growing rights-based activism of the Supreme Court after 1985, publicly stating so upon resigning in 1988.

[3]L'Heureux-Dubé tends to support Charter claims on equality rights but tends to oppose Charter claims on legal rights (of criminally accused); see Morton, Russell, and Riddell, "Canadian Charter."

[4]Sopinka tends to support Charter claims on legal rights (of the criminally accused) but tends to oppose Charter claims on equality; see Morton, Russell, and Riddell, "Canadian Charter."

tice of Canada v. Borowski, the last of the three cases, Justice Martland summarized the new standing test that was derived in part from the earlier cases:

> I interpret these cases as deciding that to establish status as a plaintiff in a suit seeking a declaration that legislation is invalid, if there is a serious issue as to its invalidity, a person need only to show that he is affected by it directly *or that he has a genuine interest as a citizen in the validity of the legislation and that there is no other reasonable and effective manner in which the issue may be brought before the Court.*[52]

The standing trilogy concerned constitutional challenges; the Supreme Court extended its liberal standing doctrine to nonconstitutional interpretation in *Finlay v. Minister of Finance of Canada*.[53] With those changes, the Canadian Supreme Court's standing doctrine became "among the most liberal" in the world.[54] It is clearly more liberal than the United States Supreme Court's policy on standing, which limits standing to parties suffering an actual injury even when the result is that a plausibly unconstitutional law goes unchallenged.[55] Significantly, the key developments in Canadian standing doctrine occurred well before passage of the Charter in 1982, and the only important post-1982 innovation extended the earlier developments to *nonconstitutional* matters, which are beyond the purview of the Charter.

Conclusion

Canada's adoption in 1982 of the Charter of Rights and Freedoms seems to overshadow nearly every other influence on the Canadian Supreme Court's agenda. For most observers, the Charter—indeed the Charter alone—transformed Canadian politics in a number of ways. It introduced into Canada a previously foreign fascination with individual rights; it generated a growing tide of individual rights litigation; and it created a new willingness among judges to act creatively in the name of rights. If the Charter's influence is so substantial, and is so independent of any other influence, we should find that the Supreme Court's agenda changed abruptly *after* 1982 and that no significant changes in the agenda occurred before that year.

In the next chapter I show that most observers have overestimated the Charter's independent influence on Canadian judicial politics and that we must consider, in addition, the influence of the support structure for legal mobilization, which began to grow two decades before 1982.

TEN

Canada's Dramatic Rights Revolution

and Its Sources

The source for Canada's dramatic rights revolution, it is commonly believed, is the Canadian Charter of Rights and Freedoms. In addition to creating a host of new constitutional rights, the Charter authorized judges to overturn administrative practices *and laws* that are found to be inconsistent with its principles. Moreover, the Canadian Supreme Court has responded: the Court's agenda is now dominated by rights cases, and the Court has developed a rich body of law that applies and expands the rights promised by the Charter. However, many of the changes commonly attributed to the Charter in fact began many years before its passage in 1982; the development of a vibrant support structure for legal mobilization helps to explain the origins of the Canadian rights revolution in the seventies, the passage and nature of the Charter itself, and the strength of the rights revolution in the eighties.

Although Canadian observers nearly universally attribute profound effects to the Charter, F. L. Morton and Rainer Knopff have recently argued that the effects often attributed to the Charter alone are also the result of active political pressure by the "Court Party," an informal coalition of rights-advocacy groups, lawyers, and judges.[1] As Morton has written, "the *Charter* itself is not so much the cause of the revolution as the means through which it is carried out."[2] My analysis here builds on their research but it differs in important ways; my analysis tracks pre-1982 changes in the judicial agenda more fully and argues that the development of the support structure constitutes a democratization of access to the Supreme Court.

The Canadian Rights Revolution
Understanding the timing and nature of key developments in the Canadian rights revolution helps to clarify the sources of that revolution. I rely on a variety of measures, which generally tell much the same story: significant changes in the Canadian Supreme Court's agenda

Figure 10.1   Issue Agenda of the Canadian Supreme Court

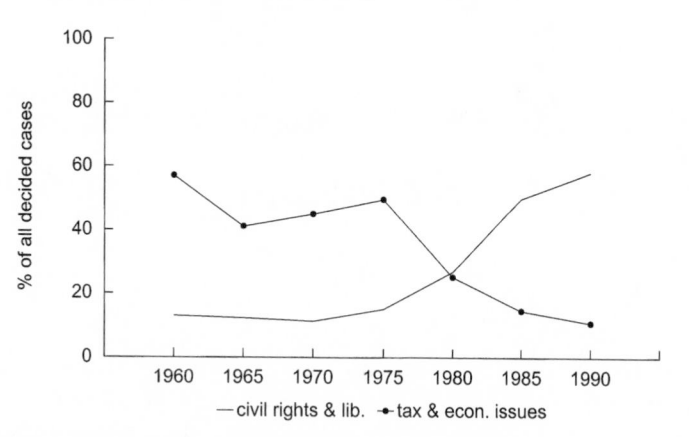

N = 1960, 77; 1965, 73; 1970, 80; 1975, 119; 1980, 119; 1985, 68; 1990, 110.

(with some exceptions) began in the early seventies and continued at rates that were largely unaffected by adoption of the Charter in 1982.

Overview

First, the Supreme Court's issue agenda changed dramatically between 1960 and 1990 (fig. 10.1). The proportion of the agenda devoted to rights claims grew, and the proportion devoted to tax cases and ordinary economic disputes declined.[3] Both developments clearly began to occur before adoption of the Charter in 1982. Rights cases constituted 13 percent or less of the Court's agenda before 1975 and about 60 percent by 1990. However, the 86 percent growth rate that occurred between 1980 and 1985 was only marginally faster than the 78 percent growth rate that occurred between 1975 and 1980. Similarly, the proportion of the Court's agenda devoted to tax and ordinary economic issues began to decline abruptly after 1975 but before adoption of the Charter in 1982.[4]

Second, the Canadian Supreme Court's exercise of judicial review also increased between 1960 and 1990, but again, much of the growth preceded passage of the Charter. Figure 10.2 presents the number of cases in which the Court *considered whether* to overturn a law as well as the number of cases in which it *did* overturn a law. The largest increase in the number of decisions striking down a law occurred between 1975 (one case) and 1980 (five cases). After 1980, although the number of laws struck down increased, the rate of growth leveled off.[5] The number of cases in which litigants asked the Court to exercise judicial review, on the other hand, grew significantly after passage of the Charter.

Figure 10.2   Exercise of Judicial Review by the Canadian Supreme Court

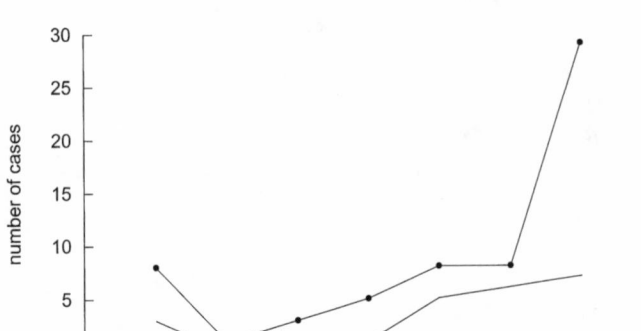

—law overturned —•plea to overturn

Although the growth apparently originated in the late sixties or early seventies, between 1985 and 1990 the number of requests for judicial review increased dramatically. In 1985 the Court decided eight cases centering on a request for the exercise of judicial review; in 1990 it decided almost thirty such cases.

It is also telling to compare the number of Charter cases on the agenda with the number of non-Charter rights cases. Even after passage of the Charter, the proportion of cases involving rights claims *not* founded on that document continued to expand (fig. 10.3). There was a substantial increase in non-Charter rights cases in 1985 over 1980; in fact, a surprisingly small proportion of the cases in 1985 were decided on Charter grounds, probably in part because of the time lag that would be involved in bringing Charter cases through several levels of the judicial system. By 1990, of course, the Charter had become the main foundation for rights decisions by the Supreme Court. But it is clear that, for much of the period before the late eighties, rights claims developed without reliance on the Charter.

Similarly, the proportion of cases decided on "higher law" grounds—including non-Charter constitutional law (dealing mainly with federalism, or the relationship between the provincial and federal governments), the 1960 Bill of Rights, and the common-law standard of natural justice—began to increase before 1982, although part of that growth reflects an increase in the number of federalism cases decided by the Supreme Court.[6] After 1982 the proportion of higher-law cases in each of the non-Charter categories declined as the proportion of cases involving the Charter increased. By 1990 Charter cases began to replace non-Charter cases on the agenda, although even in 1990 a

Figure 10.3   Non–Charter Rights Decisions of the Canadian Supreme Court

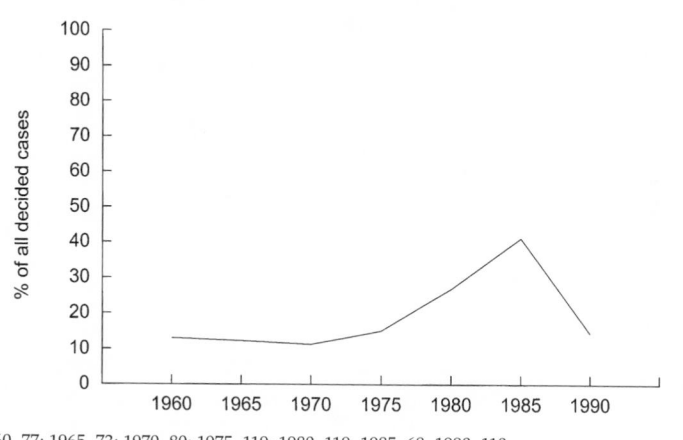

N = 1960, 77; 1965, 73; 1970, 80; 1975, 119; 1980, 119; 1985, 68; 1990, 110.

Figure 10.4   Higher-Law Foundations for Decisions of the Canadian Supreme Court

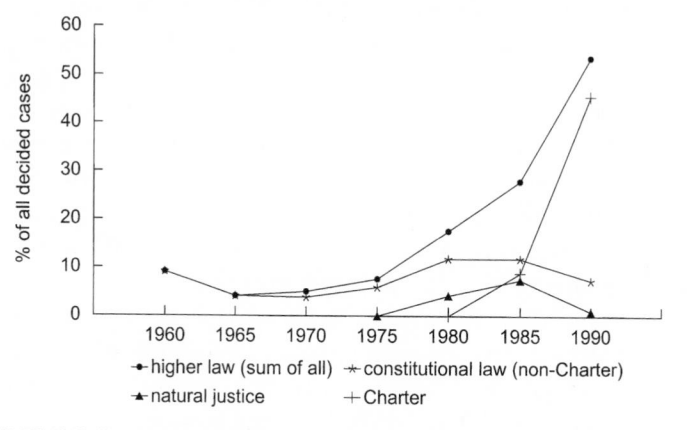

N = 1960, 77; 1965, 73; 1970, 80; 1975, 119; 1980, 119; 1985, 68; 1990, 110.

significant portion of higher-law cases were not based on the Charter (fig. 10.4).

It is also useful to examine the proportion of cases brought by individuals, who often must rely on external sources of support to reach the Supreme Court. Over the period of the study, the presence of individuals has increased and the presence of businesses has decreased (fig. 10.5). Significantly, the growing presence of individual litigants began before passage of the Charter in 1982 and the rate of growth did not increase after passage of the Charter.

The incidence of third-party intervention in Supreme Court cases also grew after 1960 (fig. 10.6). Third-party intervention in Canada is

Figure 10.5   Individuals and Businesses vs. Governmental Parties in the Canadian
Supreme Court

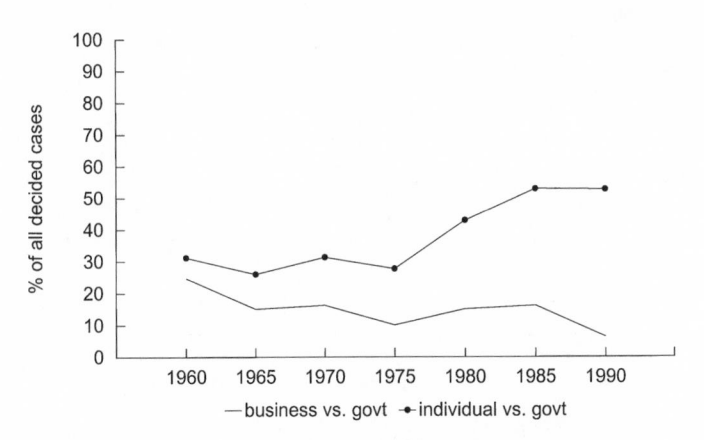

$N = $ 1960, 77; 1965, 73; 1970, 80; 1975, 119; 1980, 119; 1985, 68; 1990, 110.

analogous to amicus curiae participation in the United States, and its
extent is often taken as an indicator of the degree to which the Supreme
Court has become politicized. Although it is commonly believed that
third-party interventions began to increase only after passage of the
Charter in 1982, Ian Brodie found that the increase began before passage of the Charter.[7] My data, too, clearly indicate that trends in intervention by third parties began before passage of the Charter. Some
growth is apparent as early as 1975, and substantial changes are un-
deniable by 1980. The Court can reject petitions to intervene, and it
tended to rebuff interest groups' attempts at intervention until the
mid-eighties, when it opened the process in response to increasing
pressure from rights-advocacy groups.[8]

The total number of cases brought to the Court also grew significantly over the period of this study, but almost all of the growth occurred before 1982 (fig. 10.7). The Court's docket is composed of two
broad categories, leave-to-appeal applications (over which the justices
have complete discretion) and appeals by right (which the Court theo-
retically must hear). As noted in the previous chapter, a statutory
change in the Supreme Court's jurisdiction in 1975 shifted much of the
Court's docket to the discretionary category. As a result, the number of
leave applications filed per year began to grow around 1975, and the
number of appeals began to drop. The drop in appeals, however, did
not entirely compensate for increases in the number of leave applications, and so the total number of cases coming to the Court rose substantially between the mid-seventies and early eighties. The period of
significant growth ended in the early eighties, before passage of the

Figure 10.6   Third-Party Intervenors in the Canadian Supreme Court

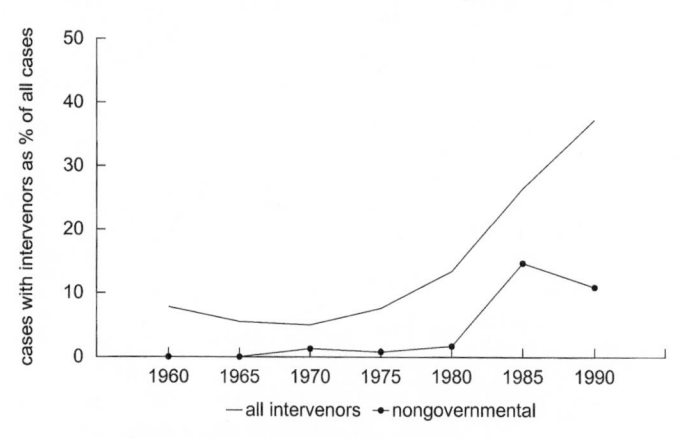

N = 1960, 77; 1965, 73; 1970, 80; 1975, 119; 1980, 119; 1985, 68; 1990, 110.

Figure 10.7   Number of Cases Filed with the Canadian Supreme Court

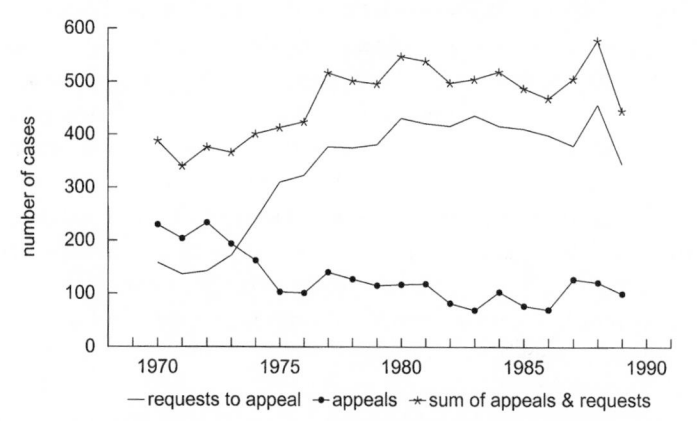

Source: Calculated from Bushnell, "Leave to Appeal Applications" (1982 and 1986); and *Bulletins of the Supreme Court of Canada.*

Charter, and that event produced no new spurt in the number of cases brought to the Court.[9] This evidence strongly suggests that patterns in appellate litigation have reflected influences other than mere passage of the Charter.

The Criminal Procedure Agenda

As with changes in the aggregate agenda, changes in the agenda on criminal procedure had their roots before passage of the Charter. Between 1960 and 1990, the proportion of the Court's agenda devoted to procedural rights claims of criminal defendants or prisoners grew

Figure 10.8   Criminal Procedure and Prisoner Rights Agenda of the Canadian
Supreme Court

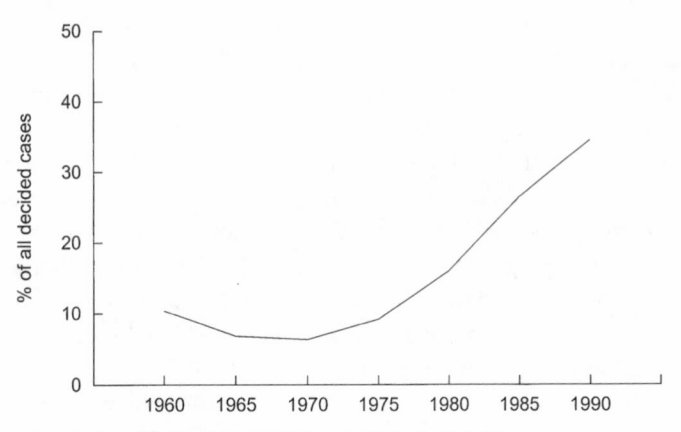

N = 1960, 77; 1965, 73; 1970, 80; 1975, 119; 1980, 119; 1985, 68; 1990, 110.

from roughly 10 percent to 33 percent. Most of the cases involved
rights guaranteed by the new Charter of Rights. Claims by criminal
defendants formed the bulk of the Court's rights agenda in the mid-
seventies, when the size of the rights agenda began to grow.[10] The pace
of growth was rapid, and virtually all of the growth occurred after
1975 (fig. 10.8).

The Court's criminal rights agenda changed substantively as well as
quantitatively. By the late eighties, as Robert Harvie and Hamar Foster
have observed, the Canadian Supreme Court had produced a revolution in criminal procedure case law comparable to that wrought by the
Warren Court in the United States.[11] In cases involving the right to
counsel, the privilege against self-incrimination, the right against unreasonable search and seizure, the use in criminal proceedings of prior
testimony, and the exclusion of evidence from criminal proceedings,
the Court has interpreted the Charter rights of the criminal suspect
broadly.[12] By the mid-eighties, the Court's expansive interpretation of
the criminal procedure rights contained in the Charter provided a
strong incentive for defendants to mount appeals to the Supreme
Court.

Although the Charter provided a new foundation for criminal procedure litigation, some of the document's innovations had precedents
in earlier statutes or judicial decisions. Before the Charter there were
statutory rights to have counsel, to be free of improper search and
seizure, to be informed of charges, and to have speedy trials; the Charter strengthened each. There was no statutory basis for excluding rele-

vant evidence from criminal proceedings, but the process of creating such a right had begun in *Rothman v. The Queen* in 1981, when Justice Antonio Lamer argued in a concurring opinion that evidence should be excluded from trial if the manner in which it was obtained would "shock" the community and diminish respect for the administration of justice.[13] The Charter's exclusionary rule establishes a right that is far broader than that early suggestion—it gives judges authority to exclude evidence "obtained in a manner that infringed or denied any rights or freedoms guaranteed by this Charter" if admitting such evidence would "bring the administration of justice into disrepute."[14] Nevertheless, it is clear from Justice Lamer's 1981 concurrence that the new judicial attitude preceded adoption of the Charter and thus was not a creation of that document alone.

Consistent judicial support for criminal procedure claims, however, did not occur early enough to explain the growth in the criminal procedure agenda that occurred in the mid-seventies. Although Bora Laskin, a liberal activist, became chief justice in 1974 and could count on the support of at least two other justices (see table 9.1), until the mid-eighties the Court as a whole remained largely unfriendly to rights claims advanced by criminal defendants. Vigorous dissents by Laskin and others, however, may have suggested to criminal lawyers that the Court might, in the future, become more receptive to their claims.[15]

In the end, then, both the Charter and judicial support for expanded criminal procedure rights undoubtedly opened new possibilities for criminal defendants and their lawyers. But the independent influence of either the Charter or the judges should not be exaggerated. The Court's new liberalism on criminal procedure began emerging *before* adoption of the Charter. But the growth of a judicial agenda on criminal procedure began emerging *before* the Court's new liberalism. As I explore in more detail shortly, the rights revolution in criminal procedure is understandable only if we look not only at the Charter and the judges but also at the support structure for legal mobilization.

The Women's-Rights Agenda

Changes in the agenda with respect to women's-rights claims occurred later than the changes related to criminal procedure claims. As late as 1970, the Canadian Supreme Court had decided only one important case hinging on women's rights;[16] by 1990, however, it was not uncommon for scholars to characterize women's rights as the leading component of the Court's equality rights agenda and the leading example of the politicization of the judicial process. Equality rights form the sym-

bolic core of the new Charter, creating what Alan Cairns calls the "Charter Canadians"—the groups, among them women, identified for constitutional protection in the Charter's equality guarantees.[17] Similarly, Knopff and Morton have called the Court's post-Charter abortion rights cases the paradigmatic example of the growing role of interest groups in litigation.[18]

The substance of the Supreme Court's decisions indeed changed substantially between the seventies and the eighties. Before passage of the Charter, the Supreme Court consistently refused to support women's-rights claims. In the mid-seventies, Jeanette Lavell and Yvonne Bedard, two status Indians (individuals having legal status as Indians under federal treaties or laws), challenged a provision of the federal Indian Act that allowed tribes to remove Indian women but not Indian men from their tribal status list if they married non-status Indians. The Federal Court of Appeal in Lavell's case struck down the challenged portion of the law on the grounds that it violated the equality clause of the Canadian Bill of Rights, but the Supreme Court, in a 5–4 decision in the combined *Lavell-Bedard* case, upheld the law.[19] In the second important women's-rights case under the Bill of Rights in the seventies, *Bliss v. Attorney-General of Canada*, Stella Bliss challenged a provision of the Unemployment Insurance Act that denied unemployment benefits to pregnant women during the final eight weeks of pregnancy and first six weeks after birth. Both the Federal Court of Appeal and the Supreme Court unanimously upheld the law.[20] Finally, in *Murdoch v. Murdoch*, the Supreme Court refused to overturn a trial court's ruling that a woman divorcing her husband after severe beatings was not entitled to half of the value of the couple's ranch, even though she had worked side by side with her husband to develop the ranch.[21]

In the eighties, by contrast, the Supreme Court' decisions were substantially more supportive of women's rights.[22] The Court struck down laws in key cases where the women's movement opposed the laws. For instance, the Court rejected the law criminalizing abortion (although on relatively narrow procedural grounds).[23] Similarly, the Supreme Court upheld laws against vigorous challenge in key cases where the most powerful parts of the women's movement favored the laws. For instance, the Court upheld federal censorship of some types of pornography.[24] Particularly since the Court's landmark decision in *Andrews v. Law Society of British Columbia* (1989), the judicial interpretation of the Charter's right to equality appears to have shifted from a general concern about unequal treatment of *any* individual compared with another "similarly situated" individual to a concern specifically about

classification based on immutable characteristics, especially sex and race.[25]

Nonetheless, focusing only on the Charter's formal provisions and on the Supreme Court's substantive decisions leads to a distorted image of the Court's agenda. In spite of the symbolic first place of women's rights in the Charter, women's-rights cases were never a significant *quantitative* part of the agenda, even after 1982. In my sample, no cases raised women's-rights claims in 1985, and only 3 percent of the Court's decisions involved such claims in 1990.

Further, women appear as litigants in *any* kind of case only rarely. Even after passage of the Charter, women appeared as individual participants in only 12 percent of all decided cases in 1985 and only 14 percent of decided cases in 1990. The disparity partly reflects the strong presence of criminal cases, most of which involve male defendants. Yet that is not a complete explanation, as criminal cases constitute about half of all decided cases. Thus women, along with women's-rights claims, remain comparatively underrepresented in the Supreme Court of Canada.

The rights revolution in the Canadian Supreme Court thus began to grow in the seventies and continued to strengthen in the eighties. The criminal procedure component of that agenda, in particular, grew rapidly after the early seventies. The women's-rights component, although developing for the first time in the eighties, remains relatively small. These patterns are best understood as a reflection of Canada's support structure for legal mobilization.

The Impact of the Support Structure for Legal Mobilization

The Support Structure's Main Components

RIGHTS-ADVOCACY ORGANIZATIONS. Rights-advocacy organizations appeared on the Canadian scene in a relatively short space of time, roughly between the late sixties and the early eighties. Before 1970, business and agricultural groups dominated the Canadian interest-group system.[26] After that year the number of nonproducer advocacy organizations, and particularly rights-advocacy organizations, virtually exploded.[27] The development partly reflected the growth of rights consciousness in Canadian society, which was surveyed in the previous chapter, but it also reflected the growing availability of resources for rights-advocacy organizing.

Civil liberties groups in particular grew in numbers, prominence, and strength after the late sixties. The two principal civil liberties or-

ganizations, the British Columbia Civil Liberties Association and the Canadian Civil Liberties Association, were founded in 1962 and 1964, respectively, but only became relatively active after about 1970. Between 1970 and 1985, a number of regional civil liberties organizations also formed, among them the Civil Liberties Association, National Capitol Region, in 1968; the Manitoba Association for Rights and Liberties in 1970; the St. John Charter Rights and Civil Liberties Association in 1971; the Vancouver Island Human Rights Coalition in 1982; and the Victoria Civil Liberties Association in 1983.

Civil rights groups also grew in numbers and strength after the late sixties. In the area of women's rights, major organizations were formed in 1972, 1973, 1974, and 1985. The major aboriginal rights organizations also formed in the late sixties and early seventies. Of 239 major aboriginal political organizations existing in 1993, forty-three were formed in the sixties, ninety-two in the seventies, and twenty-eight in the eighties.[28] The Advocacy Resource Centre for the Handicapped, a leading organization advocating expanded rights for the handicapped, was formed in 1980.

The leading rights-advocacy groups have served as the focal points for growing networks of sympathetic lawyers and organizers, and they have supported rights-advocacy litigation. For instance, during the seventies both the British Columbia Civil Liberties Association and the Canadian Civil Liberties Association (CCLA) developed networks of sympathetic lawyers who agreed to take cases without fee or for reduced fees and who apparently pooled their legal expertise to push cases through the courts.[29] Their efforts concentrated on battling abuses of power by public authorities. During the late seventies, the CCLA lawyers worked on a campaign against raids of political organizations by the Royal Canadian Mounted Police; on a court challenge to police wiretapping; against a criminal prosecution of a gay newspaper; on a court challenge to a criminal code provision authorizing the holding of the insane "at the pleasure" of provincial governments; and on a court challenge regarding search warrants.[30] In addition to participating in cases challenging law enforcement practices, CCLA lawyers were also involved in a range of cases in other areas of the law.

The timing of the CCLA's case-support efforts is significant for the questions animating this study: did the leading rights-advocacy organization respond either to passage of the Charter in 1982 or to the growing liberalism of the justices in the eighties? In fact, the level of CCLA activity in the Supreme Court remained largely unchanged by those developments. In the eight years before 1982, the CCLA intervened in

five Supreme Court cases, while in the eight years following 1982, it intervened in six Supreme Court cases.[31] On the other hand, the organization's efforts seem to have become more systematic after passage of the Charter.

Rights-advocacy organizations, therefore, provided support for development of the rights revolution in the Supreme Court of Canada, but their efforts began long *before* passage of the Charter. The organizations provided financial support and helped to coordinate legal campaigns; they encouraged the addition of rights claims to cases that otherwise would have focused on more mundane matters; and they provided the organizational core for a broader growth in networks of lawyers and of communication and support for rights litigation in general.

As this discussion has suggested, Canadian rights-advocacy organizations are primarily liberal or egalitarian in orientation. To a significant extent this reflects deliberate policies by the national government to cultivate liberal advocacy organizations. The Canadian Department of the Secretary of State, under the direction of Trudeau's liberal government in the late sixties, developed an aggressive program to finance citizens' advocacy organizations focusing on such issues as women's rights, language rights, and multiculturalism.[32] Nonetheless, several conservative organizations support litigation, among them the National Citizens' Coalition and REAL Women, but they have enjoyed much less success than liberal groups because, as Morton and Knopff observe, "they are decidedly swimming against the ideological tide."[33]

GOVERNMENT SOURCES OF FINANCING.   The national and provincial governments have developed a variety of programs that finance rights litigation and advocacy. The Canadian legal aid programs are a mixture of "judicare" plans, in which defendants receive certificates of aid that are used to retain any lawyer of the defendant's choice, and plans modeled on the neighborhood legal services idea from the United States. In the decade after 1965, in a major policy revolution, the Canadian provinces created legal aid programs that finance both civil and criminal cases. The rapidity of the development cannot be overstated. Ontario organized an official legal aid program in 1966; by 1976 all the provinces had created legal aid programs (see table 10.1). The federal government contributed to the rapid growth by helping to subsidize the new programs.[34]

Spending on court cases by the new legal aid programs increased dramatically in the seventies, from around $14 million in 1970–71 to

Table 10.1   Provincial Legal Aid Plans

Province	Incorporation of Organization
Ontario	1966
British Columbia	1970
Northwest Territories	1971
Nova Scotia	1971
Manitoba	1972
New Brunswick	1972
Alberta	1973
Québec	1973
Newfoundland	1973
Saskatchewan	1974
Yukon Territories	1975
Prince Edward Island	1973 (criminal)*
	1979 (some civil)*

Source: National Legal Aid Research Centre, *Justice Information Report.*
*Prince Edward Island organized, but did not formally incorporate, a legal aid program on these dates.

Figure 10.9   Legal Aid Expenditures (Ontario)

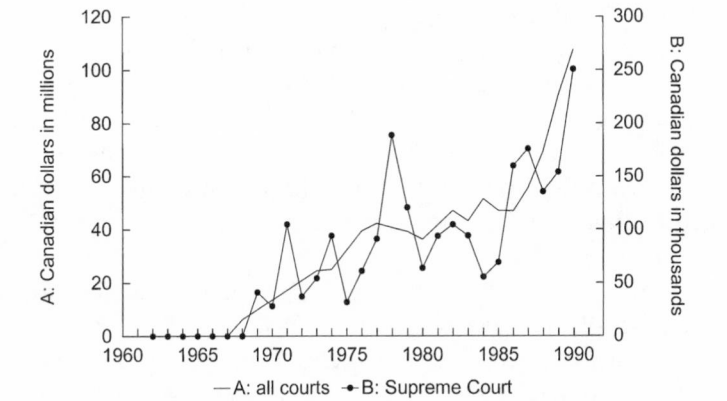

—A: all courts ⟶B: Supreme Court

Source: Ontario Legal Aid Plan Annual Reports, adjusted for inflation.

over $70 million just after the middle of that decade.[35] The level of funding by the Ontario Legal Aid Program, the oldest and largest of the provincial programs, illustrates that growth (fig. 10.9). The level of funding grew between 1970 and 1977, and then grew rapidly again in the late eighties.[36]

The Court Challenges Program, a set of funds created specifically for financing test cases on language rights and equality rights, is another government-sponsored legal aid program that began before passage of the Charter. The Program was established in 1978 to finance court

cases on language rights protected under the Constitution Act 1867; since then, it has "supported almost every major language law case at the [Supreme] Court."[37] The government added an equality rights component to the Program in 1985 to finance cases under the equality provisions in the Charter of Rights. Between 1985 and 1992, the year of the Program's temporary elimination by Brian Mulroney's government, the equality component of the Program provided financing for 178 court cases at all levels of the system, including twenty-four cases in the Supreme Court.[38] Trends in Court Challenges funding and case support across time are not easily identified, although it is clear that the language component of the program supported some cases before passage of the Charter.[39] It is also clear, however, that the creation of the equality component of the program in 1985 resulted directly from the desire of interest groups and government officials to implement the equality rights in the Charter.[40] Conservative groups have criticized the Court Challenges Program for supporting only liberal causes, and the government briefly eliminated the Program's financing from 1992–1994.

The national government's Department of Indian Affairs and Northern Development (DIAND) also began sponsoring test-case litigation before adoption of the Charter. DIAND began funding court cases in 1965, but the agency significantly increased its funding for litigation in the late seventies, financing about twenty-five test cases before 1982.[41] DIAND has provided financial support for most of the aboriginal rights cases that have reached the Canadian Supreme Court.[42]

THE LEGAL PROFESSION. Several highly significant changes in the legal profession have occurred since 1945, with the most important developments occurring between the mid-sixties and the early eighties. First, Canada's system of legal education changed dramatically as the importance and autonomy of law schools increased. In Canada, as in the United States, training for the practice of law shifted from apprenticeship, a system in which legal education is dominated by the relatively conservative interests of the practicing bar, to law schools. Ten of Canada's twenty law schools were created after World War II, and the number of full-time law professors increased dramatically, almost doubling between 1971 and 1982 alone.[43] As the importance and autonomy of the law schools increased, legal training increasingly emphasized theoretical and constitutional issues.[44] By 1982, the year of the Charter's adoption, Canadian law professors were remarkably young (the median age was 38) and generally supportive of a growing

Figure 10.10   The Canadian Lawyer Population

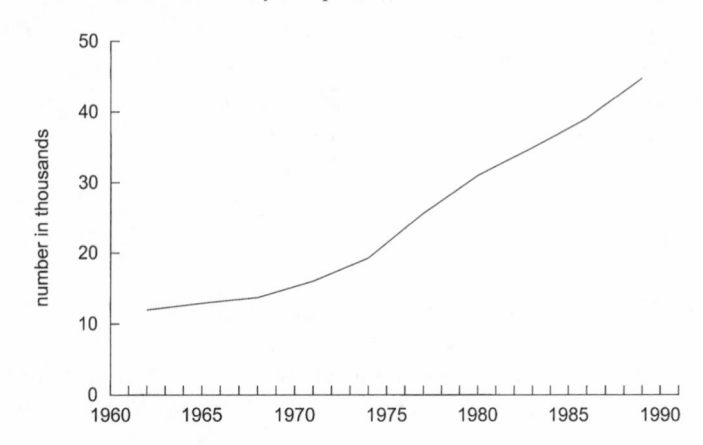

Source: Stager and Arthurs, *Lawyers in Canada,* 146.

policy-making role for the judiciary on civil liberties and civil rights.[45] For instance, in a survey conducted in 1982–83, 18 percent of law professors reported working for a law reform commission and 25 percent reported working for a public interest or community group.[46]

The growth of law schools also provided an institutional base for critical scholarship and advocacy on constitutional issues. Bora Laskin, chief justice of the Supreme Court from 1973–1984, led the push in the fifties and sixties for scholarly critique and advocacy. In 1951 he attributed the Supreme Court's conservatism to "the conservative tradition of the Canadian legal profession . . . [and] the late development of university law schools."[47] By the eighties, by contrast, many in the growing cohort of law school professors actively pursued advocacy scholarship favoring liberal judicial interpretation of civil rights and liberties.[48]

Additionally, in the decade after 1970, Canada's lawyer population grew dramatically and began to diversify, and lawyers increasingly engaged in advocacy activities. The most significant growth of the Canadian lawyer population occurred between 1971 and 1981, when the number more than doubled.[49] As figure 10.10 illustrates, the lawyer population grew at a faster pace before 1981 than after that year; thus adoption of the Charter induced no unprecedented growth in the number of lawyers.

In the seventies the Canadian legal profession also began to diversify in terms of ethnic origin and sex. In 1961, almost 80 percent of all Canadian lawyers were from either British or French backgrounds; by 1971, that proportion had declined to 74 percent; and by 1981 it had

dropped to 68 percent.[50] The proportion of lawyers from British ethnic origins, in particular, declined from over 56 percent in 1961 to under 45 percent in 1981. Ethnic minorities constituted only about a fifth of the total number of lawyers in 1961, but they constituted almost a third of the total by 1981. The rate of growth in the representation of women in the legal profession is even more dramatic than the growing proportion of ethnic minorities. In 1961, women accounted for only 3 percent of all lawyers; their number grew to 5 percent in 1971, 15 percent in 1981, and 22 percent in 1986.[51]

The structure of legal practice also began to change in the seventies as the number and size of large law firms began to grow. Both the number of large firms and the number of lawyers working in them have grown at a significantly faster pace than the number of lawyers in general.[52]

GOVERNMENT RIGHTS-ENFORCEMENT AGENCIES.   Another component of the support structure is the provincial and national government agencies that have acted as advocates of the new civil rights and liberties. Beginning in the mid-sixties, the Canadian provinces and the national government began adopting comprehensive human rights codes prohibiting private discrimination on a broad range of grounds; along with these codes, they created human rights commissions having jurisdiction as quasi-judicial administrative agencies to hear discrimination claims, from which there are appeals to the regular courts.[53] Additionally, in the late sixties several provinces and the federal government created law reform commissions that provide continuing advice to legislatures on legal reform. Both the human rights commissions and the law reform commissions became institutional sites for liberal rights advocacy, and there has been a fluid interchange of talent and legal resources among these governmental agencies, the law schools, and private rights-advocacy organizations.[54]

Taken together, these changes in Canada's interest-group system, in governmental financing of litigation, and in the legal profession, combined with the creation of government rights-enforcement agencies, fundamentally transformed the Canadian support structure for legal mobilization *before adoption of the Charter in 1982*. Those changes in the support structure profoundly influenced the Supreme Court's agenda. This may be illustrated by litigation trends under the 1960 Bill of Rights and the Charter. The Bill of Rights, as noted in the previous chapter, had become nearly irrelevant by the mid-seventies, in part

due to the Supreme Court's refusal to use it to strike down legislation. Some scholars have suggested that patterns of litigation under the Bill of Rights responded directly to the Supreme Court's unfriendly policy, and that litigants abandoned their reliance on the statute after discovering that the Court would not support them; using a similar line of analysis, these scholars suggest that litigants increasingly relied on the Charter as they discovered the Supreme Court's apparent friendliness to that document.[55]

If the different judicial receptions of the two documents determined their fate, we should expect litigants to have responded directly to judicial decisions. In particular, all other things being equal, we should expect to find similar litigation patterns under the Bill of Rights immediately after 1960 and under the Charter after 1982, with the patterns diverging only *after* the Supreme Court's level of support for claims under each of the documents became clear. The data do not support that hypothesis. For all of the sixties, as figure 10.11 illustrates, the *entire* number of cases based on the Bill of Rights in *all* Canadian courts was less than ten per year, and there was no substantial decline immediately after the Supreme Court's first unfavorable decision in 1963. By contrast, the number of cases based on the Charter in 1982, its year of passage, was nearly two hundred, and in 1983 nearly four hundred. The vast difference between the number of cases based on the Bill of Rights in the early sixties and the number of cases based on the Charter in the early eighties is striking. Even before the Supreme Court refused to read the Bill of Rights broadly, litigants failed to rely on it; and even before the Court began to read the Charter broadly, litigants had begun to file hundreds of Charter cases.[56] The higher number of Charter cases resulted primarily from the greater availability of resources for rights litigation in the early eighties than in the early sixties.[57]

The Support Structure and the Rights of the Accused
Canadian law on criminal procedure, as we saw earlier, underwent a major rights revolution in the eighties, in spite of the frustration of earlier efforts to reform a criminal law system that had remained largely unchanged since its creation in the late nineteenth century. After the failure of those legislative reform efforts, the rights revolution in criminal procedure took off within the judiciary.

After 1982, of course, the Charter provided new foundations for appeal by criminal defendants and thus for that revolution in criminal procedure—but the Charter's criminal procedure provisions themselves were, in good measure, a creation of the civil liberties lobby.

Figure 10.11   Number of Cases Citing the Canadian Bill of Rights or the Charter in
the First Decade of Each

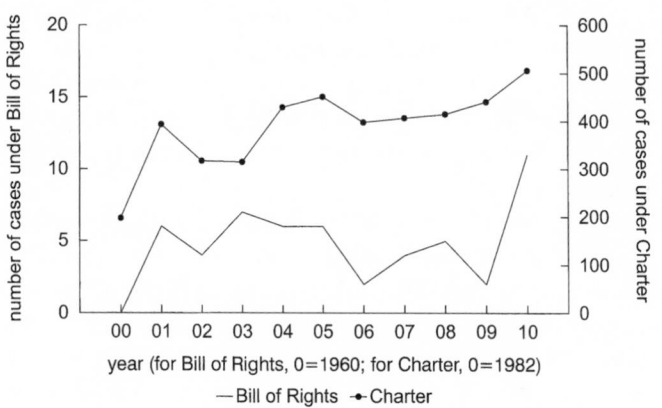

year (for Bill of Rights, 0=1960; for Charter, 0=1982)

— Bill of Rights ◆ Charter

Source: Case reporter search conducted with Lexis.

Leading officials and members of the Canadian Civil Liberties Association participated in drafting important provisions of the Charter.[58] The
CCLA representatives argued for, and got, fundamental revisions of
the Charter's wording on search and seizure and exclusion of evidence,
detention and imprisonment, the right to counsel, and jury trials.[59] The
CCLA also argued for, and got, a provision that guaranteed remedy
of rights violations in the courts (the original proposal contained no
mechanism for remedy). Jean Chrétien, the federal justice minister and
Trudeau-government spokesman on Charter matters, upon introduc-
ing a greatly revised draft Charter in 1981, acknowledged the key role
of the civil liberties organizations in shaping the new document.[60] Indeed, it was in his interest to do so—for the federal government increasingly depended on the civil liberties and civil rights lobby as allies in cultivating public support for the Charter against recalcitrant
provincial governments.[61]

   As early as 1982, rights-advocacy groups had also begun taking
steps to support litigation over the Charter's criminal procedure provisions. Their publicity on the matter indicates a clear recognition of the
role of outside groups in the process of judicial interpretation: the
CCLA observed that its caseload was likely to increase, and the organization announced plans to set up a litigation-support fund and called
on lawyers to step forward to cooperate in the development of suitable
cases for appellate review.[62]

   Although adoption of the Charter thus spurred new rights-advocacy
efforts in the area of criminal procedure, the adoption of the Charter

alone is an insufficient explanation for the criminal procedure revolution. For one thing, most criminal defendants have little money and would be incapable of pursuing appeals on their own. The Charter, by itself, provided no additional financial resources for appeal. And, just as importantly, patterns over time in the Court's criminal procedure agenda simply do not support a conclusion that the Charter alone produced the criminal procedure revolution. As illustrated in figure 10.8 above, the early phase of the Court's growing attention to the rights of the accused occurred well before passage of the Charter. Because a substantial part of the growth in the size of the criminal procedure agenda occurred before 1982, the explanation for that growth must lie, at least in part, outside of the Charter.

The key force in addition to the Charter has been growth in government-provided legal aid available to support appeals by criminal defendants. These resources expanded dramatically in the seventies and continued to grow in the eighties, and they supported a rising tide of rights claims by criminal defendants. Canadian legal aid covers criminal defense as well as civil disputes; about half the Canadian legal aid expenditure is on criminal matters. If the defendant's claim is deemed meritorious by a panel of lawyers, the Canadian plans provide assistance for appeals up through the court hierarchy. In Ontario, the plan covers all costs associated with appeal.[63]

Lawyers who were active in criminal defense and human-rights work in the seventies corroborate that the expansion of legal aid fueled the criminal procedure revolution. When I interviewed lawyers and asked them how the new criminal procedure cases managed to get to the Supreme Court in the mid- and late-seventies, they typically replied, "legal aid." And the significance of the CCLA's fundraising efforts should not be exaggerated: in the eighties, as in the seventies, legal aid provided the key financial support for most of the criminal procedure cases in which the CCLA became involved.[64] Clayton Ruby, a leading Supreme Court litigator in criminal defense matters said, "Oh, it was legal aid, of course. None of those cases could have gotten to the Canadian Supreme Court without it."[65]

The growth of the support structure for legal mobilization thus helps to explain key developments in the criminal procedure revolution. As early as the 1970s, rights-advocacy organizations, principally the CCLA, developed networks of lawyers working on criminal procedure. They, and criminal defense lawyers in general, relied on the substantial growth of legal aid after the sixties to gain financial support for an increasing number of criminal procedure appeals to the Supreme

Court in the 1970s and on into the 1980s. And then in 1982, the CCLA's lobbying efforts significantly affected the drafting of the Charter's provisions on criminal procedure, which, when adopted, provided the constitutional foundation for the Supreme Court's great transformation of Canadian law on criminal procedure.[66]

The Support Structure and Women's Rights

As we saw above, the Supreme Court devoted increasing attention and support to women's rights in the eighties, although women's-rights cases remain a relatively small part of the Court's overall agenda. Changes in the support structure for mobilization of women's rights help to explain these developments.

Women's-rights groups in Canada exploded in number and organizational power in the seventies. The numbers tell part of the story. Of the groups included in the Canadian Women's Movement Archives at Ottawa University, roughly a third were formed between 1970 and 1974, another 24 percent between 1975 and 1979, and another 12 percent between 1980 and 1984. The most rapid growth in the number of women's-rights organizations thus occurred in the early and midseventies and began to taper off by the early eighties.[67]

Several of the new Canadian women's groups, in contrast to the women's movement in the past, became highly institutionalized by the late seventies, with professional staffs and substantial organizational resources. Thus, the National Association of Women and the Law grew out of a national conference on women's rights in 1974 and by the late seventies had developed a strong organizational presence as a center for research on women's rights and a clearinghouse for information on the topic. The association periodically brought experts and others together for conferences on women's rights. Similarly, the National Action Committee on the Status of Women, an umbrella organization of hundreds of women's groups throughout the country, was formed in 1972 and had achieved a strong organizational presence by the midseventies. By the early eighties, the Canadian women's movement was an organized, institutionalized phenomenon consisting of a large number of organizations, some with substantial financial and organizational resources. Significantly, the women's organizations received substantial financial support from the Canadian government as part of its long-term plan to invigorate citizens' groups.[68]

The number and organization of women lawyers also increased significantly after 1970. Big changes clearly were afoot in the legal profes-

sion in the seventies. The number of female lawyers grew from 309 in 1961, to 780 in 1971; then it exploded to 5,175 in 1981, and 9,410 in 1986.[69] As in the United States, the legal profession in Canada became significantly more open to women—but the change preceded passage of the Charter.

In the seventies, the limited financial support available for women's-rights litigation came from a variety of sources. The plaintiffs relied primarily on the growing availability of civil legal aid to support their cases in the Supreme Court. Of the important women's-rights cases in the seventies, only *Murdoch* did not rely on some form of legal aid.[70] In general, legal aid was more crucial for case support than were women's organizations; the women's movement devoted very little attention to the courts in the seventies, and when women's groups did support court cases the support came after the cases were already moving up the judicial hierarchy. Nevertheless, all of the important women's-rights cases of the seventies were supported in one form or another by organizations in the women's movement and by other sympathetic organizations. The *Lavell-Bedard* case received organizational support from the fledgling National Action Committee, and, as Leslie Pal and F. L. Morton have shown, the Bliss case demonstrated the development of a broad network of groups with a growing capability to support strategic litigation.[71] A coalition of unions, women's-rights organizations, and a governmental-supported legal clinic provided financial, legal, and coordinating support for Bliss's case.[72] Although Bliss's claim did not prevail, the strength and organization of the coalition illustrates the growing power of the women's movement by the late seventies.

Frustration over defeats in cases like *Bliss* provided a key impetus for creating the Charter.[73] Leaders of the women's movement, reflecting on the failures of their early and rather tentative forays into constitutional litigation, turned their attention and energy to placing favorable provisions in the Charter and then to using those provisions to gain favorable judicial rulings. Beverly Baines, in an influential analysis published just as the women's movement began turning its attention more fully to the courts at the end of the seventies, argued that women's-rights advocates needed to work toward enactment of more favorable statutory or, preferably, constitutional language.[74] Baines argued in favor of developing new legal guarantees of equality "sufficiently detailed to convey to the judges a meaning for equality that corresponds to women's expectations."[75] Baines's analysis, which fo-

cused on women's rights in particular, served as a rallying cry for the growing women's movement to support passage of the Charter as well as to influence its provisions.[76]

By October 1980, when Trudeau began his last and ultimately successful attempt to enact a constitutional bill of rights, women's interest groups were among the best organized and most powerful of any of the noneconomic interest groups in Canada. The Canadian women's movement thus responded with vigor, organization, and sophisticated legal analysis to Trudeau's Charter proposal.[77] Several leading Toronto law firms allowed important women lawyers on their staffs to devote their time and legal expertise to work on the Charter's provisions.[78] Their participation in the Charter drafting process proved crucial for determining the eventual nature of the document, both for inserting language favorable to women's interests and for defending that language against removal by the provinces.

The result was a document on its face substantially favorable to women's rights, containing three key provisions of potential use by women's-rights litigators, one banning discrimination based on race, sex, and other immutable characteristics, another specifically exempting affirmative action programs from that prohibition, and a third devoted exclusively to guaranteeing that the Charter's rights apply equally to males and females.[79] In the process of developing those guarantees, women's-rights organizations played a key role in strengthening public and provincial government support for the Charter.[80]

The political process of struggle over the Charter's language further strengthened the growing support structure for legal mobilization. As Rosemary Billings observed, "At bottom . . . the greatest achievement of women's constitutional struggle may not have been the rewriting of the law, but the process of strengthening mass collective action. . . ."[81] One result of the strengthening of women's groups was the invigoration of their legal strategies.

Within two years of passage of the Charter, members of leading women's interest groups in Canada had formed the Women's Legal Education and Action Fund, or LEAF, a fund dedicated specifically to supporting women's-rights litigation. The organizers of LEAF believed that, without an organization devoted to constitutional litigation and interpretation, Charter interpretation would be dominated by "the big boys" and would not be responsive to women's interests.[82] That belief was based on their experience in participating in the Charter negotiation process, in which they became deeply frustrated with the male

negotiators' and constitutional scholars' unwillingness to support broad constitutional provisions against sex discrimination. Those experiences led to a conviction that the gains made during the Charter drafting process would be lost unless women participated directly in the process of interpreting and developing the Charter through litigation, constitutional scholarship, and judicial decisions.[83] But to do so, women's-rights advocates recognized that they would need a strong organizational capacity and substantial financial resources in order to support women's-rights lawsuits.

The history of public-interest litigation in the United States influenced the LEAF organizers. Sherene Razack notes that one of the key women's Charter negotiators had considered the experience of U.S. women's legal funds in March 1981, even before passage of the Charter. In May 1981, the Canadian Advisory Council on the Status of Women commissioned a study on the usefulness of a litigation fund for women's-rights claims.[84] The study, done by three of the most influential of the feminist legal activists and eventually released in 1984 just before formation of LEAF, detailed the experience of several Canadian and several American public-interest litigation organizations and concluded with suggestions for how to form and use a women's litigation fund.[85] In addition, the feminist legal activists organized several "study days," during which several American legal experts reported on the U.S. experience with regard to women's-rights litigation.[86] The organizers also consulted the developing Canadian experience with strategic litigation and built on it as well. As a key report concluded, "Canadian women have a good history on which to build a strategy for utilizing the Canadian Charter of Rights and Freedoms."[87]

LEAF sponsored its first test cases in the spring of 1985, and since then the organization has become a leading source of funding and legal expertise for women's-rights litigation. The first LEAF case reached the Supreme Court in 1988; by the middle of 1992, LEAF supported or participated in at least sixteen cases that reached the Supreme Court, and more than eighty others that were decided by lower courts.[88] The cases included many of the most important cases on women's-rights in the Supreme Court (see table 10.2). Significantly, LEAF's support for cases coincides with the appearance of women's-rights claims on the Supreme Court agenda: before LEAF support, women's-rights cases appeared only occasionally but, after the beginning of that support, women's-rights claims formed a regular part of the Court's rights agenda.

The extension of the Canadian rights revolution into the area of

Table 10.2   Cases Supported by LEAF in the Canadian Supreme Court

Case	Subject	Year
R. v. Canadian Newspapers Co. Ltd.	identification of sex assault victims	1988
Andrews v. Law Society of British Columbia	definition of equality	1989
Borowski v. Attorney-General for Canada	abortion	1989
Brooks v. Canada Safeway Ltd.	discrimination on basis of pregnancy	1989
Janzen v. Platy Enterprises Ltd.	sex harassment	1989
R. v. Keegstra	hate speech	1990
Taylor v. Canadian Human Rights Commission	hate speech	1990
Tremblay v. Daigle	abortion	1990
R. v. Seaboyer and Gayme	rape shield laws	1991
R. v. Sullivan and Lemay	legal status of fetus	1991
R. v. Butler	pornography	1992
Canadian Council of Churches v. Canada (Minister of Employment and Immigration)	interest group standing	1992
K. M. v. H. M.	limitation periods and incest	1992
Moge v. Moge	support after divorce	1992
Norberg v. Wynrib	doctor/patient sex assault (civil suit)	1992
Schachter v. Canada	maternity and childcare unemployment benefits	1992

Source: Compiled from LEAF documents.

women's rights thus largely grew out of the development of a support structure around the issue. A large and well-organized network of women's rights-advocacy organizations and lawyers existed by the end of the seventies, and they supported a scattering of cases but became increasingly frustrated with the judicial response. Their efforts in the Charter-drafting process and in the development of LEAF have since greatly influenced the judicial agenda on women's rights. Yet the Supreme Court nonetheless hears relatively few women's-rights cases, in significant part because few women's-rights organizations other than LEAF have taken on the task of supporting such cases.[89]

Conclusion

A dramatic rights revolution has occurred in Canada in the last several decades. The Canadian Supreme Court is now a major constitutional policy-maker, focuses much of its attention on civil rights and liberties, increasingly decides cases brought by individuals who are supported by interest groups and government financing, increasingly faces complex disputes involving large numbers of parties, increasingly relies on higher-law foundations for its decisions, increasingly entertains requests to strike down laws, and increasingly does strike down laws and administrative acts in the name of rights.

This broadly based transformation is commonly attributed to Canada's recent adoption of the Charter of Rights and Freedoms or, secondarily, to the efforts of liberal justices on the Supreme Court. The evidence presented here, however, indicates that the Charter's influence as an independent force is commonly exaggerated and that judicial liberals gained control of the Court too late to have done more than encourage already existing developments.

Undoubtedly, the shift to a largely discretionary docket in 1975 significantly contributed to the agenda transformation. When the Court gained discretion over its docket, it began abruptly moving private disputes from its agenda, making way for a growth in the agenda on public law in general and civil liberties and rights in particular. This shift occurred even though judicial liberals were in the minority on the Court at the time and remained so until after the mid-eighties. The experience of the Canadian Supreme Court in this respect closely parallels that of other courts, in particular the United States Supreme Court, that have gained discretionary control over their agendas. Certainly the 1975 Canadian legislation that granted the Supreme Court a largely discretionary docket directed the Court to select cases on the basis of their "public importance." But what is a matter of public importance is open to some interpretation; in both the United States and Canada, when given the choice, judges have chosen rights cases.

Also, undoubtedly the Charter provided new constitutional foundations for both rights advocates' legal claims and judicial policy making; and, admittedly, had Canadian judges refused to give legal force to the Charter's provisions, the growing rights revolution would have remained stunted. Although the majority of Supreme Court justices did not actively encourage the rights revolution until the mid-eighties, some justices in the seventies clearly favored broader judicial support for civil rights and liberties. Additionally, majorities of the court made several decisions that significantly opened access to the Court's agenda. In the late seventies, the Court relaxed its rules on standing, allowing individuals and groups to pursue public-interest lawsuits, and in the mid-eighties the Court opened its doors to third-party intervention by interest groups. These decisions surely contributed to the development of sustained judicial attention to civil rights and liberties. The Charter and judicial attitudes, then, constitute part of the explanation for Canada's rights revolution. But the growing pressure for greater judicial policy making on civil liberties and rights undoubtedly came from outside the judiciary.

This chapter has shown that the development of the rights revolu-

tion rested heavily on the growth of a support structure for legal mobilization. All of the main elements of the support structure—rights-advocacy organizations, sources of financing (particularly government-provided aid), lawyers, and supportive government agencies—either newly emerged or grew substantially in the seventies. Those developments provided the foundation for the rights revolution: they supported a steadily growing number of rights cases, they greatly contributed to the development of rights provisions in the Charter, they developed the scholarship that supported a vigorous judicial role in interpreting the Charter, and they brought new cases under the Charter that provided the judges with the opportunities to enforce, expand, and create the new rights.

In the end, the support structure provided the foundation for the Charter itself and for creative judicial enforcement and development of the rights contained in the Charter. As James Madison recognized more than two centuries ago, bills of rights are not self-activating precisely because ordinary individuals typically do not have the capacity to pursue a rights-based lawsuit. But a support structure in civil society may fill that gap and may fuel the development of a rights revolution.

ELEVEN

Conclusion: Constitutionalism, Judicial Power, and Rights

The basic lesson of this study is that rights are not gifts: they are won through concerted collective action arising from both a vibrant civil society and public subsidy. Rights revolutions originate in pressure from below in civil society, not leadership from above. But, as I have argued throughout this book, only certain kinds of pressure from below, particularly organized support for rights litigation, are likely to support sustained judicial attention to civil liberties and civil rights; and support from judicial elites is hardly irrelevant. In the end, the rights revolution developed and reached its greatest height and strength through an interaction between supportive judges and the support structure for rights-advocacy litigation.

That observation has important implications for theories of constitutionalism, judicial power, and rights. In standard understandings of constitutionalism, there is a deep tension between democracy and rights, and between the powers of democratic majorities and appointed judges.[1] Participants in any constitutional democracy thus wrestle with a difficult dilemma. On the one hand, they seek to ensure that their constitution constrains arbitrary political power. This is not easily done, for recent history is littered with failed constitutions. On the other hand, they seek to ensure that their constitution does not rigidly shackle democratic majorities. But many commentators argue that the more effectively constitutional structures constrain political power, the less the system is democratic.

Although the constitutional dilemma is vexing with respect to any type of constitutional restriction, including the separation of powers, it is especially acute with respect to constitutional rights. Two major criticisms have been leveled at constitutional rights. Some skeptics argue that constitutional rights that are intended to protect individuals or minorities are merely parchment barriers, ineffective against political power.[2] Other critics allege just the opposite, that constitutional

rights too greatly constrain democratic majorities.[3] Much of the writing on the proper role of judges in a constitutional democracy similarly assumes either, on the one hand, that judges lead by adapting the constitution to changing circumstances, or, on the other, that they follow by faithfully applying the "original intent" of the constitution's creators. In each of its forms, the dilemma of constitutional rights and judicial power is intractable because its poles seem to be so far apart.[4]

One solution to this dilemma is that particular constitutional rights, even when created and enforced by unelected judges, serve democracy by improving the fairness of the democratic process.[5] Yet that theory, and indeed most recent defenses of judicial power by constitutional theorists, accepts the assumption that judges exercise great power over democratic majorities; indeed, it is the belief that judges exercise great power that motivates much constitutional theorizing about the proper limits of that power.

This book, by contrast, has addressed the dilemma by analyzing the political and social conditions for sustained judicial attention to rights. Undoubtedly, constitutional rights (and higher-law rights in general) are undemocratic *under some conditions* and are merely parchment barriers *under some conditions*. For instance, if only the wealthy, or only large private business corporations, have the organizational and financial capacity to mobilize constitutional law in their favor, then judicial policy making in the area of constitutional rights is likely to be undemocratic in the extreme. Only rights of interest to those select groups will be developed through judicial interpretation; for the rest of the population, rights will remain merely promises on paper. The conditions under which constitutional rights are developed and applied through judicial interpretation, therefore, are of great significance.

The central problem of most sweeping criticisms of constitutionalism and rights like those summarized briefly above, then, is that they are unconditional in nature. By claiming that rights are always merely parchment barriers, or are always set in stone, such unconditional analyses commonly miss the opportunity to explore the contingent conditions that shape the development of constitutional rights and judicial power in practice.

The most important implication of this study is that there is a third alternative to rights as "parchment" or "stone": rights are conditioned on the extent of a support structure for legal mobilization. Under conditions in which the support structure is deep and vibrant, judicial attention to rights may be sustained and vigorous; under conditions

in which a support structure is shallow and weak, judicial attention to rights is likely to be intermittent and ineffective. Additionally, constitutional rights have proven to be remarkably variable over time. In those instances when constitutional rights have remained undeveloped through judicial interpretation, that is because rights advocates have had little capacity for pursuing their claims in the courts. But when rights have been developed through sustained litigation, the foundation for those limits is not judicial fiat but a broad support structure in civil society. Constitutional rights provisions, as *legal* guarantees, and judicial attention to rights are, therefore, constituted in cooperation with civil society.

Constitutional rights in general, and rights revolutions in particular, thus rest on a support structure that has a broad base in civil society. In the countries in this study, the leading pressure for building a rights revolution initially came from outside of the judiciary, principally from organized rights advocates. In the United States, most of the the key rights created during the rights revolution had been the subject of significant organizing pressure for some time before the Supreme Court took them up. In Canada, liberal supporters of expanded judicial protection for individual rights gained broad support and then pressed such issues on a hesitant Supreme Court, which eventually acquiesced and turned its attention to the new rights claims. Similarly, in Britain there had been growing concern about abuses of administrative discretion long before judges began to turn their attention to the issue. In India, the judicial rights agenda grew dramatically in the mid-seventies when, during the Emergency, the government imprisoned many members of the middle and upper classes. The experience brought home to these new victims an experience with arbitrary governmental power that had long been familiar to many members of the lower classes, and the new victims used their greater resources to mobilize a response. They subsidized rights-advocacy organizations, which proliferated and flourished, and they challenged their own preventive detention in court.

The continuation of nascent rights revolutions beyond their initial phases has also depended on broad support outside the judiciary. In each of the countries in this study, the judicial rights agenda has grown in a sustained way only to the extent that it has been supported by continued, organized efforts in civil society. And those efforts, centered in rights-advocacy organizations, government-provided legal aid, and the racial and sexual diversification of the legal profession, have been strong only to the extent that they have reflected either col-

lective support or broad undercurrents of democratization. Thus the widespread growth of rights-advocacy organizations, government-provided legal aid, statutes authorizing the award of attorneys' fees to successful rights plaintiffs, and the racial and sexual diversification of the legal profession, all reflect either collective support or democratizing trends. The crucial role of such resources in sustaining a rights revolution is evident in the countries in this study. Particularly in the United States and Canada, the support structure, once born, continued to grow, and that growth fueled the growing rights revolution in the two countries. The depth of the support structure has been more attenuated in Britain, and the judicial agenda has reflected that attenuation. In India, with the end of the Emergency in 1977, the middle and upper classes and opposition political parties withdrew their support from rights-advocacy organizations, many of which collapsed as a result. Although the Indian Supreme Court attempted through an unprecedented burst of judicial activism to lead a rights revolution, the effort fell short because it lacked a broad and deep support structure in civil society.

Although resources for legal mobilization thus play a crucial role, other forces are not irrelevant. Some structural characteristics of the judicial system greatly condition the potential for a rights revolution. The procedural hurdles placed in the path of criminal appeals in Britain have surely limited the development of significant judicial attention to criminal procedure in that country. Additionally, judicial control over the docket is clearly an important and perhaps even a necessary condition for a judicial rights revolution. If judges cannot eliminate routine economic disputes from their agenda, their attention is dominated by the many cases raising such issues. Thus, the Indian Supreme Court, which lacks control over its docket, focuses much of its attention on routine disputes; by contrast, after the U.S. and Canadian supreme courts gained significant control of their dockets (in 1925 and 1975, respectively), their attention shifted toward broader issues in public law, particularly individual rights.

Another important factor is judicial leadership, but its effects are complex and not dominant. In the early stages of the process, judicial support is neither necessary nor sufficient for development of a rights revolution. Thus, the earliest phases of the rights revolutions in the countries examined here all began in a context of judicial indifference or hostility. Organized support for rights cases may propel such cases onto the judicial agenda even in the absence of support from the judges. Litigants facing unsympathetic judges, moreover, often have

held out hope that they may persuade the judges of the rightness of their cause and, as a variety of cases discussed throughout this book have shown, sometimes they have achieved that goal. But ultimately, in order to sustain a rights revolution, judicial support is necessary—although it is not sufficient. As the experiences of both Canada and the United States indicate, the decisions of liberal judges encouraged further litigation by rights-advocacy lawyers and organizations. As the Indian experience again illustrates, this dynamic feedback between judicial decisions and external groups has occurred, however, only where the support structure is sufficiently strong to generate continued litigation. Obviously, the presence of a strong support structure cannot ensure that judges will ultimately support rights claims. But a strong support structure can reassure judges that if they do support rights claims, they will not be bereft of allies in the event of political attacks.

Bills of rights have contributed, too. Although it is common to argue that bills of rights empower judiciaries, that may be only a secondary effect of a much stronger relationship between popular movements and bills of rights. Judiciaries seem capable of deriving legitimacy from sources other than a bill of rights; and constituencies of support for judiciaries have not always been oriented toward a bill of rights. But in systems in which there exist broad constitutional rights guarantees, popular movements seem especially capable of using contradictions between political practice and constitutional promise as a means for organizing support for their causes.[6] And when such movements have had access to resources for legal mobilization, they have turned to the courts, creating the conditions for a new range of judicial activity. Thus a bill of rights provides popular movements with a potential tool for tying judicial power to their purposes.

The variation among these four countries indicates that the growth of a support structure is not an inevitable outgrowth of other characteristics of society but is, instead, contingent on learning and political strategy. Certainly support structures have not emerged as an automatic consequence of industrialization or modernization. India's support structure undoubtedly is the weakest among the countries in this study. But Britain too, a country that industrialized and modernized long ago, until very recently had a very limited support structure. Support structures thus appear to grow out of a wide range of complex factors. The development of rights consciousness surely is a necessary condition. Additionally, support structure development depends on a process of social learning regarding the techniques of organiza-

tional development and strategic litigation. The availability of resources for these efforts is crucial, and so patrons—typically private
foundations and wealthy individuals—have played key roles in the
start-up of rights-advocacy organizations. Political support for
government-provided legal aid also has played a key role. Some of
these factors clearly reflect the availability of disposable wealth in a
society, and so industrialization arguably may condition their development. But industrialization is not sufficient, for much of the process
depends on the efforts of rights advocates.

Nonetheless, the efforts of rights advocates may not bear fruit with
equal ease in civil-law countries. Certainly, even in civil-law courts
something like a support structure is likely to be essential for the mobilization of rights claims by individuals. Nonetheless, the influence of
the support structure is likely to be greatest in common-law systems
where rights-advocacy lawyers can cultivate precedents and build on
them. Where judicial decision making relies little or not at all on precedent, as in civil-law systems, however, the growth dynamic arising out
of the strategic cultivation of precedent is likely to be undercut.

Because learning, resources, and political strategy are so crucial to
these processes (at least in common-law countries), it is clear that no
single political ideology has an inevitable monopoly on support for
litigation. Indeed, as support structures have developed to their fullest
extent, as in the United States, they have developed diverse agendas.
Just as civil liberties advocates in the twenties and thirties adopted
many of the strategic litigation techniques used by the railroads and
other corporations, by the late seventies political conservatives were
adopting many of the techniques used by civil liberties advocates.[7]
Even among liberal rights advocates, differences have arisen. In recent
controversies over pornography, proponents of freedom of speech
sometimes clash with proponents of women's rights. Similarly, in controversies over procedures in trials involving violence against women,
proponents of the rights of the accused sometimes differ with proponents of women's rights. Thus, as Paul Sniderman, Peter Russell, Joseph Fletcher, and Philip Tetlock have observed, the development of
women's-rights claims has introduced new tensions into debates over
rights.[8] But these tensions exist mainly as a result of an increasingly
diverse body of litigants.

The new constitutional rights thus have developed, in sum, out of a
democratization of access to the judiciary. In 1915 the universe of litigants capable of pursuing sustained, strategic litigation consisted primarily of businesses. By the seventies that universe had expanded sig-

nificantly in several countries and included not only businesses but criminal defendants, women, political dissenters, and members of minority religions and races, among others. That expansion in access transformed the field of strategic litigation.

The democratization of access to the judicial agenda, however, remains limited in important ways. In India, which is dominated by a state bureaucracy and plagued by great economic inequality, there remain great limits on access to the judicial agenda. Indian rights-advocacy groups and official legal aid, for instance, suffer from chronic underfunding. No support structure is static, however, and the continued efforts of rights-advocacy organizations, along with the growth of India's middle class, may generate the resources necessary for development of a broader support structure. In Canada and Britain too, although resource shortages are not as great as in India, rights-advocacy groups nonetheless still face significant financial limitations. Their legal professions and interest-group systems have developed the organizational structures capable of supporting sustained rights litigation, but resource limitations still limit the extent and frequency of litigation campaigns. By contrast, in the United States the political environment, the large population, and the size and diverse structure of the legal profession seem ideally suited for the growth of independent, nonparty organizations and other sources of support for sustained rights-based litigation.

Nonetheless, even in the United States there remain significant limits to the democratization of access to courts. One of the most important is the relative lack of support for strategic litigation by the truly poor; as a consequence, there is little litigation aimed at improving the conditions of the least well-off. Rights litigation, as some critics have observed, benefits primarily the "haves," those groups possessing the resources necessary to pursue litigation.[9] Thus, before the development of government-sponsored legal defense services, the rights of the accused generally failed to reach the appellate judicial agenda. Similarly, rights claims based on poverty or economic class still fail to reach the judicial agenda.

It may be objected that the failure of the courts to address issues related to economic deprivation results from the liberal-individualist bias of American society and law and not the lack of resources for litigation on such issues. But the Supreme Court, in fact, entertained a relatively large number of claims framed around the issue of economic deprivation *when those legal claims received the support of a government litigation-support program*, the Legal Services Program.[10] The Court's at-

tention to such claims declined rapidly when program funding was cut. The Supreme Court's opposition to rights based on indigence or class surely contributed to the failure of such issues to take a place on the judicial agenda,[11] but the Court majority at one time opposed other extensions of rights only to reverse itself and support those rights after facing mounting litigation. Before the twenties, for instance, few Americans would have predicted that the United States Supreme Court would expand rights-based protections for freedom of speech, yet it did so; before the fifties, few would have predicted that the Court would intervene substantially in state criminal procedure, yet it did so; after the Court's decision in *Bowers v. Hardwick* in 1986, few observers would have predicted that the Court soon would accept an equal protection claim based on sexual preference, yet in *Romer v. Evans* (1996), during a litigation campaign by several rights-advocacy organizations, a far more conservative Court appeared to do just that;[12] before the eighties, British legal scholars generally denied that the House of Lords would interfere in the management of prisons or strike down a parliamentary statute, yet since then it has taken each step. To say, in retrospect, that the basic principles of American or English law allowed or even demanded those developments, whereas the same principles now limit attention to issues related to poverty, is to fail to recognize the formidable legal barriers to the development of those earlier issues, and to fail to understand the nature of the forces that propelled exactly those previously neglected issues over the jurisprudential barricades and onto the agenda.

What are the prospects for the future? Opponents of the rights agenda have attacked the support structure for years, and their attacks are increasingly successful. Some sources of funding for rights litigation have recently been cut or are increasingly under threat. For instance, there have been deep cuts in legal aid in a number of western countries. In Canada, the government eliminated funding for the Court Challenges Program in 1992 (although it has since been reinstated) and, by the mid-nineties, some provinces were considering deep cuts in their legal aid programs. In Britain, in the late eighties the government radically changed the eligibility criteria for legal aid, producing sharp cuts in the number of people eligible for such assistance, and in 1997 the government began a drastic restructuring of the program. In the United States, by the mid-nineties the federal legal aid program faced the threat of deep cuts or outright elimination.

Whether the rights agenda will suffer as a result depends on the extent to which the support structure in each country rests primarily

on government aid. For some rights claims, the support structure has multiple foundations but, for others, the structure appears to depend nearly entirely on government aid. In each of the countries in this study, appeals by criminal defendants and prisoners, for example, depend almost entirely on legal defender programs sponsored or aided by government. The capacity of nongovernmental resources to fill the gap left by the erosion of government aid varies greatly from country to country. In Britain, Canada, and India the few public-interest groups that have supported rights litigation remain relatively weak and lacking in resources. In the United States, the leading rights-advocacy organizations remain relatively well resourced and capable of supporting rights litigation at all levels of the judicial system. Those organizations fill a very different role than legal aid in the United States, however, and although some civil liberties and civil rights issues likely will continue to reach the highest courts, issues supported by legal aid likely will receive less and less judicial attention.

Rights, in sum, are not simply judicial gifts to isolated individual supplicants. Rights result from collective efforts and a support structure in civil society. But, for the same reason, rights are not magical solutions to any or all problems; they seem particularly incapable of addressing the growing problem of economic inequality in many advanced industrialized countries.

This study, then, has mixed lessons for constitutional democracies. Neither a written constitution, a rights-supportive culture, nor sympathetic judges is sufficient for sustained judicial attention to and support for rights. Protection of civil liberties and civil rights depend, in addition, on a support structure in civil society. Without a support structure, even the clearest constitutional rights guarantees are likely to become meaningless in the courts; but a vibrant support structure can extend and expand the feeblest of rights. Participants in constitutional democracy would do well to focus their efforts not only on framing or revising constitutional provisions, and not only on selecting the judges who interpret them, but also on shaping the support structure that defends and develops those rights in practice.

Selected Constitutional or Quasi-Constitutional Rights Provisions for the United States, India, Britain, and Canada

U.S. Constitution: The Bill of Rights and Other Selected Amendments

Amendment I (1791)

Congress shall make no law respecting an establishment of religion, or prohibiting the free exercise thereof; or abridging the freedom of speech, or of the press; or the right of the people peaceably to assemble, and to petition the government for a redress of grievances.

Amendment II (1791)

A well regulated militia, being necessary to the security of a free state, the right of the people to keep and bear arms, shall not be infringed.

Amendment III (1791)

No soldier shall, in time of peace be quartered in any house, without the consent of the owner, nor in time of war, but in a manner to be prescribed by law.

Amendment IV (1791)

The right of the people to be secure in their persons, houses, papers, and effects, against unreasonable searches and seizures, shall not be violated, and no warrants shall issue, but upon probable cause, supported by oath or affirmation, and particularly describing the place to be searched, and the persons or things to be seized.

Amendment V (1791)

No person shall be held to answer for a capital, or otherwise infamous crime, unless on a presentment or indictment of a grand jury, except in cases arising in the land or naval forces, or in the militia, when in

actual service in time of war or public danger; nor shall any person be subject for the same offense to be twice put in jeopardy of life or limb; nor shall be compelled in any criminal case to be a witness against himself, nor be deprived of life, liberty, or property, without due process of law; nor shall private property be taken for public use, without just compensation.

Amendment VI (1791)
In all criminal prosecutions, the accused shall enjoy the right to a speedy and public trial, by an impartial jury of the state and district wherein the crime shall have been committed, which district shall have been previously ascertained by law, and to be informed of the nature and cause of the accusation; to be confronted with the witnesses against him; to have compulsory process for obtaining witnesses in his favor, and to have the assistance of counsel for his defense.

Amendment VII (1791)
In suits at common law, where the value in controversy shall exceed twenty dollars, the right of trial by jury shall be preserved, and no fact tried by a jury, shall be otherwise reexamined in any court of the United States, than according to the rules of the common law.

Amendment VIII (1791)
Excessive bail shall not be required, nor excessive fines imposed, nor cruel and unusual punishments inflicted.

Amendment IX (1791)
The enumeration in the Constitution, of certain rights, shall not be construed to deny or disparage others retained by the people.

Amendment X (1791)
The powers not delegated to the United States by the Constitution, nor prohibited by it to the states, are reserved to the states respectively, or to the people.

Amendment XIII (1865)
Section 1. Neither slavery nor involuntary servitude, except as a punishment for crime whereof the party shall have been duly convicted, shall exist within the United States, or any place subject to their jurisdiction.

Section 2. Congress shall have power to enforce this article by appropriate legislation.

Amendment XIV (1868)

Section 1. All persons born or naturalized in the United States, and subject to the jurisdiction thereof, are citizens of the United States and of the state wherein they reside. No state shall make or enforce any law which shall abridge the privileges or immunities of citizens of the United States; nor shall any state deprive any person of life, liberty, or property, without due process of law; nor deny to any person within its jurisdiction the equal protection of the laws.

Section 2. Representatives shall be apportioned among the several states according to their respective numbers, counting the whole number of persons in each state, excluding Indians not taxed. But when the right to vote at any election for the choice of electors for President and Vice President of the United States, Representatives in Congress, the executive and judicial officers of a state, or the members of the legislature thereof, is denied to any of the male inhabitants of such state, being twenty-one years of age, and citizens of the United States, or in any way abridged, except for participation in rebellion, or other crime, the basis of representation therein shall be reduced in the proportion which the number of such male citizens shall bear to the whole number of male citizens twenty-one years of age in such state.

Section 3. No person shall be a Senator or Representative in Congress, or elector of President and Vice President, or hold any office, civil or military, under the United States, or under any state, who, having previously taken an oath, as a member of Congress, or as an officer of the United States, or as a member of any state legislature, or as an executive or judicial officer of any state, to support the Constitution of the United States, shall have engaged in insurrection or rebellion against the same, or given aid or comfort to the enemies thereof. But Congress may by a vote of two-thirds of each House, remove such disability.

Section 4. The validity of the public debt of the United States, authorized by law, including debts incurred for payment of pensions and bounties for services in suppressing insurrection or rebellion, shall not be questioned. But neither the United States nor any state shall assume or pay any debt or obligation incurred in aid of insurrection or rebellion against the United States, or any claim for the loss or emancipation of any slave; but all such debts, obligations and claims shall be held illegal and void.

Section 5. The Congress shall have power to enforce, by appropriate legislation, the provisions of this article.

Amendment XV (1870)

Section 1. The right of citizens of the United States to vote shall not be denied or abridged by the United States or by any state on account of race, color, or previous condition of servitude.

Section 2. The Congress shall have power to enforce this article by appropriate legislation.

Amendment XIX (1920)

The right of citizens of the United States to vote shall not be denied or abridged by the United States or by any state on account of sex.

Congress shall have power to enforce this article by appropriate legislation.

Constitution of India: Fundamental Rights

Right to Equality

Article 14. Equality before law.

The State shall not deny to any person equality before the law or the equal protection of the laws within the territory of India.

Article 15. Prohibition of discrimination on grounds of religion, race, caste, sex or place of birth.

(1) The State shall not discriminate against any citizen on grounds only of religion, race, caste, sex, place of birth or any of them.

(2) No citizen shall, on grounds only of religion, race, caste, sex, place of birth or any of them, be subject to any disability, liability, restriction or condition with regard to—

(a) access to shops, public restaurants, hotels and places of public entertainment; or

(b) the use of wells, tanks, bathing ghats, roads and places of public resort maintained wholly or partly out of State funds or dedicated to the use of the general public.

(3) Nothing in this article shall prevent the State from making any special provision for women and children.

(4) Nothing in this article or in clause (2) of article 29 shall prevent the State from making any special provision for the advancement of any socially and educationally backward classes of citizens or for the Scheduled Castes and the Scheduled Tribes.

Article 16. Equality of opportunity in matters of public employment.

(1) There shall be equality of opportunity for all citizens in matters relating to employment or appointment to any office under the State.

(2) No citizen shall, on grounds only of religion, race, caste, sex, descent, place of birth, residence or any of them, be ineligible for, or discriminated against in respect of, any employment or office under the State.

(3) Nothing in this article shall prevent Parliament from making any law prescribing, in regard to a class or classes of employment or appointment to an office under the Government of, or any local or other authority within, a State or Union territory, any requirement as to residence within that State or Union territory prior to such employment or appointment.

(4) Nothing in this article shall prevent the State from making any provision for the reservation of appointments or posts in favour of any backward class of citizens which, in the opinion of the State, is not adequately represented in the services under the State.

(5) Nothing in this article shall affect the operation of any law which provides that the incumbent of an office in connection with the affairs of any religious or denominational institution or any member of the governing body thereof shall be a person professing a particular religion or belonging to a particular denomination.

Article 17. Abolition of untouchability.

"Untouchability" is abolished and its practice in any form is forbidden. The enforcement of any disability arising out of "Untouchability" shall be an offence punishable in accordance with law.

Article 18. Abolition of titles.

(1) No title, not being a military or academic distinction, shall be conferred by the State.

(2) No citizen of India shall accept any title from any foreign State.

(3) No person who is not a citizen of India shall, while he holds any office of profit or trust under the State, accept without the consent of the President any title from any foreign State.

(4) No person holding any office of profit or trust under the State shall, without the consent of the President, accept any present, emoluments, or office of any kind from or under any foreign State.

Right to Freedom

Article 19. Protection of certain rights regarding freedom of speech, etc.

(1) All citizens shall have the right—
    (a) to freedom of speech and expression;

(b) to assemble peaceably and without arms;

(c) to form associations or unions;

(d) to move freely throughout the territory of India;

(e) to reside and settle in any part of the territory of India; [and]

(g) to practise any profession, or to carry on any occupation, trade or business.

(2) Nothing in sub-clause (a) of clause (1) shall affect the operation of any existing law, or prevent the State from making any law, in so far as such law imposes reasonable restrictions on the exercise of the right conferred by the said sub-clause in the interests of the sovereignty and integrity of India,] the security of the State, friendly relations with foreign States, public order, decency or morality, or in relation to contempt of court, defamation or incitement to an offence.

(3) Nothing in sub-clause (b) of the said clause shall affect the operation of any existing law in so far as it imposes, or prevent the State from making any law imposing, in the interest of the sovereignty and integrity of India or public order, reasonable restrictions on the exercise of the right conferred by the said sub-clause.

(4) Nothing in sub-clause (c) of the said clause shall affect the operation of any existing law in so far as it imposes, or prevent the State from making any law imposing, in the interests of the sovereignty and integrity of India or public order or morality, reasonable restrictions on the exercise of the right conferred by the said subclause.

(5) Nothing in sub-clauses (d) and (e) of the said clause shall affect the operation of any existing law in so far as it imposes, or prevent the State from making any law imposing, reasonable restrictions on the exercise of any of the rights conferred by the said sub-clauses either in the interests of the general public or for the protection of the interests of any Scheduled Tribe.

(6) Nothing in sub-clause (g) of the said clause shall affect the operation of any existing law in so far as it imposes, or prevent the State from making any law imposing, in the interests of the general public, reasonable restrictions on the exercise of the right conferred by the said sub-clause, and, in particular, nothing in the said sub-clause shall affect the operation of any existing law in so far as it relates to, or prevent the State from making any law relating to,—

(i) the professional or technical qualifications necessary for practising any profession or carrying on any occupation, trade or business, or

(ii) the carrying on by the State, or by a corporation owned or controlled by the State, of any trade, business, industry or service,

whether to the exclusion, complete or partial, of citizens or otherwise.

Article 20. Protection in respect of conviction for offences.

(1) No person shall be convicted of any offence except for violation of a law in force at the time of the commission of the Act charged as an offence, nor be subjected to a penalty greater than that which might have been inflicted under the law in force at the time of the commission of the offence.

(2) No person shall be prosecuted and punished for the same offence more than once.

(3) No person accused of any offence shall be compelled to be a witness against himself.

Article 21. Protection of life and personal liberty.

No person shall be deprived of his life or personal liberty except according to procedure established by law.

Article 22. Protection against arrest and detention in certain cases.

(1) No person who is arrested shall be detained in custody without being informed, as soon as may be, of the grounds for such arrest nor shall he be denied the right to consult, and to be defended by, a legal practitioner of his choice.

(2) Every person who is arrested and detained in custody shall be produced before the nearest magistrate within a period of twentyfour hours of such arrest excluding the time necessary for the journey from the place of arrest to the court of the magistrate and no such person shall be detained in custody beyond the said period without the authority of a magistrate.

(3) Nothing in clauses (1) and (2) shall apply—

(a) to any person who for the time being is in enemy alien; or

(b) to any person who is arrested or detained under any law providing for preventive detention.

(4) No law providing for preventive detention shall authorise the detention of a person for a longer period than three months unless—

(a) an Advisory Board consisting of persons who are, or have been, or are qualified to be appointed as, Judges of a High Court has reported before the expiration of the said period of three months that there is in its opinion sufficient cause for such detention:

Provided that nothing in this sub-clause shall authorise the deten-

tion of any person beyond the maximum period prescribed by any law made by Parliament under sub-clause (b) of clause (7); or

(b) such person is detained in accordance with the provisions of any law made by Parliament under subclauses (a) and (b) of clause (7).

(5) When any person is detained in pursuance of an order made under any law providing for preventive detention, the authority making the order shall, as soon as may be, communicate to such person the grounds on which the order has been made and shall afford him the earliest opportunity of making a representation against the order.

(6) Nothing in clause (5) shall require the authority making any such order as is referred to in that clause to disclose facts which such authority considers to be against the public interest to disclose.

(7) Parliament may by law prescribe—

(a) the circumstances under which, and the class or classes of cases in which, a person may be detained for a period longer than three months under any law providing for preventive detention without obtaining the opinion of an Advisory Board in accordance with the provisions of sub-clause (a) of clause (4);

(b) the maximum period for which any person may in any class or classes of cases be detained under any law providing for preventive detention; and

(c) the procedure to be followed by an Advisory Board in an inquiry under sub-clause (a) of clause (4).

Right against Exploitation
Article 23. Prohibition of traffic in human beings and forced labour.

(1) Traffic in human beings and begar and other similar forms of forced labour are prohibited and any contravention of this provision shall be an offence punishable in accordance with law.

(2) Nothing in this article shall prevent the State from imposing compulsory service for public purposes, and in imposing such service the State shall not make any discrimination on grounds only of religion, race, caste or class or any of them.

Article 24. Prohibition of employment of children in factories, etc.

No child below the age of fourteen years shall be employed to work in any factory or mine or engaged in any other hazardous employment.

Right to Freedom of Religion
Article 25. Freedom of conscience and free profession, practice and propagation of religion.

(1) Subject to public order, morality and health and to the other provisions of this Part, all persons are equally entitled to freedom of conscience and the right freely to profess, practise and propagate religion.

(2) Nothing in this article shall affect the operation of any existing law or prevent the State from making any law—

(a) regulating or restricting any economic, financial, political or other secular activity which may be associated with religious practice;

(b) providing for social welfare and reform or the throwing open of Hindu religious institutions of a public character to all classes and sections of Hindus.

Explanation I.—The wearing and carrying of kirpans shall be deemed to be included in the profession of the Sikh religion.

Explanation II.—In sub-clause (b) of clause (2), the reference to Hindus shall be construed as including a reference to persons professing the Sikh, Jaina or Buddhist religion, and the reference to Hindu religious institutions shall be construed accordingly.

Article 26. Freedom to manage religious affairs.

Subject to public order, morality and health, every religious denomination or any section thereof shall have the right—

(a) to establish and maintain institutions for religious and charitable purposes;

(b) to manage its own affairs in matters of religion;

(c) to own and acquire movable and immovable property; and

(d) to administer such property in accordance with law.

Article 27. Freedom as to payment of taxes for promotion of any particular religion.

No person shall be compelled to pay any taxes, the proceeds of which are specifically appropriated in payment of expenses for the promotion or maintenance of any particular religion or religious denomination.

Article 28. Freedom as to attendance at religious instruction or religious worship in certain education institutions.

(1) No religious instruction shall be provided in any educational institution wholly maintained out of State funds.

(2) Nothing in clause (1) shall apply to an educational institution which is administered by the State but has been established under any endowment or trust which requires that religious instruction shall be imparted in such institution.

(3) No person attending any educational institution recognised by

the State or receiving aid out of State funds shall be required to take part in any religious instruction that may be imparted in such institution or to attend any religious worship that may be conducted in such institution or in any premises attached thereto unless such person or, if such person is a minor, his guardian has given his consent thereto.

Cultural and Educational Rights
Article 29. Protection of interests of minorities.

(1) Any section of the citizens residing in the territory of India or any part thereof having a distinct language, script or culture of its own shall have the right to conserve the same.

(2) No citizen shall be denied admission into any educational institution maintained by the State or receiving aid out of State funds on grounds only of religion, race, caste, language or any of them.

Article 30. Right of minorities to establish and administer educational institutions.

(1) All minorities, whether based on religion or language, shall have the right to establish and administer educational institutions of their choice.

(1A) In making any law providing for the compulsory acquisition of any property of an educational institution established and administered by a minority, referred to in clause (1), the State shall ensure that the amount fixed by or determined under such law for the acquisition of such property is such as would not restrict or abrogate the right guaranteed under that clause.

(2) The State shall not, in granting aid to educational institutions, discriminate against any educational institution on the ground that it is under the management of a minority, whether based on religion or language.

Right to Constitutional Remedies
Article 32. Remedies for enforcement of rights conferred by this Part.

(1) The right to move the Supreme Court by appropriate proceedings for the enforcement of the rights conferred by this Part is guaranteed.

(2) The Supreme Court shall have power to issue directions or orders or writs, including writs in the nature of habeas corpus, mandamus, prohibition, quo warranto and certiorari, whichever may be appropriate, for the enforcement of any of the rights conferred by this Part.

(3) Without prejudice to the powers conferred on the Supreme Court by clauses (1) and (2), Parliament may by law empower any other court

to exercise within the local limits of its Jurisdiction all or any of the powers exercisable by the Supreme Court under clause (2).

(4) The right guaranteed by this article shall not be suspended except as otherwise provided for by this Constitution.

Article 34. Restriction on rights conferred by this Part while martial law is in force in any area.

Notwithstanding anything in the foregoing provisions of this Part, Parliament may by law indemnify any person in the service of the Union or of a State or any other person in respect of any act done by him in connection with the maintenance or restoration of order in any area within the territory of India where martial law was in force or validate any sentence passed, punishment inflicted, forfeiture ordered or other act done under martial law in such area.

Britain: The Treaty of Rome (to which the United Kingdom is a signatory)

Article 119
Each Member State shall during the first stage ensure and subsequently maintain the application of the principle that men and women should receive equal pay for equal work.

For the purpose of this Article, "pay" means the ordinary basic or minimum wage or salary and any other consideration, whether in cash or in kind, which the worker receives, directly or indirectly, in respect of his employment from his employer.

Equal pay without discrimination based on sex means:
> (a) that pay for the same work at piece rates shall be calculated on the basis of the same unit of measurement;
> (b) that pay for work at time rates shall be the same for the same job.

The Canadian Charter of Rights and Freedoms
Part 1 of the Constitution Act, 1982

Whereas Canada is founded upon principles that recognize the supremacy of God and the rule of law:

Guarantee of Rights and Freedoms
1. The Canadian Charter of Rights and Freedoms guarantees the rights and freedoms set out in it subject only to such reasonable limits

prescribed by law as can be demonstrably justified in a free and democratic society.

Fundamental Freedoms

2. Everyone has the following fundamental freedoms:

(a) freedom of conscience and religion;

(b) freedom of thought, belief, opinion and expression, including freedom of the press and other media of communication;

(c) freedom of peaceful assembly; and

(d) freedom of association.

Democratic Rights

3. Every citizen of Canada has the right to vote in an election of members of the House of Commons or of a legislative assembly and to be qualified for membership therein.

4. (1) No House of Commons and no legislative assembly shall continue for longer than five years from the date fixed for the return of the writs at a general election of its members.

(2) In time of real or apprehended war, invasion or insurrection, a House of Commons may be continued by Parliament and a legislative assembly may be continued by the legislature beyond five years if such continuation is not opposed by the votes of more than one-third of the members of the House of Commons or the legislative assembly, as the case may be.

5. There shall be a sitting of Parliament and of each legislature at least once every twelve months.

Mobility Rights

6. (1) Every citizen of Canada has the right to enter, remain in and leave Canada.

(2) Every citizen of Canada and every person who has the status of a permanent resident of Canada has the right

(a) to move to and take up residence in any province; and

(b) to pursue the gaining of a livelihood in any province.

(3) The rights specified in subsection (2) are subject to

(a) any laws or practices of general application in force in a province other than those that discriminate among persons primarily on the basis of province of present or previous residence; and

(b) any laws providing for reasonable residency requirements as a qualification for the receipt of publicly provided social services.

(4) Subsections (2) and (3) do not preclude any law, program or activity that has as its object the amelioration in a province of conditions of individuals in that province who are socially or economically disadvantaged if the rate of employment in that province is below the rate of employment in Canada.

Legal Rights

7. Everyone has the right to life, liberty and security of the person and the right not to be deprived thereof except in accordance with the principles of fundamental justice.

8. Everyone has the right to be secure against unreasonable search or seizure.

9. Everyone has the right not to be arbitrarily detained or imprisoned.

10. Everyone has the right on arrest or detention

(a) to be informed promptly of the reasons therefor;

(b) to retain and instruct counsel without delay and to be informed of that right; and

(c) to have the validity of the detention determined by way of habeas corpus and to be released if the detention is not lawful.

11. Any person charged with an offence has the right

(a) to be informed without unreasonable delay of the specific offence;

(b) to be tried within a reasonable time;

(c) not to be compelled to be a witness in proceedings against that person in respect of the offence;

(d) to be presumed innocent until proven guilty according to law in a fair and public hearing by an independent and impartial tribunal;

(e) not to be denied reasonable bail without just cause;

(f) except in the case of an offence under military law tried before a military tribunal, to the benefit of trial by jury where the maximum punishment for the offence is imprisonment for five years or a more severe punishment;

(g) not to be found guilty on account of any act or omission unless, at the time of the act or omission, it constituted an offence under Canadian or international law or was criminal according to the general principles of law recognized by the community of nations;

(h) if finally acquitted of the offence, not to be tried for it again and, if finally found guilty and punished for the offence, not to be tried or punished for it again; and

(i) if found guilty of the offence and if the punishment for the offence has been varied between the time of commission and the time of sentencing, to the benefit of the lesser punishment.

12. Everyone has the right not to be subjected to any cruel and unusual treatment or punishment.

13. A witness who testifies in any proceedings has the right not to have any incriminating evidence so given used to incriminate that witness in any other proceedings, except in a prosecution for perjury or for the giving of contradictory evidence.

14. A party or witness in any proceedings who does not understand or speak the language in which the proceedings are conducted or who is deaf has the right to the assistance of an interpreter.

Equality Rights

15. (1) Every individual is equal before and under the law and has the right to the equal protection and equal benefit of the law without discrimination and, in particular, without discrimination based on race, national or ethnic origin, colour, religion, sex, age or mental or physical disability.

(2) Subsection (1) does not preclude any law, program or activity that has as its object the amelioration of conditions of disadvantaged individuals or groups including those that are disadvantaged because of race, national or ethnic origin, colour, religion, sex, age or mental or physical disability.

Official Languages of Canada

16. (1) English and French are the official languages of Canada and have equality of status and equal rights and privileges as to their use in all institutions of the Parliament and government of Canada.

(2) English and French are the official languages of New Brunswick and have equality of status and equal rights and privileges as to their use in all institutions of the legislature and government of New Brunswick.

(3) Nothing in the Charter limits the authority of Parliament or a legislature to advance the equality of status or use of English and French.

17. (1) Everyone has the right to use English or French in any debates and other proceedings of Parliament.

(2) Everyone has the right to use English or French in any debates and other proceedings of the legislature of New Brunswick.

18. (1) The statutes, records and journals of Parliament shall be

printed and published in English and French and both language versions are equally authoritative.

(2) The statutes, records and journals of the legislature of New Brunswick shall be printed and published in English and French and both language versions are equally authoritative.

19. (1) Either English or French may be used by any person in, or in any pleading in or process issuing from, any court established by Parliament.

(2) Either English or French may be used by any person in, or in any pleading in or process issuing from, any court of New Brunswick.

20. (1) Any member of the public in Canada has the right to communicate with, and to receive available services from, any head or central office of an institution of the Parliament or government of Canada in English or French, and has the same right with respect to any other office of any such institution where

(a) there is a significant demand for communications with and services from that office in such language; or

(b) due to the nature of the office, it is reasonable that communications with and services from that office be available in both English and French.

(2) Any member of the public in New Brunswick has the right to communicate with, and to receive available services from, any office of an institution of the legislature or government of New Brunswick in English or French.

21. Nothing in sections 16 to 20 abrogates or derogates from any right, privilege or obligation with respect to the English and French languages, or either of them, that exists or is continued by virtue of any other provision of the Constitution of Canada.

22. Nothing in section 16 to 20 abrogates or derogates from any legal or customary right or privilege acquired or enjoyed either before or after the coming into force of this Charter with respect to any language that is not English or French.

Minority Language Educational Rights
23. (1) Citizens of Canada

(a) whose first language learned and still understood is that of the English or French linguistic minority population of the province in which they reside, or

(b) who have received their primary school instruction in Canada in English or French and reside in a province where the lan-

guage in which they received that instruction is the language of the English or French linguistic minority population of the province, have the right to have their children receive primary and secondary school instruction in that language in that province.

(2) Citizens of Canada of whom any child has received or is receiving primary or secondary school instruction in English or French in Canada, have the right to have all their children receive primary and secondary school instruction in the same language.

(3) The right of citizens of Canada under subsections (1) and (2) to have their children receive primary and secondary school instruction in the language of the English or French linguistic minority population of a province

(a) applies wherever in the province the number of children of citizens who have such a right is sufficient to warrant the provision to them out of public funds of minority language instruction; and

(b) includes, where the number of those children so warrants, the right to have them receive that instruction in minority language educational facilities provided out of public funds.

Enforcement

24. (1) Anyone whose rights or freedoms, as guaranteed by this Charter, have been infringed or denied may apply to a court of competent jurisdiction to obtain such remedy as the court considers appropriate and just in the circumstances.

(2) Where, in proceedings under subsection (1), a court concludes that evidence was obtained in a manner that infringed or denied any rights or freedoms guaranteed by this Charter, the evidence shall be excluded if it is established that, having regard to all the circumstances, the admission of it in the proceedings would bring the administration of justice into disrepute.

General

25. The guarantee in this Charter of certain rights and freedoms shall not be construed so as to abrogate or derogate from any aboriginal, treaty or other rights or freedoms that pertain to the aboriginal peoples of Canada including

(a) any rights or freedoms that have been recognized by the Royal Proclamation of October 7, 1763; and

(b) any rights or freedoms that may be acquired by the aboriginal peoples of Canada by way of land claims settlement.

26. The guarantee in this Charter of certain rights and freedoms shall not be construed as denying the existence of any other rights or freedoms that exist in Canada.

27. This Charter shall be interpreted in a manner consistent with the preservation and enhancement of the multicultural heritage of Canadians.

28. Notwithstanding anything in this Charter, the rights and freedoms referred to in it are guaranteed equally to male and female persons.

29. Nothing in this Charter abrogates or derogates from any rights or privileges guaranteed by or under the Constitution of Canada in respect of denominational, separate or dissentient schools.

30. A reference in this Charter to a province or to the legislative assembly or legislature of a province shall be deemed to include a reference to the Yukon Territory and the Northwest Territories, or to the appropriate legislative authority thereof, as the case may be.

31. Nothing in this Charter extends the legislative powers of any body or authority.

Application of Charter

32. (1) This Charter applies

(a) to the Parliament and government of Canada in respect of all matters within the authority of Parliament including all matters relating to the Yukon Territory and Northwest Territories; and

(b) to the legislature and government of each province in respect of all matters within the authority of the legislature of each province.

(2) Notwithstanding subsection (1), section 15 shall not have effect until three years after this section comes into force.

33. (1) Parliament or the legislature of a province may expressly declare in an Act of Parliament or of the legislature, as the case may be, that the Act or a provision thereof shall operate nothwithstanding a provision included in section 2 or sections 7 to 15 of this Charter.

(2) An Act or a provision of an Act in respect of which a declaration made under this section is in effect shall have such operation as it would have but for the provision of this Charter referred to in the declaration.

(3) A declaration made under subsection (1) shall cease to have

effect five years after it comes into force or on such earlier date as may be specified in the declaration.

(4) Parliament or a legislature of a province may re-enact a declaration made under subsection (1).

(5) Subsection (3) applies in respect of a re-enactment made under subsection (4).

NOTES

Citations to case reporters use the abbreviations listed below.

AC	Law Reports, Appeal Cases (United Kingdom)
AIR . . . SC	All India Reporter, Supreme Court Division
All ER	All England Law Reports
D.L.R.	Dominion Law Reports (Canada)
ECR	European Court Reports
EHRR	European Human Rights Reports
F. Supp.	Federal Supplement (United States)
IRLR	Industrial Relations Law Reports (England)
ICR	Industrial Court Reports (England)
KB	Law Reports, King's Bench Division
La. Ann.	Louisiana Annual Reports
QB	Law Reports, Queen's Bench Division
SCALE	Supreme Court Almanac (India)
SCC	Supreme Court Cases (India)
SCR	Supreme Court Reports (India)
S.C.R.	Supreme Court Reports (Canada)
U.S.	United States Reports
WLR	Weekly Law Reports (England)

Chapter One

1. *Monroe v. Pape,* 365 U.S. 167 (1961). The victim's wife and her lover were eventually convicted of the crime. "Negro Family Wins Right to Sue Police Officers," *Chicago Tribune,* Feb. 21, 1961, p. 17; Thomas J. Klitgaard, "The Civil Rights Acts and Mr. Monroe," *California Law Review* 49:145–71 (1961). A federal jury eventually awarded the Monroes $13,000 in damages. *Monroe v. Pape,* 221 F. Supp. 635, 638–39 (1963). Although the number of officers has been widely reported as thirteen, the actual number apparently was nine. Ibid.

2. The Court's decision was announced almost four months before the Court's landmark decision in *Mapp v. Ohio,* 367 U.S. 643 (1961) (and over a month before *Mapp* was argued). The *Mapp* decision, which held that illegally seized evidence must be excluded from state criminal trials, is now recognized as the beginning of the criminal procedure revolution. *Monroe,* although not a criminal procedure decision, addressed policy questions that were very similar

to those addressed in *Mapp:* how may unlawful police activity be controlled? Coming as it did before *Mapp*, and indeed in the absence of any change in membership on the Court, the *Monroe* decision was unexpected.

3. 325 U.S. 91 (1945). The Court in *Screws* ruled that, in order to convict an official under 18 U.S.C. §242 (which makes it a federal crime to act under "color of law" to deprive any individual of constitutional or other federal rights), prosecutors must show beyond a reasonable doubt that the official had a "specific intent" to violate the victim's rights. The "specific intent" standard was very difficult to meet in most cases. As late as 1960, United States Justice Department officials believed that the standard posed a major obstacle to police brutality prosecutions and convictions. See John T. Elliff, *The United States Department of Justice and Individual Rights, 1937–1962* (New York: Garland, 1987), 569. Yet it must be noted that the justices who supported the difficult standard for conviction created by *Screws* did so because they believed that standard to be necessary in order to save the statute from challenges that it was void for vagueness (that it gave officials no adequate notice of what kinds of actions were to be illegal).

4. In *Monroe*, the Court repudiated the *Screws* standard for cases involving civil, not criminal liability; Justice Douglas's majority opinion declared that the civil rights statute authorizing civil lawsuits (42 U.S.C. §1983) "should be read against the background of tort liability that makes a man responsible for the natural consequences of his actions." That new standard for civil actions against police brutality and other deprivations of civil rights significantly eased the burden of proof for plaintiffs, and the number of civil lawsuits brought under the statute grew significantly. Nonetheless, constitutional tort litigants still face significant obstacles. See Theodore Eisenberg and Stewart Schwab, "The Reality of Constitutional Tort Litigation," *Cornell Law Review* 72:641–95 (1987). See also David H. Rosenbloom and Rosemary O'Leary, *Public Administration and Law* (New York: Marcel Dekker, 1997).

5. Richard L. Pacelle, Jr., *The Transformation of the Supreme Court's Agenda: From the New Deal to the Reagan Administration* (Boulder: Westview Press, 1991), 138.

6. Much of this development in the United States is documented in Pacelle, *Transformation;* C. Herman Pritchett, *The Roosevelt Court: A Study in Judicial Politics and Values, 1937–1947* (New York: Macmillan, 1948); C. Herman Pritchett, *Civil Liberties and the Vinson Court* (Chicago: University of Chicago Press, 1954); and Jeffrey Segal and Harold Spaeth, *The Supreme Court and the Attitudinal Model* (Cambridge: Cambridge University Press, 1993).

7. Pacelle, *Transformation*, 138.

8. Gerald R. Rosenberg, *The Hollow Hope: Can Courts Bring About Social Change?* (Chicago: University of Chicago Press, 1991). The landmark school desegregation ruling, *Brown v. Board of Education*, in particular has been eroded in practice. See Gary Orfield, Susan E. Eaton, and the Harvard Project on School Desegregation, *Dismantling Desegregation: The Quiet Reversal of Brown v. Board of Education* (New York: New Press, 1996).

9. See, for instance, Bruce Ackerman, *We the People: Foundations* (Cambridge: Harvard University Press, 1991); Lee Epstein and Joseph F. Kobylka, *The Su-*

preme Court and Legal Change: Abortion and the Death Penalty (Chapel Hill: University of North Carolina Press, 1992); Kermit L. Hall, *The Magic Mirror: Law in American History* (New York: Oxford University Press, 1989); Michael J. Klarman, "Rethinking the Civil Rights and Civil Liberties Revolutions," *Virginia Law Review* 82:1–67 (1996); Robert G. McCloskey, *The American Supreme Court*, 2d ed., ed. Sanford Levinson (Chicago: University of Chicago Press, 1994); Mark V. Tushnet, *The NAACP's Legal Strategy against Segregated Education, 1925–1950* (Chapel Hill: University of North Carolina Press, 1987); Clement E. Vose, *Constitutional Change: Amendment Politics and Constitutional Litigation since 1900* (Lexington, Mass.: Lexington Books, 1972); and many others.

10. Robert H. Bork, *The Tempting of America: The Political Seduction of the Law* (New York: Free Press, 1990), 9, 11.

11. Ibid., 3; William J. Quirk and R. Randall Bridwell, *Judicial Dictatorship* (New Brunswick, N.J.: Transaction, 1995). For a more sophisticated analysis along the same line, see James Allan, "Bills of Rights and Judicial Power—A Liberal's Quandary," *Oxford Journal of Legal Studies* 16:337–52 (1996).

12. John Hart Ely, *Democracy and Distrust: A Theory of Judicial Review* (Cambridge: Harvard University Press, 1980).

13. See, e.g., *Reynolds v. Sims*, 377 U.S. 533 (1964), and *Baker v. Carr*, 369 U.S. 186 (1962).

14. Ely, *Democracy and Distrust*, 120–24.

15. Susan Sterett, *Creating Constitutionalism? The Politics of Legal Expertise and Administrative Law in England and Wales* (Ann Arbor: University of Michigan Press, 1997). Several scholars have examined such developments more broadly. Mauro Cappelletti, for example, argued that the role of constitutional courts in many countries is experiencing a fundamental transformation toward rights-based activism. See "Repudiating Montesquieu? The Expansion and Legitimacy of 'Constitutional Justice,'" *Catholic University Law Review* 35:1–30 (1985). Most of the western European countries, in fact, have granted to courts of one sort or another the power of judicial review over legislation, and some (but not all) of those courts have used their power broadly to develop unwritten but nonetheless foundational principles of human rights. See Louis Favoreu, "Constitutional Review in Europe," in *Constitutionalism and Rights: The Influence of the United States Constitution Abroad*, ed. Louis Henkin and Albert J. Rosenthal (New York: Columbia University Press, 1990); and Alec Stone, *The Birth of Judicial Politics in France* (Oxford: Oxford University Press, 1992). For a comprehensive analysis of developments in judicial policy making in many countries, see C. Neal Tate and Torbjorn Vallinder, eds., *The Global Expansion of Judicial Power* (New York: New York University Press, 1995).

16. Rosenberg, *The Hollow Hope*.

17. 347 U.S. 483 (1954).

18. Rosenberg, *The Hollow Hope*, 103–4.

19. Michael W. McCann, *Rights at Work: Pay Equity Reform and the Politics of Legal Mobilization* (Chicago: University of Chicago Press, 1994).

20. Marc Galanter, "The Radiating Effects of Courts," in *Empirical Theories about Courts*, ed. Keith O. Boyum and Lynn Mather (New York: Longman, 1983), 136.

21. Mark V. Tushnet, *Making Civil Rights Law: Thurgood Marshall and the Supreme Court, 1936–1961* (New York: Oxford University Press, 1994), 56–66; Elliff, *Department of Justice.*

22. ACLU—Illinois Division, *Secret Detention by the Chicago Police* (Glencoe, Ill.: Free Press, 1959), discussed in Samuel Walker, *In Defense of American Liberties: A History of the ACLU* (New York: Oxford University Press, 1990), 248–49.

23. S. Walker, *In Defense of American Liberties,* 249.

24. *Monell v. Department of Social Services,* 436 U.S. 658 (1978); Conrad K. Harper, "The Overthrow of *Monroe v. Pape:* A Chapter in the Legacy of Thurgood Marshall," *Fordham Law Review* 61:39–48 (1992). See also *Owen v. City of Independence,* 445 U.S. 622 (1980).

Chapter Two

1. The precise meaning of "judicial independence" is open to endless debate; the criteria mentioned here are threshold requirements. See Owen M. Fiss, "The Right Degree of Independence," in *Transition to Democracy in Latin America: The Role of the Judiciary,* ed. Irwin P. Stotzky (Boulder: Westview Press, 1993), 55–72; Christopher M. Larkins, "Judicial Independence and Democratization: A Theoretical and Conceptual Analysis," *American Journal of Comparative Law* 44:605–26 (1996).

2. Allan, "Bills of Rights"; P. S. Atiyah and Robert S. Summers, *Form and Substance in Anglo-American Law* (Oxford: Oxford University Press, 1987), 238–39; Kenneth M. Holland, ed., *Judicial Activism in Comparative Perspective* (New York: St. Martin's Press, 1991).

3. Louis Henkin and Albert J. Rosenthal, eds., *Constitutionalism and Rights: The Influence of the U.S. Constitution Abroad* (New York: Columbia University Press, 1991).

4. Favoreu, "Constitutional Review in Europe," 42–43. Similarly, in other European countries, the critics of judicial policy making have opposed the adoption of bills of rights precisely because such documents are thought to empower judges.

5. Granville Austin, *The Indian Constitution: Cornerstone of a Nation* (Delhi: Oxford University Press, 1966), 103–6.

6. See, for example, Michael Mandel, *The Charter of Rights and the Legalisation of Politics in Canada* (Toronto: Thompson, 1989).

7. Michael Zander, *A Bill of Rights?* 3d ed. (London: Sweet & Maxwell, 1985).

8. See, for instance, James Allan's discussion of "raw judicial power" in "Bills of Rights," 347–51.

9. James Madison, *The Papers of James Madison,* vol. 12 (Charlottesville: University Press of Virginia, 1979), 207.

10. Rainer Knopff and F. L. Morton, *Charter Politics* (Scarborough, Ont.: Nelson Canada, 1992); F. L. Morton, "The Political Impact of the Canadian Charter of Rights and Freedoms," *Canadian Journal of Political Science* 20:31–55 (1987).

11. James Madison, *The Papers of James Madison,* vol. 11 (Charlottesville: University Press of Virginia, 1977), 298–99; see also Madison, *Papers,* vol. 12, 204–5.

12. Vivien Hart, *Bound by Our Constitution: Women, Workers, and the Minimum Wage* (Princeton: Princeton University Press, 1994), 174; Hendrik Hartog, "The

Constitution of Aspiration and 'The Rights That Belong to Us All,'" *Journal of American History* 74:1013–34 (1987).

13. Mark MacGuigan, "The Development of Civil Liberties in Canada," *Queen's Quarterly* 72:273 (1965), quoted in Cynthia Williams, "The Changing Nature of Citizen Rights," in *Constitutionalism, Citizenship, and Society in Canada*, ed. Alan Cairns and Cynthia Williams (Toronto: University of Toronto Press, 1985), 107.

14. David Adamany and Joel B. Grossman, "Support for the Supreme Court as a National Policymaker," *Law and Policy Quarterly* 5:405–37 (1983).

15. A. V. Dicey, *Introduction to the Study of the Law of the Constitution*, 10th ed. (London: Macmillan, 1961), 198–202. Dicey identified another limitation of bills of rights. A government intent on tyranny, he argued, is easily capable of wiping out a bill of rights in a single action; but to destroy the common law's remedies, a government must eradicate virtually the entire common law and the legal culture with which it is intertwined. Ibid.

16. James Madison, *The Papers of James Madison*, vol. 10 (Chicago: University of Chicago Press, 1977), 211–12, emphasis added. See also Jack N. Rakove, "Parchment Barriers and the Politics of Rights," in *A Culture of Rights: The Bill of Rights in Philosophy, Politics, and Law–1791 and 1991*, ed. Michael J. Lacey and Knud Haakonssen (Cambridge: Cambridge University Press, 1991), 136. Madison's doubts about a bill of rights reflected in part his belief that such rights promises were likely to be far less effective than structural mechanisms for restraining governmental power. Structural mechanisms, particularly the separation of powers and federalism, tied the individual interests of officials to the institutional resources of branches of the government, thus enabling officials to effectively defend their interests. A bill of rights, by contrast, as the quoted statement indicates, provided individuals with no institutional resources for pursuing their interests. For further discussion, see Charles R. Epp, "Do Bills of Rights Matter? The Canadian Charter of Rights and Freedoms," *American Political Science Review* 90:766 (1996).

17. Segal and Spaeth, *Attitudinal Model*, 69–72.

18. Gerhard Casper and Richard A. Posner, *The Workload of the Supreme Court* (Chicago: American Bar Foundation, 1976); Felix Frankfurter and James M. Landis, *The Business of the Supreme Court: A Study in the Federal Judicial System* (New York: Macmillan, 1927).

19. Burton M. Atkins and Henry R. Glick, "Environmental and Structural Variables as Determinants of Issues in State Courts of Last Resort," *American Journal of Political Science* 20:97–115 (1976); Robert A. Kagan, Bliss Cartwright, Lawrence M. Friedman, and Stanton Wheeler, "The Business of State Supreme Courts, 1870–1970," *Stanford Law Review* 30:121–56 (1977).

20. Robert Yates, "Letters of Brutus" (letter no. 15, 1788), in *The Origins of the American Constitution: A Documentary History*, ed. Michael Kammen (New York: Penguin Books, 1986), 356.

21. Segal and Spaeth, for instance, devote their discussion of the United States Supreme Court's civil liberties agenda to a history of turnover in the Court's membership. See *Attitudinal Model*, 97–118.

22. Louis Hartz, *The Liberal Tradition in America* (San Diego: Harcourt, Brace, Jovanovich, 1955), 9.

23. Mary Ann Glendon, *Rights Talk: The Impoverishment of Political Discourse* (New York: Free Press, 1991).

24. Ibid.

25. Jack Donnelly, *Universal Human Rights in Theory and Practice* (Ithaca, N.Y.: Cornell University Press, 1989).

26. Cappelletti, "Repudiating Montesquieu?"

27. Elizabeth Heger Boyle, "Litigants, Lawbreakers, Legislators: Using Political Frames to Explain Cross-National Variation in Legal Activity" (Ph.D. diss., Stanford University, 1996). See also, more generally, Walter W. Powell and Paul J. DiMaggio, eds., *The New Institutionalism in Organizational Analysis* (Chicago: University of Chicago Press, 1991).

28. Herbert Wechsler, "Toward Neutral Principles of Constitutional Law," *Harvard Law Review* 73:33 (1959). He asked rhetorically (clearly presuming that the answer was obvious), "Does enforced separation of the sexes discriminate against females merely because it may be the females who resent it and it is imposed by judgments predominantly male?" Ibid.

29. See Elisabeth Clemens's analysis of the complex interaction between beliefs about organizational possibilities and resource mobilization in the historical development of interest groups. She argues that interest-group organizing grew out of the discovery and development of a new "organizational repertoire"—new understandings about how political pressure might be mobilized and channeled. Elisabeth S. Clemens, *The People's Lobby: Organizational Innovation and the Rise of Interest Group Politics in the United States, 1890–1925* (Chicago: University of Chicago Press, 1997), 41–64.

30. For discussions of this issue, see Frances Kahn Zemans, "Legal Mobilization: The Neglected Role of the Law in the Political System," *American Political Science Review* 77:690–703 (1983); Mark Kessler, "Legal Mobilization for Social Reform: Power and the Politics of Agenda Setting," *Law & Society Review* 24:121–43 (1990); Susan E. Lawrence, *The Poor in Court: The Legal Services Program and Supreme Court Decision Making* (Princeton: Princeton University Press, 1990); and Susan M. Olson, "Interest Group Litigation in Federal District Court: Beyond the Political Disadvantage Theory," *Journal of Politics* 52:854–82 (1990).

31. H. W. Perry, Jr., *Deciding to Decide: Agenda Setting in the United States Supreme Court* (Cambridge: Harvard University Press, 1991), 230–34.

32. 347 U.S. 483 (1954).

33. J. Harvie Wilkinson, *From Brown to Bakke: The Supreme Court and School Integration, 1954–1978* (New York: Oxford University Press, 1979).

34. Marc Galanter, "Why the Haves Come Out Ahead: Speculations on the Limits of Social Change," *Law & Society Review* 9:95–160 (1974). Galanter's hypothesis has been tested most directly by examining the win/loss records of different kinds of litigants in head-to-head conflict in court. In general (there are some exceptions), "upperdog" litigants fare better than "underdogs." The research based on the theory includes Peter McCormick, "Party Capability Theory and Appellate Success in the Supreme Court of Canada, 1949–1992," *Canadian Journal of Political Science* 26:523–40 (1993); Donald R. Songer and Reginald S. Sheehan, "Who Wins on Appeal? Upperdogs and Underdogs in the United States Courts of Appeals," *American Journal of Political Science*

36:235–58; Stanton Wheeler, Bliss Cartwright, Robert A. Kagan, and Lawrence M. Friedman, "Do the 'Haves' Come Out Ahead? Winning and Losing in State Supreme Courts, 1870–1970," *Law & Society Review* 21:403–45 (1987); Stacia L. Haynie, "Resource Inequalities and Litigation Outcomes in the Philippine Supreme Court," *Journal of Politics* 56:752–72 (1994); Mary L. Voncansek, "Winners and Losers before the European Court of Justice: Litigant Status and Ideology" (unpublished paper on file with author); and Burton M. Atkins, "Party Capability Theory and Judicial Decisions: A Multivariate Perspective on the Structure of Intervention Behavior by the English Court of Appeal," *American Journal of Political Science* 35:881–903 (1991). Atkins also found, however, that party capability, measured by type of litigant, did not significantly influence mobilization of appeals in the English judicial system. See his "Alternative Models of Appeal Mobilization in Judicial Hierarchies," *American Journal of Political Science* 37:780–98 (1993). The research on the United States Supreme Court finds that party type is not closely associated with degree of success on the merits, perhaps for the reason that in that court judicial preferences have a larger impact on case outcomes. See Reginald S. Sheehan, William Mishler, and Donald R. Songer, "Ideology, Status, and the Differential Success of Direct Parties before the Supreme Court," *American Political Science Review* 86:464–71 (1992). There is some evidence indicating that groups may fare no better on the merits than nongroup litigants. See Lee Epstein and C. K. Rowland, "Debunking the Myth of Interest Group Invincibility in the Courts," *American Political Science Review* 85:205–17 (1991). But whether differences in resources lie behind differences in the victory ratios of different *types* of litigants has not been explored adequately.

35. The litigation-related activities of organized interest groups are surveyed in L. Epstein and Kobylka, *Supreme Court and Legal Change*, 24–32. See also Gregory A. Caldeira and John R. Wright, "Organized Interests and Agenda-Setting in the U.S. Supreme Court," *American Political Science Review* 82:1109–27 (1988); Galanter, "Why the Haves Come Out Ahead"; Wasby, *Race Relations Litigation*.

36. Cornell W. Clayton, *The Politics of Justice: The Attorney General and the Making of Legal Policy* (Armonk, N.Y.: M. E. Sharpe, 1992).

37. See, for instance, Lawrence, *The Poor in Court*.

38. Robert A. Kagan, "Do Lawyers Cause Adversarial Legalism? A Preliminary Inquiry," *Law & Social Inquiry* 19:1–62 (1994); Kevin T. McGuire, *The Supreme Court Bar: Legal Elites in the Washington Community* (Charlottesville: University Press of Virginia, 1993).

39. See, e.g., Richard L. Abel and Phillip S. C. Lewis, eds., *Lawyers in Society, Volume I: The Common Law World* (Berkeley: University of California Press, 1988).

40. Clemens, *People's Lobby*.

41. Tushnet, *NAACP's Legal Strategy*; Richard Kluger, *Simple Justice: The History of Brown v. Board of Education and Black America's Struggle for Equality* (New York: Vintage, 1977); Clement E. Vose, *Caucasians Only: The Supreme Court, the NAACP, and the Restrictive Covenant Cases* (Berkeley: University of California Press, 1959); Wasby, *Race Relations Litigation*; S. Walker, *In Defense of American Liberties*; Frank J. Sorauf, *The Wall of Separation: The Constitutional Poli-*

tics of Church and State (Princeton: Princeton University Press, 1976); Karen O'Connor, *Women's Organizations' Use of the Courts* (Lexington, Mass.: Lexington Books, 1980).

42. M. James Penton, *Jehovah's Witnesses in Canada: Champions of Freedom of Speech and Worship* (Toronto: Macmillan, 1976).

43. *Drake v. Chief Adjudication Officer,* Case 150/85 [1987] QB 166 (ECJ). The Act had prevented married women from receiving assistance allocated to caregivers for disabled persons. See Roger Smith, "How Good Are Test Cases?" in *Public Interest Law,* ed. Jeremy Cooper and Rajeev Dhavan (Oxford, Basil Blackwell, 1986), 271–85; Carol Harlow and Richard Rawlings, *Pressure through Law* (London: Routledge, 1992).

44. Marc Galanter and Thomas Palay, *Tournament of Lawyers: The Transformation of the Big Law Firm* (Chicago: University of Chicago Press, 1991); Abel and Lewis, *Lawyers in Society.*

45. Stephen Wasby, "How Planned is 'Planned Litigation'?" *American Bar Foundation Research Journal* 1984:83–138.

46. Ruth B. Cowan, "Women's Rights through Litigation: An Examination of the American Civil Liberties Union Women's Rights Project, 1971–1976," *Columbia Human Rights Law Review* 8:383 (1976).

47. Wasby, *Race Relations Litigation,* 96.

48. For an important early discussion of comparative research of judicial systems, see C. Neal Tate, "Judicial Institutions in Cross-National Perspective: Toward Integrating Courts into the Comparative Study of Politics," in *Comparative Judicial Systems: Challenging Frontiers in Conceptual and Empirical Analysis,* ed. John R. Schmidhauser (London: Butterworths, 1987). Each of the countries is a crucial addition to the study because each contributes significant variation to the dependent variable (extent of attention to rights) and to the independent variables (the various factors thought to be most important in influencing attention to rights). This research design thus combines elements of the most-similar and most-different comparative methods. For a discussion of the most-similar and most-different comparative designs, see John P. Frendreis, "Explanation of Variation and Detection of Covariation: The Purpose and Logic of Comparative Analysis," *Comparative Political Studies* 16:255–72 (1983).

49. Pacelle, *Transformation.*

50. Burton M. Atkins has shown that there are important systematic differences between published and unpublished cases decided by the British Court of Appeal. Accordingly, my evidence for the supreme courts that produce some unpublished decisions, those of Britain and India, relies on both published and unpublished decisions. See Burton M. Atkins, "Selective Reporting and the Communication of Legal Rights in England," *Judicature* 76:58–67, and "Communication of Appellate Decisions: A Multivariate Model for Understanding the Selection of Cases for Publication," *Law & Society Review* 24:1171–96 (1990).

Chapter Three

1. Glendon, *Rights Talk,* 1.

2. Jesse H. Choper, *Judicial Review and the National Political Process* (Chicago: University of Chicago Press, 1980), 64, 128.

3. The data presented in figure 3.1 are taken from Pacelle, *Transformation*, and from additional data generously supplied by Richard Pacelle, for which I am grateful.

4. Paul L. Murphy, *The Meaning of Freedom of Speech: First Amendment Freedoms from Wilson to FDR* (Westport, Conn.: Greenwood Press, 1972).

5. 245 U.S. 60 (1917).

6. *Schenck v. United States*, 249 U.S. 47 (1919); *Abrams v. United States*, 250 U.S. 616 (1919); *Debs v. United States*, 249 U.S. 211 (1919); *Frohwerk v. United States*, 249 U.S. 204 (1919).

7. *Gilbert v. Minnesota*, 254 U.S. 325 (1920); *Gitlow v. New York*, 268 U.S. 652 (1925); *Fiske v. Kansas*, 274 U.S. 380 (1927).

8. *Pierce v. Society of Sisters*, 268 U.S. 510 (1925); *Meyer v. Nebraska*, 262 U.S. 390 (1923).

9. *Near v. Minnesota*, 283 U.S. 697 (1931); *Powell v. Alabama*, 287 U.S. 45 (1932).

10. The Court handed down several important civil rights and liberties decisions before 1917, particularly *Minor v. Happersett*, 88 U.S. 162 (1875) (law prohibiting women from voting found not to violate the citizenship and privileges and immunities clauses of the Fourteenth Amendment, the Guarantee Clause, the due process clause of the Fifth Amendment, or the prohibition against bills of attainder); *United States v. Cruikshank*, 92 U.S. 542 (1876) (federal civil rights statute improperly invoked to convict defendants of participation in armed mob that killed over a hundred black men over a disputed election; the decision narrowed congressional authority to criminalize armed violence against blacks in the South); *Strauder v. West Virginia*, 100 U.S. 303 (1880) (state statute expressly limiting jury service to white males found to violate equal protection); the *Civil Rights Cases*, 109 U.S. 3 (1883) (portions of Civil Rights Act of 1875 prohibiting discrimination in private accommodations and the like found to be beyond congressional authority, which is limited to "state action"); *Hurtado v. California*, 110 U.S. 516 (1884) (Fifth Amendment's guarantee of grand jury indictment in capital cases not applicable to state cases under the Fourteenth Amendment); *Yick Wo v. Hopkins*, 118 U.S. 356 (1886) (law applied in a discriminatory manner found to violate equal protection); *Plessy v. Ferguson*, 163 U.S. 537 (1896) (law requiring racial segregation on railroad cars found not to violate equal protection); *Maxwell v. Dow*, 176 U.S. 581 (1900) (state conviction for robbery by jury of eight, not twelve, and without indictment by grand jury, found not to violate privileges and immunities and due process clauses); and *Twining v. New Jersey*, 211 U.S. 78 (1908) (privilege against self-incrimination found not to be incorporated in the Fourteenth Amendment as limitation on states).

11. David M. Rabban, "The First Amendment in Its Forgotten Years," *Yale Law Journal* 90:514–95 (1981).

12. *United States v. Cruikshank*, 92 U.S. 542 (1876); *Ex parte Jackson*, 96 U.S. 727 (1877); *Ex parte Curtis*, 106 U.S. 371 (1882); *Spies v. Illinois*, 123 U.S. 131 (1887); *Davis v. Beason*, 133 U.S. 333 (1890); *In re Rapier*, 143 U.S. 110 (1892); *Rosen v. United States*, 161 U.S. 29 (1896) (*Rosen* concerned mailing of obscene materials, but no free speech issues were raised by either party or the Court); *Davis v. Massachusetts*, 167 U.S. 43 (1897); *American School of Magnetic Healing v. McAnnulty*, 187 U.S. 94 (1902); *Public Clearing House v. Coyne*, 194 U.S. 497 (1904);

Turner v. Williams, 194 U.S. 279 (1904); *Halter v. Nebraska,* 205 U.S. 34 (1907) (*Halter* concerned what would now be considered commercial speech issues, although neither the defendant, the government, nor the Court raised free speech issues); *Patterson v. Colorado,* 205 U.S. 454 (1907); *Gompers v. Bucks Stove & Range Co.,* 221 U.S. 418 (1911); *United States v. Press Publishing Co.,* 219 U.S. 1 (1911); *Lewis Publishing Co. v. Morgan,* 229 U.S. 288 (1913); *Fox v. Washington,* 236 U.S. 273 (1915); and *Mutual Film Corp. v. Industrial Commission of Ohio,* 236 U.S. 230 (1915).

13. *Hoyt v. Florida,* 368 U.S. 57 (1961).

14. 381 U.S. 479 (1965).

15. I treat the abortion cases as women's-rights cases because of the centrality of issues related to reproductive freedom in the women's movement. See, e.g., Kristin Luker, *Abortion and the Politics of Motherhood* (Berkeley: University of California Press, 1984).

16. Stephen M. Griffin, *American Constitutionalism* (Princeton: Princeton University Press, 1996); Morton Keller, "Powers and Rights: Two Centuries of American Constitutionalism," *Journal of American History* 74:675–94 (1987).

17. 32 U.S. (7 Pet.) 243 (1833).

18. William E. Nelson, *The Fourteenth Amendment: From Political Principle to Judicial Doctrine* (Cambridge: Harvard University Press, 1988).

19. Hartog, "Constitution of Aspiration."

20. *Slaughterhouse Cases,* 83 U.S. (16 Wall.) 36 (1873); *Minor v. Happersett,* 88 U.S. 162 (1875); *Civil Rights Cases,* 109 U.S. 3 (1883).

21. The Nineteenth Amendment, guaranteeing the right to vote regardless of sex, of course was added in 1920; but it has not been part of the constitutional foundation for the judicial rights revolution.

22. Hartog, "Constitution of Aspiration."

23. William M. Wiecek, *The Sources of Antislavery Constitutionalism in America, 1760–1848* (Ithaca, N.Y.: Cornell University Press, 1977).

24. Hartog, "Constitution of Aspiration," 1030.

25. Nelson, *Fourteenth Amendment,* 13–39.

26. David M. Rabban, "The IWW Free Speech Fights and Popular Conceptions of Free Expression before World War I," *Virginia Law Review* 80:1055–1158 (1994); David M. Rabban, "The Free Speech League, the ACLU, and Changing Conceptions of Free Speech in American History," *Stanford Law Review* 45:47–114 (1992).

27. Rabban, "IWW Free Speech Fights," 1081–86, 1098–1102.

28. The statement is from Amos Pinchot, a progressive journalist, and is quoted in Rabban, "IWW Free Speech Fights," 1084–85.

29. *State v. Goodwin,* 37 La. Ann. 713 (1885), noted in John W. Wertheimer, "Free-Speech Fights: The Roots of Modern Free-Expression Litigation in the United States" (Ph.D. diss., Princeton University, 1992), 64.

30. Rabban, "Free Speech League," 88–97.

31. Wertheimer, "Free-Speech Fights"; John W. Wertheimer, "*Mutual Film* Revisited: The Movies, Censorship, and Free Speech in Progressive America," *The American Journal of Legal History* 37:158–89 (1993). See also Alexis J. Anderson, "The Formative Period of First Amendment Theory, 1870–1915," *The American Journal of Legal History* 24:56–75 (1980).

32. Undoubtedly the Supreme Court responds at least marginally to public opinion. See Roy B. Flemming and B. Dan Wood, "The Public and the Supreme Court: Individual Justice Responsiveness to American Policy Moods," *American Journal of Political Science* 41:468–98 (1997). See also William Mishler and Reginald Sheehan, "The Supreme Court as a Counter-Majoritarian Institution? The Impact of Public Opinion on Supreme Court Decisions," *American Political Science Review* 87:87–101 (1993).

33. Alexis de Tocqueville, *Democracy in America*, ed. J. P. Mayer (New York: Harper & Row, 1969), 150.

34. McCloskey, *American Supreme Court*, 209.

35. In public opinion polls, respondents' stated willingness to vote for a woman for president, for instance, jumped dramatically in the late sixties and early seventies, from 55 percent of survey respondents in 1963 to 80 percent of respondents by 1974. George H. Gallup, *The Gallup Poll: Public Opinion 1935–1971*, vol. 13 (New York: Random House, 1972), 1846; Floris W. Wood, *An American Profile—Opinions and Behavior, 1972–89* (Detroit: Gale Research, 1990), 541.

36. See, for example, David G. Barnum, "The Supreme Court and Public Opinion: Judicial Decision-Making in the Post—New Deal Period." *Journal of Politics* 47:652–66 (1985); Hazel Erskine, "The Polls: Race Relations," *Public Opinion Quarterly* 26:137 (1956); Glendon, *Rights Talk.*

37. In 1920, for instance, the *Literary Digest* denounced "America's High Tide of Crime" (*Literary Digest*, Dec. 11, 1920, 11–12). In 1921, articles appeared on "Accounting for the Crime Wave" (*Literary Digest*, Aug. 27, 1921, 30) and "Meeting the Crime Wave" (J. Gollomb, *Nation*, Jan. 19, 1921, 80–83). Since that period, fear of a "crime wave" has been fairly continual.

38. Sam B. Warner and Henry B. Cabot, "Changes in the Administration of Criminal Justice During the Past Fifty Years," *Harvard Law Review* 50:583 (1937), quoted in Lawrence M. Friedman, *Crime and Punishment in American History* (New York: Basic Books, 1993), 303.

39. In 1916, for instance, *Outlook* published an article by "An Exconvict" characterizing "Criminal Lawyers as a Cause of Crime" (*Outlook*, Dec. 27, 1916, 911–13); in 1927, William Johnson argued that "Law Protects the Criminal" (*Good Housekeeping*, March 1927, 20–21); in 1931, M. N. Davis demanded, "Let the Police Have the Breaks Rather Than the Criminal" (*American City*, March 1931, 102); in 1934, J. Beatty criticized the "Guardians of Crime: Lawyers Who Defend Criminals" (*American Magazine*, Sept. 1934, 81–82); in 1940, J. Edgar Hoover previewed a currently popular theme, "Crime's Law School: Combing the Prison Lawbooks to Find Loopholes for Freedom" (*American Magazine*, Nov. 1940, 55); and in 1945, still more than fifteen years before the Supreme Court's criminal procedure revolution, V. W. Peterson blasted the "Unreasonable Leniency of Criminal Justice" ("Case Dismissed: Unreasonable Leniency of Criminal Justice," *Atlantic Monthly*, April 1945, 69–74).

40. A. B. Hart, "Use of Torture in America's Prisons," *Current History*, Nov. 1931, 249–50; and A. M. Turano, "Brutalities by the Police," *American Mercury*, July 1934, 341–50.

41. V. W. Peterson, "Case Dismissed: Unreasonable Leniency of Criminal Justice," *Atlantic Monthly*, April 1945, 69–74.

42. See Segal and Spaeth, *Attitudinal Model.*

43. Casper and Posner, *Workload of the Supreme Court,* 19 (citing research by Mary Cornelia Porter).

44. Act of Feb. 13, 1925, ch. 229, 43 Stat. 93.

45. Casper and Posner, *Workload of the Supreme Court,* 20, table 2.6.

46. Frankfurter and Landis, *Study in the Federal Judicial System.*

47. Saul Brenner, "The New Certiorari Game," *Journal of Politics* 41:649–55 (1979); Saul Brenner and John F. Krol, "Strategies in Certiorari Voting on the United States Supreme Court," *Journal of Politics,* 51:828 (1989); Segal and Spaeth, *Attitudinal Model,* 165–207.

48. Gregory A. Caldeira, John R. Wright, and Christopher J. W. Zorn, "Strategic Voting and Gatekeeping in the Supreme Court" (paper presented at the annual meeting of the American Political Science Association, Aug. 29–Sept. 1, 1996, San Francisco).

49. Lee Epstein, Jeffrey A. Segal, and Timothy Johnson, "The Claim of Issue Creation on the U.S. Supreme Court," *American Political Science Review* 90:845–52 (1996).

50. Caldeira and Wright, "Organized Interests"; Caldeira, Wright, and Zorn, "Strategic Voting;" Perry, *Deciding to Decide;* Doris Marie Provine, *Case Selection in the United States Supreme Court* (Chicago: University of Chicago Press, 1980).

51. Perry, *Deciding to Decide,* 230–34. These indicators of legal conflict at the very least fit uncomfortably with the judge-centered model; more plausibly, they are deeply inconsistent with it. In "Organized Interests" Caldeira and Wright suggest that the justices seek cases involving legal conflict in lower courts because such cases enhance their own policy-making power. Perry (*Deciding to Decide,* 246–60), however, argues that these factors are important because the justices believe it to be their institutional responsibility to decide such cases in order to maintain coherence and consistency in the interpretation of federal law. At the very least, the indicators (presence of legal conflict, intercircuit disagreement) more directly measure *legal* factors than attitudinal factors, because they are not direct measures of the *policy* importance of cases but instead are measures of the presence of legal conflict. Segal and Spaeth seem to concur: "the justices . . . refuse to decide . . . meritless cases"; they acknowledge the importance of legal conflict in lower courts as virtually a prerequisite for a case to reach the Court's agenda. Segal and Spaeth, *Attitudinal Model,* 70, 195–99.

52. Perry, *Deciding to Decide,* 218.

53. Ibid., 221.

54. Ibid., 218.

55. Joel B. Grossman, "Agenda Formation on a Policy Active Supreme Court" (unpublished paper on file with author, n.d.). The agenda is constructed over a number of months, and the decisions of a number of actors influence the eventual aggregate outcome. The process is as follows: The Court now employs what is called the "cert. pool," a group of law clerks from each of the justices (except for Stevens) who assist the justices in selecting cases for the Court's agenda. The clerks divide the incoming certiorari petitions among themselves. Each clerk writes a separate memo to the justices on each of the petitions assigned to him or her. The chief justice selects from among the petitions those that he considers most worthy of review and places them on the "discuss list." This list is circulated among the justices, and they may add cases

to the list. The approximately 70 percent of petitions that never reach the discuss list are automatically denied review. In special conferences in late September, before the beginning of the Court's October term, and in conferences on Wednesday and Friday during the regular term, the justices vote on whether to grant or deny certiorari in the numerous petitions on the discuss list. There is little time during the conferences for discussions about the merits of the various petitions, and the justices rely on the clerks' memos in deciding how to vote. Under the "Rule of Four," if four of the nine justices vote to grant certiorari, a case is scheduled for argument. Thus, although each justice may vote to select some cases based on his or her policy preferences, the balance of those policy preferences may be poorly reflected in the aggregate agenda that emerges at the end of the serially conducted, bureaucratic agenda-setting process.

56. Segal and Spaeth, *Attitudinal Model*, 97–118.

57. *Palko v. Connecticut*, 302 U.S. 319 (1937); *United States v. Carolene Products Co.*, 304 U.S. 144 (1938); *Mapp v. Ohio*, 367 U.S. 643 (1961); Segal and Spaeth, *Attitudinal Model*, 97, 102, 107. The famous Footnote Four of *Carolene Products* confirmed that henceforth the Supreme Court would presume the constitutionality of economic regulations, but it also declared that the same presumption would not be accorded to legislation that on its face violated a specific constitutional provision, particularly one contained in the Bill or Rights, or if the legislation were directed at particular religions, national or ethnic minorities, or "discrete and insular minorities" that were systematically excluded from the political process. The footnote is commonly viewed as identifying the Court's emerging role as a defender of the rights of minorities (although only four justices concurred in the opinion containing the footnote).

58. Although by 1920 Holmes vigorously favored freedom of speech, he dissented from the Court's ruling in *Meyer v. Nebraska*, 262 U.S. 390 (1923), which protected the right of parents to educate their children in modern languages other than English.

59. Admittedly Harlan Stone (appointed in 1925), Charles Hughes (reappointed to the Court in 1930 after his resignation in 1916), and Benjamin Cardozo (appointed in 1932 to replace Holmes) in some cases favored the expansion of constitutional protection for rights. But with the votes only of Holmes/Cardozo, Brandeis, Stone, and Hughes, the Court never contained a majority clearly in favor of the expansion of constitutional protection for rights during the period from 1916 through 1937; in most cases there were far fewer than four in favor of such expansion.

60. Felix Frankfurter and James M. Landis, "The Business of the Supreme Court at October Term, 1930," *Harvard Law Review* 45:271 (1930), 286–87.

61. Calculated from Felix Frankfurter and James M. Landis, "The Business of the Supreme Court at the October Term, 1934," *Harvard Law Review* 49:68 (1935), 80–81.

62. See, in particular, *Stromberg v. California*, 283 U.S. 359 (1931), *Near v. Minnesota*, 283 U.S. 697 (1931); *Powell v. Alabama*, 287 U.S. 45 (1932).

63. 347 U.S. 483 (1954).

64. Bernard Schwartz, ed., *The Warren Court: A Retrospective* (New York: Oxford University Press, 1996); Mark Tushnet, ed., *The Warren Court in Historical and Political Perspective* (Charlottesville: University Press of Virginia, 1993); and

John Downing Weaver, *Warren: The Man, the Court, the Era* (Boston: Little, Brown, 1967).

65. Until 1961 the Supreme Court hesitated to impose significant constitutional requirements on state criminal trials. In *Barron v. Baltimore*, 32 U.S. (7 Pet.) 243 (1833), the Supreme Court had decided that the Bill of Rights in general did not apply to the states. The Fourteenth Amendment appeared to many observers of the time as effecting an extension of the Bill of Rights to the states but others disagreed, including a majority on the Supreme Court, which rejected that view in the *Slaughterhouse Cases*, 83 U.S. (16 Wall.) 36, in 1873. A little over ten years later, in *Hurtado v. California*, 110 U.S. 516 (1884), the Court refused to require that felony charges in state trials be initiated by grand jury indictment as the Bill of Rights required for the federal courts. The Court's refusal to apply the Bill of Rights to state governments continued in the early twentieth century. In *Twining v. New Jersey*, 211 U.S. 78 (1908), the Court ruled that states could compel a defendant to testify against himself in spite of the Fifth Amendment protection against self-incrimination in federal trials. Even while the Supreme Court refused to apply the Bill of Rights against the states, the Court supported some rights claims advanced by criminal defendants. In federal trials, the justices gradually expanded procedural protections under the Fifth Amendment's due process clause, among them the exclusionary rule requiring that illegally seized evidence be excluded from federal trials, *Weeks v. United States*, 232 U.S. 383 (1914); the prohibition on police seizure of items other than the "fruits" or "instrumentalities" of a crime, *Gouled v. United States*, 255 U.S. 298 (1921); the requirement of a warrant for police searches, *Agnello v. United States*, 269 U.S. 20 (1925); and the requirement that the police must have probable cause to gain a search warrant, *Byars v. United States*, 273 U.S. 28 (1927). Then, in a major step in 1938, the Court created a constitutional right to counsel for defendants charged with felonies under federal laws, *Johnson v. Zerbst*, 304 U.S. 458 (1938).

66. The Court held that race may not be used to exclude people from state juries, *Strauder v. West Virginia*, 100 U.S. 303 (1880); that state trials dominated by mob pressures violate the Fourteenth Amendment's guarantee of due process, *Moore v. Dempsey*, 261 U.S. 86 (1923); that federal courts may overturn a guilty verdict where evidence is insufficient to support the verdict, *Fiske v. Kansas*, 274 U.S. 380 (1927); that in capital cases due process requires the provision of legal counsel to indigent defendants, *Powell v. Alabama*, 287 U.S. 45 (1932); and that state authorities may not use methods that "shock the conscience" in their interrogation of criminal suspects, *Brown v. Mississippi*, 297 U.S. 278 (1936). By the thirties, the Supreme Court had developed a "fair hearing" standard covering state criminal trials, which the Court used until 1961 when it replaced the standard with the federal case law interpreting the Bill of Rights. See Richard C. Cortner, *The Supreme Court and the Second Bill of Rights: The Fourteenth Amendment and the Nationalization of Civil Liberties* (Madison: University of Wisconsin Press, 1981), 124–76.

67. 332 U.S. 46 (1947); Adamson had been convicted of murder and sentenced to death after a trial in which the prosecutor drew the jury's attention to the defendant's failure to testify. The Supreme Court, in a 5–4 vote, refused to accept Adamson's argument that this violated his right against self-incrimination under the Fifth and Fourteenth Amendments and rejected Jus-

tice Black's dissent arguing in favor of total incorporation of the Bill of Rights.

68. 367 U.S. 643 (1961). The new liberal majority actually first came together in 1960. The case was *Elkins v. United States*, 364 U.S. 206 (1960), in which the Court excluded from a federal trial, for the first time, evidence that had been illegally obtained by state officials; prior to *Elkins*, while the Court excluded from federal trials evidence that was illegally obtained by federal officials, it allowed the use of evidence illegally obtained by state officials. This approach was known as the "silver platter doctrine." See Cortner, *Second Bill of Rights*, 177–78.

69. 372 U.S. 335 (1963).

70. 297 U.S. 278 (1936).

71. 368 U.S. 57 (1961).

72. In *Reed*, 404 U.S. 71 (1971), the Burger Court struck down the offending statute on the relatively narrow ground that the statute's preference was "arbitrary" and therefore unacceptable under the rational basis test, the lowest level of scrutiny under the Fourteenth Amendment. The decision was regarded, nonetheless, as a major breakthrough for women's rights. Over the next few years the Court struggled to agree on what test—the ordinary rational-basis test, the strict-scrutiny test applied to race-based discrimination, or a test somewhere in between—to apply to sex-based discrimination. Although the Court ruled in favor of a women's-rights claim in *Frontiero v. Richardson*, 411 U.S. 677 (1973), the majority rejected the application of the strict-scrutiny standard in that case. The Court eventually settled on a vague, middle-level, "heightened scrutiny" standard in 1976, requiring that sex-based classifications be substantially related to an important government purpose and narrowly tailored to serve that purpose. See *Craig v. Boren*, 429 U.S. 190 (1976). But how broadly such a test would be applied remained unclear, subject to shifting votes among the justices. Nonetheless, the new opening offered by *Reed* and *Frontiero* signaled that the justices would carefully consider sex-discrimination claims.

73. Stewart supported civil rights claims in 58 percent of the split decisions in which he participated (only five of the Warren Court's seventeen justices had lower support scores for civil rights than Stewart); Fortas and Warren, by contrast, supported such claims in 82.7 and 82.6 percent of such cases respectively (and only four of the Warren Court's justices—among them Fortas—had higher support scores for civil rights than Warren). Segal and Spaeth, *Attitudinal Model*, 246–47, table 6.6.

74. Admittedly, the Court in *Dandridge v. Williams*, 397 U.S. 471 (1970), affirmed its earlier decision in *Goesaert v. Cleary*. It is plausible that the justices could have drawn a distinction between such "protective" legislation and legislation, as in *Reed*, that had no plausible protective purpose. So the *Dandridge* decision does not necessarily rule out the possibility that a majority of justices might have been sympathetic to sex discrimination claims prior to the seventies, had many such cases reached the Court.

Chapter Four

1. Alfred D. Chandler, Jr., *The Visible Hand: The Managerial Revolution in American Business* (Cambridge: Harvard University Press, 1977); Alfred D. Chandler, Jr., "The United States: Seedbed of Managerial Capitalism," in *Managerial Hier-*

archies: *Comparative Perspectives on the Rise of the Modern Industrial Enterprise,* ed. Alfred D. Chandler, Jr. and Herman Daems (Cambridge: Harvard University Press, 1980); Martin Sklar, *The Corporate Reconstruction of American Capitalism, 1890–1916: The Market, the Law, and Politics* (Cambridge: Cambridge University Press, 1988).

2. Herbert Croly, *The Promise of American Life* (Indianapolis: Bobbs-Merrill, 1965) 105–17, 351–54.

3. Howard Gillman, *The Constitution Besieged: The Rise and Demise of Lochner Era Police Powers Jurisprudence* (Durham: Duke University Press, 1993), 147–93.

4. Chandler, *Visible Hand,* and "Seedbed of Managerial Capitalism."

5. Chandler, "Seedbed of Managerial Capitalism," 30–35.

6. Richard C. Cortner, *The Iron Horse and the Constitution: The Railroads and the Transformation of the Fourteenth Amendment* (Westport, Conn.: Greenwood Press, 1993).

7. *Munn v. Illinois,* 94 U.S. 113 (1877) ("the *Granger Cases*").

8. Cortner, *Iron Horse,* p. xii.

9. Gillman, *Constitution Besieged;* Melvin I. Urofsky, "Myth and Reality: The Supreme Court and Protective Legislation in the Progressive Era," *Yearbook— Supreme Court Historical Society* 1983:55.

10. C. Peter Magrath, *Morrison R. Waite* (New York: Macmillan, 1963), 178, quoted in Cortner, *Iron Horse,* 3.

11. Louis Brandeis, "The Opportunity in the Law," in *Business—A Profession* (Boston: Small, Maynard, 1914), 337–38.

12. Woodrow Wilson, *The Papers of Woodrow Wilson,* vol. 21 (1910), ed. Arthur S. Link (Princeton: Princeton University Press, 1976), 70, 79.

13. John P. Heinz and Edward O. Laumann, *Chicago Lawyers: The Social Structure of the Bar* (New York: Russell Sage Foundation, 1982).

14. Theron Strong, *Landmarks of a Lawyer's Lifetime* (New York: Dodd, Mead, 1914), 378, quoted in Galanter and Palay, *Tournament of Lawyers,* 16.

15. William E. Nelson, *The Fourteenth Amendment: From Political Principle to Judicial Doctrine* (Cambridge: Harvard University Press, 1988), 8.

16. 247 U.S. 251 (1918).

17. Rabban, "Free Speech League."

18. Ibid., 74.

19. In "Free Speech League," 89–96, Rabban documents legal defenses of John Turner, Emma Goldman, Margaret Sanger, William Sanger, IWW organizers arrested during the San Diego and New Jersey free speech fights, Max Eastman, Upton Sinclair, an anarchist group calling itself the Home Colony, and Jay Fox.

20. 236 U.S. 273 (1915); Rabban, "Free Speech League," 95–96.

21. S. Walker, *In Defense of American Liberties,* 22–23. Although Rabban acknowledges Schroeder's "key role" in the League, he argues that historians have underestimated the League's influence and have exaggerated Schroeder's role in the association. Rabban, "Free Speech League," 49 n. 8, 73–74.

22. David Barry Brudnoy, "Liberty's Bugler: The Seven Ages of Theodore Schroeder" (Ph.D. diss., Brandeis University, 1971), 246 n. 1, citing the views of Joseph Ishill, a friend of Schroeder's. Other evidence from Schroeder's contemporaries calls into question Rabban's view that the League was substan-

tially more than a vehicle for Schroeder. In 1912 Lincoln Steffens wrote to Schroeder, "annoyed at how lax the rest of the directors of the League had become. Steffens thought Schroeder was being too polite to come right out and say so." Ibid., 212. Brudnoy observed that Schroeder's correspondence and papers mention the League only in a "few places" and that the correspondence clearly indicates "that he was its only full-time activist." Ibid., 145.

23. Ibid., 145 (emphasis in original).

24. *Mutual Film Corp. v. Industrial Commission of Ohio*, 236 U.S. 230 (1915). See Wertheimer, "*Mutual Film* Revisited."

25. Rabban, "IWW Free Speech Fights," 1071, 1115–20.

26. S. Walker, *In Defense of American Liberties*.

27. P. Murphy, *Freedom of Speech*, 118.

28. Ibid., 163.

29. S. Walker, *In Defense of American Liberties*, 47.

30. The significant role of the ACLU state affiliates is explored in Donald J. Farole, Jr., *Interest Groups and Judicial Federalism: Organizational Litigation in State Judiciaries* (Westport, Conn.: Praeger, 1998).

31. P. Murphy, *Freedom of Speech*, 131–32; S. Walker, *In Defense of American Liberties*, 47, 51–114.

32. Dicta are statements in a judicial decision that are not essential to the holding of the decision and therefore have no precedential value. Nonetheless, dicta often carry great significance as indications of decisions the court may make in the future.

33. 268 U.S. 652 (1925).

34. 274 U.S. 357 (1927). The ACLU had also sponsored *Ruthenberg v. Michigan*, which became moot because Ruthenberg died while the case was under consideration. The dissent Justice Brandeis had drafted for *Ruthenberg* was turned into his famous concurrence in *Whitney* (and the Court eventually endorsed Brandeis's speech-action distinction in *Brandenburg v. Ohio*, 395 U.S. 444, 1969).

35. 274 U.S. 380 (1927).

36. 299 U.S. 353 (1937).

37. 330 U.S. 1 (1947).

38. 338 U.S. 25 (1949).

39. 283 U.S. 359 (1931).

40. 287 U.S. 45 (1932).

41. 310 U.S. 296 (1940).

42. 283 U.S. 697 (1931).

43. S. Walker, *In Defense of American Liberties*, 91.

44. The NAACP filed an *amicus* brief in *Guinn v. United States*, 238 U.S. 347 (1915).

45. *Buchanan v. Warley*, 245 U.S. 60 (1917).

46. *Nixon v. Herndon*, 273 U.S. 536 (1926).

47. The NAACP eventually received only a little more than $20,000 from the grant due to the Fund's growing financial difficulties in the thirties. Nonetheless, the grant greatly assisted the NAACP in developing its long-term strategy against racial segregation. See Tushnet, *NAACP's Legal Strategy*, 17.

48. The NAACP and the LDF worked closely together for much of their

early history. They shared many of the same directors until 1954, when the two boards of directors became totally separate (due to pressure from an IRS investigation). But even then they continued to cooperate until 1956, when strains began to develop over how to proceed with desegregation litigation. The two organizations eventually split entirely, with the LDF pursuing desegregation efforts in the South and the NAACP pursuing similar litigation in the North. See Tushnet, *Making Civil Rights Law*, 27, 310–11.

49. Tushnet, *Making Civil Rights Law*; Vose, *Caucasians Only*.

50. Dan T. Carter, *Scottsboro: A Tragedy of the American South*, rev. ed. (Baton Rouge: Louisiana State University Press, 1979).

51. 287 U.S. 45 (1932).

52. This summary of the Jehovah's Witnesses' use of the legal system in the United States relies on William Shepard McAninch, "A Catalyst for the Evolution of Constitutional Law: Jehovah's Witnesses in the Supreme Court," *Cincinnati Law Review* 55:997 (1987). The sect went by several other names before settling on its present one in 1931.

53. Ibid., 1008.

54. The convictions were overturned after the Witnesses had served a year of the sentences. A case arising out of the prosecution, *Ex parte Hudgings*, 249 U.S. 378 (1919), eventually reached the Supreme Court as a challenge to a contempt citation. See McAninch, "Jehovah's Witnesses," 1009–12, for discussion of the Espionage Act case.

55. Wasby, *Race Relations Litigation*, 46–75.

56. Joyce Gelb, *Feminism and Politics: A Comparative Perspective* (Berkeley: University of California Press, 1989).

57. O'Connor, *Women's Organizations*, Karen O'Connor and Lee Epstein, "Beyond Legislative Lobbying: Women's Rights Groups and the Supreme Court." *Judicature* 67:134–43 (1989).

58. Karen O'Connor and Lee Epstein, *Public Interest Law Groups: Institutional Profiles* (Westport, Conn.: Greenwood Press, 1989), 151, 208, 211. It should be noted, however, that the initial efforts of the NOW-LDF were hampered by internal dissent. See O'Connor and L. Epstein, "Beyond Legislative Lobbying," 136.

59. The numbers are derived from O'Connor and L. Epstein, *Public Interest Law Groups*, and Lee Epstein, *Conservatives in Court* (Knoxville: University of Tennessee Press, 1985). *Conservatives in Court* also lists a small number of conservative organizations that have supported court cases *challenging* women's rights.

60. Cowan, "Women's Rights." Although women's rights organizations contributed significantly to the judicial revolution in women's rights, many of the Supreme Court cases involving women's rights were not brought directly by such organizations. O'Connor and Epstein reported that only 29 percent of the sixty-three gender discrimination cases considered from the Court's 1969 term through its 1980 term were brought by interest groups (and most of those were supported by the ACLU's Women's Rights Project). O'Connor and L. Epstein, "Beyond Legislative Lobbying," 139.

61. Cynthia Fuchs Epstein, *Women in Law*, 2d ed. (Urbana: University of Illinois Press, 1993), 137.

62. The liberal NAACP and the radical ILD greatly disagreed over the tactics and some of the goals in the defense of the Scottsboro Boys. See D. Carter, *Scottsboro*, 54–58, 61–62, 77–80, 93–96. Similarly, the NAACP's request for a relatively large grant from the Garland Fund generated a great dispute among the Fund's directors over whether the NAACP's proposed litigation strategy against racial segregation would aid the cause of labor organizing. Roger Baldwin opposed the grant on the grounds that the strategy would not aid the radical labor movement, but he was narrowly defeated and the NAACP received the grant. See Tushnet, *NAACP's Legal Strategy*, 7–14.

63. Galanter and Palay, *Tournament of Lawyers*, 1–3.

64. Ibid., 14–15.

65. Richard L. Abel, *American Lawyers* (New York: Oxford University Press, 1989), 40–44.

66. Jerold Auerbach, *Unequal Justice; Lawyers and Social Change in Modern America* (New York: Oxford University Press, 1976), 74–101; William R. Johnson, *Schooled Lawyers: A Study in the Clash of Professional Cultures* (New York: New York University Press, 1978), 164–70.

67. Gillman, *Constitution Besieged*, 147–93.

68. 372 U.S. 335 (1963).

69. Daniel John Meador, *Preludes to Gideon: Notes on Appellate Advocacy, Habeas Corpus, and Constitutional Litigation* (Charlottesville, Va.: Michie, 1967).

70. Abel, *American Lawyers*, 201.

71. By 1920 virtually all of the new law schools were open to women as well. Ibid., 90.

72. Ibid., 78–80; Auerbach, *Unequal Justice*, 211–15; Maxwell Bloomfield, "From Deference to Confrontation: The Early Black Lawyers of Galveston, Texas, 1895–1920," in *The New High Priests: Lawyers in Post–Civil War America*, ed. Gerard W. Gawalt (Westport, Conn.: Greenwood Press, 1984).

73. Abel, *American Lawyers*, 86, 280.

74. Auerbach, *Unequal Justice*; Bloomfield, "From Deference to Confrontation"; D. Carter, *Scottsboro*; S. Walker, *In Defense of American Liberties*.

75. William V. Rowe, "Legal Clinics and Better Trained Lawyers—A Necessity," *Illinois Law Review* 11:602–3 (1917), quoted in Auerbach, *Unequal Justice*, 107.

76. George Wickersham, *American Bar Association Journal*, March 1922, 8, quoted in Auerbach, *Unequal Justice*, 115–16.

77. Auerbach, *Unequal Justice*; Abel, *American Lawyers*.

78. Auerbach, *Unequal Justice*, 219.

79. P. Murphy, *Freedom of Speech*, 79.

80. Ann Fagan Ginger and Eugene M. Tobin, eds., *The National Lawyers Guild: From Roosevelt through Reagan* (Philadelphia: Temple University Press, 1988).

81. Elliff, *Department of Justice*, 91–92.

82. Barbara Curran and Clara N. Carson, *The Lawyer Statistical Report: The U.S. Legal Profession in the 1990s* (Chicago: American Bar Foundation, 1994).

83. Data are from Curran and Carson, *Lawyer Statistical Report*, and a letter from Curran and Carson on file with the author. It is nearly impossible to construct an annual series of data on the total lawyer population; the lawyer population is available in three-year intervals from the mid-fifties to 1970, but

then there is a ten-year gap until 1980, followed by a five-year gap until 1985, followed by a three-year gap until 1988, and a two-year gap until 1990. Admittedly the estimates presented in the figure do not provide a measure of the growth of the female legal profession as a whole; rather, they provide a measure of the pace of female entrance into the legal profession. That pace was roughly constant through the fifties and early sixties but quickened significantly after about 1965.

84. 335 U.S. 464 (1948).

85. C. Epstein, *Women in Law,* 37–45, 130–61.

86. 410 U.S. 113 (1973).

87. Deborah L. Markowitz, "In Pursuit of Equality: One Woman's Work to Change the Law," *Women's Rights Law Reporter* 11:73–97 (1989); *Reed v. Reed,* 404 U.S. 71 (1971).

88. The following discussion is based on Gloria Garrett Samson, *The American Fund for Public Service: Charles Garland and Radical Philanthropy, 1922–1941* (Westport, Conn.: Greenwood Press, 1996).

89. Samson, *American Fund,* 19–20.

90. S. Walker, *In Defense of American Liberties,* 70–71.

91. Richard Magat, *The Ford Foundation at Work: Philanthropic Choices, Methods, and Styles* (New York: Plenum, 1979), 194–95.

92. Quoted in Auerbach, *Unequal Justice,* 55.

93. Special Committee of the Association of the Bar of the City of New York, *Equal Justice for the Accused* (Garden City, N.Y.: Doubleday, 1959), 44.

94. *Powell v. Alabama,* 287 U.S. 45 (1932).

95. Quoted in D. Carter, *Scottsboro,* 163.

96. Ibid.

97. The British government in 1949 adopted the Legal Aid and Advice Act, which provided legal aid in civil cases, and the British plan seems to have encouraged the U.S. legal profession into renewed agitation around the issue of legal aid. Nonetheless, the British plan provided little support for criminal defendants until the sixties. J. R. Spencer, *Jackson's Machinery of Justice,* 8th ed., Cambridge: Cambridge University Press, 1989), 474.

98. Special Committee, *Equal Justice,* 38–39.

99. 372 U.S. 335 (1963).

100. Jonathan Casper, *Lawyers before the Warren Court: Civil Liberties and Civil Rights, 1957–66* (Urbana: University of Illinois Press, 1972), 89.

101. Lawrence, *The Poor in Court,* 9.

102. Lawrence, *The Poor in Court;* Warren E. George, "Development of the Legal Services Corporation," *Cornell Law Review* 61:681–730 (1976).

103. Robert V. Percival and Geoffrey P. Miller, "The Role of Attorney Fee Shifting in Public Interest Litigation," *Law & Contemporary Problems* 47:233 (1984); Note, "Attorneys' Fees: Exceptions to the American Rule," *Drake Law Review* 25:717 (1976).

104. Karen O'Connor and Lee Epstein, "Bridging the Gap between Congress and the Supreme Court: Interest Groups and the Erosion of the American Rule Governing the Award of Attorneys' Fees," *Western Political Quarterly* 38:241 (1985).

105. Stewart J. Schwab and Theodore Eisenberg, "Explaining Constitutional

Tort Litigation: The Influence of the Attorney Fees Statute and the Government as Defendant," *Cornell Law Review* 73:733, table 4 (1988).

106. Rebecca Mae Salokar, *The Solicitor General: The Politics of Law* (Philadelphia: Temple University Press, 1992), 114.

107. Ibid., 108.

108. Clayton, *Politics of Justice*, 67–68.

109. Caldeira and Wright, "Organized Interests"; Perry, *Deciding to Decide*.

110. Salokar, *Solicitor General*, 29.

111. Clayton, *Politics of Justice*; Robert G. Dixon, "The Attorney General and Civil Rights, 1870–1964," in *Roles of the Attorney General of the United States*, ed. Luther A. Huston, Arthur Selwyn Miller, Samuel Krislov, and Robert G. Dixon (Washington, D.C.: American Enterprise Institute, 1968); Philip Elman, "The Solicitor General's Office, Justice Frankfurter, and Civil Rights Litigation, 1946–1960: An Oral History." *Harvard Law Review* 100:817–52 (1987).

112. Elliff, *Department of Justice*, 66, 71–73.

113. The case ended in a hung jury and the Justice Department, after initial efforts to pursue the case again, dropped it; nonetheless, the case focused much attention on the coalfield disputes and, after the case was closed, a number of the mine operators signed a contract with the United Mine Workers. See Elliff, *Department of Justice*, 75–76.

114. Ibid., 93–95. See also Robert K. Carr, *Federal Protection of Civil Rights: Quest for a Sword* (Ithaca, N.Y.: Cornell University Press, 1947).

115. Elliff, *Department of Justice*, 99–126, 156–80; Dixon, "Attorney General and Civil Rights," 110–12. The Supreme Court's decision in *Screws* (1945) upheld the constitutionality of the Civil Rights Act and prosecutions under it but handicapped such prosecutions by requiring for conviction that the defendant have a specific intent to deprive the victim of his or her constitutional rights—a difficult standard to meet.

116. Clayton, *Politics of Justice*, 128; Elman, "Solicitor General's Office," 818–19.

117. 334 U.S. 1 (1948).

118. Clayton, *Politics of Justice*, 129–31; Elliff, *Department of Justice*, 323–33.

119. Elman, "Solicitor General's Office," 822–45.

120. Clayton, *Politics of Justice*, 131–37; Dixon, "Attorney General and Civil Rights," 114–17.

121. Dixon, "Attorney General and Civil Rights," 114.

122. Clayton, *Politics of Justice*, 126–27, 135.

123. Ibid., 126.

124. Michal Belknap, *Federal Law and Southern Order: Racial Violence and Constitutional Conflict in the Post-Brown South* (Athens: University of Georgia Press, 1987), 19.

125. By contrast, even as late as 1990 the English Equal Opportunities Commission could not initiate suits in its own name and had to rely on use of nominal plaintiffs. Significantly, in 1994 the House of Lords ruled in favor of the EOC's claim to initiate such suits (see chapter 8).

126. Joan Hoff, *Law, Gender, and Injustice: A Legal History of U.S. Women* (New York: New York University Press, 1991), 234.

127. Wasby, *Race Relations Litigation*, 26–45; McCann, *Rights at Work*.

128. *Near v. Minnesota*, 283 U.S. 697 (1931); *Stromberg v. California*, 83 U.S. 359 (1931); *Powell v. Alabama*, 287 U.S. 45 (1932).

129. P. Murphy, *Freedom of Speech*; S. Walker, *In Defense of American Liberties*, 79–92.

130. 347 U.S. 483 (1954).

131. Wasby, *Race Relations Litigation*, 32; McCann, *Rights at Work*.

132. 372 U.S. 335 (1963).

133. Ibid., 42–43. The cases were, respectively, *National Association for the Advancement of Colored People v. Button*, 371 U.S. 415 (1963), and *Newman v. Piggie Park Enterprises*, 390 U.S. 400 (1968).

134. *Alyeska Pipeline Service Co. v. Wilderness Society*, 421 U.S. 240 (1975).

135. Wasby, *Race Relations Litigation*, 31.

136. Ibid., 28.

137. The following discussion is based on S. Walker, *In Defense of American Liberties*, 87–88.

138. Ibid., 87.

139. Elliff, *Department of Justice*; Carr, *Quest for a Sword*.

140. O'Connor, *Women's Organizations*.

141. *Schenck v. United States*, 249 U.S. 47 (1919).

142. Fred D. Ragan, "Justice Oliver Wendell Holmes, Jr., Zechariah Chafee, Jr., and the Clear and Present Danger Test for Free Speech: The First Year, 1919," *Journal of American History* 58:24 (1971); Rabban, "First Amendment"; Rabban, "The Emergence of Modern First Amendment Doctrine," *University of Chicago Law Review* 50:1205 (1983); Gerald Gunther, "Learned Hand and the Origins of Modern First Amendment Doctrine: Some Fragments of History," *Stanford Law Review* 27:719 (1975).

143. Ragan, "Oliver Wendell Holmes"; Rabban, "First Amendment" and "Emergence"; Gunther, "Learned Hand."

144. 330 U.S. 1 (1947).

145. J. Woodford Howard, Jr., "On the Fluidity of Judicial Choice," *American Political Science Review* 62:43–56, 54 (1968).

146. 100 U.S. 303 (1880). The Court undermined the *Strauder* precedent in *Virginia v. Rives*, 100 U.S. 313 (1880), decided the same year, which held that the absence of blacks from juries, even though a repeated occurrence, did not in itself constitute a violation of the equal protection clause. Nonetheless, there was little subsequent litigation testing the practical conflict between the two decisions.

Chapter Five

1. See, e.g., *Kishore Singh v. State of Rajasthan*, (1981) 1 SCC 503.

2. *People's Union for Democratic Rights v. Union of India*, AIR 1982 SC 1473.

3. *M. H. Hoskot v. State of Maharashtra*, AIR 1978 SC 1548, reaffirmed in *Hussainara Khatoon v. State of Bihar*, AIR 1979 SC 1369.

4. *M. C. Mehta v. Union of India*, AIR 1988 SC 1037; *M. C. Mehta v. Union of India*, AIR 1988 SC 1115.

5. Rajeev Dhavan, *Justice on Trial: The Supreme Court Today* (Allahabad: Wheeler, 1980), chapter 1. See also Carl Baar, "Social Action Litigation in India: The Operation and Limits of the World's Most Active Judiciary," in *Comparative*

Judicial Review and Public Policy, ed. Donald W. Jackson and C. Neal Tate (Westport, Conn.: Greenwood Press, 1992).

6. Paul R. Brass, "The Punjab Crisis and the Unity of India," in *India's Democracy: An Analysis of Changing State-Society Relations,* ed. Atul Kohli (Princeton: Princeton University Press, 1988).

7. Ghanshyam Shah, "Grass-Roots Mobilization in Indian Politics," in *India's Democracy,* ed. Kohli.

8. Arend Lijphart, "The Puzzle of Indian Democracy: A Consociational Interpretation," *American Political Science Review* 90:258–68 (1996).

9. See, for example, Madhu Kishwar and Ruth Vanita, "Indian Women: A Decade of New Ferment," in *India Briefing, 1989,* ed. Marshall M. Bouton and Philip Oldenburg (Boulder: Westview Press, 1989), on which this discussion of the paradox is based.

10. A widely reported figure is one to two such "dowry deaths" per day in Delhi. See Nandita Gandhi and Nandita Shah, *The Issues at Stake: Theory and Practice in the Contemporary Women's Movement in India* (New Delhi: Kali for Women, 1992), 52–61. That figure, however, may be somewhat high. A study of 179 unnatural deaths in New Delhi in a one-year period in 1981 and 1982 found that 12 percent were dowry-related and that one-third of those were clearly murder (the other two-thirds are listed as suicide, but the characterization of a dowry death as "suicide" is a commonly made by relatives and widely disputed by women's-rights advocates). See M. S. Khan and R. Ray, "Dowry Death," *Indian Journal of Social Work* 45:303–7 (1984). Advocates for women's rights generally believe that the number of deaths related to dowry has increased since 1982. A study by the Department of Woman and Child Development concluded that the reported number of dowry-related deaths in India grew from 2209 in 1988 to 4006 in 1989. Soli Sorabjee, "Women, Constitution and the Courts," in *Women, Law and Social Change,* ed. Shamsuddin Shams (New Delhi: Ashish Publishing House, 1991). On the practice of dowry generally, see M. N. Srinivas, *Some Reflections on Dowry* (New Delhi: Oxford University Press, 1984); and Rehana Ghadially and Pramod Kumar, "Bride-Burning: The Psycho-Social Dynamics of Dowry Deaths," in Rehana Ghadially, ed., *Women in Indian Society: A Reader* (New Delhi: Sage, 1988).

11. Sohaila Abdulali, "Rape in India: An Empirical Picture," in *Women in Indian Society: A Reader,* ed. Rehana Ghadially (New Delhi: Sage, 1988).

12. Gandhi and Shah, *Issues at Stake,* 49–51.

13. Lloyd I. Rudolph and Susanne Hoeber Rudolph, *In Pursuit of Lakshmi: The Political Economy of the Indian State* (Chicago: University of Chicago Press, 1987), 21–23, 412–13 n. 6.

14. Paul R. Brass, *The Politics of India Since Independence* (Cambridge: Cambridge University Press, 1990), 13.

15. Kuldeep Mathur, "The State and the Use of Coercive Power in India," *Asian Survey* 32:344 (1992). For instance, according to Mathur, the number of armed police battalions grew from 66 in 1963 to 144 in 1983. The Assam Rifles grew from 21 battalions in 1983–84 to 31 battalions only four years later; the Indo-Tibetan Police Force grew from 9 battalions in 1981–82 to 14 in 1985–86; the Border Security Force, originally created for defense of the India-Pakistani border but increasingly used for maintenance of internal order, grew from 25

battalions in 1967 to 92 battalions in 1987–88; and the Central Reserve Police Force, with wide authority for maintaining internal security, including the authority to take "preventive action," grew from 66 battalions in 1981–82 to 83 in 1987.

16. Ibid., 345–46.

17. Ibid., 346.

18. The various laws are the Preventive Detention Act (1950–1971), the Maintenance of Internal Security Act (1971–1977), the National Security Act (1980 to the present). The National Security Act was significantly tightened in 1984.

19. (1950) SCR 88.

20. In 1973, reporting the first reliable figures on the number of detainees, the first Amnesty International report on India cited the detention of some seventeen thousand civilians in West Bengal and many others in India's far northwest region bordering Pakistan. The second Amnesty International report (1973–74) concluded that there were about twenty thousand political prisoners in West Bengal, of whom only two thousand had been charged with any offense in court, and that up to thirty thousand trade unionists were detained during a railway strike. In 1974, Amnesty International again reported more than fifteen thousand detainees in West Bengal. By the late seventies, Amnesty began reporting that there was clear evidence that both national and state governments routinely used torture against political detainees and sometimes killed them. The national government repealed its preventive detention statute in 1977 but reenacted another in 1980. In its 1981 report, Amnesty charged that the national government had resumed the use of detention against students, trade unionists, and members of opposition political parties. See the Amnesty International reports reproduced in A. R. Desai, ed., *Violation of Democratic Rights in India*, vol. 1 (Bombay: Popular Prakashan, 1986), 193–95, 201–24. See also Asia Watch, *Police Killings and Rural Violence in Andhra Pradesh* (New York: Asia Watch, 1992).

21. Amnesty International reports, various years, reproduced in Desai, *Violation*, 187–238; Amnesty International, "Torture in the Eighties: An Amnesty International Report," reproduced in Desai, *Violation*, 254.

22. *People's Union for Civil Liberties Bulletin*, March–April 1982.

23. Amnesty International, *India: Torture, Rape, and Deaths in Custody* (New York: Amnesty International, 1992); also see continuing reports and analysis in the *People's Union for Civil Liberties Bulletin*, every edition for 1986, 1987, 1988, 1989, 1990, 1991, 1992, 1993.

24. Sudip Majumdar, "Deaths in Police Custody," in Desai, *Violation*, 307–12.

25. Granville Austin, "The Constitution, Society, and Law," in *India Briefing, 1993*, ed. Philip Oldenburg (Boulder: Westview Press, 1993), 126.

26. See the numerous reports and articles reproduced in Desai, *Violation*, in particular Sam Rajappa, "Kerala's Concentration Camps;" Prabhat Dasgupta, "A Catalogue of Repression June 1977–May 1978"; Sudip Majumdar, "Deaths in Police Custody"; Arun Shourie, "Lethal Custodians"; and People's Union for Civil Liberties, "Murder by Encounter"; as well as the reports on particular states contained in the same collection.

27. Gandhi and Shah, *Issues at Stake*, especially chapter 3, "Violence Becomes a Political Issue."

28. Soli Sorabjee, "Women, Constitution and the Courts."

29. The Indian Foreign Service had such a policy until 1979, and the Indian national airline requires stewardesses to resign if they marry within four years of joining the airline.

30. Gandhi and Shah, *Issues at Stake*, 183–85.

31. Ibid., 192–93.

32. Amnesty International report on India, reprinted in Desai, *Violation*, 196.

33. Brass, *Politics of India*; see also various selections in Atul Kohli, ed., *India's Democracy: An Analysis of Changing State-Society Relations* (Princeton: Princeton University Press, 1988).

34. Smitu Kothari, "Social Movements and the Redefinition of Democracy," in Oldenburg, *India Briefing, 1993*.

35. Amnesty International report on India, reprinted in Desai, *Violation*, 200.

36. Nani Palkhivala, quoted in Upendra Baxi, *The Indian Supreme Court and Politics* (Lucknow: Eastern Book Co., 1980), 73.

37. Smitu Kothari, "The Human Rights Movement in India: A Critical Overview," in *Rethinking Human Rights: Challenges for Theory and Action*, ed. Smitu Kothari and Harsh Sethi (Delhi: Lokayan, 1991).

38. Marc Galanter, *Law and Society in Modern India* (New York: Oxford University Press, 1989), 279.

39. My discussion of the Constitution is based on Austin, *Indian Constitution*.

40. Among the significant changes in constitutional interpretation created by the post-1978 Supreme Court was a growing emphasis on the Directive Principles. While admitting that the Constitution defines them as nonjusticiable, the Supreme Court nonetheless came to declare that the Fundamental Rights must be interpreted in the context of the Directive Principles, thus increasing the egalitarian component of the Fundamental Rights.

41. V. N. Shukla, *Constitution of India*, 9th ed., ed. Mahendra P. Singh (Lucknow, India: Eastern Book Co., 1994), 185.

42. Ibid., 189–90.

43. *Ariel v. State*, AIR 1954 SC 15.

44. Lalit Chari, "Police Repression and the Criminal Law," in Desai, *Violation*, 87.

45. Sylvia M. Hale, "The Status of Women in India," *Pacific Affairs* 62:371 (1989).

46. This discussion is based on Archana Parashar, *Women and Family Law Reform in India* (New Delhi: Sage, 1992).

47. Shyamla Pappu, Chandramani Chopra, and Mohini Giri, "Women and the Law," in *Problems and Concerns of Indian Women*, ed. B. K. Pal (New Delhi: ABC Publishing, 1987), 132–33.

48. Anika Rahman, "Religious Rights versus Women's Rights in India: A Test Case for International Human Rights Law," in *Columbia Journal of Transnational Law* 28:473 (1990).

49. Parashar, *Women*.

50. Austin, *Indian Constitution*, 80–81.

51. Galanter, *Law and Society*, 279.

52. For accounts see K. S. Hegde, *Crisis in Indian Judiciary* (Bombay: Sindhu, 1973), and Kuldip Nayar, ed., *Supersession of Judges* (New Delhi: Indian Book Co., 1973).

53. Austin, *Indian Constitution*, 164–65.

54. Ibid., 169.

55. Quoted in Durga Das Basu, *Introduction to the Constitution of India*, 15th ed. (New Delhi: Prentice-Hall of India, 1993), 122.

56. Indian Const., Art. 131.

57. Ibid., Art. 133.

58. Ibid., Art. 136.

59. Ibid., Art. 21. For a discussion of the Constituent Assembly debate, see Dhavan, *Justice on Trial*, 17; Austin, *Indian Constitution*, 103–6.

60. *A. K. Gopalan v. State of Madras*, AIR 1950 SC 27.

61. Basu, *Constitution of India*, 147–48.

62. Data obtained from the Registrar of the Supreme Court of India, Annual Statement, 1990.

63. The 1972 provision limiting appeals in civil cases to "substantial question[s] of law of general importance," noted earlier, was another attempt to deal with the Supreme Court's workload. However, giving *state* High Court justices the power to make this determination is of limited value in reducing the Supreme Court's workload and contributes nothing to the Supreme Court's ability to shape its own agenda.

64. Basu, *Constitution of India*, 276 n. 1.

65. Rajeev Dhavan, *The Supreme Court of India: A Socio-Legal Critique of Its Juristic Techniques* (Bombay: N. M. Tripathi, 1977).

66. Formally, the process is an unencumbered one, based entirely on appointment by the president with no confirmation process. To be eligible, a person must be an Indian citizen and either a distinguished jurist, a High Court judge for at least five years, or an advocate in a High Court for at least ten years. The Constitution requires the president to consult various officials before making his decision; for appointing the chief justice the consultation must include whichever judges of the Supreme Court and the High Courts he chooses; for appointing puisne (associate) justices the president must consult the government's ministers and the chief justice. There is no minimum age, but the mandatory retirement age is 65.

67. George Gadbois, Jr., "The Supreme Court of India as a Political Institution," in *Judges and the Judicial Power*, ed. Rajeev Dhavan, R. Sudarshan, and Salman Khurshid (Bombay: N. M. Tripathi, 1985).

68. Admittedly, identifying the attitudes and policy preferences of the Indian Supreme Court justices is more difficult than for the other courts in this study. For one thing, observers of the Indian Supreme Court rarely attempt to analyze the views of individual justices. Gadbois, "Supreme Court," 261. In part this is due to the tendency of Indian legal scholars and lawyers to hold a narrowly formalistic, Blackstonian view of the nature of law. Marc Galanter, *Competing Equalities: Law and the Backward Classes in India* (Delhi: Oxford University Press, 1984), 483–86; Gadbois, "Supreme Court," 261. Systematic research also has been discouraged by more practical factors, in particular the structure and traditions of the Supreme Court. Research on judicial attitudes typically relies on cases in which not all justices agree on the outcome, which makes possible analysis of ideological disagreements among judges. Yet past research has shown that Indian Supreme Court justices rarely dissent and, when they do, they typically reverse themselves and join the majority in later cases on the

same issue. Dhavan, *Supreme Court of India*, 32–35. Thus, even in highly publicized issues, "it is difficult to locate the philosophical responses of all the judges with any certainty." Dhavan, *Justice on Trial*, 204. Additionally, the low retirement age, the consequent rapid turnover among the justices, and the division into small benches contribute to an institutional fragmentation that impedes the development of a consistent judicial philosophy.

69. This is the standard interpretation of the Supreme Court's approach to property rights. Rajeev Dhavan has suggested that the standard interpretation is not entirely accurate because, of the many cases challenging restrictions on the use or ownership of property, the Court only rarely opposed the government's position. See Dhavan, *Supreme Court*.

70. *Kesavananda Bharati v. State of Kerala*, AIR 1973 SC 1461.

71. When the next opening for chief justice occurred, the government declined to fill the vacancy on the basis of seniority, which had been until then common practice, because the most senior justices had ruled against the government's property rights amendment, and the government instead selected Justice Ray, one of the dissenters, for the position. Additionally, the government appointed a number of other "committed" justices, as they were called, for positions on the Supreme Court. Several of those justices, principally V. R. Krishna Iyer, D. A. Desai, O. Chinnappa Reddy, M. P. Thakkar, and P. N. Bhagwati, became forceful egalitarians during their service on the Court.

72. The amendment also declared that the Directive Principles should take precedence over the Fundamental Rights in cases of conflict.

73. Baxi, *Court and Politics*, 70–76.

74. Ibid., 34.

75. For discussions of this development, see Rajeev Dhavan, "Law As Struggle: Notes on Public Interest Law in India" (Institute for Legal Studies Working Paper no. ILS 5–3, Madison, Wisc., 1993); Jamie Cassels, "Judicial Activism and Public Interest Litigation in India: Attempting the Impossible?" *American Journal of Comparative Law* 37:495 (1989); Carl Baar, "Social Action Litigation."

76. Ibid., 121.

77. *Minerva Mills v. Union of India*, AIR 1980 SC 1789. Nonetheless, in 1978 the first post-Emergency government had removed the property right entirely from among the Fundamental Rights, and the Supreme Court did not challenge this amendment.

78. *Maneka Gandhi v. Union of India*, AIR 1978 SC 597. In particular, the reinterpretation led by Justices Bhagwati and Krishna Iyer connected the meaning of Article 21's due process guarantee with Article 14's equality guarantees and Article 19's protections of fundamental liberties, so that Article 21 came to be used as a means for evaluating the substance of legislation and administrative action in light of equality and liberty. For a summary of the jurisprudential developments surrounding Article 21, see David G. Barnum, "Article 21 and Policy Making Role of Courts in India: An American Perspective," *Journal of the Indian Law Institute* 30:19 (1988).

79. Shukla, *Constitution of India*, 70.

80. *Maneka Gandhi v. Union of India*, AIR 1978 SC 597.

81. Many "undertrials," as they are called in India, were found to have been imprisoned waiting trial for periods far longer than the maximum sentence

for the crimes for which they were charged. The practice was vigorously rejected in *Hussainara Khatoon v. Home Secretary, Bihar,* AIR 1979 SC 1360.

82. *Sunil Batra v. Delhi Administration,* AIR 1978 SC 1675. In that case, Justice Krishna Iyer stated, "True our Constitution has no 'due process' clause . . . but . . . after *Cooper* . . . and *Maneka Gandhi* . . . , the consequence is the same" (quoted in Shukla, *Constitution of India,* 171).

83. *Mithu v. State of Punjab,* AIR 1983 SC 473.

84. *Ramana Dayaram Shetty v. International Airport Authority,* AIR 1979 SC 1628.

85. *M. H. Hoskot v. State of Maharashtra,* AIR 1978 SC 1548. This decision was reaffirmed in the famous case of *Hussainara Khatoon v. State of Bihar,* AIR 1979 SC 1369 (1979).

86. One newspaper editor reported, "[A justice] asked a lawyer to ask me to ask the reporter to go to these areas, get affidavits from some of the victims who are still alive and some of them who were dead, from their families. The affidavits were got compiled [*sic*], sent and [the justice] entertained a writ. Eight months later some one came to me saying that the same judge had sent him . . . to ask me to ask the correspondent to file such and such information in a letter through so and so. . . . A third time a civil rights activist asked that the same thing be done. He said the same judge had asked him." This judge was later shown to be Bhagwati. Arun Shourie, quoted in S. K. Agrawala, *Public Interest Litigation in India: A Critique* (Bombay: N. M. Tripathi, 1987), 16 n. 55.

87. *S. P. Gupta v. Union of India,* AIR 1982 SC 149; *People's Union for Democratic Rights v. Union of India,* AIR 1982 SC 1473.

88. *S. P. Gupta* (1982), n. 66.

89. Article 32 contains the Constitutional guarantee of direct access to the Supreme Court by claimants alleging violations of Fundamental Rights.

90. *M. C. Mehta v. Union of India,* AIR 1988 SC 1037; *M. C. Mehta v. Union of India,* AIR 1988 SC 1115.

91. Cassels, "Judicial Activism," 505–6.

92. *Anil Yadav v. State of Bihar* ("Bhagalpur Blindings Case"), (1981) 1 SCC 622.

93. *A. K. Gopalan v. State of Madras,* AIR 1950 SC 27.

94. *Charles Sobraj v. Superintendent, Central Jail, Tihar,* AIR 1978 SC 1514; *Sunil Batra v. Delhi Administration,* AIR 1978 SC 1675; *Sunil Batra v. Delhi Administration,* AIR 1980 SC 1579.

95. *Francis Coralie Mullin v. The Administrator, Union Territory of Delhi,* AIR 1981 SC 746; *Rakesh Kaushik v. B. L. Vig, Superintendent, Central Jail, Delhi,* AIR 1981 SC 746; *Sunil Batra v. Delhi Administration,* AIR 1980 SC 1579.

96. *Francis Coralie Mullin* (1981).

97. *Hussainara Khatoon v. Home Secretary, State of Bihar,* AIR 1979 SC 1360.

98. *Joint Women's Programme v. State of Rajasthan,* AIR 1987 SC 2060.

99. *Sheela Barse v. State of Maharashtra,* (1983) 2 SCC 96.

100. *Upendra Baxi v. State of Uttar Pradesh,* (1983) 2 SCC 308.

101. *Rathinam v. State of Gujarat,* case begun in early eighties and tracked by the Supreme Court through 1993. Reported in (1993) 2 SCALE 631.

102. *Randhir Singh v. Union of India,* (1982) 1 SCC 618.

103. Many of the cases deal with discrimination against married women.

See generally Ratna Kapur and Brenda Cossman, "On Women, Equality, and the Constitution: Through the Looking Glass of Feminism," *National Law Journal* 1:1 (1993). In one of the earliest cases, *Bombay Labour Union v. International Franchise*, AIR 1966 SC 942, the Supreme Court relied on the constitutional equality guarantees to uphold a woman's challenge to her dismissal upon marriage by a state-affiliated business. In 1979, a senior Indian Foreign Service officer challenged her dismissal upon marriage as a violation of her constitutional equality rights, and in *C. B. Muthamma v. Union of India*, AIR 1979 SC 1868, the Supreme Court upheld her claim, rejecting the Foreign Service's policy of firing women upon marriage. In 1983, in *Sanjit Roy v. State of Rajasthan*, AIR 1983 SC 328, a public interest case brought by a social worker, the Supreme Court struck down as a violation of the equality guarantees a state's policy of paying women engaged in famine relief work less than men so engaged, which the state had justified as an emergency measure necessitated by the famine. In *MacKinnon MacKenzie & Co. v. Audrey D'Costa*, AIR 1987 SC 1281, the Court held that, under the Equal Remuneration Act of 1976, female stenographers must be paid the same wage as male stenographers.

104. *Maya Devi v. State of Maharashtra*, (1986) 1 SCR 743.

105. *Mohammad Ahmad Kan v. Shah Bano*, AIR 1985 SC 945.

106. AIR 1986 SC 1011.

107. Asghar Ali Engineer, ed., *The Shah Bano Controversy* (Hyderabad, India: Orient Longman, 1987).

108. Parashar, *Women*, 216, 315 n. 7.

109. Chandramani Chopra, Supreme Court lawyer, interview by author, New Delhi, Dec. 20, 1993; members of Multiple Action Research Group, interview by author, New Delhi, Dec. 16, 1993.

110. *Air India v. Nergesh Meerza*, AIR 1981 SC 1829. The Supreme Court, in a ruling surprising for its arbitrary reasoning, held that the jobs of pursers and hostesses were sufficiently different to prevent the difference in retirement ages from violating the equality guarantee, and that the requirement to quit if married within the first four years was justifiable as contributing to the country's family planning policies. However, the Court struck down an additional requirement that women quit when they become pregnant because it "interfere[d] with and diverte[d] the ordinary course of human nature" and constituted "an open insult to Indian womanhood—the most sacrosanct and cherished institution." Ibid., quoted in Kapur and Cossman, "On Women," 26–27. In another surprising decision, the Court in 1987 upheld over an equality challenge Air India's policy of terminating air hostesses at a younger age if they worked exclusively within India than if they worked on international flights (a policy intended to bring Air India into compliance with the labor laws of other countries), when the airline assured the Court that, regardless of its formal policy, it would terminate international hostesses at the same age as domestic hostesses to meet constitutional standards. *Lena Khan v. Union of India*, AIR 1987 SC 1515.

111. Baxi, "Taking Suffering Seriously," in *Judges and the Judicial Power*, edited by Rajeev Dhavan, R. Sudarshan, and Salman Khurshid (Bombay: N. M. Tripathi, 1985), 303–4.

112. Cassels reports that the Supreme Court received 23,772 public interest

letters between January 1, 1987, and March 31, 1988, a staggering load of claims. Cassels, "Judicial Activism," 508.

113. Baxi, "Taking Suffering Seriously," 300.

114. The remarkable freedom to act creatively resulted from the relatively unique structural conditions of the Indian Supreme Court. As noted earlier, the Court's enormous workload, the large number of justices, and the fragmentation into small benches contribute to inconsistency in voting patterns, Dhavan, *Supreme Court of India,* but those structural conditions also allowed the egalitarian activists to create their own judicial agenda. See Baxi, "Taking Suffering Seriously," 297, 311–12 n. 67. For example, as chief justice, Bhagwati directed all public interest petitions to his constitutional bench, thus controlling their admission to the Court. Baxi, "Taking Suffering Seriously."

115. P. N. Bhagwati, "Judicial Activism and Public Interest Litigation," *Columbia Journal of Transnational Law* 23:561 (1985).

116. Smitu Kothari, interview by author, Delhi, Dec. 17, 1993.

117. Rajeev Dhavan, interview by author, New Delhi, Dec. 19, 1993.

118. The Indian Supreme Court's support for rights claims is measured here, as for the other courts in this study, as the proportion of rights claims in which the Court's decision favors the interest of the rights claimant.

119. Baxi, "Taking Suffering Seriously," 289.

Chapter Six

1. For data on the Court's public agenda, I rely on a random sample of the *All India Reporter's* (AIR's) selection of Supreme Court cases for 1960, 1965, 1970, 1975, 1980, 1985, and 1990. The AIR publishes some 300 to 400 Supreme Court cases annually, out of which I selected a random sample of approximately 100 cases for each of the seven sample years.

2. For data on the Supreme Court's routine agenda, I rely on the Supreme Court Registrar's records of the number of cases filed and disposed of within the Court's Article 32 jurisdiction, which deals with Fundamental Rights claims. The Article 32 statistics are a blunt measure, for they are an aggregation of all Fundamental Rights claims and thus tell us little about changes across time in the kinds of rights claims brought to the Court. Nonetheless the Registrar's statistics include the total number of cases coming to the Court, something that no case reporter can achieve.

3. The data reported in figure 6.2 differ significantly from all previously published data on the Indian Supreme Court's agenda. That is because previously published data suffer from a shared problem that significantly overcounts the number of Fundamental Rights cases. The error results from the fact that Indian law has no class action mechanism but, with the growth of the Supreme Court's populist jurisprudence beginning in 1977, the Court began to combine into single consolidated cases the ostensibly separate claims of numerous individuals, thus creating something like a class action. For instance, a consolidated case might represent the discrimination claims of a thousand workers at a government construction site. Such consolidated cases were confined largely to petitions brought under the Article 32 Fundamental Rights jurisdiction. Unfortunately, previously available data consisted of official Supreme Court statistics that counted each individual claim within a con-

solidated case as a single case. By 1986 the Registrar of the Supreme Court had determined that such a method of counting produced a distorted understanding of the Court's workload, and so he ordered the method of counting changed to consider each consolidated set of claims as a single case. Members of the Registrar's staff, interview by author, New Delhi, Dec. 12, 1993. Widely published statistics based on the Supreme Court's old counting system not surprisingly showed a rapid growth in the Fundamental Rights agenda after 1978. For example, Rajeev Dhavan, in a careful analysis of the Supreme Court's data, found that the fastest growing segment of its docket in the late seventies was petitions under Article 32 of the Constitution, the mechanism for bringing Fundamental Rights claims directly to the Court. Rajeev Dhavan, *Litigation Explosion in India* (Bombay: N. M. Tripathi, 1986), 60–61. Dhavan reported that cases brought under the Fundamental Rights jurisdiction constituted 9.49 percent of all cases filed in 1979, 27.59 percent in 1980, 37.76 percent in 1981, and 46.4 percent in 1982, suggesting that "[t]here is no doubt that the Fundamental Rights jurisdiction is becoming a major jurisdiction within the Supreme Court." *Litigation Explosion,* 61, 80. At my request, the Registrar recalculated the number of Fundamental Rights cases prior to 1986 using the new method, and the revised statistics are the basis for figure 6. 2. The figure includes only data for case institutions (filings), because the data for case disposals appear to have remaining problems related to counting methods.

4. Lloyd I. Rudolph and Susanne Hoeber Rudolph, *The Modernity of Tradition* (Chicago: University of Chicago Press, 1967). Quite a range of independent organizations had participated in the struggle for independence but most disbanded after 1947 as their leaders' efforts went into supporting Prime Minister Nehru's nation-building strategies. S. Kothari, "Social Movements."

5. S. Kothari, "Social Movements," 139; see also D. L. Sheth and Harsh Sethi, "The NGO Sector in India: Historical Context and Current Discourse," *Voluntas* 2, no. 2:49 (1991); Siddhartha Sen, "Non-Profit Organisations in India: Historical Development and Common Patterns," *Voluntas* 3, no. 2:175 (1992).

6. An earlier civil liberties organization, the Civil Liberties Union, was formed in the early thirties to provide legal aid to supporters of national independence from Britain but was "short-lived," according to S. Kothari, "Human Rights Movement."

7. Ibid., 142–43.

8. Sheth and Sethi, "NGO Sector," 54, 55.

9. Snehalata Reddy, *A Prison Diary* (Mysore, India: Human Rights Committee, 1977), 14.

10. Baxi, "Taking Suffering Seriously," 297.

11. S. Kothari, "Social Movements," 141.

12. Ibid., 151.

13. Few civil liberties organizations existed before the Emergency. The first post-Independence organizations were formed in the early seventies in response to increasing brutality by the police and security forces against leftist dissidents and guerillas, commonly called Naxalites.

14. "Civil Liberties and Democratic Rights Groups: A Listing," *Lokayan Bulletin* 5:4–5 (1987), reprinted in Desai, *Violation,* 309.

15. Ibid.

16. Committee for the Protection of Democratic Rights, "The Civil Liberties Movement: A Perspective," in Desai, *Violation*, 284.

17. Jyoti Punwani, "At What Stage is the Civil Rights Movement?" in Desai, *Violation*, 299; V. M. Tarkunde, "In Defence of Freedom," in *Expanding Governmental Lawlessness and Organized Struggles*, ed. A. R. Desai (Bombay: Popular Prakashan, 1991), 306.

18. Committee, "Civil Liberties Movement," 287.

19. Rudolph and Rudolph, *Lakshmi*, 247.

20. S. Kothari, "Social Movements"; Rajni Kothari, "Decline of Parties and Rise of Grassroots Movements," in *State Against Democracy: In Search of Humane Governance*, ed. Rajni Kothari (New York: New Horizons Press, 1989).

21. Rudolph and Rudolph, *Lakshmi*, 21–23.

22. Ibid., 247.

23. "Civil Liberties Organisations in Andhra Pradesh," in Desai, *Violation*, 294.

24. Ibid.

25. The two groups are named, respectively, the People's Union for Civil Liberties and the People's Union for Democratic Rights.

26. Sheth and Sethi," NGO Sector," 58 (note omitted).

27. S. Kothari, "Human Rights Movement," 87.

28. "Civil Liberties and Democratic Rights Groups: A Listing," in *Lokayan Bulletin* 5:4–5 (1987), *reprinted in* Desai, *Violation*, 309.

29. Galanter, *Law and Society*, 279.

30. Ibid., 282–83.

31. Ibid.

32. J. S. Gandhi, "Past and Present: A Sociological Portrait of the Indian Legal Profession," in Abel and Lewis, *Lawyers in Society*, 369–82; J. S. Gandhi, *Sociology of the Legal Profession, Law, and Legal System: The Indian Setting* (Delhi: Gian, 1987); Robert L. Kidder, "Formal Litigation and Professional Insecurity: Legal Entrepreneurship in South India," *Law & Society Review* 9:11 (1974); T. K. Oommen, "The Legal Profession in India: Some Sociological Perspectives," in *The Legal Profession: A Preliminary Study of the Tamilnadu Bar*, ed. N. R. Madhava Menon (New Delhi: Bar Council of India Trust, 1984), 20–21.

33. Oommen, "Legal Profession," 20–21.

34. Ibid., 20, table II.

35. Ibid., 19; N. R. Madhava Menon, S. Rama Rao, S. Sudarsen, "Legal Profession in Tamil Nadu: A Sociological Survey," in Menon, *Tamilnadu Bar*, 143; Gandhi, "Past and Present," 380.

36. Indian Const., Art. 39A.

37. *M. H. Hoskot v. State of Maharashtra*, AIR 1978 SC 1548, reaffirmed in *Hussainara Khatoon v. State of Bihar*, AIR 1979 SC 1369.

38. See the history of the legal aid movement in S. S. Sharma, *Legal Aid to the Poor: The Law and Indian Legal System* (New Delhi: Deep & Deep, 1993), 64–82.

39. Dhavan, "Law as Struggle," 31.

40. Data from the Supreme Court Legal Aid Committee.

41. This is the universal consensus drawn from interviews conducted by the author in 1993 with Supreme Court and High Court lawyers in New Delhi and numerous representatives of rights-advocacy organizations, including Shy-

amla Pappu, Nov. 20, 1993; four anonymous New Delhi High Court lawyers, Dec. 12, 1993; Jose Verghese, Nov. 24, 1993; Geeta Luthra and Pinky Anand, Nov. 22, 1993; Rajeev Dhavan, Dec. 19, 1993; Smitu Kothari (in Delhi), Dec. 17, 1993; Rajiv Vora, Nov. 30, 1993; Jyotsna Chatterji, Dec. 1, 1993. On the other hand, several lawyers acknowledged that legal aid has made it possible for the poorest of the poor to gain representation on some occasions. Anonymous New Delhi High Court lawyer, interview by author, Dec. 12, 1993; Geeta Luthra and Pinky Anand, interview by author, Nov. 22, 1993.

42. Galanter, *Law and Society*, 290.

43. Dhavan, "Law as Struggle," 40–41.

44. Punwani, "At What Stage," 298.

45. Ibid., 301.

46. *PUCL Bulletin* 6, no. 7 (July 1986).

47. Punwani, "At What Stage," 298.

48. Mary Fainsod Katzenstein, "Organizing against Violence: Strategies of the Indian Women's Movement," *Pacific Affairs* 62:56 (1989); Vibhuti Patel, "Emergence and Proliferation of Autonomous Women's Groups (1974–1984)," in *A Decade of Women's Movement in India*, ed. Neera Desai (Bombay: Himalaya Publishing House, 1988), 117–29; see also Gandhi and Shah, *Issues at Stake;* Nandita Haksar, "Violation of Democratic Rights of Women," in *Expanding Governmental Lawlessness and Organized Struggles*, ed. A. R. Desai (Bombay: Popular Prakashan, 1991), 262–67.

49. *Tukaram v. State of Maharashtra*, AIR 1979 SC 185.

50. For discussions of the role of the Mathura rape case in catalyzing the women's movement, see Katzenstein, "Organizing against Violence"; and Gandhi and Shah, *Issues at State.*

51. Upendra Baxi, Lotika Sarkar, Vasudha Dhagamwar, and Ragunath Kelkar, "An Open Letter to the Chief Justice of India," *Supreme Court Cases (Journal)* 1:17 (1979). Baxi reported "The 'quality' national press refused to publish our Open Letter on the bizarre ground that it was not 'news!'" (The incident had occurred seven years earlier.) See Upendra Baxi, *Inhuman Wrongs and Human Rights: Unconventional Essays* (New Delhi: Har-Anand, 1994), 71.

52. "Rape: The Victim is the Accused," *Manushi*, no. 442–46 (Dec. 1979–Jan. 1980), referring to a letter by Upendra Baxi, Lotika Sarkar, Vasudha Dhagamwar, and Raghunath Kelkar to the Chief Justice. By Baxi's account, women's-rights organizations hesitated to take up the issue until after other grassroots organizations had picked it up and after the letter itself had become a subject of controversy. Baxi, *Inhuman Wrongs*, 71.

53. See "The New Rape Bill—Legislating Rape 'Out of Existence'!" *Manushi*, no. 7:38–45 (1981).

54. Madhu Kishwar, "Never Say Die: Fight for Justice from an Unjust Judicial System," *Manushi*, no. 71:2–10 (1992) (on a case argued by Geeta Luthra and Pinky Anand); "Our Rights and Wrongs: Such Lofty Sympathy for a Rapist! A Recent Judgment by Justice Krishna Iyer," *Manushi*, no. 5:35–36 (1980) (publicizing a case in which a Supreme Court justice reduced the sentence of a rapist).

55. "Appeal to Supreme Court—Enquiry into Vimla's Death in Hyderabad," *Manushi*, no. 20:41–42 (1984); Geeta Luthra and Pinky Anand, "Torture is Abet-

ment of Suicide—Supreme Court Sets New Precedent," *Manushi,* nos. 54–55:22–24 (1989).

56. "The Delhi Nari Niketan—Protection Worse than Imprisonment," *Manushi,* no. 10:18–32 (1982). See also *Upendra Baxi v. State of Uttar Pradesh,* (1983) 2 SCC 308; *Sheela Barse v. Secretary, Children Aid Society,* (1987) 3 SCC 50; *Upendra Baxi v. State of Uttar Pradesh* AIR 1987 SC 191.

57. The one exception is the unified response to the Muslim Women's (Protection) Act (passed by Parliament to overrule the Shah Bano decision); fourteen women's organizations, led by the All India Women's Conference, filed a constitutional challenge to the Act, which the Supreme Court has yet to bring up for hearing.

58. Ratna Kapur, interview by author, New Delhi, Dec. 20, 1993.

59. Katzenstein, "Organizing Against Violence," 53.

60. Madhu Kishwar, interview by author, New Delhi, Dec. 10, 1993.

61. Geeta Luthra and Pinky Anand, interview by author, New Delhi, Nov. 22, 1993.

62. Chandramani Chopra, interview by author, New Delhi, Dec. 20, 1993.

63. Senior advocates make up the upper rung of the Indian bar and are analogous to Queen's Counsel in England.

64. Jyotsna Chatterji, interview by author, New Delhi, Dec. 1, 1993.

65. Ratna Kapur, "From Theory to Practice: Reflections on Legal Literacy Work with Women in India," in *Legal Literacy: A Tool for Women's Empowerment,* ed. Margaret Schuler and Sakuntala Kadirgamar-Rajasingham (New York: United Nations Development Fund for Women, 1992).

66. The structure of access to the Supreme Court, while appearing to aid previously excluded groups, paradoxically may limit their impact. By allowing easy access, the Supreme Court provides a structure in which litigants are not encouraged to carefully develop case strategies and in which the Court's attention to any one case is limited. Cases simply pop in easily and therefore very little organizational planning goes into developing them prior to the court appearance. Planning focuses instead on narrow legal arguments once in court. In addition, the few cases brought by rights-advocacy groups and lawyers are overwhelmed by the vastly larger numbers of cases continually brought by other interests, and their impact is diluted.

67. Chief Justice M. N. Venkatachaliah, interview by author, Nov. 25, 1993.

68. As one sympathetic critic put it: "It was a happy development on the Indian scene that the Emergency gave rise to movements of civil liberties and democratic rights. Their presence cannot be ignored now. . . . Human rights groups would however do well to take some stock-taking, assessing the nature and extent of impact that more than a decade of selective, *ad hoc* investigative reporting, publishing and litigating on Human Rights violations might have had on laws, institutions, public conscience and action programmes of political parties in the country." Iqbal A. Ansari, "Human Rights in India," *PUCL Bulletin,* December 1990, 9.

Chapter Seven

1. The legal jurisdictions of the United Kingdom (U.K.) are complex and potentially confusing. The U.K. is constituted by Great Britain and Northern

Ireland (along with some islands). Great Britain, in turn, comprises England, Wales, and Scotland. Within the U.K. there are three distinct court systems: England and Wales share one, and Scotland and Ireland each have their own. Yet the Appellate Committee of the House of Lords is the court of final appeal for each of the court systems. Although my discussion of the political context includes some matters implicating the U.K. as a whole (particularly the conflict in Northern Ireland, because of its implications for civil liberties within Great Britain), I have focused most of my attention on Great Britain and hence will generally refer to "Britain."

2. [1993] AC 534.

3. [1993] 3 All ER 537 (HL).

4. *R. v. Secretary of State for Transport, ex parte Factortame Ltd.* [1990] 2 AC 85; *R. v. Secretary of State for Transport, ex parte Factortame Ltd.* [1991] AC 603; and *R. v. Secretary of State for Employment, ex parte EOC* [1994] 1 All ER 910. In *Factortame*, after initial hesitation, the House of Lords granted an interim injunction suspending a parliamentary statute. The decision was a major development in the growing supremacy of European law over British law. See P. P. Craig, "Sovereignty of the United Kingdom Parliament after *Factortame*," *Yearbook of European Law* 11:221 (1991). The 1994 *EOC* case is especially significant because the Law Lords directly suspended parts of the offending statute under the judicial review procedure, now widely used by litigants challenging administrative actions, and because they granted standing to the Equal Opportunities Commission, a statutory agency that had suffered no direct injury but merely asked to challenge the statute in the abstract on behalf of working women. The Law Lords rejected the British statute because it distinguished between part-time workers (who are disproportionately women) and full-time workers in its policy on benefits and dismissal. The government's barrister had argued that using European law to reject the British law would be bringing judicial review in through the back door. See Richard Gordon, "Judicial Review and Equal Opportunities," *Public Law* 1994:217.

5. "Profound Judgment," *Times* (London), March 5, 1994, Features section.

6. Thomas Wilson, *Ulster: Conflict and Consent* (Oxford: Basil Blackwell, 1989).

7. Dilip Hiro, *Black British White British: A History of Race Relations in Britain* (London: Grafton, 1991); Shamit Saggar, *Race and Politics in Britain* (London: Harvester Wheatsheaf, 1992); John Solomos, *Race and Racism in Contemporary Britain* (London: Macmillan, 1989).

8. Hiro, *Black British White British*, p. ix.

9. Hiro, *Black British White British*; Solomos, *Race and Racism*.

10. Anthony M. Messina, *Race and Party Competition in Britain* (Oxford: Clarendon Press, 1989).

11. On the Immigration Law Practitioners Association, see Sterett, *Creating Constitutionalism?* 163–64.

12. See, for example, Clive Walker and Keir Starmer, eds., *Justice in Error* (London: Blackstone Press, 1993); K. D. Ewing and C. A. Gearty, *Freedom under Thatcher: Civil Liberties in Modern Britain* (Oxford: Clarendon Press, 1990).

13. Home Office, *Criminal Statistics* (London: Her Majesty's Stationery Office, annual).

14. Wilson, *Ulster.*

15. Saggar, *Race and Politics*, 84–85.

16. April Carter, *The Politics of Women's Rights* (London: Longman, 1988).

17. Bernard Crick, *The Reform of Parliament* (London: Weidenfeld and Nicholson, 1966), 2–3.

18. Ibid., 181–82.

19. Dicey, *Introduction.* P. P. Craig, *Administrative Law*, 2d ed. (London: Sweet & Maxwell, 1989), 3–11; P. P. Craig, *Public Law and Democracy in the United Kingdom and the United States of America* (New York: Oxford University Press, 1990), 13–29.

20. *Local Government Board v. Arlidge* [1915] AC 120.

21. Sir Stephen Sedley, "The Sound of Silence: Constitutional Law without a Constitution," *Law Quarterly Review* 110:274 (1994).

22. See, for instance, The Hon. Sir John Laws, "Law and Democracy," *Public Law* 1995:72–93.

23. Samuel E. Finer, *Comparative Government* (London: Allen Lane, 1970), 157.

24. A. G. Jordan and J. Richardson, *Government and Pressure Groups in Britain* (Oxford: Oxford University Press, 1987), 128, 192–97.

25. Ibid., 251–52; 141.

26. The conventional wisdom is at least in part an oversimplification; groups have used litigation to accomplish a number of objectives. See Harlow and Rawlings, *Pressure through Law.* For the conventional wisdom, see Joseph L. Badaracco, *Loading the Dice: A Five-Country Study of Vinyl Chloride Regulation* (Boston: Harvard Business School Press, 1985); David Vogel, *National Styles of Regulation: Environmental Policy in Great Britain and the United States* (Ithaca, N.Y.: Cornell University Press, 1986).

27. Rodney Brazier, *Constitutional Reform* (Oxford: Clarendon Press, 1991); Joseph Jaconelli, *Enacting a Bill of Rights: The Legal Problems* (Oxford: Clarendon Press, 1980); Zander, *Bill of Rights?*

28. For an extended discussion, see Mark Evans, *Charter 88: A Successful Challenge to the British Political Tradition?* (Aldershot, Eng.: Dartmouth, 1995).

29. "UK Soon to Adopt Human Rights Law," *The Lawyer* (London), July 8, 1997, p. 3; David Pannick, QC, "How to Judge a Human Rights Bill," *Times* (London), Aug. 12, 1997, Features section.

30. On these developments generally, see The Rt. Hon. Lord Browne-Wilkinson, "The Infiltration of a Bill of Rights," *Public Law* 1992:397–410; Anthony Lester, QC, "English Judges as Law Makers," *Public Law* 1993:269–90; Sedley, "Sound of Silence"; Sir John Laws, "Is the High Court the Guardian of Fundamental Constitutional Rights?" *Public Law* 1993:59; Bernard Schwartz, *Lions over the Throne: The Judicial Revolution in English Administrative Law* (New York: New York University Press, 1987).

31. Schwartz, *Lions;* H. W. R. Wade, *Administrative Law*, 6th ed. (Oxford: Clarendon Press, 1988); Lester, "English Judges."

32. J. D. B. Mitchell, "The Causes and Effects of the Absence of a System of Public Law in the United Kingdom," *Public Law* 1965:102.

33. On the general development, see Schwartz, *Lions;* Craig, *Administrative*

Law; Jeffrey L. Jowell and Dawn Oliver, eds., *New Directions in Judicial Review* (London: Stevens & Sons, 1988); Sedley, "Sound of Silence."

34. *Council of Civil Service Unions and others v. Minister for the Civil Service* [1984] 3 All ER 935 (HL) (*"GCHQ* case").

35. Ibid., 950.

36. [1925] AC 578.

37. [1964] AC 40.

38. [1948] 1 KB 223.

39. "MR" stands for "Master of the Rolls." Master of the Rolls is the title for the president of the Court of Appeal.

40. In clarifying what that meant, Lord Greene stated: "For instance, a person entrusted with a discretion must, so to speak, direct himself properly in law. He must call his own attention to the matters which he is bound to consider. He must exclude from his consideration matters which are irrelevant to what he has to consider. If he does not obey those rules, he may truly be said, and often is said, to be acting 'unreasonably.' Similarly, there may be something so absurd that no sensible person could ever dream that it lay within the powers of the authority." *Associated Provincial Picture Houses,* [1948] 1 KB at 229.

41. *Bromley LBC v. Greater London Council* [1983] 1 AC 768.

42. Louis Blom-Cooper, "The New Face of Judicial Review: Administrative Changes in Order 53," *Public Law* 1985:250. For a rich discussion of the development of Order 53, see Susan Sterett, "Keeping the Law Up to Date: The Idiom of Legalism and the Reform of Administrative Law in England and Wales," *Law & Social Inquiry* 15:749–54 (1991).

43. Blom-Cooper, "New Face."

44. Maurice Sunkin, "The Incidence and Effect of Judicial Review Procedures against Central Government in the United Kingdom," in *Comparative Judicial Review and Public Policy,* ed. Donald W. Jackson and C. Neal Tate (Westport, Conn.: Greenwood Press, 1992); Maurice Sunkin, "What Is Happening to Applications for Judicial Review?" *Modern Law Review* 50:432 (1987); Lee Bridges, Maurice Sunkin, and George Meszaros, *Judicial Review in Perspective* (London: Cavendish, 1995).

45. Marc Galanter developed the term "case congregations" to describe types of cases that lawyers and judges come to see as having similar sources, characteristics, and problems. Case congregations typically experience a period of substantial growth. See Marc Galanter, "Case Congregations and Their Careers," *Law & Society Review* 24:371 (1990). On the rise of administrative procedure litigation, see Jerold Waltman and Priscilla Machado, "Postindustrialism and the Changing Face of Administrative Litigation in England, 1960–1985," *Social Science Journal* 29:185–98 (1992).

46. This discussion is based on *European Court of Human Rights: Survey of Activities, 1959–1989* (Strasbourg, France: Council of Europe, 1990); Spencer, *Machinery of Justice,* 429–33; and Christopher McCrudden and Gerald Chambers, "Conclusions," in *Individual Rights and the Law in Britain,* ed. Christopher McCrudden and Gerald Chambers (Oxford: Oxford University Press, 1993), 570–79.

47. On the latter, see Donald W. Jackson, *The United Kingdom Confronts the*

European Convention on Human Rights (Gainesville: University Press of Florida, 1997), 64–81.

48. McCrudden and Chambers, "Conclusions," p. 571.

49. McCrudden and Chambers, "Conclusions"; Jackson, *United Kingdom Confronts*.

50. R. R. Churchill, "Aspects of Compliance with Findings of the Committee of Ministers and Judgements of the Court with Reference to the United Kingdom," in *The European Convention on Human Rights: Aspects of Incorporation*, ed. J. P. Gardner (London: British Institute of Comparative Law, 1992).

51. Herbert M. Kritzer, "Courts, Justice, and Politics in England," in *Courts, Law, and Politics in Comparative Perspective*, ed. Herbert Jacob, Erhard Blankenburg, Herbert M. Kritzer, Doris Marie Provine, and Joseph Sanders (New Haven: Yale University Press, 1995).

52. N. Bratza, "The Treatment and Interpretation of the European Convention on Human Rights: Aspects of Incorporation," in *European Convention on Human Rights: Aspects of Incorporation*, ed. J. P. Gardner (London: British Institute of Comparative Law, 1992).

53. *Derbyshire County Council v. Times Newspapers Ltd.* [1993] AC 534.

54. In 1993, the Treaty of European Union at Maastricht established the European Union, which is constituted by three independent elements, the European Community, the Common Foreign and Security Policy, and Justice and Home Affairs, all under the umbrella of the European Council of Heads of State and Government. The legal system operates within the European Community, and hence my discussion will be confined to the EC.

55. Gerhard Casper, "The Emerging Constitution of the European Community," *Law School Record of the University of Chicago Law School* 24:5–12 (1978); Eric Stein, "Lawyers, Judges, and the Making of a Transnational Constitution," *American Journal of International Law* 75:1–27 (1981); Martin Shapiro, "The European Court of Justice," in *Euro-Politics: Institutions and Policymaking in the "New" European Community*, ed. Alberta M. Sbragia (Washington, D.C.: Brookings Institution, 1992).

56. The fact that the Commission's proposals, according to critics, largely avoided the miscarriage issue but extended the powers of the police and limited the rights of defendants (such as proposing to abolish the right to silence in criminal trials, now enacted into law) has itself become a subject of some controversy.

57. The authoritative summary of the law is Michael Zander, *The Police and Criminal Evidence Act 1984*, 2d ed. (London: Sweet & Maxwell, 1991).

58. David Feldman, "Regulating Treatment of Suspects in Police Stations: Judicial Interpretations of Detention Provisions in the Police and Criminal Evidence Act 1984," *Criminal Law Review* (1990); D. Birch, "The PACE Hots Up: Confessions and Confusions under the 1984 Act," *Criminal Law Review* (1989); R. May, "Fair Play at Trial: An Interim Assessment of S. 78 of the Police and Criminal Evidence Act 1984," *Criminal Law Review* 1988:722–30; A. A. S. Zuckerman, "Illegally Obtained Evidence: Discretion as a Guardian of Legitimacy," in *Current Legal Problems 1987* (London: Stevens, 1987).

59. Michael Zander, *Cases and Materials on the English Legal System*, 5th ed. (London: Weidenfeld & Nicolson, 1988), 559.

60. A. T. H. Smith, "Criminal Appeals in the House of Lords," *Modern Law Review* 47:133 (1984).

61. Ibid.

62. Spencer, *Machinery of Justice*, 201–2.

63. JUSTICE, *Evidence to the Royal Commission on Criminal Justice* (London: JUSTICE, 1991), 29.

64. Ibid., 25.

65. Ibid.

66. Kate Malleson, "Review of the Appeal Process" (report to The Royal Commission on Criminal Justice, London: Her Majesty's Stationery Office, 1993). Malleson's evidence rejects the view advanced by the standard text on the English judicial system, which claims that the Court interprets the "miscarriage" proviso to mean that "no reasonable jury, properly directed, could have failed to convict. . . . A case may reek of guilt, but the Court of Appeal may be unable to say that a jury would infallibly have convicted, and may therefore feel bound to quash the conviction." See J. R. Spencer, *Machinery of Justice*, 206–7.

67. Quoted in W. B. Creighton, *Working Women and the Law* (London: Mansell, 1979), 67.

68. Ibid., 73–75.

69. Elizabeth Meehan, *Women's Rights at Work: Campaigns and Policy in Britain and the United States* (London: Macmillan, 1985).

70. Colin Bourn and John Whitmore, *Race and Sex Discrimination*, 2d ed. (London: Sweet & Maxwell, 1993), 9–10.

71. 401 U.S. 424 (1971).

72. B. A. Hepple, "Judging Equal Rights," *Current Legal Problems* 36:71–90 (1983).

73. Council Directive 74/117/EEC (Feb. 10, 1975).

74. Council Directive 76/207/EEC (Feb. 9, 1976).

75. Council Directives 79/7/EEC (Dec. 19, 1978) (social security); 86/378/EEC (July 24, 1986) (occupational social security policies); 86/613/EEC (Dec. 11, 1986) (self-employed enterprises, including agricultural work).

76. Evelyn Ellis, *Sex Discrimination Law* (Aldershot, Eng.: Gower, 1988).

77. Case 43/75 [1976] ECR 455.

78. Case 152/84 [1986] 2 ECR 723. See Bourn and Whitmore, *Race and Sex*, 21–24.

79. Sally J. Kenney, *For Whose Protection? Reproductive Hazards and Exclusionary Policies in the United States and Britain* (Ann Arbor: University of Michigan Press, 1992), 87.

80. Ibid., 89–91.

81. Sedley, "Sound of Silence," 270.

82. Browne-Wilkinson, "Infiltration of a Bill of Rights." See also Ferdinand Mount, *The British Constitution Now: Recovery or Decline* (London: Heineman, 1992), 230. For an insightful analysis of the growing effect of European law on English courts, see Kritzer, "Courts, Justice and Politics."

83. Alan Paterson, *The Law Lords* (London: Macmillan, 1982); Robert S. Stevens, *Law and Politics: The House of Lords as a Judicial Body, 1800–1976* (Chapel Hill: University of North Carolina Press, 1978); and J. A. G. Griffith, *Judicial*

Politics Since 1920: A Chronicle (Oxford: Blackwell, 1993). Recent appointments, however, may shift the Law Lords slightly to the left. See David Rose, "UK— Silent Revolution: Judges with Radical Views," *Observer* (London), May 9, 1993.

84. House of Lords, "Practice Statement (Judicial Precedent)" [1966] 1 *Weekly Law Reports* 1234. In *London Street Tramways v. London County Council* [1898] AC 375, the Law Lords had declared that they had no authority to over-rule their own precedents and henceforth were to be bound by stare decisis. On the Practice Statement, see Paterson, *Law Lords*, 143–53.

85. Stevens, *Law and Politics*. Similarly, Louis Blom-Cooper and Gavin Drewry have observed that the Appellate Committee is the site of "final appeal." See *Final Appeal: A Study of the House of Lords in Its Judicial Capacity* (Oxford: Oxford University Press, 1972).

86. Paterson, *Law Lords*, 11–12.

87. Jerold Waltman, "Judicial Activism in England," in Holland, *Judicial Activism;* David Feldman, "Public Law Values in the House of Lords," *Law Quarterly Review* 106:246 (1990); Atiyah and Summers, *Form and Substance*.

88. Joni Lovenduski, *Women and European Politics* (Amherst: University of Massachusetts Press, 1986), 216–19.

89. Recent research on the judicial role of the Lord Chancellor shows that all Lord Chancellors since the late forties have participated as judges in a small percentage of cases, about 10–15 percent over the period as a whole. The Lord Chancellors serving in the late seventies and the eighties apparently increased their level of participation in cases somewhat. See Anthony Bradney, "The Judicial Activity of the Lord Chancellor 1946–1987: A Pellet," *Journal of Law and Society* 16:360 (1989).

90. Classifications are based, where possible, on scholarly research on the Law Lords; where that was not possible, I relied on other characterizations of their views by legal scholars or by long-time colleagues (in obituaries). Sources for the classification are David Robertson, "Judicial Ideology in the House of Lords: A Jurimetric Analysis," *British Journal of Political Science* 12:1–25 (1982); Griffith, *Judicial Politics;* Stevens, *Law and Politics;* Feldman, "Public Law Values"; *The Dictionary of National Biography: 1971–1980* (Oxford: Oxford University Press, 1986); *The Dictionary of National Biography: 1981–1985* (Oxford: Oxford University Press, 1990); *Obituaries of the Times, 1951–60, 1961–70, 1971–75;* and *Annual Obituary,* 1980, 1985, 1989, 1990. The classification and its sources are admittedly sketchy by the standards of American political science. Apart from the study by David Robertson, there has been no systematic statistical research on the voting patterns of Law Lords. But, if such research on the American Supreme Court is any guide, journalists' characterizations of judicial attitudes generally are not wide of the mark established by statistical measurement. See Jeffrey A. Segal and Albert D. Cover, "Ideological Values and the Votes of U.S. Supreme Court Justices," *American Political Science Review* 83:557–65 (1989). Additionally, the classification in the table is based on the sort of evidence available to lawyers and other judges in the British court system, evidence on which they may base their decisions about appealing cases to the House of Lords.

91. See, in particular, Paterson, *Law Lords;* Stevens, *Law and Politics;* and Griffith, *Judicial Politics*.

92. Quoted in Stevens, *Law and Politics*, 468 n. 141.

93. Paterson, *Law Lords*, 144–53.

94. See Stevens, *Law and Politics;* Griffith, *Judicial Politics;* and J. A. G. Griffith, *The Politics of the Judiciary*, 4th ed. (London: Fontana, 1991). Griffith's two books also document the more recent apparent return to conservatism by the Law Lords. See also Atiyah and Summers, *Form and Substance.*

95. Stevens, *Law and Politics*, 588.

96. Ibid.

97. Ibid., 586, quoting John Paine.

98. Feldman, "Public Law Values."

99. Burton M. Atkins, "Alternative Models," 785.

100. Occasionally a case reaches the Lords by "leapfrogging" the Court of Appeal, coming directly from the High Court; doing so requires a certificate from the High Court that the case involves a point of law of general public importance as well as leave to appeal from the House of Lords.

101. *Judicial Statistics* (London: Her Majesty's Stationery Office, 1991), 10, table 1.5.

102. The number of leave-to-appeal petitions, however, is sharply limited by the requirement in criminal cases that the Criminal Division of the Court of Appeal, the court below the House of Lords in the judicial hierarchy, must certify that the case contains a point of law of general public importance in order for the prospective appellant even to have the option of petitioning the House of Lords for leave to appeal. Additionally, the House of Lords does not have complete control over its docket in that the Court of Appeal has the authority to grant leave to appeal to the Law Lords.

Chapter Eight

1. The data for the study of the agenda of the Appellate Committee of the House of Lords consist of a coding of a variety of information from (a) all Appellate Committee cases reported in *Appeal Cases* in five-year intervals from 1960 to 1990, and (b) all Appellate Committee cases decided in those years as recorded in the House of Lords Records Office. The number of decided cases in my sample for each of the years is slightly higher than the number listed in *Civil Judicial Statistics* and *Judicial Statistics* due to the inclusion in *Appeal Cases* of some cases decided in the prior year.

2. Tax cases include any in which a private party and a government party dispute the levying of a tax. Ordinary economic cases, following Pacelle's definition, include torts, contracts, wills and estates, insurance, and other disputes generally pitting private parties against other private parties. See Pacelle, *Transformation of the Supreme Court's Agenda.*

3. The increase in ordinary economic cases in 1990 does not appear to be centered in only one type of case but occurs in contracts, personal and property torts, and disputes over titles and real property. The increase interestingly also includes one tort of "misfeasance in public office," a recently developed mechanism for controlling official discretion.

4. [1964] AC 1254.

5. [1974] AC 878.

6. M. Trebilgas-Davey, "Miscarriages of Justice within the English Legal Sys-

tem," *New Law Journal* 141:608 (1991); John Jackson, "Due Process," in *Individual Rights and the Law in Britain*, ed. Christopher McCrudden and Gerald Chambers (Oxford: Oxford University Press, 1994).

7. *R. v. Sang* [1980] AC 402.

8. [1984] AC 437.

9. *McKee v. Chief Constable of Northern Ireland* [1985] 1 All ER 1 (HL).

10. The following discussion is based on Martin Loughlin and Peter M. Quinn, "Prisons, Rules, and Courts: A Study in Administrative Law," *Modern Law Review* 56:497 (1993); Martin Loughlin, "The Underside of the Law: Judicial Review and the Prison Disciplinary System," *Current Legal Problems* 46:23 (1993); and Stephen Livingstone and Tim Owen, *Prison Law* (Oxford: Clarendon Press, 1993).

11. *Becker v. Home Office* [1972] 2 All ER 682, quoted in Loughlin, "Underside," 41.

12. *Golder v. United Kingdom*, (1975) 1 EHRR 524, Series A, No. 18.

13. [1983] 1 AC 1.

14. *R. v. Secretary of State for the Home Department, ex parte Anderson* [1984] 1 All ER 920 (QB).

15. [1979] QB 425.

16. [1988] 1 All ER 485.

17. Creighton, *Working Women*, 68.

18. *Roberts v. Cleveland Area Health Authority* [1979] 1 WLR 754; *Duke v. Reliance Systems Ltd.* [1988] AC 618.

19. *R. v. Birmingham City Council, ex parte Equal Opportunities Commission* [1989] AC 1155; *James v. Eastleigh Borough Council* [1990] 2 AC 751.

20. *Rainey v. Greater Glasgow Health Board* [1987] AC 224. On this decision, the House of Lords followed precedent established by the European Court of Justice in *Bilka-Kaufhaus GmbH v. Weber von Hartz*, Case 170/84 [1986] ECR 1607.

21. *Hayward v. Cammell Laird Shipbuilders Ltd.* [1988] IRLR 257.

22. *Pickstone v. Freemans PLC* [1988] 3 WLR 265.

23. Rajeev Dhavan and Martin Partington, "Co-optation or Independent Strategy? The Role of Social Action Groups," in *Public Interest Law*, ed. Jeremy Cooper and Rajeev Dhavan (Oxford: Basil Blackwell, 1986), 243–44.

24. Tony Prosser, *Test Cases for the Poor* (London: Child Poverty Action Group, 1983); Smith, "How Good Are Test Cases?"

25. Barbara Cohen and Marie Staunton, "In Pursuit of a Legal Strategy: The National Council for Civil Liberties," in Cooper and Dhavan, *Public Interest Law*, 290, 294; Mark Lilly, *The National Council for Civil Liberties: The First Fifty Years* (London: Macmillan, 1984).

26. John Wadham, Legal Director of Liberty, interview by author, London, October 20, 1993.

27. Dhavan and Partington, *Co-optation*, 244.

28. Ian Martin, "Combining Casework and Strategy: The Joint Council for the Welfare of Immigrants," in Cooper and Dhavan, *Public Interest Law*, 261–70; Sterett, *Creating Constitutionalism*, 163–64.

29. Dhavan and Partington, "Co-optation" 246–47.

30. Ibid., 247.

31. Mike Stephens, *Community Law Centres* (Aldershot, Eng.: Avebury, 1990), 28.

32. Ibid., 78, 114.

33. The following discussion is based on Spencer, *Machinery of Justice*, 463–90.

34. Herbert M. Kritzer, "The English Experience with the English Rule: How 'Loser Pays' Works, What Difference It Makes, and What Might Happen Here" (Disputes Processing Research Program Working Paper, Madison, Wisc.: Institute for Legal Studies, 1992).

35. This observation applies only to civil lawsuits. Criminal defendants are never liable for the prosecutor's costs.

36. The full headline reads: "No smoke without fire: Legal aid has been granted to 200 smokers considering suing British cigarette companies on health grounds," (by Jeremy Watson) *Scotland on Sunday* (Edinburgh), Feb. 5, 1995, p. 8; see also "Legal aid for the Arts Club banned," *Evening Standard* (London), Oct. 28, 1997, p.10 (award of legal aid for a man challenging being banned from a drinking club); John Steele, "Robber given legal aid to sue Home Secretary," *Daily Telegraph* (London), Sept. 25, 1997, p.17 (award of legal aid to a prisoner challenging his security status); Bruce McKain, "No legal aid for widow of smoking death man," *Herald* (Glasgow), Feb. 16, 1995, p. 9; "Amputee smoker refused legal aid," *Herald* (Glasgow), July 10, 1995, p. 4; Luke Harding, "Forget Excalibur, Arthur is armed with legal aid," *Daily Mail* (London), June 10, 1995, p. 3 (about a Druid named Arthur Pendragon who was granted legal aid for challenging, on religious grounds, access restrictions around Stonehenge); "Three-month-old baby wins legal aid," *Evening Standard* (London), Aug. 11, 1995, p. 16 (about a grant of legal aid to a child whose asthma allegedly was exacerbated by pollution).

37. Mike McConville, Jacqueline Hodgson, Lee Bridges, and Anita Pavlovic, *Standing Accused: The Organisation and Practices of Criminal Defence Lawyers in Britain* (Oxford: Clarendon Press, 1994), 1–9; Lee Bridges, "The Professionalization of Criminal Justice," *Legal Action*, August 1992, 7.

38. Michael Murphy, "Civil Legal Aid Eligibility Estimates, 1979–90," unpublished paper, London School of Economics, reprinted in part as appendix 1 in Legal Action Group, *A Strategy for Justice* (London: Legal Action Group, 1992).

39. Richard L. Abel, *The Legal Profession in England and Wales* (Oxford: Basil Blackwell, 1988), 68–72, 137–68.

40. Ibid., 74–85.

41. Ibid., 170–76.

42. Ibid., 104.

43. Ibid., table 2.24, p. 423.

44. Michael Jeeves and Julie Macfarlane, "Rethinking Legal Education," in Cooper and Dhavan, *Public Interest Law*, 394–413.

45. In 1969 about 20 percent of criminal defendants charged with indictable offenses in magistrates' courts were supported by legal aid, but by 1986 over 80 percent were so supported, according to the Legal Action Group, *A Strategy for Justice* (London: Legal Action Group, 1992).

46. Spencer, *Machinery of Justice*, 479.

47. JUSTICE, "Evidence"; Liberty, *Let Justice Be Done: Evidence to the Royal Commission on Criminal Justice* (London: Liberty, 1991).

48. McConville et al., *Standing Accused.*

49. The following discussion is based on McConville et al., *Standing Accused,* 270–98.

50. Ibid., 275.

51. JUSTICE, *Miscarriages of Justice* (London: JUSTICE, 1989), 2.

52. The number of long-term prisoners roughly doubled after 1980. The long-term prisoners, especially lifers, began to believe that they had little to lose by litigating, and several became the plaintiffs in the prisoner-rights litigation of the eighties. Adam Sampson, Deputy Director, Prison Reform Trust, interview by author, London, Sept. 28, 1993; Kate Akester, solicitor involved in many of the prisoner-rights cases, interview by author, London, Oct. 23, 1993.

53. Akester (interview).

54. Ibid.

55. Ibid.

56. Akester (interview); Tim Owen, interview by author, London, October 29, 1993; anonymous High Court judge, interview by author, undisclosed location, October 26, 1993.

57. Akester (interview).

58. Bob Hepple, "The Judicial Process in Claims for Equal Pay and Equal Treatment in the United Kingdom," in *Women, Employment, and European Equity Law,* ed. Christopher McCrudden (London: Eclipse, 1987), 150. In the eighties, the EOC was on record as opposing extension of legal aid for representation in tribunals, "presumably because it want[ed] to retain control of a substantial proportion of discrimination litigation." Ibid.

59. This analysis is supported by a wide range of scholarship on the British women's movement. See, in particular, Meehan, *Women's Rights at Work,* 155; Gelb, *Feminism and Politics;* Paul Byrne, "The Politics of the Women's Movement," in *Women in Politics,* ed. Joni Lovenduski and Pippa Norris (New York: Oxford University Press, 1996), 57–72; Joni Lovenduski and Vicky Randall, *Contemporary Feminist Politics: Women and Power in Britain* (New York: Oxford University Press, 1993), 93–132; Sheila Rowbotham, Lynne Segal, and Hilary Wainwright, *Beyond the Fragments: Feminism and the Making of Socialism* (London: Merlin, 1979); Susan Atkins, "Women's Rights," in Cooper and Dhavan, *Public Interest Law,* 333–34.

60. Meehan, *Women's Rights at Work,* 155; Gelb, *Feminism and Politics.*

61. Gelb, *Feminism and Politics;* Meehan, *Women's Rights at Work,* 129. Among the structures that Meehan identifies as enhancing women's-group involvement in the United States is the amicus curiae brief, which allows nonparties to communicate directly with courts; such a mechanism is lacking in the British court system.

62. Gelb, *Feminism and Politics.*

63. Harlow and Rawlings, *Pressure through Law,* 166–68.

64. Vera Sacks, "The Equal Opportunities Commission—Ten Years On," *Modern Law Review* 49:560 (1986).

65. S. Atkins, "Women's Rights," 36.

66. Anonymous solicitor, interview by author, London, Oct. 11, 1993.

67. Harlow and Rawlings, *Pressure through Law*, 284–85.

68. Ibid.

69. Ibid., 285.

70. Meehan, *Women's Rights at Work*; Ellis, *Sex Discrimination Law*; Sacks, "Equal Opportunities Commission."

71. Sacks, "Equal Opportunities Commission"; others, notably Erika Szyszczak, "The Future of Women's Rights: The Role of European Community Law," in *The Yearbook of Social Policy*, ed. M. Brenton and C. Ungerson (London: Routledge,1986), lauded the EOC for developing an effective litigation strategy using EC law.

72. Ellis, *Sex Discrimination Law*, 243.

73. Kenney, *For Whose Protection*, 92–93.

74. See Graham K. Wilson, *The Politics of Safety and Health* (Oxford: Oxford University Press, 1985); and David Vogel, *National Styles of Regulation* (Ithaca, N.Y.: Cornell University Press, 1986). For a review of the research, see Robert A. Kagan, "Adversarial Legalism and American Government," *Journal of Policy Analysis and Management* 10:369–406 (1991).

75. Alice Leonard, Deputy Legal Advisor of the EOC, interview by author, London, Oct. 21, 1993. On developments in the running battle, see also Frances Gibb, "Equality Watchdog Seeks EC Decision," *Times* (London), Aug. 24, 1993, Home News section; Barrie Clement, "Women's Pay Battle to Go to Europe; Equality Body's Patience Runs Out," *Independent* (London), Aug. 24, 1993, p. 3; Barrie Clement and Patricia Wynn Davies, "Equal Pay for Women Curbed by Ministers" *Independent* (London), Oct. 11, 1993, 1.

76. Leonard (interview).

77. Katherine O'Donovan and Erika Szyszczak, *Equality and Sex Discrimination Law* (Oxford: Basil Blackwell, 1988), 122–52.

78. *Macarthy's Ltd. v. Smith*, Case 129/79 [1980] ECR 1275 (on the standard of comparison in equal pay cases); *Garland v. British Rail Engineering Ltd.*, Case 12/81 [1982] ECR 359 (on the definition of retirement benefits, which often were given unequally to men and women, and the direct applicability of the definition); and *Marshall* [1986] (on unequal retirement ages for men and women, and on the direct effect of EC Directives, which are addressed only to governments and not individuals).

79. The ECJ decision in *Marshall* [1986] forced the British government to pass the Sex Discrimination Act of 1986, mandating equal retirement ages for men and women.

80. *Commission of the European Communities v. United Kingdom*, Case 61/81 [1982] ECR 2601.

81. *R. v. Secretary of State for Employment, ex parte EOC*, [1994] 1 All ER 910; see Clare Dyer and Patrick Wintour, "Part-Timers Win Rights: Women Gain Most From Lords Ruling," *Guardian* (London), March 4, 1994, p. 1; Barrie Clement and Patricia Wynn Davies, "Law Biased Against Part-Time Workers, Lords Rule," *Independent* (London), March 4, 1994, p. 3; "UK Part-Time Work Rules 'in Breach of EU Law'" *Financial Times* (London), March 4, 1994, p. 6; "Profound Judgment."

270 Notes to Pages 154–158

82. Kate Akester, interview by author, London, Oct. 23, 1993.

Chapter Nine

1. *R. v. Askov* [1990] 2 S.C.R. 1199 held that a twenty-three-month delay is "unreasonable" under section 11(b) of the Charter of Rights and Freedoms; Ontario's decision to stay or drop numerous charges is discussed in W. A. Bogart, *Courts and Country: The Limits of Litigation and the Social and Political Life of Canada* (Toronto: Oxford, 1994), 208.

2. See, for example, Knopff and Morton, *Charter Politics*, 4.

3. *Morgentaler v. The Queen* [1976] 1 S.C.R. 616.

4. *R. v. Morgentaler* [1988] 1 S.C.R. 30; the political and legal campaigns around the two cases, as well as similar campaigns by abortion opponents, are explored in rich and fascinating detail in F. L. Morton, Morgentaler v. Borowski: *Abortion, the Charter, and the Courts* (Toronto: McClelland & Stewart, 1992).

5. F. L. Morton, Peter H. Russell, and Michael J. Withey, "The Supreme Court's First One Hundred Charter of Rights Decisions: A Statistical Analysis," *Osgoode Hall Law Journal* 30:1–56 (1989); F. L. Morton, Peter H. Russell, and Troy Riddell, "The Canadian Charter of Rights and Freedoms: A Descriptive Analysis of the First Decade, 1982–1992," *National Journal of Constitutional Law* 5:1–60 (1995).

6. A representative case from the seventies is *The Queen v. Wray* [1971] S.C.R. 272. By 1985, in *R. v. Therens* [1985] 1 S.C.R. 613, the Court had reversed course and excluded any breathalyzer evidence obtained in a police station before the accused was informed of his right to counsel; many other cases hinging on exclusion of evidence soon followed.

7. Most previous research, however, has not explicitly tested alternative explanations for that transformation but has assumed that it resulted primarily from adoption of the Charter in 1982. But see F. L. Morton, "The Charter Revolution and the Court Party," in *The Impact of the Charter on the Public Policy Process*, ed. Patrick Monahan and Marie Finkelstein (North York, Ont.: York University Centre for Public Law and Public Policy, 1993); and F. L. Morton and Rainer Knopff, "The Supreme Court as the Vanguard of the Intelligentsia: The Charter Movement as Post-Materialist Politics," in *Two Hundred Years of Canadian Constitutionalism*, ed. Janet Ajzenstat (Ottawa: Canadian Study of Parliament Group, 1993).

8. Louis Hartz, *The Founding of New Societies* (New York: Harcourt, 1969); Gad Horowitz, *Canadian Labour in Politics* (Toronto: University of Toronto Press, 1968); Seymour Martin Lipset, *Continental Divide: The Values and Institutions of the United States and Canada* (New York: Routledge, 1990).

9. Lipset, *Continental Divide*, 1–18.

10. Ibid., 90–116, 136–40.

11. Ibid., 172–92.

12. Alan C. Cairns, *Charter versus Federalism: The Dilemmas of Constitutional Reform* (Montreal: McGill-Queen's University Press, 1992), 17.

13. This observation should not be pushed too far: the geographical expansion of land ownership by some religious sects occasioned provincial legislation that limited further expansion, particularly legislation by Alberta limiting land purchases by Hutterites. See William Janzen, *Limits on Liberty: The Experi-*

ence of Mennonite, Hutterite, and Doukhobor Communities in Canada (Toronto: University of Toronto Press, 1990).

14. Ibid., 11–32.

15. Williams, "Citizen Rights," 100–107.

16. Ibid., 105.

17. Ibid., 113.

18. Ibid., 107–10, 113–15.

19. Ibid., 113.

20. Maxwell Cohen, "Human Rights: Programme or Catchall? A Canadian Rationale," *Canadian Bar Review,* December 1968, 557, quoted in Williams, "Citizen Rights," 99.

21. Rainer Knopff and F. L. Morton, "Nation-Building and the Canadian Charter of Rights and Freedoms," in *Constitutionalism, Citizenship, and Society in Canada,* ed. Alan Cairns and Cynthia Williams (Toronto: University of Toronto Press, 1985).

22. Roy Romanow, John Whyte and Howard Leeson, *Canada Notwithstanding: The Making of the Constitution 1976–1982* (Toronto: Carswell/Methuen, 1984); Keith Banting and Richard Simeon, eds., *And No One Cheered: Federalism, Democracy, and the Constitution Act* (Toronto: Methuen, 1983).

23. Canadian Const., §93 (educational rights) and §133 (language rights).

24. Peter H. Russell, "The Growth of Canadian Judicial Review and the Commonwealth and American Experiences," in *Comparative Judicial Review and Public Policy,* ed. Donald W. Jackson and C. Neal Tate (Westport, Conn.: Greenwood Press, 1992).

25. See Frank Scott, "The Consequences of the Privy Council Decisions," *Canadian Bar Review* 15:485–94 (1937).

26. Arthur Maloney, "The Supreme Court and Civil Liberties," *Criminal Law Quarterly* 18:202 (1976).

27. Bogart, *Courts and Country,* 257.

28. Knopff and Morton, *Charter Politics,* 1.

29. See, for instance, Knopff and Morton, *Charter Politics,* and Bogart, *Courts and Country.*

30. Bogart, *Courts and Country,* 301–3; Knopff and Morton, *Charter Politics,* 26–29; Morton, "Political Impact."

31. Martin L. Friedland, "R. S. Wright's Model Criminal Code: A Forgotten Chapter in the History of the Criminal Law," *Oxford Journal of Legal Studies* 1:307 (1981); D. H. Brown, *The Genesis of the Canadian Criminal Code of 1892* (Toronto: University of Toronto Press, 1989).

32. By convention, the governor-general in council has commuted the few death sentences handed down by judges. See B. Welling and L. A. Hipfner, "Cruel and Unusual? Capital Punishment in Canada," *University of Toronto Law Journal* 26:55–83 (1976).

33. Martin L. Friedland, *Double Jeopardy* (Oxford: Clarendon Press, 1969), 229–30.

34. See, for example, Law Reform Commission of Canada, *Police Powers: Search and Seizure in Criminal Law Enforcement* (Ottawa: The Law Reform Commission of Canada, 1983).

35. *In re Meaning of the Word "Persons"* [1928] S.C.R. 276. On the other hand,

most of the provinces by that point allowed women to serve in provincial legislatures.

36. *Edwards v. Attorney-General for Canada* [1930] AC 124 (PC).

37. Walter S. Tarnopolsky, *The Canadian Bill of Rights,* 2d ed. (Toronto: McClelland & Stewart, 1975), 69, 84–85 nn. 219–26.

38. Ibid., 74.

39. Royal Commission on the Status of Women, *Report of the Royal Commission on the Status of Women* (Ottawa: Information Canada, 1970).

40. *Murdoch v. Murdoch* [1975] 1 S.C.R. 423.

41. For a discussion of adoption of such provisions in the common-law provinces, see A. J. McLean, "Matrimonial Property—Canadian Common Law Style," *University of Toronto Law Journal* 31:363–435 (1981). Québec passed similar reform legislation in 1980.

42. James G. Snell and Frederick Vaughan, *The Supreme Court of Canada: History of the Institution* (Toronto: University of Toronto Press, 1985); Ian Bushnell, "Leave to Appeal Applications to the Supreme Court of Canada: A Matter of Public Importance," *Supreme Court Law Review* 3:479 (1982); Knopff and Morton, "Nation-Building."

43. Knopff and Morton, "Nation-Building."

44. Ian Bushnell, *The Captive Court: A Study of the Supreme Court of Canada* (Montreal: McGill-Queen's University Press, 1992). The Canadian Supreme Court differs from the U.S. Court in several other ways. The Prime Minister directly appoints Supreme Court justices; they face no confirmation by Parliament; there is a deeply entrenched convention producing regional representation on the Court; and oral arguments in cases may run for a day or more, compared to the standard total of one hour allotted to oral arguments in the U.S. Court.

45. Snell and Vaughan, *Supreme Court,* 206–8.

46. W. H. McConnell, *Commentary on the British North America Act* (Toronto: Macmillan,1977).

47. [1963] S.C.R. 651.

48. John Cavarazon, quoted in Maloney, "Supreme Court and Civil Liberties."

49. [1970] S.C.R. 282.

50. In *Singh v. Minister of Employment and Immigration* [1985] 1 S.C.R. 177, four justices relied on the Bill of Rights to strike down the procedures used by the Department of Employment and Immigration for determining the validity of claims of refugee status; three other justices relied on the Charter to reach the same end. Reflecting on the history of judicial interpretation of the Bill of Rights in a 1985 Supreme Court case applying the new Charter, Justice Gerald Ledain suggested that courts narrowly interpreted the Bill of Rights "because it did not reflect a clear constitutional mandate to make judicial decisions having the effect of limiting or qualifying the traditional sovereignty of Parliament." *R. v. Therens* [1985] 1 S.C.R. 613. By contrast, of course, the Charter of Rights appeared to carry such a clear constitutional mandate.

51. *Thorson v. Attorney-General of Canada* [1975] 1 S.C.R. 138; *Nova Scotia Board of Censors v. McNeil* [1976] 2 S.C.R. 265; and *Minister of Justice of Canada v. Borowski* [1981] 2 S.C.R. 575.

52. *Borowski* [1981] 2 S.C.R. at 598.

53. [1986] 2 S.C.R. 607.

54. W. A. Bogart, "Understanding Standing, Chapter IV: *Minister of Finance of Canada vs. Finlay,"* *Supreme Court Law Review* 10:377 (1988).

55. *Valley Forge Christian College v. Americans United for Separation of Church and State, Inc.,* 454 U.S. 464 (1982). More recently, the U.S. Court limited standing under statutes to parties who can demonstrate actual injury. See *Lujan v. Defenders of Wildlife,* 504 U.S. 555 (1992).

Chapter Ten

1. Morton, "Charter Revolution"; Morton and Knopff, "The Supreme Court as the Vanguard of the Intelligentsia."

2. Morton, "Charter Revolution," 181.

3. The proportion of the agenda devoted to rights that I report here is somewhat higher than that reported by Morton, Russell, and Riddell, "Descriptive Analysis," probably because my analysis is not limited to Charter cases and because I use, as a base, only full decisions (one page or more of opinion). Ordinary economic issues, as defined here, include all tax disputes (unless they raise a rights claim) and a range of ordinary private disputes, among them contracts, torts, wills and estates, and the like.

4. There is also some evidence that the Court's ordinary economic cases are themselves shifting toward a focus on rights. For example, in *Norberg v. Wynrib* [1992] 2 S.C.R. 226, a tort case, the decision centered on the issue of sex discrimination. Thus, the trends presented in figure 10.1 likely understate the extent of the transformation from ordinary economic issues to rights issues (I am indebted to Ian Brodie for this observation).

5. Even at the height of its judicial-review activity in 1990, the Supreme Court overturned fewer than ten federal and provincial laws. In contrast, the U.S. Supreme Court struck down about sixteen state laws and just under two federal laws per year in the 1980s. For the U.S. figures, see Lawrence Baum, *The Supreme Court,* 4th ed. (Washington, D.C.: Congressional Quarterly Press, 1992), 188–90. On the other hand, there are far fewer provinces than states to generate potential conflict with Supreme Court policy, and so we might expect the use of judicial review to be somewhat less frequent in Canada than in the United States.

6. Patrick Monahan, *Politics and the Constitution: The Charter, Federalism, and the Supreme Court of Canada* (Toronto: Carswell, 1987), 18–21; Peter H. Russell, "The Supreme Court and Federal-Provincial Relations: The Political Use of Legal Resources," *Canadian Public Policy* 11:161–70 (1985).

7. Ian Ross Brodie, "Charting the Growth of Interest Group Activity in the Supreme Court of Canada" (paper presented at the annual meeting of the Law and Society Association, Toronto, 1995); Ian Ross Brodie, "Interest Groups and the Charter of Rights and Freedoms: Interveners at the Supreme Court of Canada" (master's thesis, University of Calgary, 1992).

8. Brodie, "Charting the Growth"; Jillian Welch, "No Room at the Top: Interest Group Intervenors and Charter Litigation in the Supreme Court of Canada," *University of Toronto Faculty Law Review* 43:204–31 (1985); Kenneth P. Swan, "Intervention and Amicus Curiae Status in Charter Litigation," in *Char-*

ter Cases, 1986–1987, ed. Gerald A. Beaudoin (Cowansville, Québec: Les Editions Yvon Blais, 1987), 95–112; Sharon Lavine, "Advocating Values: Public Interest Intervention in Charter Litigation," *National Journal of Constitutional Law* 2:27–62 (1992).

9. The surprising absence of significant growth in the number of leave applications in the 1980s may have resulted from the Supreme Court's refusal to abandon oral hearings on leave to appeal applications, which placed time restrictions on the number of applications that could be heard. Nonetheless, if the Charter had the direct effect commonly attributed to it, one easily might imagine not the lack of change that in fact occurred but instead a growing backlog of applications after 1982.

10. This observation parallels a similar discovery by Pacelle on the prominence of criminal defendants' rights claims in the earliest stages of development of the U.S. Supreme Court's rights agenda.

11. Robert Harvie and Hamar Foster, "Ties That Bind? The Supreme Court of Canada, American Jurisprudence, and the Revision of Canadian Criminal Law under the Charter," *Osgoode Hall Law Review* 28:729–88 (1990).

12. Ibid.

13. [1981] 1 S.C.R. 640, at 697.

14. Charter of Rights and Freedoms, sec. 24(2).

15. In *Hogan v. The Queen* [1974] 48 D.L.R. (3d) 427, the Supreme Court, over a dissent by Laskin and Spence, ruled that a man taken to a police station to obtain an alcohol breath sample had no right to consult his lawyer before giving the sample even though the lawyer was present in the station; in *Caccamo v. The Queen* [1975] 54 D.L.R. (3d) 685, the Court, over a dissent by Spence, held that evidence not disclosed to the defense could nevertheless be introduced by surprise at trial; in *Morgentaler v. The Queen* [1976] 1 S.C.R. 616, the Court, over dissents by Laskin, Judson, and Spence, upheld the unusual decision of the Court of Appeal in overturning a jury's acquittal of a doctor for performing an abortion—but the dissenters based their dissent on narrow grounds rather than on the grounds that the federal abortion law was unconstitutional as a violation of the Bill of Rights or on federalism grounds. But in *Kienapple v. The Queen* [1975] 1 S.C.R. 729, the Court, in a 5–4 decision led by Laskin, overturned the conviction of a man on a second charge based on an act (rape) for which he had already been convicted. The decision produced the "Kienapple principle," that a single criminal act cannot give rise to multiple charges for the same offense. Allan Hutchinson and Neil Withington observed that, in the late seventies, the Supreme Court showed increasing interest in the process by which police obtained confessions of guilt. Surveying a series of cases, they noted that the Court, while unable to develop a clear legal doctrine on the matter, appeared willing to overturn convictions based on confessions obtained in ways the majority deemed to violate common-law rights. See Allan C. Hutchinson and Neil R. Withington, "*Horvath v. The Queen:* Reflections on the Doctrine of Confessions," *Osgoode Hall Law Review* 18:146 (1980).

16. The case was the notorious *Persons Case* in 1928, in which the Court ruled unanimously that women were not "persons" qualified to join the Canadian Senate under the British North America Act (*In re Meaning of the Word "Persons"* [1928] S.C.R. 276). In the words of the *Ottawa Evening Journal,* the Court's deci-

sion made the Court as well as the law appear an ass. See Snell and Vaughan, *Supreme Court*, 142. The Judicial Committee of the Privy Council overturned the decision in *Edwards v. Attorney-General of Canada* [1930] AC 125.

17. Cairns, *Charter versus Federalism*.

18. Knopff and Morton, *Charter Politics*, 261; see also Morton, *Morgentaler*.

19. *Attorney-General of Canada v. Lavell, Isaac v. Bedard* [1973] 38 D.L.R. (3d) 481.

20. [1979] 1 S.C.R. 183.

21. *Murdoch v. Murdoch* [1975] 1 S.C.R. 423.

22. See Peter W. Hogg, *Constitutional Law of Canada*, 3d ed. (Scarborough, Ont: Carswell, 1992), 1186–88; Knopff and Morton, *Charter Politics*. Some women's-rights advocates, however, have been very critical of the impact of the Charter on women's-rights claims. See Gwen Brodsky and Shelagh Day, *Canadian Charter Equality Rights for Women: One Step Forward or Two Steps Back?* (Ottawa: Canadian Advisory Council on the Status of Women, 1989).

23. *R. v. Morgentaler* [1988] 1 S.C.R. 30.

24. *R. v. Butler* [1992] 1 S.C.R. 452.

25. [1989] 1 S.C.R. 143. For discussion, see Hogg, *Constitutional Law*, 1160–79.

26. Robert Presthus, *Elites in the Policy Process* (Toronto: Macmillan, 1974).

27. Paul Pross, ed, *Pressure Group Behaviour in Canadian Politics* (Toronto: McGraw-Hill, Ryerson, 1975); Khayyam Z. Paltiel, "The Changing Environment and Role of Special Interest Groups," *Canadian Public Administration* 25:198–210 (1982).

28. James S. Frideres, *Native Peoples in Canada* (Scarborough, Ont.: Prentice-Hall, 1993), 288.

29. This discussion is based on the organizations' official newsletters and the author's interviews with Bill Black (Ottawa, May 19, 1993) and A. Alan Borovoy (Toronto, May 27, 1993), lawyers who were heavily involved with the organizations at the time..

30. *CCLA News Notes*, May 1977; ibid., March 1978; ibid., June 1980; ibid., Sept. 1980; ibid., Nov. 1980.

31. The interventions are listed in the affidavit of A. Alan Borovoy to the Supreme Court of Canada requesting leave to intervene in the case of *Butler v. The Queen*, court file no. 22191, 1991. Three of the five interventions before passage of the Charter involved matters of criminal due process.

32. Leslie Pal, *Interests of State: The Politics of Language, Multiculturalism, and Feminism in Canada* (Montreal: McGill-Queen's University Press, 1993).

33. Morton and Knopff, "The Supreme Court as the Vanguard," 70.

34. Frederick H. Zemans, "Legal Aid and Advice in Canada," *Osgoode Hall Law Journal* 16:663–93 (1978).

35. Frederick H. Zemans, "Canada," in *Perspectives on Legal Aid: An International Survey*, ed. Frederick H. Zemans (Westport, Conn.: Greenwood Press, 1979), 93, 122 n. 2.

36. Some of the growth in legal aid in the late eighties may have been due to the Supreme Court's decision in *Singh v. Minister of Employment and Immigration* [1985] 1 S.C.R. 177, which required the government to conduct hearings before deporting illegal immigrants and to ensure that immigrants have counsel in such hearings (I am indebted to Ian Brodie for this observation).

37. Brodie, "Interest Groups and the Charter."

38. Court Challenges Program, *Court Challenges Program Annual Report, 1991–92* (Ottawa: Court Challenges Program, 1992).

39. Ibid.

40. Brodie, "Interest Groups and the Charter."

41. E. L. Oscapella and Associates, "Legal Liaison and Support Study: Test Case Funding Program" (study prepared for the Department of Indian Affairs and Northern Development, 1988); Milligan and Company, "Evaluation of the Test Case Funding Program" (report prepared for the Department of Indian Affairs and Northern Development, 1989).

42. Anonymous lawyers for several native rights organizations, interviews by author, Ottawa, June 4 and June 10, 1993.

43. David A. A. Stager and Harry W. Arthurs, *Lawyers in Canada* (Toronto: University of Toronto Press, 1990), 90, 302–3.

44. Bushnell, *Captive Court*, 281–82, 341–42, 343–46; Stager and Arthurs, *Lawyers in Canada*, 84–91.

45. Stager and Arthurs, 303.

46. Ibid., 304.

47. Bora Laskin, "The Supreme Court of Canada: A Final Court of and for Canadians," *Canadian Bar Review* 29:1046 (1951).

48. Morton and Knopff, "Supreme Court as the Vanguard," 61, 72–75.

49. Stager and Arthurs, *Lawyers in Canada*, 149.

50. Ibid., 148–54.

51. Ibid., 148–50.

52. Ibid., 170–77

53. Rainer Knopff, *Human Rights and Social Technology: The New War on Discrimination* (Ottawa: Carleton University Press, 1990), 36–40; Walter S. Tarnopolsky, *Discrimination and the Law in Canada* (Toronto: de Boo, 1982), 25–37, 434–39.

54. Reva Devins, "A Perspective from the Ontario Human Rights Commission," in *The Impact of the Charter on the Public Policy Process*, ed. Patrick Monahan and Marie Finkelstein (North York, Ont.: York University Centre for Public Law and Public Policy, 1993); Morton, "Charter Revolution," 193–94; Morton and Knopff, "Supreme Court as the Vanguard," 72.

55. Knopff and Morton, *Charter Politics*.

56. It is true that although the Bill of Rights applies only to the federal government, the Charter applies to both federal and provincial governments, and we should therefore expect a greater number of cases under the Charter. But the difference in the number of cases is very large, strongly suggesting that some other factor led to the higher number of cases under the Charter.

57. Although temporal priority and correlation alone cannot prove causation, the weakness of the primary alternative explanations, those focusing on judicial attitudes and adoption of the Charter, lends credibility to the support-structure hypothesis.

58. The civil liberties lobby at the Charter negotiation process included Walter Tarnopolsky, member of the CCLA Board, J. S. Midanik, past CCLA president, and A. Alan Borovoy, CCLA Executive Director and General Counsel.

59. The original proposed wording of the search and seizure provision was,

"Everyone has the right not to be subjected to search or seizure except on grounds, and in accordance with procedures, established by law"; the revised wording is, "Everyone has the right to be secure against unreasonable search or seizure." The originally proposed Charter would have denied courts the authority to exclude from trial illegally obtained evidence: "No provision of this Charter, other than [the section on self-incrimination] affects the laws respecting the admissibility of evidence in any proceedings or the authority of parliament or a legislature to make laws in relation thereto"; the final Charter does not include that proviso. Regarding detention, the original Charter's wording was, "Everyone has the right not to be detained or imprisoned except on grounds, and in accordance with procedures, established by law"; the final Charter reads, "Everyone has the right not to be arbitrarily detained or imprisoned." Regarding rights of suspects upon arrest, the original proposal read, "Everyone has the right on arrest or detention (a) to be informed promptly of the reasons therefor; (b) to retain and instruct counsel without delay"; the final Charter reads, "Everyone has the right on arrest or detention (a) to be informed promptly of the reasons therefor; (b) to retain and instruct counsel without delay and to be informed of that right; (c) to have the validity of the detention determined by way of *habeas corpus* and to be released if the detention is not lawful." Regarding bail, the original Charter read, "Anyone charged with an offence has the right not to be denied reasonable bail except on grounds, and in accordance with procedures, established by law"; the final Charter reads, "Any person charged with an offence has the right . . . (e) not to be denied reasonable bail without just cause." The original proposal contained no guarantee of trial by jury; the final Charter reads, "Any person charged with an offence has the right . . . (f) except in case of an offence under military law tried before a military tribunal, to the benefit of trial by jury where the maximum punishment for the offence is imprisonment for five years or a more severe punishment." In each matter, CCLA lawyers argued for the more expansive version of the right, explicitly favoring judicial enforcement of procedural rights in the criminal justice process. *CCLA News Notes,* February 1981.

60. See *CCLA News Notes,* February 1981.

61. Romanow, Whyte, and Leeson, *Canada Notwithstanding,* 121; Rainer Knopff and F. L. Morton, "Nation-Building," 151.

62. *CCLA News Notes,* April 1982.

63. George Bigger, Ontario Legal Aid Plan, interview by author, Toronto, May 14, 1993.

64. A. Alan Borovoy, CCLA General Counsel, interview by author, Toronto, May 27, 1993.

65. Clayton Ruby, interview by author, Toronto, May 27, 1993. Interviews with A. Alan Borovoy (Toronto, May 27, 1993) and Bill Black (Ottawa, May 19, 1993), both rights lawyers, supported that view.

66. The Charter's provision on the exclusion from court of illegally obtained evidence, for instance, has been used avidly by defense lawyers in challenges to police procedures. Morton, Russell, and Withey, "First One Hundred," 33–36; Morton, Russell, and Riddell, "Descriptive Analysis."

67. These figures were calculated by the author from a review of information about the fifty-one national women's groups included in the archives for their

importance in the Canadian women's movement. Some other evidence suggests that significant growth continued into the early eighties. A recent history of the National Action Committee on the Status of Women, a national umbrella organization whose membership consists primarily of other organizations, concluded that its membership grew most rapidly from 1984 to 1987, so that by 1988 it had about six hundred organizational members. See Jill Vickers, Pauline Rankin, and Christine Appelle, *Politics As If Women Mattered: A Political Analysis of the National Action Committee on the Status of Women* (Toronto: University of Toronto Press, 1993), 4.

68. See, in particular, Pal, *Interests of State.*

69. Stager and Arthurs, *Lawyers in Canada,* 149 table 6.5.

70. Elizabeth M. Atcheson, Mary A. Eberts, Beth Symes, with Jennifer Stoddart, *Women and Legal Action: Precedents, Resources, and Strategies for the Future* (Ottawa: Canadian Advisory Council on the Status of Women, 1984).

71. [1979] 1 S.C.R. 183.

72. Among those in the coalition were the Service, Office, and Retail Workers Union of Canada, the B.C. Federation of Labour, women's organizations from Québec, Ottawa, and Manitoba, and the Vancouver Community Legal Assistance Society. The Public Interest Advocacy Centre coordinated the efforts and fund-raising for the case. See Pal and Morton, *"Bliss v. Attorney-General of Canada:* From Legal Defeat to Political Victory," *Osgoode Hall Law Journal* 24: 141–60 (1986).

73. Ibid.

74. See Beverly Baines, "Women, Human Rights, and the Constitution," in *Women and the Constitution in Canada,* ed. Audrey Doerr and Micheline Carrier (Ottawa: Canadian Advisory Council on the Status of Women, 1981) for the definitive analysis of the weakness of the Supreme Court's interpretation of the Canadian Bill of Rights from the perspective of the women's movement.

75. Ibid., 58.

76. Penney Kome, *The Taking of Twenty-Eight: Women Challenge the Constitution* (Toronto: Women's Press, 1983); Sherene Razack, *Canadian Feminism and the Law: The Women's Legal Education and Action Fund and the Pursuit of Equality* (Toronto: Second Story Press, 1991).

77. Chaviva Hosek, "Women and the Constitutional Process," in Banting and Simeon, *And No One Cheered;* Romanow, Whyte, and Leeson, *Canada Notwithstanding;* Kome, *Taking of Twenty-Eight.*

78. Razack, *Canadian Feminism.*

79. Charter of Rights and Freedoms, sections 15(1); 15(2); and 28.

80. Hosek, "Women and the Constitutional Process."

81. Kome, *Taking of Twenty-Eight,* 13.

82. Razack, *Canadian Feminism,* 36–46.

83. Razack, *Canadian Feminism.*

84. Ibid., 36.

85. Atcheson et al., *Women and Legal Action.*

86. Razack, *Canadian Feminism,* 39. Razack does not identify the American experts.

87. Atcheson et al., *Women and Legal Action,* 42.

88. Some of the cases remained under appeal at the close of this study. The information on LEAF cases is taken from LEAF publications.

89. This may depend to a great extent on the evaluation of LEAF strategy by other women's organizations. At least one major women's-rights organization indicated that it did not support court cases because LEAF was satisfactorily carrying that burden. Huguette Léger, Parliamentary Liaison for the National Action Committee on the Status of Women, interview by author, Ottawa, May 13, 1993. At least one interviewee, however, indicated that some women's organizations were displeased with LEAF support for legislation banning pornography and were reevaluating the de facto authorization of LEAF to speak for the women's movement in court. Anonymous interviewee, interview by author, Ottawa, May 21, 1993.

Chapter Eleven

1. Walter F. Murphy, "Constitutions, Constitutionalism, and Democracy," in *Constitutionalism and Democracy: Transitions in the Contemporary World*, ed. Douglas Greenberg, Stanley N. Katz, Melanie Beth Oliviero, and Steven C. Wheatley (New York: Oxford University Press, 1993).

2. Madison, *Papers*, vol. 10, 211–12. A similar argument was developed more recently by Robert Dahl, "Decision-Making in a Democracy: The Supreme Court as a National Policy Maker," *Journal of Public Law* 6:279 (1957).

3. Allen, "Bills of Rights"; Stephen Sedley, "The Sound of Silence: Constitutional Law without a Constitution," *Law Quarterly Review* 110:270–91 (1994); Bork, *Tempting of America*; Robert H. Wiebe, *Self-Rule: A Cultural History of American Democracy* (Chicago: University of Chicago Press, 1995), 226.

4. Stephen M. Griffin has nicely articulated this difficulty in "Constitutionalism in the United States: From Theory to Politics," in *Responding to Imperfection: The Theory and Practice of Constitutional Amendment*, ed. Sanford Levinson (Princeton: Princeton University Press, 1995).

5. Ely, *Democracy and Distrust*.

6. See, for instance, the discussion in Hartog, "Constitution of Aspiration"; for related observations, see McCann, *Rights at Work*; V. Hart, *Bound by Our Constitution*.

7. L. Epstein, *Conservatives in Court*.

8. Paul M. Sniderman, Peter H. Russell, Joseph F. Fletcher, and Philip E. Tetlock, *The Clash of Rights: Liberty, Equality, and Legitimacy in Pluralist Democracy* (New Haven: Yale University Press, 1996).

9. Bogart, *Courts and Country*, 270; Andrew Petter, "Canada's Charter Flight: Soaring Backward into the Future," *Journal of Law & Society* 16:151–65 (1989); Mandel, *Legalisation of Politics*.

10. Lawrence, *The Poor in Court*.

11. In *Dandridge v. Williams*, 397 U.S. 471 (1970), the Supreme Court refused to develop a fundamental constitutional right to public assistance. In *San Antonio Independent School District v. Rodriguez*, 411 U.S. 1 (1973), a case involving state funding of public schools, the Court ruled that wealth is not a suspect classification subject to strict scrutiny.

12. *Bowers v. Hardwick*, 478 U.S. 186 (1986); *Romer v. Evans*, 116 S. Ct. 1620 (1996).

BIBLIOGRAPHY

Abdulali, Sohaila. "Rape in India: An Empirical Picture." In *Women in Indian Society: A Reader,* edited by Rehana Ghadially. New Delhi: Sage, 1988.

Abel, Richard L. *American Lawyers.* New York: Oxford University Press, 1989.

————. *The Legal Profession in England and Wales.* Oxford: Basil Blackwell, 1988.

————. "United States: The Contradictions of Professionalism." In *Lawyers in Society, Vol. I: The Common Law World,* edited by Richard L. Abel and Philip S. C. Lewis. Berkeley: University of California Press, 1988.

Abel, Richard L., and Phillip S. C. Lewis, eds. *Lawyers in Society, Vol. I: The Common Law World.* Berkeley: University of California Press, 1988.

ACLU–Illinois Division. *Secret Detention by the Chicago Police.* Glencoe, IL: Free Press, 1959.

Adamany, David, and Joel B. Grossman. "Support for the Supreme Court as a National Policymaker." *Law and Policy Quarterly* 5:405–37 (1983).

Agrawala, S. K. *Public Interest Litigation in India: A Critique.* Bombay: N. M. Tripathi, 1987.

Allen, James. "Bills of Rights and Judicial Power—A Liberal's Quandary." *Oxford Journal of Legal Studies* 16:337–52 (1996).

Amnesty International. *India: Torture, Rape and Deaths in Custody.* New York: Amnesty International, 1992.

————. "Torture in the Eighties: An Amnesty International Report." In *Violation of Democratic Rights in India,* edited by A. R. Desai. Bombay: Popular Prakashan, 1986.

"Amputee smoker refused legal aid." *Herald* (Glasgow), July 10, 1995, p. 4.

Anderson, Alexis J. "The Formative Period of First Amendment Theory, 1870–1915." *The American Journal of Legal History* 24:56–75 (1980).

Ansari, Iqbal A. "Human Rights in India." *PUCL Bulletin,* December 1990.

"Appeal to Supreme Court—Enquiry into Vimla's Death in Hyderabad." *Manushi,* no. 20:41–42 (1984).

Asia Watch, *Police Killings and Rural Violence in Andhra Pradesh* (New York: Asia Watch, 1992).

Associations Unlimited (on compact disc). Detroit: Gale Research, 1993.

Atcheson, Elizabeth M., Mary A. Eberts, Beth Symes, with Jennifer Stoddart. *Women and Legal Action: Precedents, Resources, and Strategies for the Future.* Ottawa: Canadian Advisory Council on the Status of Women, 1984.

Atiyah, P. S., and Robert S. Summers. *Form and Substance in Anglo-American Law.* Oxford: Oxford University Press, 1987.

Atkins, Burton M. "Alternative Models of Appeal Mobilization in Judicial Hierarchies." *American Journal of Political Science* 37:780–98 (1993).

———. "Communication of Appellate Decisions: A Multivariate Model for Understanding the Selection of Cases for Publication." *Law & Society Review* 24:1171–96 (1990).

———. "Party Capability Theory and Judicial Decisions: A Multivariate Perspective on the Structure of Intervention Behavior by the English Court of Appeal." *American Journal of Political Science* 35:881–903 (1991).

———. "Selective Reporting and the Communication of Legal Rights in England." *Judicature* 76:58–67 (1992).

Atkins, Burton M., and Henry R. Glick. "Environmental and Structural Variables as Determinants of Issues in State Courts of Last Resort." *American Journal of Political Science* 20:97–115 (1976).

Atkins, Susan. "Women's Rights." In *Public Interest Law,* edited by Jeremy Cooper and Rajeev Dhavan (Oxford: Basil Blackwell, 1986).

Auerbach, Jerold. *Unequal Justice: Lawyers and Social Change in Modern America.* New York: Oxford University Press, 1976.

Austin, Granville. "The Constitution, Society, and Law." In *India Briefing, 1993,* edited by Philip Oldenburg. Boulder: Westview Press, 1993.

———. *The Indian Constitution: Cornerstone of a Nation.* Oxford: Oxford University Press, 1966.

Baar, Carl. "Judicial Activism in Canada." In *Judicial Activism in Comparative Perspective,* edited by Kenneth M. Holland. New York: St. Martin's Press, 1991.

———. "Social Action Litigation in India: The Operation and Limits of the World's Most Active Judiciary." In *Comparative Judicial Review and Public Policy,* edited by Donald W. Jackson and C. Neal Tate. Westport, Conn.: Greenwood Press, 1992.

Badaracco, Joseph L. *Loading the Dice: A Five-Country Study of Vinyl Chloride Regulation.* Boston: Harvard Business School Press, 1985.

Baines, Beverly. "Women, Human Rights, and the Constitution." In *Women and the Constitution in Canada,* edited by Audrey Doerr and Micheline Carrier. Ottawa: Canadian Advisory Council on the Status of Women, 1981.

Banting, Keith, and Richard Simeon, eds. *And No One Cheered: Federalism, Democracy, and the Constitution Act.* Toronto: Methuen, 1983.

Barnum, David G. "Article 21 and Policy Making Role of Courts in India: an American Perspective." *Journal of the Indian Law Institute* 30:19 (1988).

———. "The Supreme Court and Public Opinion: Judicial Decision-Making in the Post–New Deal Period." *Journal of Politics* 47:652–66 (1985).

Barnum, David G., John L. Sullivan, and Maurice Sunkin. "Constitutional and Cultural Underpinnings of Political Freedom in Britain and the United States." *Oxford Journal of Legal Studies* 12:362–79 (1992).

Basu, Durga Das. *Introduction to the Constitution of India.* 15th ed. New Delhi: Prentice-Hall of India, 1993.

Baum, Lawrence. "Measuring Policy Change in the U.S. Supreme Court." *American Political Science Review* 82:905–12 (1988).

———. "Review Article: Research on the English Judicial Process." *British Journal of Political Science* 7:511 (1978).

———. *The Supreme Court.* 4th ed. Washington, D.C.: Congressional Quarterly Press, 1992.

Baxi, Upendra. *Inhuman Wrongs and Human Rights: Unconventional Essays.* New Delhi: Har-Anand Publications, 1994.

———. *Courage, Craft, and Contention: The Supreme Court in the 1980s.* Bombay: N. M. Tripathi, 1985.

———. "Taking Suffering Seriously." In *Judges and the Judicial Power,* edited by Rajeev Dhavan, R. Sudarshan, and Salman Khurshid. Bombay: N. M. Tripathi, 1985.

———. *The Indian Supreme Court and Politics.* Lucknow: Eastern Book Company, 1980.

Baxi, Upendra, Lotika Sarkar, Vasudha Dhagamwar, and Ragunath Kelkar. "An Open Letter to the Chief Justice of India." *Supreme Court Cases (Journal)* 1:17 (1979).

Beaney, William M. *The Right to Counsel in the American States.* Ann Arbor: University of Michigan Press, 1955.

Beatty, David. *Talking Heads and the Supremes: The Canadian Production of Constitutional Review.* Toronto: Carswell, 1990.

Beatty, J. "Guardians of Crime: Lawyers Who Defend Criminals." *American Magazine,* Sept. 1934, 81–82.

Belknap, Michal. *Federal Law and Southern Order: Racial Violence and Constitutional Conflict in the Post-Brown South.* Athens: University of Georgia Press, 1987.

Bhagwati, P. N. "Judicial Activism and Public Interest Litigation." *Columbia Journal of Transnational Law* 23:561 (1985).

Birch, Di. "The PACE Hots Up: Confessions and Confusions under the 1984 Act." *Criminal Law Review* 1989:95–116.

Blom-Cooper, Louis. "The New Face of Judicial Review: Administrative Changes in Order 53." *Public Law* 1985:250.

Blom-Cooper, Louis, and Gavin Drewry. *Final Appeal: A Study of the House of Lords in Its Judicial Capacity.* Oxford: Oxford University Press, 1972.

Bloomfield, Maxwell. "From Deference to Confrontation: The Early Black Lawyers of Galveston, Texas, 1895–1920." In *The New High Priests: Lawyers in Post-Civil War America,* edited by Gerard W. Gawalt. Westport, Conn.: Greenwood Press, 1984.

Bogart, W. A. *Courts and Country: The Limits of Litigation and the Social and Political Life of Canada.* Toronto: Oxford, 1994.

———. "Understanding Standing, Chapter IV: *Minister of Finance of Canada vs. Finlay.*" *Supreme Court Law Review* 10:377 (1988).

Bork, Robert H. *The Tempting of America: The Political Seduction of the Law.* New York: Free Press, 1990.

Borovoy, A. Alan. *When Freedoms Collide: The Case for Our Civil Liberties.* Toronto: Lester and Orpen Dennys, 1988.

Bourn, Colin, and John Whitmore. *Race and Sex Discrimination.* 2d ed. London: Sweet & Maxwell, 1993.

Boyle, Elizabeth Heger. "Litigants, Lawbreakers, Legislators: Using Political Frames to Explain Cross-National Variation in Legal Activity." Ph.D. diss., Stanford University, 1996.

Bradney, Anthony. "The Judicial Activity of the Lord Chancellor 1946–1987: A Pellet." *Journal of Law and Society* 16:360 (1989).

Brandeis, Louis. "The Opportunity in the Law." In *Business—A Profession.* Boston: Small, Maynard, 1914.

Brass, Paul R. *The Politics of India Since Independence.* Cambridge: Cambridge University Press, 1990.

———. "The Punjab Crisis and the Unity of India." In *India's Democracy: An Analysis of Changing State-Society Relations,* edited by Atul Kohli. Princeton: Princeton University Press, 1988.

Bratza, N. "The Treatment and Interpretation of the European Convention on Human Rights: Aspects of Incorporation." In *European Convention on Human Rights: Aspects of Incorporation,* edited by J. P. Gardner. London: British Institute of Comparative Law, 1992.

Brazier, Rodney. *Constitutional Reform.* Oxford: Clarendon Press, 1991.

Brenner, Saul. "The New Certiorari Game." *Journal of Politics* 41:649–55 (1979).

Brenner, Saul, and John F. Krol. "Strategies in Certiorari Voting on the United States Supreme Court." *Journal of Politics* 51:828 (1989).

Bridges, Lee. "The Professionalization of Criminal Justice." *Legal Action* (August 1992), 7.

Bridges, Lee, Maurice Sunkin, and George Meszaros, *Judicial Review in Perspective.* London: Cavendish, 1995.

British Columbia Civil Liberties Association. *Annual Reports,* 1977, 1978, 1983, 1985, 1991–92.

Brodie, Ian Ross. "Charting the Growth of Interest Group Activity in the Supreme Court of Canada." Paper presented at the annual meeting of the Law and Society Association, Toronto, 1995.

———. "Interest Groups and the Charter of Rights and Freedoms: Interveners at the Supreme Court of Canada." Master's thesis, University of Calgary, 1992.

Brodsky, Gwen, and Shelagh Day. *Canadian Charter Equality Rights for Women: One Step Forward or Two Steps Back?* Ottawa: Canadian Advisory Council on the Status of Women, 1989.

Brown, D. H. *The Genesis of the Canadian Criminal Code of 1892.* Toronto: University of Toronto Press, 1989.

Browne-Wilkinson, Right Hon. Lord. "The Infiltration of a Bill of Rights." *Public Law* 1992:397–410.

Brudnoy, David Barry. "Liberty's Bugler: The Seven Ages of Theodore Schroeder." Ph.D. diss., Brandeis University, 1971.

Bushnell, Ian. *The Captive Court: A Study of the Supreme Court of Canada.* Montreal: McGill-Queen's University Press, 1992.

———. "Leave to Appeal Applications: The 1984–85 Term." *Supreme Court Law Review* 8:383 (1986).

———. "Leave to Appeal Applications to the Supreme Court of Canada: A Matter of Public Importance." *Supreme Court Law Review* 3:479 (1982).

Byrne, Paul. "The Politics of the Women's Movement." In *Women in Politics,* edited by Joni Lovenduski and Pippa Norris. New York: Oxford University Press, 1996.

Cairns, Alan C. *Charter versus Federalism: The Dilemmas of Constitutional Reform.* Montreal: McGill-Queen's University Press, 1992.

Caldeira, Gregory A., and John R. Wright. "Organized Interests and Agenda Setting in the U.S. Supreme Court." *American Political Science Review* 82:1109–27 (1988).

Caldeira, Gregory A., John R. Wright, and Christopher J. W. Zorn, "Strategic Voting and Gatekeeping in the Supreme Court." Paper presented at the annual meeting of the American Political Science Association, Aug. 29–Sept. 1, 1996, San Francisco.

Cappelletti, Mauro. "The Law-Making Power of the Judges and Its Limits." *Monash University Law Review* 8:15 (1981).

———. "Repudiating Montesquieu? The Expansion and Legitimacy of 'Constitutional Justice,'" *Catholic University Law Review* 35:1–30 (1985).

Carr, Robert K. *Federal Protection of Civil Rights: Quest for a Sword.* Ithaca, N.Y.: Cornell University Press, 1947.

Carter, April. *The Politics of Women's Rights.* London: Longman, 1988.

Carter, Dan T. *Scottsboro: A Tragedy of the American South.* Rev. ed. Baton Rouge: Louisiana State University Press, 1979.

Casper, Gerhard. "The Emerging Constitution of the European Community." *Law School Record of the University of Chicago Law School* 24:5–12 (1978).

Casper, Gerhard, and Richard A. Posner. *The Workload of the Supreme Court.* Chicago: American Bar Foundation, 1976.

Casper, Jonathan. *Lawyers Before the Warren Court: Civil Liberties and Civil Rights, 1957–66.* Urbana: University of Illinois Press, 1972.

Cassels, Jamie. "Judicial Activism and Public Interest Litigation in India: Attempting the Impossible?" *American Journal of Comparative Law* 37:495 (1989).

CCLA News Notes, May 1977; March 1978; June, Sept., and Nov. 1980; Feb. 1981; April 1982.

Chandler, Alfred D., Jr. "The United States: Seedbed of Managerial Capitalism." In *Managerial Hierarchies: Comparative Perspectives on the Rise of the Modern Industrial Enterprise,* edited by Alfred D. Chandler, Jr. and Herman Daems. Cambridge: Harvard University Press, 1980.

———. *The Visible Hand: The Managerial Revolution in American Business.* Cambridge: Harvard University Press, 1977.

Chari, Lalit. "Police Repression and the Criminal Law." In *Violation of Democratic Rights in India,* edited by A. R. Desai. Bombay: Popular Prakashan, 1986.

Choper, Jesse H. *Judicial Review and the National Political Process.* Chicago: University of Chicago Press, 1980.

Churchill, R. R. "Aspects of Compliance with Findings of the Committee of Ministers and Judgements of the Court with Reference to the United Kingdom." In *The European Convention on Human Rights: Aspects of Incorporation,* edited by J. P. Gardner. London: British Institute of Comparative Law, 1992.

"Civil Liberties and Democratic Rights Groups: A Listing." *Lokayan Bulletin* 5:4–5 (1987).

"Civil Liberties Organisations in Andhra Pradesh." In *Violation of Democratic Rights in India*, edited by A. R. Desai.

Clayton, Cornell W. *The Politics of Justice: The Attorney General and the Making of Legal Policy*. Armonk, N.Y.: M. E. Sharpe, 1992.

Clemens, Elisabeth S. *The People's Lobby: Organizational Innovation and the Rise of Interest Group Politics in the United States, 1890–1925*. Chicago: University of Chicago Press, 1997.

Clement, Barrie. "Women's Pay Battle to Go to Europe; Equality Body's Patience Runs Out." *Independent* (London), August 24, 1993, p. 3.

Clement, Barrie, and Patricia Wynn Davies. "Equal Pay for Women Curbed by Ministers." *Independent* (London), October 11, 1993, p. 1.

———. "Law Biased Against Part-Time Workers, Lords Rule." *Independent* (London), March 4, 1994, p. 3.

Cohen, Barbara, and Marie Staunton, "In Pursuit of a Legal Strategy: The National Council for Civil Liberties." In *Public Interest Law*, edited by Jeremy Cooper and Rajeev Dhavan. Oxford: Blackwell, 1986.

Cohen, Maxwell. "Human Rights: Programme or Catchall? A Canadian Rationale." *Canadian Bar Review*, 46:554–64 (1986).

Committee for the Protection of Democratic Rights. "The Civil Liberties Movement: A Perspective." In *Violation of Democratic Rights in India*, edited by A. R. Desai. Bombay: Popular Prakashan, 1986.

Cooper, Jeremy, and Rajeev Dhavan, eds. *Public Interest Law*. Oxford: Blackwell, 1986.

Cortner, Richard C. *The Iron Horse and the Constitution: The Railroads and the Transformation of the Fourteenth Amendment*. Westport, Conn.: Greenwood Press, 1993.

———. *The Supreme Court and the Second Bill of Rights: The Fourteenth Amendment and the Nationalization of Civil Liberties*. Madison: University of Wisconsin Press, 1981.

Court Challenges Program. *Court Challenges Program Annual Report, 1991–92*. Ottawa: Court Challenges Program, 1992.

Cowan, Ruth B. "Women's Rights through Litigation: An Examination of the American Civil Liberties Union Women's Rights Project, 1971–1976." *Columbia Human Rights Law Review* 8:373–412 (1976).

Craig, P. P. *Administrative Law*. 2d ed. London: Sweet & Maxwell, 1989.

———. *Public Law and Democracy in the United Kingdom and the United States of America*. New York: Oxford University Press, 1990.

———. "Sovereignty of the United Kingdom Parliament after *Factortame*." *Yearbook of European Law* 11:221 (1991).

Creighton, W. B. *Working Women and the Law*. London: Mansell, 1979.

Crick, Bernard. *The Reform of Parliament*. London: Weidenfeld and Nicholson, 1966.

Croly, Herbert. *The Promise of American Life*. Indianapolis: Bobbs-Merrill, 1965 [1909]).

Curran, Barbara, and Clara N. Carson. *The Lawyer Statistical Report: The U.S. Legal Profession in the 1990s*. Chicago: American Bar Foundation, 1994.

Dahl, Robert. "Decision-Making in a Democracy: The Supreme Court as a National Policy Maker." *Journal of Public Law* 6:279 (1957).

Dasgupta, Prabhat. "A Catalogue of Repression, June 1977– May 1978." In *Violation of Democratic Rights in India*, edited by A. R. Desai. Bombay: Popular Prakashan, 1986.

Davis, M. N. "Let the Police Have the Breaks Rather Than the Criminal." *American City*, March 1931, 102.

"The Delhi Nari Niketan—Protection Worse than Imprisonment." *Manushi*, no. 10:18–32 (1982).

Desai, A. R. *Violation of Democratic Rights in India*. Bombay: Popular Prakashan, 1986.

Devins, Reva. "A Perspective from the Ontario Human Rights Commission." In *The Impact of the Charter on the Public Policy Process*, edited by Patrick Monahan and Marie Finkelstein. North York, Ont.: York University Centre for Public Law and Public Policy, 1993.

Dhavan, Rajeev. *Justice on Trial: The Supreme Court Today*. Allahabad: Wheeler, 1980.

———. "Law As Struggle: Notes on Public Interest Law in India." Institute for Legal Studies Working Paper no. ILS 5–3, Madison, Wisc., 1993.

———. *Litigation Explosion in India*. Bombay: N. M. Tripathi, 1986.

———. *The Supreme Court of India: A Socio-Legal Critique of Its Juristic Techniques*. Bombay: N. M. Tripathi, 1977.

Dhavan, Rajeev, and Martin Partington. "Co-optation or Independent Strategy? The Role of Social Action Groups." In *Public Interest Law*, edited by Jeremy Cooper and Rajeev Dhavan. Oxford: Blackwell, 1986.

Dicey, A. V. *Introduction to the Study of the Law of the Constitution*. 10th ed. London: Macmillan, 1961.

Dixon, Robert G. "The Attorney General and Civil Rights, 1870–1964." In *Roles of the Attorney General of the United States*, edited by Luther A. Huston, Arthur Selwyn Miller, Samuel Krislov, and Robert G. Dixon. Washington, D.C.: American Enterprise Institute, 1968.

Donnelly, Jack. *Universal Human Rights in Theory and Practice*. Ithaca, N.Y.: Cornell University Press, 1989.

Dyer, Clare, and Patrick Wintour. "Part-Timers Win Rights: Women Gain Most From Lords Ruling." *Guardian* (London), March 4, 1994, p. 1.

Eisenberg, Theodore, and Stewart Schwab. "The Reality of Constitutional Tort Litigation." *Cornell Law Review* 72:641–95 (1987).

Elliff, John T. *The United States Department of Justice and Individual Rights, 1937–1962*. New York: Garland, 1987.

Ellis, Evelyn. *Sex Discrimination Law*. Aldershot, Eng.: Gower, 1988.

Elman, Philip. "The Solicitor General's Office, Justice Frankfurter, and Civil Rights Litigation, 1946–1960: An Oral History." *Harvard Law Review* 100:817–52 (1987).

Ely, John Hart. *Democracy and Distrust: A Theory of Judicial Review*. Cambridge: Harvard University Press, 1980.

Engineer, Asghar Ali, ed. *The Shah Bano Controversy*. Hyderabad, India: Orient Longman, 1987.

Epp, Charles R. "Do Bills of Rights Matter? The Canadian Charter of Rights and Freedoms." *American Political Science Review* 90:766 (1996).

Epstein, Cynthia Fuchs. *Women in Law*. 2d ed. Urbana: University of Illinois Press, 1993.

Epstein, Lee. *Conservatives in Court*. Knoxville: University of Tennessee Press, 1985.

Epstein, Lee, and Joseph F. Kobylka. *The Supreme Court and Legal Change: Abortion and the Death Penalty*. Chapel Hill: University of North Carolina Press, 1992.

Epstein, Lee, and C. K. Rowland. "Debunking the Myth of Interest Group Invincibility in the Courts." *American Political Science Review* 85:205–17 (1991).

Epstein, Lee, Jeffrey A. Segal, and Timothy Johnson. "The Claim of Issue Creation on the U.S. Supreme Court." *American Political Science Review* 90:845–52 (1996).

Erskine, Hazel. "The Polls: Race Relations." *Public Opinion Quarterly* 26:137 (1956).

European Court of Human Rights: Survey of Activities, 1959–1989. Strasbourg, France: Council of Europe, 1990.

Evans, Mark. *Charter 88: A Successful Challenge to the British Political Tradition?* Aldershot, Eng.: Dartmouth, 1995.

Ewing, K. D., and C. A. Gearty. *Freedom under Thatcher: Civil Liberties in Modern Britain*. Oxford: Clarendon Press, 1990.

An Exconvict. "Criminal Lawyers as a Cause of Crime." *Outlook*, Dec. 27, 1916, 911–13.

Farole, Donald J., Jr. *Interest Groups and Judicial Federalism: Organizational Litigation in State Judiciaries*. Westport, Conn.: Praeger, 1998.

Favoreu, Louis. "Constitutional Review in Europe." In *Constitutionalism and Rights: The Influence of the United States Constitution Abroad*, edited by Louis Henkin and Albert J. Rosenthal. New York: Columbia University Press, 1990.

"Federal Judicial Center Report of the Study Group on the Case Load of the Supreme Court." *Federal Rules Decisions* 57:573 (1973).

Feldman, David. "Public Law Values in the House of Lords." *Law Quarterly Review* 106:246 (1990).

———. "Regulating Treatment of Suspects in Police Stations: Judicial Interpretations of Detention Provisions in the Police and Criminal Evidence Act 1984" *Criminal Law Review* 1990:452–71.

Finer, Samuel E. *Comparative Government*. London: Allen Lane, 1970.

Fiss, Owen M. "The Right Degree of Independence." In *Transition to Democracy in Latin America: The Role of the Judiciary*, edited by Irwin P. Stotzky. Boulder: Westview Press, 1993.

Flemming, Roy B., and B. Dan Wood. "The Public and the Supreme Court: Individual Justice Responsiveness to American Policy Moods." *American Journal of Political Science* 41:468–98 (1997).

Forbath, William E. "Courts, Constitutions, and Labor Politics in England and America: A Study of the Constitutive Power of Law." *Law & Social Inquiry* 16:1–34 (1991).

———. *Law and the Shaping of the American Labor Movement*. Cambridge: Harvard University Press, 1991.

Frankfurter, Felix, and James M. Landis. *The Business of the Supreme Court: A Study in the Federal Judicial System*. New York: Macmillan, 1927.

———. "The Business of the Supreme Court at October Term, 1930." *Harvard Law Review* 45:271 (1930).

———. "The Business of the Supreme Court at October Term, 1934." *Harvard Law Review* 49:68 (1935).

Franklin, Daniel P., and Michael J. Baun, eds. *Political Culture and Constitutionalism: A Comparative Approach.* Armonk, N.Y.: M. E. Sharpe, 1995.

Frendreis, John P. "Explanation of Variation and Detection of Covariation: The Purpose and Logic of Comparative Analysis." *Comparative Political Studies* 16:255–72 (1983).

Frideres, James S. *Native Peoples in Canada.* Scarborough, Ont.: Prentice-Hall, 1993.

Friedland, Martin L. *Double Jeopardy.* Oxford: Clarendon Press, 1969.

———. "R. S. Wright's Model Criminal Code: A Forgotten Chapter in the History of the Criminal Law." *Oxford Journal of Legal Studies* 1:307 (1981).

Friedman, Lawrence M. *Crime and Punishment in American History.* New York: Basic Books, 1993.

Gadbois, George, Jr. "Indian Judicial Behaviour." *Economic and Political Weekly* 5:140–66.

———. "Selection, Background Characteristics, and Voting Behaviour of Indian Supreme Court Judges, 1950–59." In *Comparative Judicial Behaviour,* edited by Glendon Schubert and David J. Danelski. New York: Oxford University Press, 1969.

———. "The Supreme Court of India as a Political Institution." In *Judges and the Judicial Power,* edited by Rajeev Dhavan, R. Sudarshan, and Salman Khurshid. London: Sweet & Maxwell, 1985.

Galanter, Marc. "Affidavit composed for the court proceedings regarding the Bhopal disaster." In *Mass Disasters and Multinational Liability: The Bhopal Case,* edited by Upendra Baxi and Thomas Paul. Bombay: N. M. Tripathi, 1986.

———. "Case Congregations and Their Careers." *Law & Society Review* 24:371 (1990).

———. *Competing Equalities: Law and the Backward Classes in India.* Delhi: Oxford University Press, 1984.

———. "Law Abounding: Legalisation Around the North Atlantic." *Modern Law Review* 55:1–24 (1992).

———. *Law and Society in Modern India.* New Delhi: Oxford University Press, 1989.

———. "The Radiating Effects of Courts." In *Empirical Theories About Courts,* edited by Keith O. Boyum and Lynn Mather. New York: Longman, 1983.

———. "Reading the Landscape of Disputes: What We Know and Don't Know (and Think We Know) about Our Allegedly Contentious and Litigious Society." *UCLA Law Review* 31:4–71 (1983).

———. "Why the Haves Come Out Ahead: Speculations on the Limits of Social Change." *Law & Society Review* 9:95–160 (1974).

Galanter, Marc, and Thomas Palay. *Tournament of Lawyers: The Transformation of the Big Law Firm.* Chicago: University of Chicago Press, 1991.

Gallup, George H. *The Gallup Poll: Public Opinion 1935–1971.* Vol. 13. New York: Random House, 1972.

Gandhi, J. S. "Past and Present: A Sociological Portrait of the Indian Legal

Profession." In *Lawyers in Society, Vol 1: The Common Law World*, edited by Richard L. Abel and Philip S. C. Lewis. Berkeley: University of California Press, 1988.

————. *Sociology of the Legal Profession, Law and Legal System: The Indian Setting.* Delhi: Gian, 1987.

Gandhi, Nandita, and Nandita Shah. *The Issues at Stake: Theory and Practice in the Contemporary Women's Movement in India.* New Delhi: Kali for Women, 1992.

Gelb, Joyce. *Feminism and Politics: A Comparative Perspective.* Berkeley: University of California Press, 1989.

George, Warren E. "Development of the Legal Services Corporation." *Cornell Law Review* 61:681–730 (1976).

Ghadially, Rehana, and Pramod Kumar. "Bride-Burning: The Psycho-Social Dynamics of Dowry Deaths." In *Women in Indian Society: A Reader*, edited by Rehana Ghadially. New Delhi: Sage, 1988.

Gibb, Frances. "Equality Watchdog Seeks EC Decision." *Times* (London), August 24, 1993, Home News section.

Gillman, Howard. *The Constitution Besieged: The Rise and Demise of Lochner Era Police Powers Jurisprudence.* Durham: Duke University Press, 1993.

Ginger, Ann Fagan, and Eugene M. Tobin, eds. *The National Lawyers Guild: From Roosevelt through Reagan.* Philadelphia: Temple University Press, 1988.

Glendon, Mary Ann. *Rights Talk: The Impoverishment of Political Discourse.* New York: Free Press, 1991.

Gollomb, J. "Meeting the Crime Wave." *Nation*, Jan. 19, 1921, 80–83.

Gordon, Richard. "Judicial Review and Equal Opportunities." *Public Law* 1994:217.

Greenberg, Jack. *Crusaders in the Courts: How a Dedicated Band of Lawyers Fought for the Civil Rights Revolution.* New York: Basic Books, 1994.

Greene, Ian. *The Charter of Rights.* Toronto: James Lorimer, 1989.

Griffin, Stephen M. *American Constitutionalism.* Princeton: Princeton University Press, 1996.

————. "Constitutionalism in the United States: From Theory to Politics." In *Responding to Imperfection: The Theory and Practice of Constitutional Amendment*, edited by Sanford Levinson. Princeton: Princeton University Press, 1995.

Griffith, J. A. G. *Judicial Politics Since 1920: A Chronicle.* Oxford: Blackwell, 1993.

————. *The Politics of the Judiciary.* 4th ed. London: Fontana, 1991.

Grossman, Joel B. "Agenda Formation on a Policy Active Court." Unpublished paper on file with author (n.d.).

Gunther, Gerald. "Learned Hand and the Origins of Modern First Amendment Doctrine: Some Fragments of History." *Stanford Law Review* 27:719 (1975).

Hakman, Nathan. "Lobbying the Supreme Court—An Appraisal of Political Science Folklore." *Fordham Law Review* 35:50–75 (1966).

————. "The Supreme Court's Political Environment: The Processing of Noncommercial Litigation." In *Frontiers of Judicial Research*, edited by Joel B. Grossman and Joseph Tanenhaus. New York: John Wiley, 1969.

Haksar, Nandita. "Violation of Democratic Rights of Women." In *Expanding Governmental Lawlessness and Organized Struggles*, edited by A. R. Desai. Bombay: Popular Prakashan, 1991.

Hale, Sylvia M. "The Status of Women in India." *Pacific Affairs* 62:364 (1989).

Hall, Kermit L. *The Magic Mirror: Law in American History.* New York: Oxford University Press, 1989.

Harding, Luke. "Forget Excalibur, Arthur is armed with legal aid." *Daily Mail* (London), June 10, 1995, p. 3.

Harlow, Carol, and Richard Rawlings. *Pressure Through Law.* London: Routledge, 1992.

Harper, Conrad K. "The Overthrow of *Monroe v. Pape:* A Chapter in the Legacy of Thurgood Marshall." *Fordham Law Review* 61:39–48 (1992).

Hart, A. B. "Use of Torture in America's Prisons." *Current History,* Nov. 1931, 249–50.

Hart, Vivien. *Bound by Our Constitution: Women, Workers, and the Minimum Wage.* Princeton: Princeton University Press, 1994.

Hartog, Hendrik. "The Constitution of Aspiration and the 'Rights That Belong to Us All.'" *Journal of American History* 74:1013–34 (1987).

Hartz, Louis. *The Founding of New Societies.* New York: Harcourt, 1969.

———. *The Liberal Tradition in America.* San Diego: Harcourt, Brace, Jovanovich, 1955.

Harvie, Robert, and Hamar Foster. "Ties That Bind? The Supreme Court of Canada, American Jurisprudence, and the Revision of Canadian Criminal Law under the Charter." *Osgoode Hall Law Review* 28:729–88 (1990).

Haynie, Stacia L. "Resource Inequalities and Litigation Outcomes in the Philippine Supreme Court." *Journal of Politics* 56:752–72 (1994).

Heard, Andrew D. "The Charter in the Supreme Court of Canada: The Importance of Which Judges Hear an Appeal." *Canadian Journal of Political Science* 24:289 (1991).

Hegde, K. S. *Crisis in Indian Judiciary.* Bombay: Sindhu, 1973.

Heinz, John P. and Edward O. Laumann. *Chicago Lawyers: The Social Structure of the Bar.* New York: Russell Sage Foundation, 1982.

Henkin, Louis, and Albert J. Rosenthal, eds. *Constitutionalism and Rights: The Influence of the U.S. Constitution Abroad.* New York: Columbia University Press, 1991.

Hepple, B. A. "Judging Equal Rights." *Current Legal Problems* 36:71–90 (1983).

———. "The Judicial Process in Claims for Equal Pay and Equal Treatment in the United Kingdom." In *Women, Employment, and European Equality Law,* edited by Christopher McCrudden. London: Eclipse, 1987.

Hiro, Dilip. *Black British White British: A History of Race Relations in Britain.* London: Grafton, 1991.

Hoff, Joan. *Law, Gender, and Injustice: A Legal History of U.S. Women.* New York: New York University Press, 1991.

Hogg, Peter W. *Constitutional Law of Canada.* 3d ed. Scarborough, Ont: Carswell. 1992.

Holland, Kenneth M., ed. *Judicial Activism in Comparative Perspective.* New York: St. Martin's Press, 1991.

Home Office. *Criminal Statistics* (London: Her Majesty's Stationery Office, annual).

Horowitz, Gad. *Canadian Labour in Politics.* Toronto: University of Toronto Press, 1968.

Hosek, Chaviva. "Women and the Constitutional Process." In *And No One Cheered: Federalism, Democracy, and the Constitution Act*, edited by Keith Banting and Richard Simeon. Toronto: Methuen, 1983.

House of Lords. "Practice Statement (Judicial Precedent)." [1966] 1 *Weekly Law Reports* 1234.

Howard, J. Woodford, Jr. "On the Fluidity of Judicial Choice." *American Political Science Review* 62:43–56 (1968).

Hutchinson, Allan C., and Neil R. Withington. "*Horvath v. The Queen*: Reflections on the Doctrine of Confessions." *Osgoode Hall Law Review* 18:146 (1980).

Jackson, Donald W. *The United Kingdom Confronts the European Convention on Human Rights*. Gainesville: University Press of Florida, 1997.

Jackson, John. "Due Process." In *Individual Rights and the Law in Britain*, edited by Christopher McCrudden and Gerald Chambers. Oxford: Oxford University Press, 1994.

Jaconelli, Joseph. *Enacting a Bill of Rights: The Legal Problems*. Oxford: Clarendon Press, 1980.

Janzen, William. *Limits on Liberty: The Experience of Mennonite, Hutterite, and Doukhobor Communities in Canada*. Toronto: University of Toronto Press, 1990.

Jeeves, Michael, and Julie Macfarlane. "Rethinking Legal Education." In *Public Interest Law*, edited by Jeremy Cooper and Rajeev Dhavan. Oxford: Blackwell, 1986.

Johnson, William R. *Schooled Lawyers: A Study in the Clash of Professional Cultures*. New York: New York University Press, 1978.

Johnson, William. "Law Protects the Criminal." *Good Housekeeping*, March 1927, 20–21.

Jordan, A. G., and J. Richardson. *Government and Pressure Groups in Britain*. Oxford: Oxford University Press, 1987.

Jordan, Grant. *The British Administrative System: Principles versus Practice*. London: Routledge, 1994.

Jowell, Jeffrey L., and Dawn Oliver, eds. *New Directions in Judicial Review*. London: Stevens & Sons, 1988.

JUSTICE. *Evidence to the Royal Commission on Criminal Justice*. London: JUSTICE, 1991.

Kagan, Robert A. "Adversarial Legalism and American Government." *Journal of Policy Analysis and Management* 10:369–406 (1991).

———. "Do Lawyers Cause Adversarial Legalism? A Preliminary Inquiry." *Law & Social Inquiry* 19:1–62 (1994).

Kapur, Ratna. "From Theory to Practice: Reflections on Legal Literacy Work with Women in India." In *Legal Literacy: A Tool for Women's Empowerment*, edited by Margaret Schuler and Sakuntala Kadirgamar-Rajasingham. New York: United Nations Development Fund for Women, 1992.

Kapur, Ratna, and Brenda Cossman. "On Women, Equality, and the Constitution: Through the Looking Glass of Feminism." *National Law Journal* 1:1 (1993).

Katzenstein, Mary Fainsod. "Organizing against Violence: Strategies of the Indian Women's Movement." *Pacific Affairs* 62:53 (1989).

Keller, Morton. "Powers and Rights: Two Centuries of American Constitutionalism." *Journal of American History* 74:675–94 (1987).

Kenney, Sally J. *For Whose Protection? Reproductive Hazards and Exclusionary Policies in the United States and Britain.* Ann Arbor: University of Michigan Press, 1992.

Kessler, Mark. "Legal Mobilization for Social Reform: Power and the Politics of Agenda Setting." *Law & Society Review* 24:121–43 (1990).

Khan, M. S., and R. Ray. "Dowry Death." *Indian Journal of Social Work* 45:303–307 (1984).

Kidder, Robert L. "Formal Litigation and Professional Insecurity: Legal Entrepreneurship in South India." *Law & Society Review* 9:11 (1974).

Kishwar, Madhu. "Never Say Die: Fight for Justice from an Unjust Judicial System." *Manushi*, no. 71:2–10 (1992).

Kishwar, Madhu, and Ruth Vanita. "Indian Women: A Decade of New Ferment." In *India Briefing, 1989,* edited by Marshall M. Bouton and Philip Oldenburg. Boulder: Westview Press, 1989.

Klarman, Michael J. "Rethinking the Civil Rights and Civil Liberties Revolutions." *Virginia Law Review* 82:1–67 (1996).

Klitgaard, Thomas J. "The Civil Rights Acts and Mr. Monroe." *California Law Review* 49:145–71 (1961).

Kluger, Richard. *Simple Justice: The History of* Brown v. Board of Education *and Black America's Struggle for Equality.* New York: Vintage, 1977.

Knopff, Rainer. *Human Rights and Social Technology: The New War on Discrimination.* Ottawa: Carleton University Press, 1990.

Knopff, Rainer, and F. L. Morton. *Charter Politics.* Scarborough, Ont.: Nelson, 1992.

———. "Nation-Building and the Canadian Charter of Rights and Freedoms." In *Constitutionalism, Citizenship, and Society in Canada,* edited by Alan Cairns and Cynthia Williams. Toronto: University of Toronto Press, 1985.

Kohli, Atul, ed. *India's Democracy: An Analysis of Changing State-Society Relations.* Princeton: Princeton University Press, 1988.

Kome, Penney. *The Taking of Twenty-Eight: Women Challenge the Constitution.* Toronto: Women's Press, 1983.

Kothari, Rajni. "Decline of Parties and Rise of Grassroots Movements." In *State Against Democracy: In Search of Humane Governance,* edited by Rajni Kothari. New York: New Horizons Press, 1989.

Kothari, Smitu. "The Human Rights Movement in India: A Critical Overview." In *Rethinking Human Rights: Challenges for Theory and Action,* edited by Smitu Kothari and Harsh Sethi. Delhi: Lokayan, 1991.

———. "Social Movements and the Redefinition of Democracy." In *India Briefing, 1993,* edited by Philip Oldenburg. Boulder: Westview Press, 1993.

Kritzer, Herbert M. "Courts, Justice, and Politics in England." In *Courts, Law, and Politics in Comparative Perspective,* edited by Herbert Jacob, Erhard Blankenburg, Herbert M. Kritzer, Doris Marie Provine, and Joseph Sanders. New Haven: Yale University Press, 1995.

———. "The English Experience with the English Rule: How 'Loser Pays' Works, What Difference It Makes, and What Might Happen Here." Disputes Processing Research Program Working Paper. Madison, Wisc.: Institute for Legal Studies, 1992.

Kritzer, Herbert M., W. A. Bogart, and Neil Vidmar. "The Aftermath of Injury:

Cultural Factors in Compensation Seeking in Canada and the United States." *Law & Society Review* 25:499–543 (1991).

Lacey, Michael J., and Knud Haakonssen, eds. *A Culture of Rights: The Bill of Rights in Philosophy, Politics, and Law—1791 and 1991.* Cambridge: Cambridge University Press, 1991.

Larkins, Christopher M. "Judicial Independence and Democratization: A Theoretical and Conceptual Analysis." *American Journal of Comparative Law* 44:605–26 (1996).

Laskin, Bora. "The Supreme Court of Canada: A Final Court of and for Canadians." *Canadian Bar Review* 29:1038–79 (1951).

Lavine, Sharon. "Advocating Values: Public Interest Intervention in Charter Litigation." *National Journal of Constitutional Law* 2:27–62 (1992).

Law Reform Commission of Canada. *Police Powers: Search and Seizure in Criminal Law Enforcement.* Ottawa: Law Reform Commission of Canada, 1983.

Lawrence, Susan E. *The Poor in Court: The Legal Services Program and Supreme Court Decision Making.* Princeton: Princeton University Press, 1990.

Laws, John. "Law and Democracy." *Public Law* 1995:72–93.

———. "Is the High Court the Guardian of Fundamental Constitutional Rights?" *Public Law* 1993:59.

Legal Action Group, *A Strategy for Justice.* London: Legal Action Group, 1992.

"Legal aid for the Arts Club banned." *Evening Standard* (London), Oct. 28, 1997, p. 10.

Lester, Anthony. "English Judges as Law Makers." *Public Law* 1993:269.

Lewis, Anthony. *Gideon's Trumpet.* New York: Vintage, 1989.

Liberty. *Let Justice Be Done: Evidence to the Royal Commission on Criminal Justice.* London: Liberty, 1991.

Lijphart, Arend. "The Puzzle of Indian Democracy: A Consociational Interpretation." *American Political Science Review* 90:258–68 (1996).

Lilly, Mark. *The National Council for Civil Liberties: The First Fifty Years.* London: Macmillan, 1984.

Lipset, Seymour Martin. *Continental Divide: The Values and Institutions of the United States and Canada.* New York: Routledge, 1990.

Livingstone, Steven, and Tim Owen. *Prison Law.* Oxford: Clarendon Press, 1993.

Lord Chancellor's Department. *Civil Judicial Statistics.* Her Majesty's Stationery Office, annual.

Lord Chancellor's Department. *Judicial Statistics.* Her Majesty's Stationery Office, annual.

Loughlin, Martin. "The Underside of the Law: Judicial Review and the Prison Disciplinary System." *Current Legal Problems* 46:23 (1993).

Loughlin, Martin, and Peter M. Quinn. "Prisons, Rules, and Courts: A Study in Administrative Law." *Modern Law Review* 56:497–527 (1993).

Lovenduski, Joni. *Women and European Politics.* Amherst: University of Massachusetts Press, 1986.

Lovenduski, Joni, and Vicky Randall. *Contemporary Feminist Politics: Women and Power in Britain.* New York: Oxford University Press, 1993.

Luker, Kristin. *Abortion and the Politics of Motherhood.* Berkeley: University of California Press, 1984.

Luthra, Geeta, and Pinky Anand. "Torture is Abetment of Suicide—Supreme Court Sets New Precedent." *Manushi*, nos. 54–55:22–24 (1989).

MacGuigan, Mark. "The Development of Civil Liberties in Canada." *Queen's Quarterly* 72:273 (1965).

Madison, James. *The Papers of James Madison*. Vol. 10. Chicago: University of Chicago Press, 1977.

———. *The Papers of James Madison*. Vol. 11. Charlottesville: University Press of Virginia, 1977.

———. *The Papers of James Madison*. Vol. 12. Charlottesville: University Press of Virginia, 1979.

Magat, Richard. *The Ford Foundation at Work: Philanthropic Choices, Methods and Styles*. New York: Plenum, 1979.

Majumdar, Sujip. "Deaths in Police Custody." In *Violation of Democratic Rights in India*, edited by A. R. Desai. Bombay: Popular Prakashan, 1986.

Malleson, Kate. "Review of the Appeal Process." Report to The Royal Commission on Criminal Justice. London: Her Majesty's Stationery Office (1993).

Maloney, Arthur. "The Supreme Court and Civil Liberties." *Criminal Law Quarterly* 18:202 (1976).

Mandel, Michael. *The Charter of Rights and the Legalisation of Politics in Canada*. Toronto: Thompson, 1989.

Markowitz, Deborah L. "In Pursuit of Equality: One Woman's Work to Change the Law." *Women's Rights Law Reporter* 11:73–97 (1989).

Martin, Ian. "Combining Casework and Strategy: The Joint Council for the Welfare of Immigrants." In *Public Interest Law*, edited by Jeremy Cooper and Rajeev Dhavan. Oxford: Blackwell, 1986.

Mathur, Kuldeep. "The State and the Use of Coercive Power in India." *Asian Survey* 32:337 (1992).

May, Richard. "Fair Play at Trial: An Interim Assessment of S. 78 of the Police and Criminal Evidence Act 1984." *Criminal Law Review* 1988:722–30.

McAninch, William Shepard. "A Catalyst for the Evolution of Constitutional Law: Jehovah's Witnesses in the Supreme Court." *Cincinnati Law Review* 55:997 (1987).

McCann, Michael W. *Rights at Work: Pay Equity Reform and the Politics of Legal Mobilization*. Chicago: University of Chicago Press, 1994.

McCloskey, Robert G. *The American Supreme Court*. 2d ed. Edited by Sanford Levinson. Chicago: University of Chicago Press, 1994.

McConnell, W. H. *Commentary on the British North America Act*. Toronto: Macmillan, 1977.

McConville, Mike, Jacqueline Hodgson, Lee Bridges, and Anita Pavlovic. *Standing Accused: The Organisation and Practices of Criminal Defence Lawyers in Britain*. Oxford: Clarendon Press, 1994.

McCormick, Peter. "Party Capability Theory and Appellate Success in the Supreme Court of Canada, 1949–1992. *Canadian Journal of Political Science* 26:523–40 (1993).

McCrudden, Christopher, and Gerald Chambers. "Conclusions." In *Individual Rights and the Law in Britain*, edited by Christopher McCrudden and Gerald Chambers. Oxford: Oxford University Press, 1993.

McGuire, Kevin T. *The Supreme Court Bar: Legal Elites in the Washington Community*. Charlottesville: University Press of Virginia, 1993.

McKain, Bruce. "No legal aid for widow of smoking death man." *Herald* (Glasgow), Feb. 16, 1995, p. 9.

McLean, A. J. "Matrimonial Property—Canadian Common Law Style." *University of Toronto Law Journal* 31:363–435 (1981).

Meador, Daniel John. *Preludes to Gideon: Notes on Appellate Advocacy, Habeas Corpus, and Constitutional Litigation.* Charlottesville, Va.: Michie, 1967.

Meehan, Elizabeth. *Women's Rights at Work: Campaigns and Policy in Britain and the United States.* London: Macmillan, 1985.

Menon, N. R. Madhava, S. Rama Rao, and S. Sudarsen. "Legal Profession in Tamil Nadu: A Sociological Survey." In *The Legal Profession: A Preliminary Study of the Tamilnadu Bar,* edited by N. R. Madhava Menon. New Delhi: Bar Council of India Trust, 1984.

Messina, Anthony M. *Race and Party Competition in Britain.* Oxford: Clarendon Press, 1989.

Milligan and Company. "Evaluation of the Test Case Funding Program." Report prepared for the Department of Indian Affairs and Northern Development, 1989.

Mishler, William, and Reginald Sheehan. "The Supreme Court as a Counter-Majoritarian Institution? The Impact of Public Opinion on Supreme Court Decisions." *American Political Science Review* 87:87–101 (1993).

Mitchell, J. D. B. "The Causes and Effects of the Absence of a System of Public Law in the United Kingdom." *Public Law* 1965:95–118.

Monahan, Patrick. *Politics and the Constitution: The Charter, Federalism, and the Supreme Court of Canada.* Toronto: Carswell, 1987.

Moog, Robert. "Indian Litigiousness and the Litigation Explosion: Challenging the Legend." *Asian Survey* 33:1136 (1993).

Morris, Terence. *Crime and Criminal Justice Since 1945.* London: Basil Blackwell, 1993.

Morton, F. L. "The Charter Revolution and the Court Party." In *The Impact of the Charter on the Public Policy Process,* edited by Patrick Monahan and Marie Finkelstein. North York, Ont.: York University Centre for Public Law and Public Policy, 1993.

———. *Morgentaler v. Borowski: Abortion, the Charter, and the Courts.* Toronto: McClelland & Stewart, 1992.

———. "The Political Impact of the Canadian Charter of Rights and Freedoms." *Canadian Journal of Political Science* 20:31–55 (1987).

Morton, F. L., and Rainer Knopff. "The Supreme Court as the Vanguard of the Intelligentsia: The Charter Movement as Post-Materialist Politics." In *Two Hundred Years of Canadian Constitutionalism,* edited by Janet Ajzenstat. Ottawa: Canadian Study of Parliament Group, 1993.

Morton, F. L., Peter H. Russell, and Troy Riddell. "The Canadian Charter of Rights and Freedoms: A Descriptive Analysis of the First Decade, 1982–1992." *National Journal of Constitutional Law* 5:1–60 (1995).

Morton, F. L., Peter H. Russell, and Michael J. Withey. "The Supreme Court's First One Hundred Charter of Rights Decisions: A Statistical Analysis." *Osgoode Hall Law Journal* 30:1–56 (1989).

Mount, Ferdinand. *The British Constitution Now: Recovery or Decline.* London: Heineman, 1992.

Murphy, Michael. "Civil Legal Aid Eligibility Estimates, 1979–90." Unpublished paper, London School of Economics, reprinted in part as appendix 1

in Legal Action Group, *A Strategy for Justice* London: Legal Action Group, 1992.

Murphy, Paul L. *The Meaning of Freedom of Speech: First Amendment Freedoms from Wilson to FDR.* Westport, Conn.: Greenwood Press, 1972.

Murphy, Walter F. "Constitutions, Constitutionalism, and Democracy." In *Constitutionalism and Democracy: Transitions in the Contemporary World,* edited by Douglas Greenberg, Stanley N. Katz, Melanie Beth Oliviero, and Steven C. Wheatley. New York: Oxford University Press, 1993.

National Legal Aid Research Centre. *Justice Information Report: Legal Aid Services in Canada 1979/80.* Ottawa: Implementation Work Group on Justice Information and Statistics, 1981.

Nayar, Kuldip, ed. *Supersession of Judges.* New Delhi: Indian Book Co., 1973.

"Negro Family Wins Right to Sue Police Officers." *Chicago Tribune.* Tuesday, Feb. 21, 1961, p. 17.

Nelson, William E. *The Fourteenth Amendment: From Political Principle to Judicial Doctrine.* Cambridge: Harvard University Press, 1988.

"New Rape Bill—Legislating Rape 'Out of Existence'!" *Manushi,* no. 7:38–45 (1981).

Nobles, Richard, David Schiff, and Nicola Shaldon. "The Inevitability of Crisis in Criminal Appeals." *International Journal of the Sociology of Law* 21:1–21 (1993).

Note. "Attorneys' Fees: Exceptions to the American Rule." *Drake Law Review* 25:717 (1976).

O'Brien, David M. *Storm Center: The Supreme Court in American Politics.* New York: Norton, 1993.

O'Connor, Karen. *Women's Organizations' Use of the Courts.* Lexington, Mass.: Lexington Books, 1980.

O'Connor, Karen, and Lee Epstein. "Bridging the Gap between Congress and the Supreme Court: Interest Groups and the Erosion of the American Rule Governing the Award of Attorneys' Fees." *Western Political Quarterly* 38:241 (1985).

———. "Amicus Curiae Participation in the U.S. Supreme Court: An Appraisal of Hakman's 'Folklore,'" *Law & Society Review* 16:701–11 (1982).

———. "Beyond Legislative Lobbying: Women's Rights Groups and the Supreme Court." *Judicature* 67:134–43 (1989).

———. *Public Interest Law Groups: Institutional Profiles.* Westport, Conn.: Greenwood Press, 1989.

O'Donovan, Katherine, and Erika Szyszczak. *Equality and Sex Discrimination Law.* Oxford: Basil Blackwell, 1988.

Olson, Susan M. "Interest Group Litigation in Federal District Court: Beyond the Political Disadvantage Theory." *Journal of Politics* 52:854–82 (1990).

Oommen, T. K. "The Legal Profession in India: Some Sociological Perspectives." In *The Legal Profession: A Preliminary Study of the Tamilnadu Bar,* edited by N. R. Madhava Menon. New Delhi: Bar Council of India Trust, 1984.

Orfield, Gary, Susan E. Eaton, and the Harvard Project on School Desegregation. *Dismantling Desegregation: The Quiet Reversal of* Brown v. Board of Education. New York: New Press, 1996.

Oscapella, E. L., and Associates. "Legal Liaison and Support Study: Test Case

Funding Program." Study prepared for the Department of Indian Affairs and Northern Development, 1988.

"Our Rights and Wrongs: Such Lofty Sympathy for a Rapist! A Recent Judgment by Justice Krishna Iyer." *Manushi*, no. 5:35–36 (1980).

Pacelle, Richard L., Jr. *The Transformation of the Supreme Court's Agenda: From the New Deal to the Reagan Administration.* Boulder: Westview Press, 1991.

Pal, Leslie. *Interests of State: The Politics of Language, Multiculturalism, and Feminism in Canada.* Montreal: McGill-Queen's University Press, 1993.

Pal, Leslie, and F. L. Morton. "*Bliss v. Attorney-General of Canada*: From Legal Defeat to Political Victory." *Osgoode Hall Law Journal* 24:141–60 (1986).

Paltiel, Khayyam Z. "The Changing Environment and Role of Special Interest Groups." *Canadian Public Administration* 25:198–210 (1982).

Pannick, David. "How to Judge a Human Rights Bill." *Times* (London), Aug. 12, 1997, Features section.

Pappu, Shyamla, Chandramani Chopra, and Mohini Giri. "Women and the Law." In *Problems and Concerns of Indian Women*, edited by B. K. Pal. New Delhi: ABC Publishing, 1987.

Parashar, Archana. *Women and Family Law Reform in India.* New Delhi: Sage, 1992.

Patel, Vibhuti. "Emergence and Proliferation of Autonomous Women's Groups (1974–1984)." In *A Decade of Women's Movement in India*, edited by Neera Desai. Bombay: Himalaya Publishing House, 1988.

Paterson, Alan. *The Law Lords.* London: Macmillan, 1982.

Penton, M. James. *Jehovah's Witnesses in Canada: Champions of Freedom of Speech and Worship.* Toronto: Macmillan, 1976.

People's Union for Civil Liberties. "Murder by Encounter." In *Violation of Democratic Rights in India.* Edited by A. R. Desai: Bombay: Popular Prakashan, 1986.

Percival, Robert V., and Geoffrey P. Miller. "The Role of Attorney Fee Shifting in Public Interest Litigation." *Law & Contemporary Problems* 47:233–47 (1984).

Perry, H. W., Jr. *Deciding to Decide: Agenda Setting in the United States Supreme Court.* Cambridge: Harvard University Press, 1991.

Peterson, V. W. "Case Dismissed: Unreasonable Leniency of Criminal Justice." *Atlantic Monthly*, April 1945, 69–74.

Petter, Andrew. "Canada's Charter Flight: Soaring Backward into the Future." *Journal of Law & Society* 16:151–65 (1989).

Pound, Roscoe. "The Scope and Purpose of Sociological Jurisprudence." *Harvard Law Review* 25:140–68 (1911).

Powell, Walter W., and Paul J. DiMaggio, eds. *The New Institutionalism in Organizational Analysis.* Chicago: University of Chicago Press, 1991.

Presthus, Robert. *Elites in the Policy Process.* Toronto: Macmillan, 1974.

Pritchett, C. Herman, and Alan F. Westin, eds. *The Third Branch of Government.* New York: Harcourt, Brace & World, 1963.

Pritchett, C. Herman. *The Roosevelt Court: A Study in Judicial Politics and Values, 1937–1947.* New York: Macmillan, 1948.

"Profound Judgment." *Times* (London), March 5, 1994, Features section.

Pross, Paul, ed. *Pressure Group Behaviour in Canadian Politics.* Toronto: McGraw-Hill, Ryerson, 1975.

Prosser, Tony. *Test Cases for the Poor.* London: Child Poverty Action Group, 1983.

Provine, Doris Marie. *Case Selection in the United States Supreme Court.* Chicago: University of Chicago Press, 1980.

Punwani, Jyoti. "At What Stage is the Civil Rights Movement?" In *Violation of Democratic Rights in India,* edited by A. R. Desai. Bombay: Popular Prakashan, 1986.

Quirk, William J., and R. Randall Bridwell. *Judicial Dictatorship.* New Brunswick, N.J.: Transaction, 1995.

Rabban, David M. "The First Amendment in Its Forgotten Years." *Yale Law Journal* 90:514–95 (1981).

———. "The Free Speech League, the ACLU, and Changing Conceptions of Free Speech in American History." *Stanford Law Review* 45:47–114 (1992).

———. "The IWW Free Speech Fights and Popular Conceptions of Free Expression Before World War I." *Virginia Law Review* 80:1055–58 (1994).

Rabin, Robert L. "Lawyers for Social Change: Perspectives on Public Interest Law." *Stanford Law Review* 28:207 (1976).

Ragan, Fred D. "Justice Oliver Wendell Holmes, Jr., Zechariah Chafee, Jr., and the Clear and Present Danger Test for Free Speech: The First Year, 1919." *Journal of American History* 58:24 (1971).

Rahman, Anika. "Religious Rights Versus Women's Rights in India: A Test Case for International Human Rights Law." *Columbia Journal of Transnational Law* 28:473 (1990).

Rajappa, Sam. "Kerala's Concentration Camps." In *Violation of Democratic Rights in India,* edited by A. R. Desai. Bombay: Popular Prakashan, 1986.

Rakove, Jack N. "Parchment Barriers and the Politics of Rights." In *A Culture of Rights: The Bill of Rights in Philosophy, Politics, and Law—1791 and 1991,* edited by Michael J. Lacey and Knud Haakonssen. Cambridge: Cambridge University Press, 1991.

"Rape: The Victim is the Accused." In *Manushi,* no. 4:42–46 (Dec. 1979–Jan. 1980).

Rawlings, Richard. "The Eurolaw Game: Some Deductions from a Saga." *Journal of Law and Society* 20:309 (1993).

Razack, Sherene. *Canadian Feminism and the Law: The Women's Legal Education and Action Fund and the Pursuit of Equality.* Toronto: Second Story Press, 1991.

Reddy, Snehalata. *A Prison Diary.* Mysore, India: Human Rights Committee, 1977.

Redlich, Norman. "Private Attorneys General: Group Action in the Fight for Civil Liberties." *Yale Law Journal* 58:574 (1949).

Robertson, David. "Judicial Ideology in the House of Lords: A Jurimetric Analysis." *British Journal of Political Science* 12:1–25 (1982).

Romanow, Roy, John Whyte, and Howard Leeson. *Canada Notwithstanding: The Making of the Constitution 1976–1982.* Toronto: Carswell/Methuen, 1984.

Rose, David. "UK—Silent Revolution: Judges with Radical Views." *Observer* (London), May 9, 1993.

Rosenberg, Gerald N. *The Hollow Hope: Can Courts Bring About Social Change?* Chicago: University of Chicago Press, 1991.

Rosenbloom, David H., and Rosemary O'Leary. *Public Administration and Law.* New York: Marcel Dekker, 1997.

Rowbotham, Sheila, Lynne Segal, and Hilary Wainwright. *Beyond the Frag-ments: Feminism and the Making of Socialism.* London: Merlin, 1979.

Rowe, William V. "Legal Clinics and Better Trained Lawyers—A Necessity." *Illinois Law Review* 11:593 (1917).

Royal Commission on Criminal Justice, *Report of the Royal Commission on Crimi-nal Justice.* London: Her Majesty's Stationery Office, 1993.

Royal Commission on the Status of Women. *Report of the Royal Commission on the Status of Women.* Ottawa: Information Canada, 1970.

Rudolph, Lloyd I., and Susanne Hoeber Rudolph. *In Pursuit of Lakshmi: The Political Economy of the Indian State.* Chicago: University of Chicago Press, 1987.

———. *The Modernity of Tradition.* Chicago: University of Chicago Press, 1967.

Russell, Peter H. "The Growth of Canadian Judicial Review and the Common-wealth and American Experiences." In *Comparative Judicial Review and Public Policy,* edited by Donald W. Jackson and C. Neal Tate. Westport, Conn.: Greenwood Press, 1992.

———. "The Supreme Court and Federal-Provincial Relations: The Political Use of Legal Resources." *Canadian Public Policy* 11:161–70 (1985).

Sacks, Vera. "The Equal Opportunities Commission—Ten Years On." *Modern Law Review* 49:560 1986).

Saggar, Shamit. *Race and Politics in Britain.* London: Harvester Wheatsheaf, 1992.

Salokar, Rebecca Mae. *The Solicitor General: The Politics of Law.* Philadelphia: Temple University Press, 1992.

Samson, Gloria Garrett. *The American Fund for Public Service: Charles Garland and Radical Philanthropy, 1922–1941.* Westport, Conn.: Greenwood Press, 1996.

Schubert, Glendon. *The Judicial Mind Revisited.* New York: Oxford University Press, 1974.

Schwab, Stewart J., and Theodore Eisenberg. "Explaining Constitutional Tort Litigation: The Influence of the Attorney Fees Statute and the Government as Defendant." *Cornell Law Review* 73:719–84 (1988).

Schwartz, Bernard. *The Warren Court: A Retrospective.* New York: Oxford Uni-versity Press, 1996.

———. *Lions over the Throne: The Judicial Revolution in English Administrative Law.* New York: New York University Press, 1987.

Scott, Frank. "The Consequences of the Privy Council Decisions." *Canadian Bar Review* 15:485–94 (1937).

Sedley, Stephen. "The Sound of Silence: Constitutional Law without a Consti-tution." *Law Quarterly Review* 110:270 (1994).

Segal, Jeffrey A., and Albert D. Cover. "Ideological Values and the Votes of U.S. Supreme Court Justices." *American Political Science Review* 83:557–65 (1989).

Segal, Jeffrey A., and Harold J. Spaeth. *The Supreme Court and the Attitudinal Model.* Cambridge: Cambridge University Press, 1993.

Sen, Siddhartha. "Non-Profit Organisations in India: Historical Development and Common Patterns." *Voluntas* 3, no. 2:175 (1992).

Shah, Ghanshyam. "Grass-Roots Mobilization in Indian Politics." In *India's De-mocracy: An Analysis of Changing State-Society Relations,* edited by Atul Kohli. Princeton: Princeton University Press, 1988.

Shapiro, Martin. "The European Court of Justice." In *Euro-Politics: Institutions and Policymaking in the "New" European Community,* edited by Alberta M. Sbragia. Washington, D.C.: Brookings Institution, 1992.

Sharma, S. S. *Legal Aid to the Poor: The Law and Indian Legal System.* New Delhi: Deep & Deep, 1993.

Sheehan, Reginald S., William Mishler, and Donald R. Songer. "Ideology, Status, and the Differential Success of Direct Parties Before the Supreme Court." *American Political Science Review* 86:464–71 (1992).

Sheth, D. L., and Harsh Sethi. "The NGO Sector in India: Historical Context and Current Discourse." *Voluntas* 2, no. 2:49 (1991).

Shourie, Arun. "Lethal Custodians." In *Violation of Democratic Rights in India,* edited by A. R. Desai. Bombay: Popular Prakashan, 1986.

Shukla, V. N. *Constitution of India.* 9th ed. Edited by Mahendra P. Singh. Lucknow, India: Eastern, 1994.

Sklar, Martin. *The Corporate Reconstruction of American Capitalism, 1890–1916: The Market, the Law, and Politics.* Cambridge: Cambridge University Press, 1988.

Smith, A. T. H. "Criminal Appeals in the House of Lords." *Modern Law Review* 47:133 (1984).

Smith, Roger. "How Good Are Test Cases?" In *Public Interest Law,* edited by Jeremy Cooper and Rajeev Dhavan. Oxford: Basil Blackwell, 1986.

Snell, James G., and Frederick Vaughan. *The Supreme Court of Canada: History of the Institution.* Toronto: University of Toronto Press, 1985.

Sniderman, Paul M., Peter H. Russell, Joseph F. Fletcher, and Philip E. Tetlock. *The Clash of Rights: Liberty, Equality, and Legitimacy in Pluralist Democracy.* New Haven: Yale University Press, 1996.

Solomos, John. *Race and Racism in Contemporary Britain.* London: Macmillan, 1989.

Songer, Donald R., and Reginald S. Sheehan. "Who Wins on Appeal? Upperdogs and Underdogs in the United States Courts of Appeals." *American Journal of Political Science* 36:235–58 (1992).

Sorabjee, Soli. "Women, Constitution, and the Courts." In *Women, Law and Social Change,* edited by Shamsuddin Shams. New Delhi: Ashish Publishing House, 1991.

Sorauf, Frank J. *The Wall of Separation: The Constitutional Politics of Church and State.* Princeton: Princeton University Press, 1976.

Special Committee of the Association of the Bar of the City of New York. *Equal Justice for the Accused.* Garden City, N.J.: Doubleday, 1959.

Spencer, J. R. *Jackson's Machinery of Justice.* 8th ed. Cambridge: Cambridge University Press, 1989.

Srinivas, M. N. *Some Reflections on Dowry.* New Delhi: Oxford University Press, 1984.

Stager, David A. A., and Harry W. Arthurs. *Lawyers in Canada.* Toronto: University of Toronto Press, 1990.

Stanbury, W. T. *Business-Government Relations in Canada: Influencing Public Policy.* Scarborough, Ont.: Nelson Canada, 1993.

"Statistical Recap of Supreme Court's Workload." *U.S. Law Week,* annually.

Steele, John. "Robber given legal aid to sue Home Secretary." *Daily Telegraph* (London), Sept. 25, 1997, p.17.

Stein, Eric. "Lawyers, Judges, and the Making of a Transnational Constitution." *American Journal of International Law* 75:1–27 (1981).

Stephens, Mike. *Community Law Centres.* Aldershot, Eng.: Avebury, 1990.

Sterett, Susan. *Creating Constitutionalism? The Politics of Legal Expertise and Administrative Law in England and Wales.* Ann Arbor: University of Michigan Press, 1997.

———. "Keeping the Law Up to Date: The Idiom of Legalism and the Reform of Administrative Law in England and Wales." *Law & Social Inquiry* 15:731 (1991).

———. "Politics and Jurisprudence in the British Courts." *Canadian Journal of Law and Jurisprudence* 1:173 (1988).

Stevens, Robert S. *Law and Politics: The House of Lords as a Judicial Body, 1800–1976.* Chapel Hill: University of North Carolina Press, 1978.

Stone, Alec. *The Birth of Judicial Politics in France.* Oxford: Oxford University Press, 1992.

Strong, Theron. *Landmarks of a Lawyer's Lifetime.* New York: Dodd, Mead, 1914.

Sunkin, Maurice. "The Incidence and Effect of Judicial Review Procedures against Central Government in the United Kingdom." In *Comparative Judicial Review and Public Policy,* edited by Donald W. Jackson and C. Neal Tate. Westport, Conn.: Greenwood Press, 1992.

———. "What Is Happening to Applications for Judicial Review?" *Modern Law Review* 50:432 (1987).

Swan, Kenneth P. "Intervention and Amicus Curiae Status in Charter Litigation." In *Charter Cases, 1986–1987,* edited by Gerald A. Beaudoin. Cowansville, Québec: Les Editions Yvon Blais, 1987.

Szyszczak, Erika. "The Future of Women's Rights: The Role of European Community Law." In *The Yearbook of Social Policy,* edited by M. Brenton and C. Ungerson. London: Routledge,1986.

Tarkunde, V. M. "In Defence of Freedom." In *Expanding Governmental Lawlessness and Organized Struggles,* edited by A. R. Desai. Bombay: Popular Prakashan, 1991.

Tarnopolsky, Walter S. *The Canadian Bill of Rights.* 2d ed. Toronto: McClelland & Stewart, 1975.

———. *Discrimination and the Law in Canada.* Toronto: de Boo, 1982.

Tate, C. Neal. "Judicial Institutions in Cross-National Perspective: Toward Integrating Courts in the Comparative Study of Politics." In *Comparative Judicial Systems: Challenging Frontiers in Conceptual and Empirical Analysis,* edited by John R. Schmidhauser. London: Butterworths, 1987.

Tate, C. Neal, and Panu Sittiwong. "Decision Making in the Canadian Supreme Court: Extending the Personal Attributes Model Across Nations." *Journal of Politics* 51:900–16 (1989).

Tate, C. Neal, and Torbjorn Vallinder, eds. *The Global Expansion of Judicial Power.* New York: New York University Press, 1995.

"Three-month-old baby wins legal aid." *Evening Standard* (London), Aug. 11, 1995, p. 16.

Tocqueville, Alexis de, *Democracy in America.* Edited by J. P. Mayer. New York: Harper & Row, 1969.

Trebilgas-Davey, M. "Miscarriages of Justice within the English Legal System." *New Law Journal* 141:608 (1991).

Turano, A. M. "Brutalities by the Police." *American Mercury,* July 1934, 341–50.

Tushnet, Mark. *Making Civil Rights Law: Thurgood Marshall and the Supreme Court, 1936–1961.* New York: Oxford University Press, 1994.

———. *The NAACP's Legal Strategy against Segregated Education, 1925–1950.* Chapel Hill: University of North Carolina Press, 1987.

Tushnet, Mark, ed. *The Warren Court in Historical and Political Perspective.* Charlottesville: University Press of Virginia, 1993.

"UK Part-Time Work Rules 'in Breach of EU Law'" *Financial Times* (London), March 4, 1994, p. 6.

"UK Soon to Adopt Human Rights Law." *The Lawyer* (London), July 8, 1997, p. 3.

Ulmer, S. Sidney. "The Decision to Grant Certiorari as an Indicator to Decision 'On the Merits'" *Polity* 4:429–47 (1972).

Urofsky, Melvin I. "Myth and Reality: The Supreme Court and Protective Legislation in the Progressive Era." *Yearbook—Supreme Court Historical Society* 1983:55.

Vickers, Jill, Pauline Rankin, and Christine Appelle. *Politics As If Women Mattered: A Political Analysis of the National Action Committee on the Status of Women.* Toronto: University of Toronto Press, 1993.

Vogel, David. *National Styles of Regulation.* Ithaca, N.Y.: Cornell University Press, 1986.

Volcansek, Mary L. "Winners and Losers Before the European Court of Justice: Litigant Status and Ideology." Unpublished paper on file with author.

Vose, Clement. *Caucasians Only: The Supreme Court, the NAACP, and the Restrictive Covenant Cases.* Berkeley: University of California Press, 1959.

———. *Constitutional Change: Amendment Politics and Constitutional Litigation since 1900.* Lexington, Mass.: Lexington Books, 1972.

Wade, H. W. R. *Administrative Law.* 6th ed. Oxford: Clarendon Press, 1988.

Walker, Clive, and Keir Starmer, eds. *Justice in Error.* London: Blackstone Press, 1993.

Walker, Jack. "The Origins and Maintenance of Interest Groups in America." *American Political Science Review* 77:390–406 (1983).

Walker, Samuel. *In Defense of American Liberties: a History of the ACLU.* New York: Oxford University Press, 1990.

Waltman, Jerold. "Judicial Activism in England." In *Judicial Activism in Comparative Perspective,* edited by Kenneth M. Holland. New York: St. Martin's Press, 1991.

Waltman, Jerold, and Priscilla Machado. "Postindustrialism and the Changing Face of Administrative Litigation in England, 1960–1985." *Social Science Journal.* 29:185–98 (1992).

Warner, Sam B., and Henry B. Cabot. "Changes in the Administration of Criminal Justice During the Past Fifty Years." *Harvard Law Review* 50:583 (1937).

Warr, Mark. "The Polls—Poll Trends: Public Opinion on Crime and Punishment." *Public Opinion Quarterly* 59:296–310 (1995).

Wasby, Stephen. *Race Relations Litigation in an Age of Complexity.* Charlottesville: University Press of Virginia, 1995.

———. "How Planned is 'Planned Litigation'?" *American Bar Foundation Research Journal* 1984:83–138.

Watson, Jeremy. "Legal Aid Has Been Granted to 200 Smokers Considering

Suing British Cigarette Companies." *Scotland on Sunday* (Edinburgh), Feb. 5, 1995, p. 8

Weaver, John Downing. *Warren: The Man, the Court, the Era.* Boston: Little, Brown, 1967.

Wechsler, Herbert. "Toward Neutral Principles of Constitutional Law." *Harvard Law Review* 73:1 (1959).

Welch, Jillian. "No Room at the Top: Interest Group Intervenors and Charter Litigation in the Supreme Court of Canada." *University of Toronto Faculty Law Review* 43:204–31 (1985).

Welling, B., and L. A. Hipfner, "Cruel and Unusual? Capital Punishment in Canada." *University of Toronto Law Journal* 26:55–83 (1976).

Wells, Richard S., and Joel B. Grossman. "The Concept of Judicial Policy-Making: a Critique." In *Journal of Public Law* 15:286 (1966).

Wertheimer, John W. "Free-Speech Fights: The Roots of Modern Free-Expression Litigation in the United States." Ph.D. diss., Princeton University, 1992.

———. "*Mutual Film* Revisited: The Movies, Censorship, and Free Speech in Progressive America." *The American Journal of Legal History* 37:158–89 (1993).

Westin, Alan F. "The United States Bill of Rights and the Canadian Charter: A Socio-Political Analysis." In *The U.S. Bill of Rights and the Canadian Charter of Rights and Freedoms,* edited by William R. McKercher. Toronto: Ontario Economic Council, 1983.

Wheeler, Stanton, Bliss Cartwright, Robert A. Kagan, and Lawrence M. Friedman. "Do the 'Haves' Come Out Ahead? Winning and Losing in State Supreme Courts, 1870–1970." *Law & Society Review* 21:403–45 (1987).

Wiebe, Robert H. *Self-Rule: A Cultural History of American Democracy.* Chicago: University of Chicago Press, 1995.

Wiecek, William M. *The Sources of Antislavery Constitutionalism in America, 1760–1848.* Ithaca, N.Y.: Cornell University Press, 1977.

Wilkinson, J. Harvie. *From Brown to Bakke: The Supreme Court and School Integration, 1954–1978.* New York: Oxford University Press, 1979.

Williams, Cynthia. "The Changing Nature of Citizen Rights." In *Constitutionalism, Citizenship, and Society in Canada,* edited by Alan Cairns and Cynthia Williams. Toronto: University of Toronto Press, 1985.

Wilson, Graham K. *The Politics of Safety and Health: Occupational Safety and Health in the United States and Britain.* Oxford: Clarendon Press, 1985.

Wilson, Thomas. *Ulster: Conflict and Consent.* Oxford: Basil Blackwell, 1989.

Wilson, Woodrow. *The Papers of Woodrow Wilson.* Vol. 21 (1910). Edited by Arthur S. Link. Princeton: Princeton University Press, 1976.

Wood, Floris W. *An American Profile—Opinions and Behavior, 1972–89.* Detroit: Gale Research, 1990.

Yates, Robert. "Letters of Brutus" (letter no. 15, 1788). In *The Origins of the American Constitution: A Documentary History.* Michael Kammen, ed., New York: Penguin, 1986.

Zander, Michael. *A Bill of Rights?* 3d ed. Oxford: Oxford University Press, 1985.

———. *Cases and Materials on the English Legal System.* 5th ed. London: Weidenfeld & Nicolson, 1988.

———. *The Police and Criminal Evidence Act 1984.* 2d ed. London: Sweet & Maxwell, 1991.

Zemans, Frances Kahn. "Legal Mobilization: The Neglected Role of the Law in the Political System." *American Political Science Review* 77:690–703 (1983).

Zemans, Frederick H. "Canada." In *Perspectives on Legal Aid: An International Survey,* edited by Frederick H. Zemans. Westport, Conn.: Greenwood Press, 1979.

———. "Legal Aid and Advice in Canada." *Osgoode Hall Law Journal* 16:663–93 (1978).

Zuckerman, A. A. S. "Illegally Obtained Evidence: Discretion as a Guardian of Legitimacy." In *Current Legal Problems 1987.* London: Stevens, 1987.

INDEX

Page references to tables and figures appear in italics.

A. K. Gopalan v. State of Madras, 74, 250n.
60, 252n. 93
ABA (American Bar Association), 56
Abel, Richard, 55, 144–45
aboriginals (Canadian): equal rights of,
168; funding cases for, 184; rights consciousness of, 159; rights organizations
for, 181; women's status and, 179
abortion: in Canada, 156–57, 165, 179,
274n. 15; in United States, 26, 29, 53,
57, 156
Abrams v. United States, 28
accused. See criminal procedure
ACLU. See American Civil Liberties
Union (ACLU)
Adamson v. California, 40, 238–39n. 67
Administration of Justice Act (1960, British), 122–23
administrative law (British), 115, 117–19,
125, 132, 154
Advocacy Resource Centre for the Handicapped (Canadian), 181
African Americans, legal training for, 55–
56. See also race; racial discrimination;
school desegregation
Agnello v. United States, 238n. 65
AIR (All India Reporter), cases in, 254n. 1
Air India v. Nergesh Meerza, 253n. 110
airline industry (Indian), sex discrimina-
tion in, 75, 88, 249n. 29, 253n. 110
Alberta (Canada): divorce case in, 165,
179, 191, 275n. 21; land purchases in,
270–71n. 13
Ali, Faizal, 105–6
Allan, James, 227n. 11
All India Reporter (AIR), cases in, 254n. 1
All India Women's Conference, 258n.
57

All India Women's Federation v. Union of India, 106
Alyeska Pipeline Service Co. v. Wilderness Society, 246n. 134
Ambedkar, B. R., 81
American Bar Association (ABA), 56
American Civil Liberties Union (ACLU):
cooperation with other rights groups,
53; development of, 21, 48, 49–50; funding and support for, 49–50, 58; judicial
policies' impact on, 8, 64–65; litigation
supported by, 50–51, 66; Monroes' suit
supported by, 10; police studied by, 9,
66; role of, 66; state affiliates of, 9, 50;
Women's Rights Project of, 52–54, 57,
149, 242n. 60
American Fund for Public Service (Gar-
land Fund), 49, 51, 53, 58, 243n. 62
American Jewish Congress, 48, 53
American Law Institute, 103
American School of Magnetic Healing v.
McAnnulty, 233–34n. 12
amicus curiae brief, use of, 175, 268n.
61
Amnesty International, 74, 76, 248n. 20
Anand, Pinky, 107, 256–57n. 41
Andhra Pradesh (India), police brutality
in, 102–3
Andhra Pradesh Civil and Democratic
Rights Association, 98
Andhra Pradesh Civil Liberties Commit-
tee, 103
Andrews v. Law Society of British Columbia,
179–80, 194
Anil Yadav v. State of Bihar (Bhagalpur Blind-
ings Case), 252n. 92
Ansari, Iqbal A., 258n. 68
Appeal Cases (British), 265n. 1

role of, 121; EOC-sponsored cases in, 152–53, 154; on sex discrimination, 124, 140

European Union, elements of, 262n. 54

Everson v. Board of Education, 50, 68

exploitation (Indian), freedom from, 214

Farole, Donald J., 241n. 30

fee-shifting statutes: in Britain, 142, 154, 267n. 35; in United States, 20, 60–61, 65

Feldman, David, 129

Fifteenth Amendment (U.S.), 210

Fifth Amendment (U.S.), 207–8, 233n. 10, 238n. 65

film industry, rights issues and, 49, 118

Finer, Samuel, 116

The Finished Mystery (Jehovah's Witnesses), 52

Finlay v. Minister of Finance of Canada, 170

First Amendment (U.S.), 50, 207. *See also* freedom of speech and the press

Fiske v. Kansas, 28, 50, 238n. 66

Fletcher, Joseph, 202

Footnote Four *(United States v. Carolene Products)*, 237n. 57

Ford Foundation, 58

Fortas, Abe, 39, 41–42, 239n. 73

Forty-Second Amendment (Indian), 84, 85, 101

Foster, Hamar, 177

foundations, funding from, 21, 24

Fourteenth Amendment (U.S.): cases related to, 38, 233n. 10; effect of, 13; implications for states, 30–31, 238n. 65; managerial business interests and, 47–48; popular ideology and, 32–33; railroad litigation and, 46; text of, 209–10. *See also* due process (U.S.)

Fourth Amendment (Indian), 84

Fourth Amendment (U.S.), 207

Fox, Jay, 240n. 19

Fox v. Washington, 48, 233–34n. 12

France, bill of rights in, 12

Francis Coralie Mullin v. The Administrator, Union Territory of Delhi, 252nn. 95–96

Frankfurter, Felix, 12, 63, 82

"freedom" (Indian), text on, 211–16. *See also* Fundamental Rights (Indian)

freedom of speech and the press: Court cases on, 28–29, 62, 67–68, 111, 204; extended to symbolic speech, 50; influences on, 21; Jehovah's Witnesses and, 21, 51–52, 66; origins of, 2, 7; pre-1918

cases on, 29, 32–33, 48–49; Warren Court support for, 39; during wartime, 28, 67

freedoms (U.S.): of assembly, 50; of religion, 7, 21, 51–52. *See also* freedom of speech and the press

Free Speech League (U.S.), 33, 48–49

Frohwerk v. United States, 28

Frontiero v. Richardson, 239n. 72

"fundamental freedoms" (Canadian), text on, 217–23

Fundamental Rights (Indian): adoption of, 23–24; components of, 77–78; consolidated cases on, 254–55n. 3; interpretation of, 80, 249n. 40; petitioning Court as, 81, 108–9; to property, 84, 251n. 77; sex discrimination under, 79; statistics on cases on, 91–92, 254–55n. 3, 254n. 2; suspension of, 85; text of, 210–17

Fund for the American Republic, 58

Gadbois, George, Jr., 250–51n. 68

Galanter, Marc: on case congregations, 261n. 45; on democracy, 77; on implementation of rights, 8; on judiciary, 80–81, 250–51n. 68; on legal aid, 102; on legal profession, 100; on litigant types, 18, 230–31n. 34

Gandhi, Indira: court packing by, 81, 84–85; emergency rule by, 76, 83–85, 89, 91, 95–98, 96–97, 103–4, 109; leadership of, 73; organizations investigated by, 102

Gandhi, Rajiv, 102

Ganges River, Indian Court on, 71, 86

Garland, Charles, 58. *See also* American Fund for Public Service

Garland Fund (American Fund for Public Service), 49, 51, 53, 58, 243n. 62

Garland v. British Rail Engineering Ltd., 269n. 78

"GCHQ" case *(Council of Civil Service Unions and others v. Minister for the Civil Service)*, 117–18, 261n. 34

gender: in British legal profession, 127, 144; in Canadian legal profession, 185–86, 190–91, 192; in Indian legal profession, 101; in U.S. legal profession, 56–58, 57, 243–44n. 83, 243n. 71. *See also* ethnicity; race; sex discrimination; women

Gideon v. Wainwright, 40, 55, 60, 64

Gilbert v. Minnesota, 28

DATE DUE

DEMCO 38-296